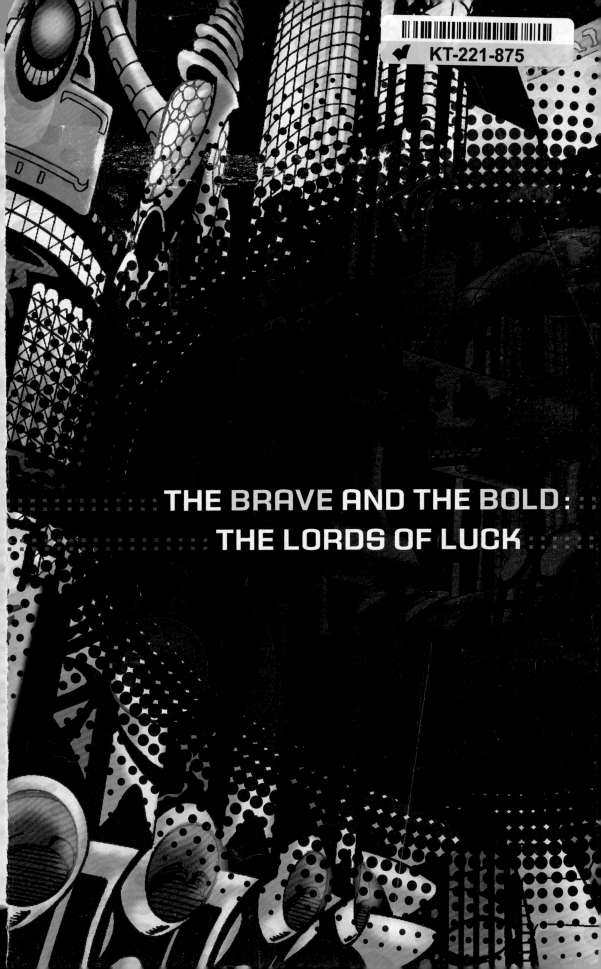

THE BRAVE AND THE BOLD:
THE LORDS OF LUCK

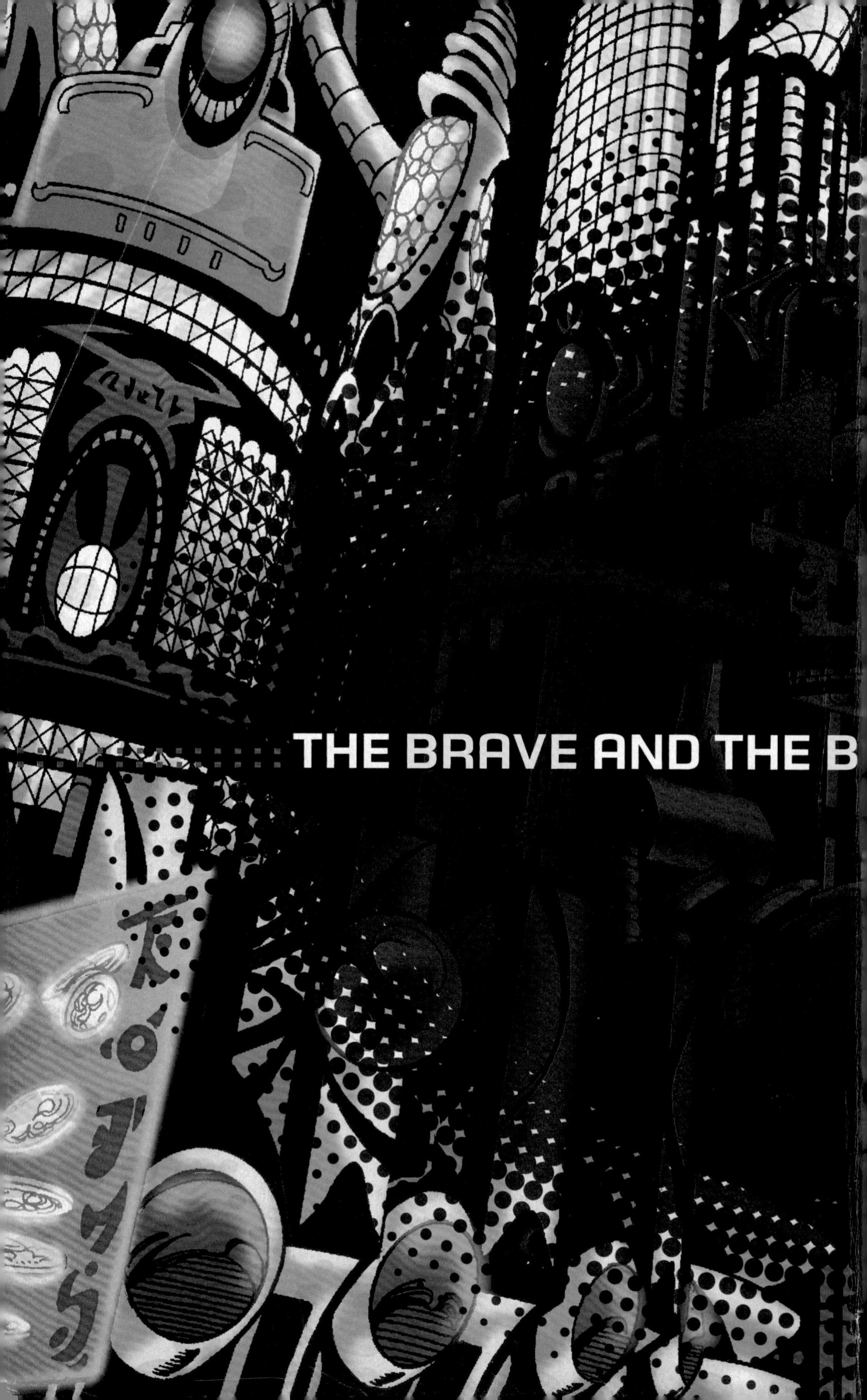
THE BRAVE AND THE B

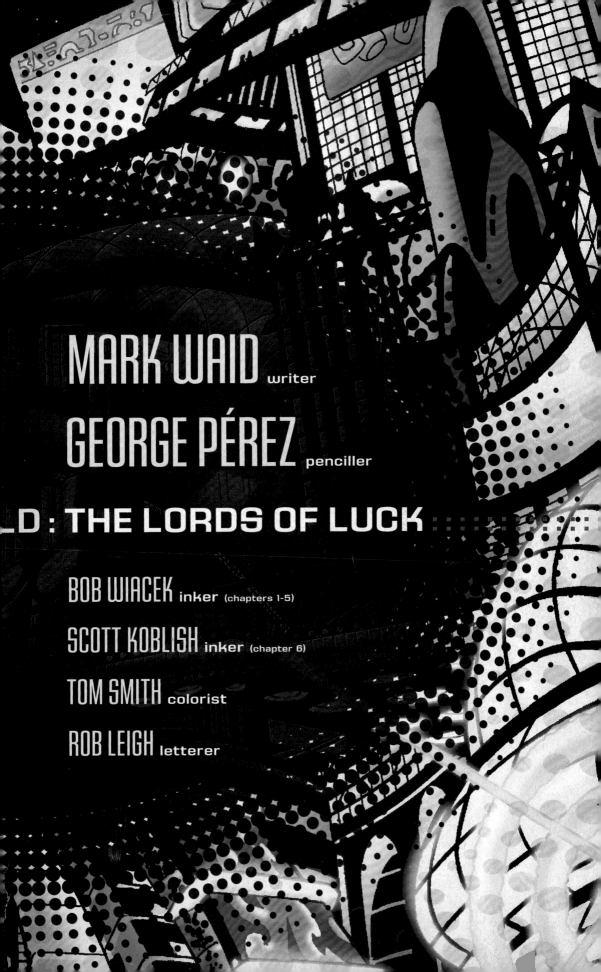

MARK WAID writer

GEORGE PÉREZ penciller

LD : THE LORDS OF LUCK

BOB WIACEK inker (chapters 1-5)

SCOTT KOBLISH inker (chapter 6)

TOM SMITH colorist

ROB LEIGH letterer

Cover art by George Pérez and Tom Smith. Publication design by Amelia Grohman.

THE BRAVE AND THE BOLD: THE LORDS OF LUCK
Published by DC Comics. Cover, introduction and compilation copyright © 2007 DC Comics. All
Rights Reserved. Originally published in single magazine form in THE BRAVE AND THE BOLD #1-6.
Copyright © 2007 DC Comics. All Rights Reserved. All characters, their distinctive likenesses and
related elements featured in this publication are trademarks of DC Comics. The stories, characters
and incidents featured in this publication are entirely fictional. DC Comics does not read or accept
unsolicited submissions of ideas, stories or artwork.

DC Comics, 1700 Broadway, New York, NY 10019   A Warner Bros. Entertainment Company
Printed in Canada. First Printing. HC ISBN: 1-4012-1503-3   HC ISBN 13: 978-1-4012-1503-3
SC ISBN: 1-4012-1588-2   SC ISBN 13: 978-1-4012-1588-0

Batman created by Bob Kane. Lobo created by Roger Slifer and Keith Giffen.

NINE HUNDRED AND SEVENTY-THREE PANELS.

Yes, I counted. I was curious. I put maybe five, six hundred panels total in my script, and I get back 973. This is a continual source of amazement for me. I've been writing comics for twenty years, and I'm constantly wrangling with artists who, as goes human nature, are looking for ways to work less hard. Not my pal George Pérez. George lives to give the readers more for their money. He's the only artist I've ever worked with that I can say this to without having to duck:

"Okay, on page eighteen, we see an enormous, splashy shot of Green Lantern and Adam Strange being attacked by an army of Hawkmen. Not just three or four Hawkmen, either — dozens of winged warriors, weapons brandished, all tearing and clawing and snarling in a midair assault above the skies of Ranagar.

"Then, in panel two..."

I'm not bringing this up to argue that more panels automatically equals better comics. I can, pretty much at random, point to any of ten thousand soul-deadening comics from the 1990s that would make a mockery of that statement. Noise is not always music. But I will absolutely declare that more George Pérez artwork automatically equals better comics, particularly when every single illustration so beautifully captures a moment or expression or moves the story along in an exciting, unexpected way.

I couldn't ask for a better partner in this project than an artist hungry to draw everyone and everything in the DC Universe. When I first pitched a BRAVE AND THE BOLD monthly—a revival of a long-running team-up series from my childhood—I proposed that we forgo the tradition of having Batman co-star in every issue and instead marquee a different pair of heroes in each installment. I like Batman as much as the next guy, but I also love Green Lantern and Supergirl and this new Blue Beetle kid and Adam Strange and so forth and so on. There's no single DC character I read as a boy who I can't now wax poetic about for a half hour. The DC heroes are just so amazing to me that I cannot wait to show you how cool each of them is, so the more, the merrier.

Likewise, George is equally obsessively compelled to draw every single comics character ever. Ever. It's true. He longs for this. Even now, after already long ago having permanently retired the record, if some other DC writer or artist thousands of miles away from George at three in the morning comes up with a new hero or villain, George's drawing hand starts to twitch in his sleep. He was particularly delighted at the prospect of drawing the new Blue Beetle simply because he hadn't before. When I confessed to George that issue six would not, in fact, co-star the planet-hopping Space Cabby and the Sun Devils, swash-bucklers of the 22nd century, because I couldn't figure out a way to shoehorn them in, I thought his giant heart would break. Instead, naturally, George figured out a way to get them in there anyway.

The story we finally put together using all these ingredients — aided superbly by inkers Bob Wiacek and Scott Koblish, colorist Tom Smith and letterer Rob Leigh—spans the breadth and depth of the DC Universe, taking you through space and time to meet (or, depending on your age, be reintroduced to) a veritable army of DC's most exciting superheroes and supervillains. It's a murder mystery, a space adventure, a comedy and a tragedy, and it's about a book that tells everything that ever was, is, or will be.

Because George won't rest until he draws that, too.

MARK WAID SEPTEMBER 2007

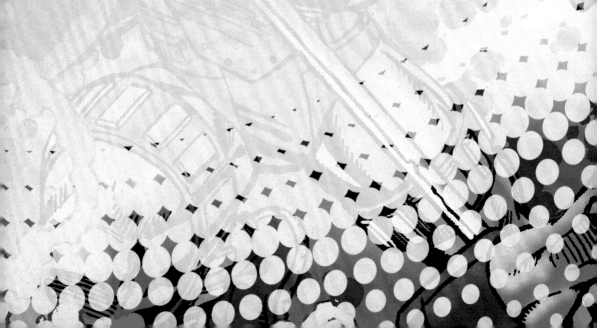

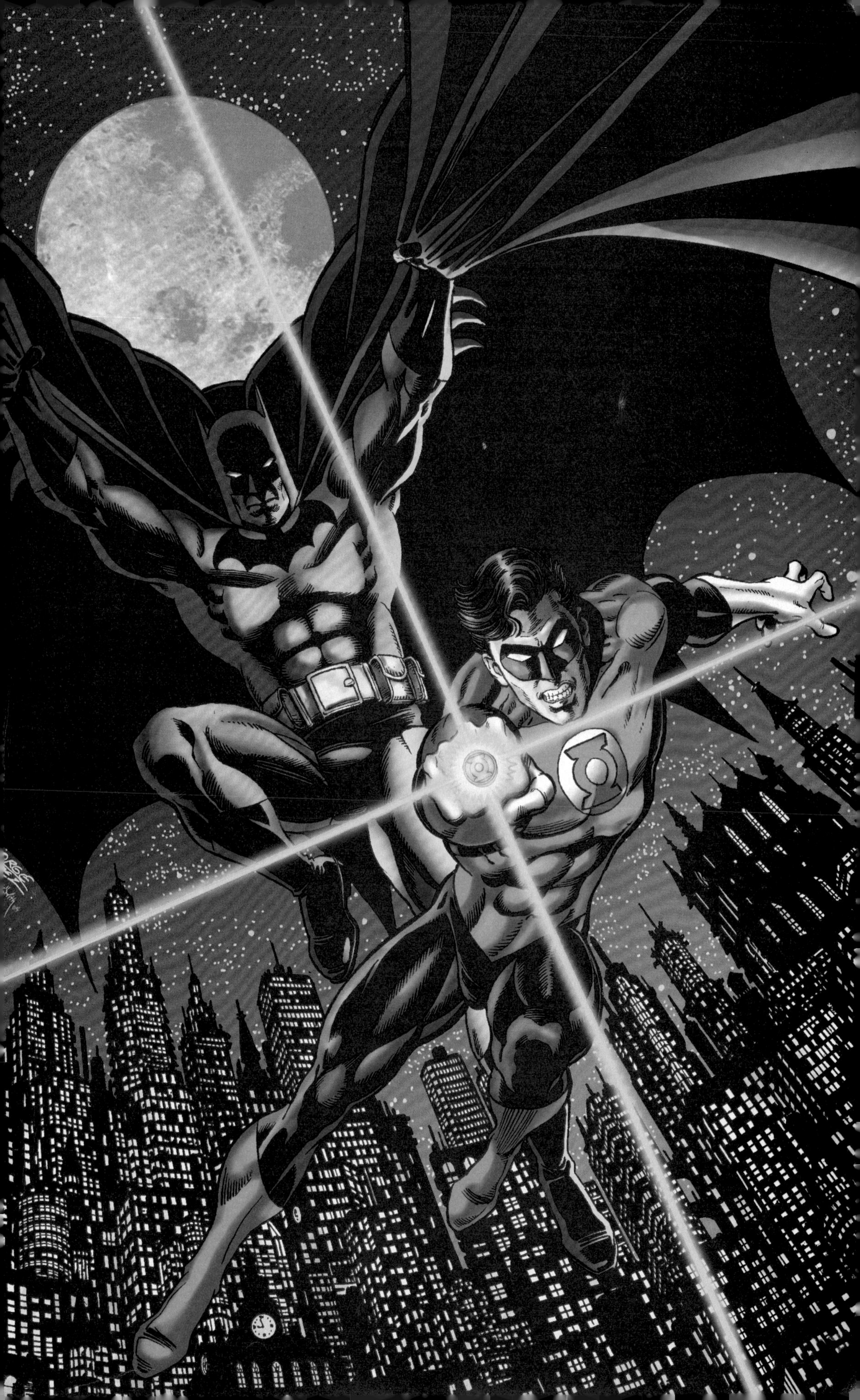

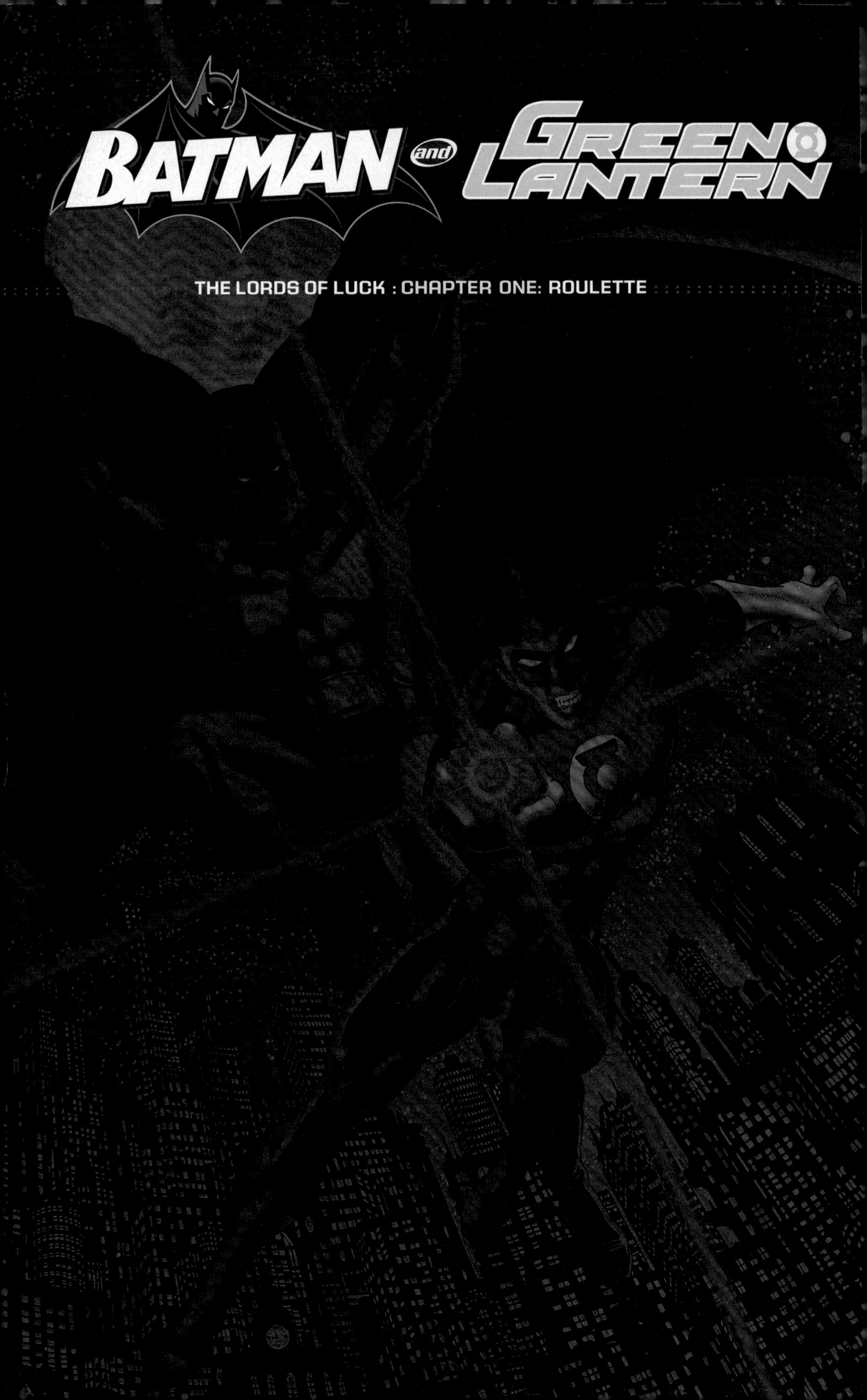
BATMAN and GREEN LANTERN
THE LORDS OF LUCK : CHAPTER ONE: ROULETTE

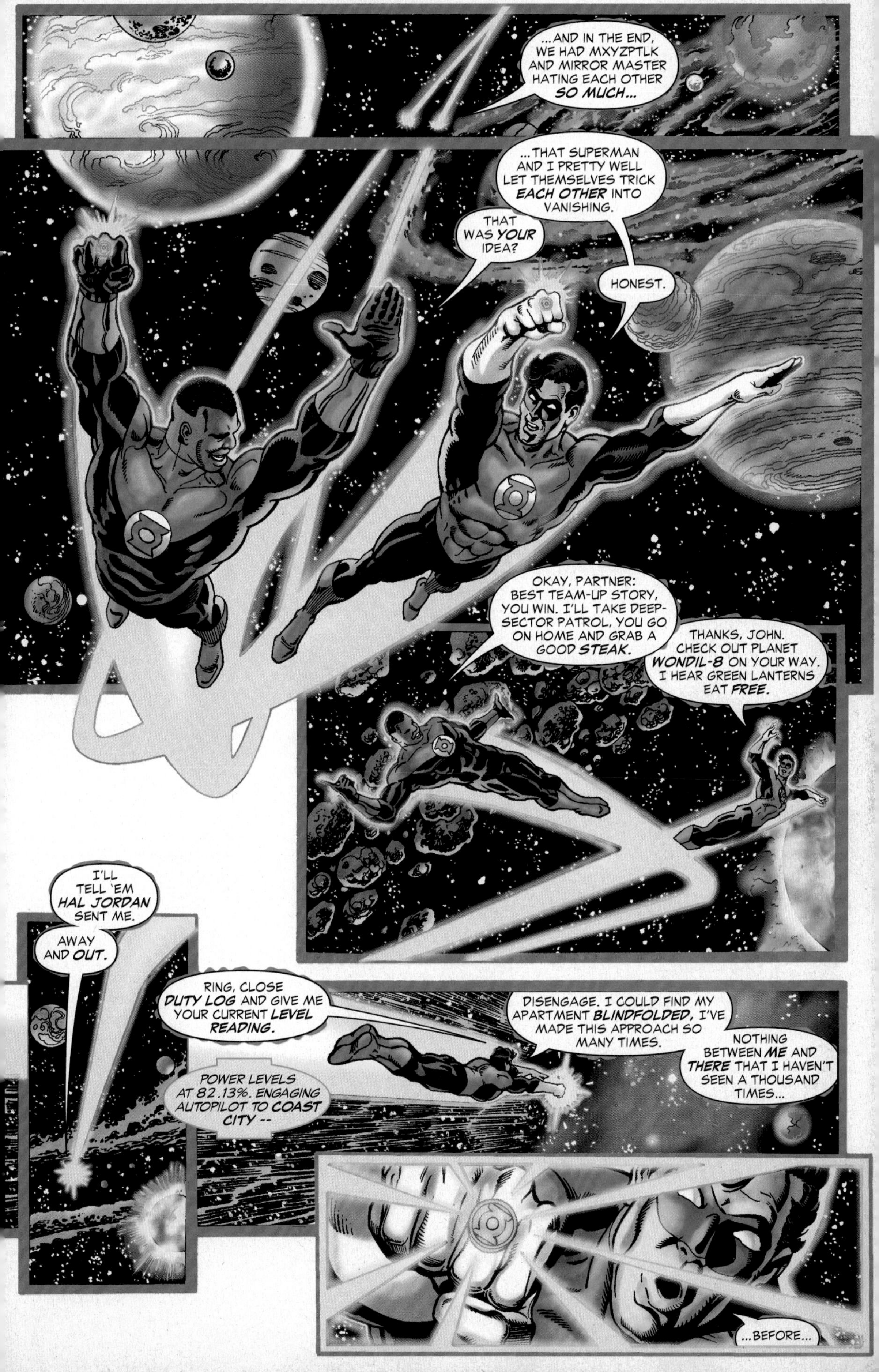

...AND IN THE END, WE HAD MXYZPTLK AND MIRROR MASTER HATING EACH OTHER SO MUCH...
...THAT SUPERMAN AND I PRETTY WELL LET THEMSELVES TRICK EACH OTHER INTO VANISHING.
THAT WAS YOUR IDEA?
HONEST.
OKAY, PARTNER: BEST TEAM-UP STORY, YOU WIN. I'LL TAKE DEEP-SECTOR PATROL, YOU GO ON HOME AND GRAB A GOOD STEAK.
THANKS, JOHN. CHECK OUT PLANET WONDIL-8 ON YOUR WAY. I HEAR GREEN LANTERNS EAT FREE.
I'LL TELL 'EM HAL JORDAN SENT ME.
AWAY AND OUT.
RING, CLOSE DUTY LOG AND GIVE ME YOUR CURRENT LEVEL READING.
POWER LEVELS AT 82.13%. ENGAGING AUTOPILOT TO COAST CITY --
DISENGAGE. I COULD FIND MY APARTMENT BLINDFOLDED, I'VE MADE THIS APPROACH SO MANY TIMES.
NOTHING BETWEEN ME AND THERE THAT I HAVEN'T SEEN A THOUSAND TIMES...
...BEFORE...

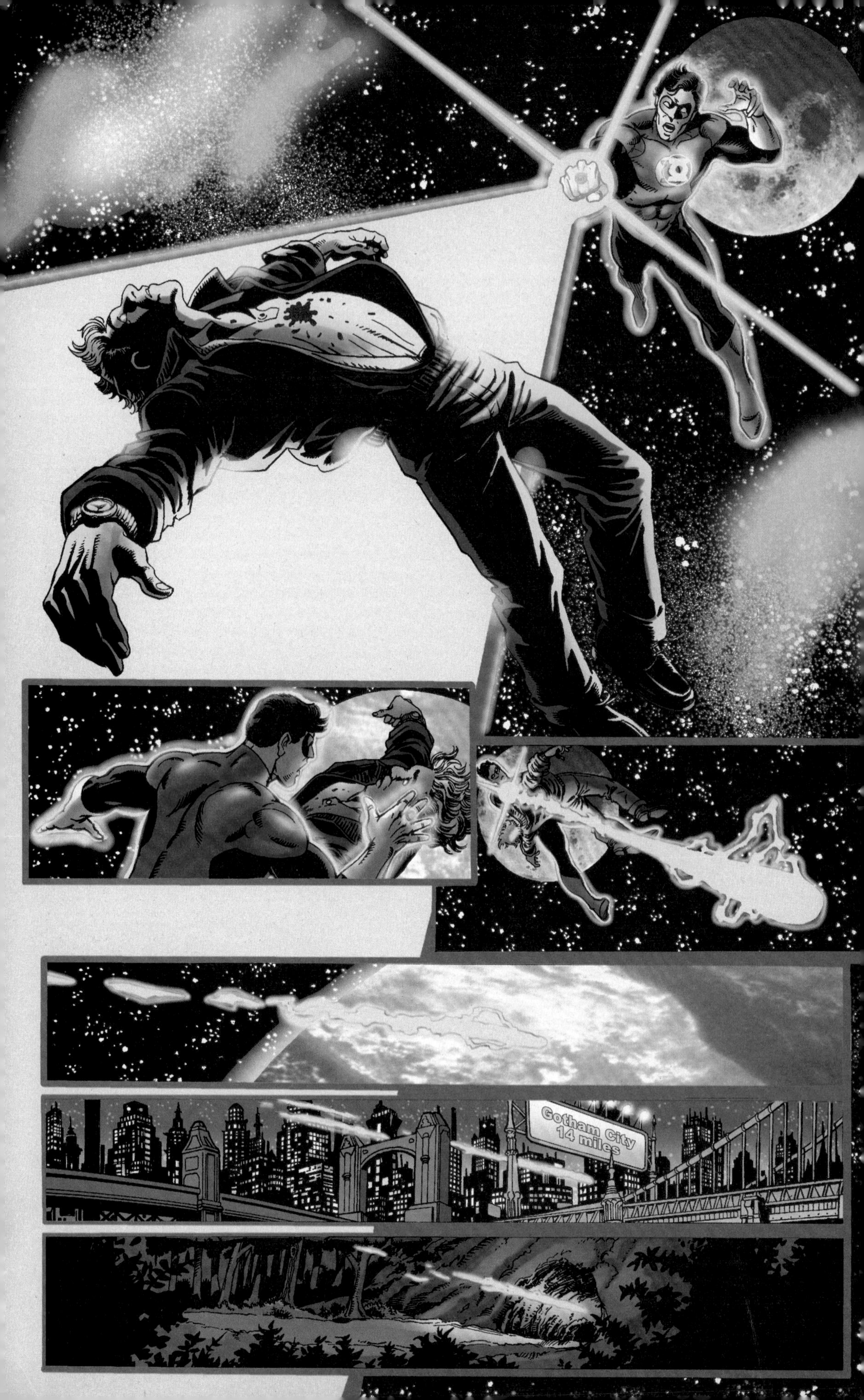
Gotham City
14 miles

BATMAN? *GREEN LANTERN.* IF YOU'RE THERE, I COULD USE A QUICK *CONSULT.*

GO AHEAD.

I HAVE A LITTLE *MYSTERY IN SPACE* HERE. YOU WON'T BELIEVE THIS, BUT APPROXIMATELY 145 MILES *ABOVE* VENICE, ITALY, I'VE FOUND A *FRESH CORPSE--*

--IN A ZONE THAT THE RING CONFIRMS HASN'T HAD *ANY ENTRANCES* OR *EXITS* SINCE I CAME THROUGH *YESTERDAY.*

VICTIM IS *CAUCASIAN HUMAN,* IN KHAKIS AND A BLUE PULLOVER SHIRT, DEAD MAYBE TWENTY MINUTES--

--BUT *NOT* FROM EXPOSURE. FROM, AS CRAZY AS THIS SOUNDS, A *GUNSHOT WOUND.*

TO THE CHEST?

AS A MATTER OF FACT, YES.

NO I.D. ON THE BODY. FINGERTIPS ARE CALLOUSED--DOES THAT TELL YOU ANYTHING?

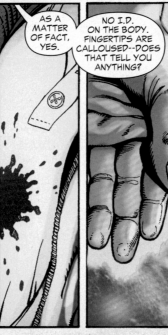

YES. HE'S A GUITARIST, HE'S ABOUT TWENTY-SIX, BLOND...

...AND WEARS HIS WATCH ON HIS RIGHT WRIST.

MY GOD, YOU REALLY *ARE* THE WORLD'S GREATEST DETECTIVE. HOW DID YOU *KNOW* ALL THAT?

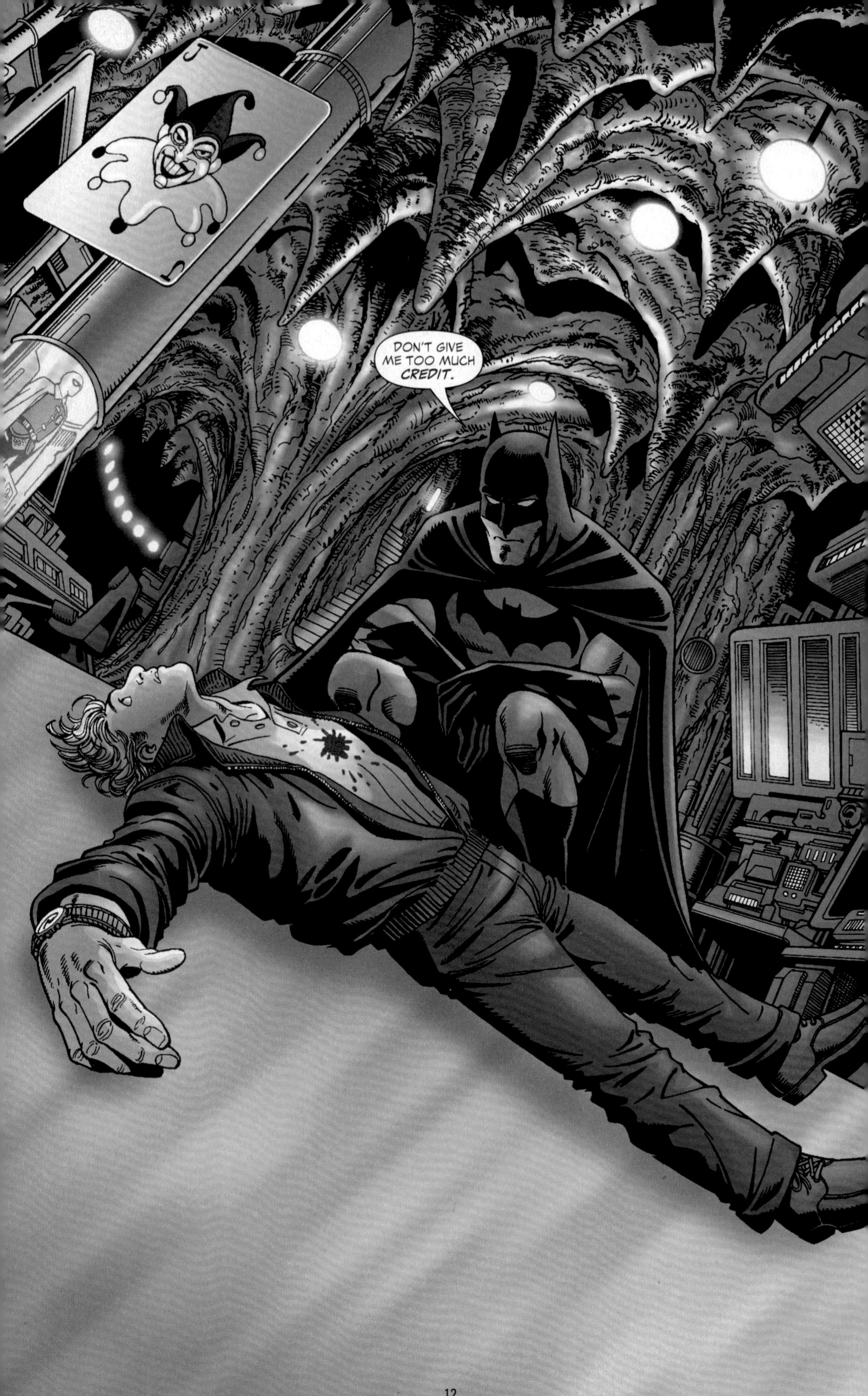
DON'T GIVE ME TOO MUCH CREDIT.

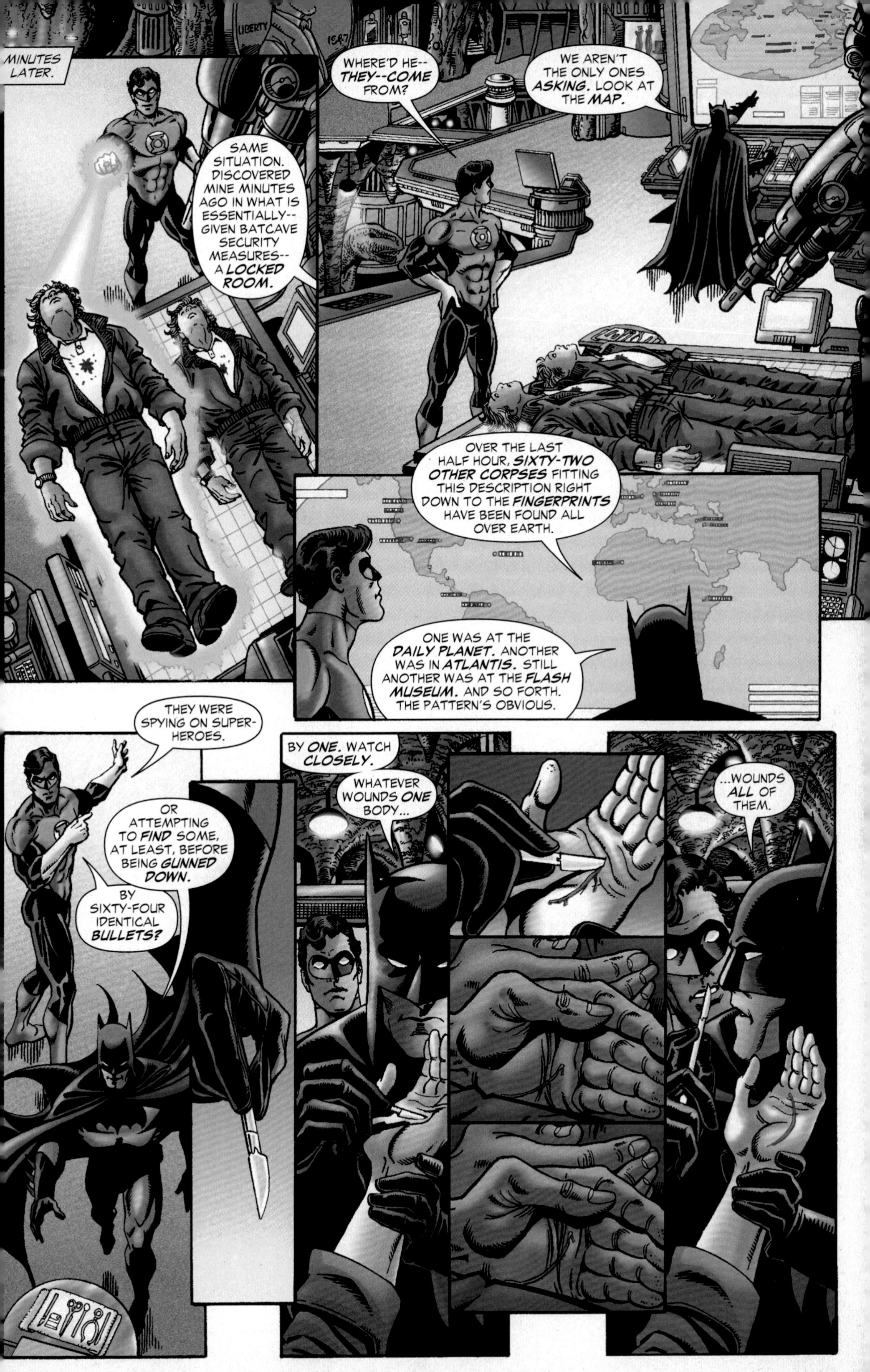
MINUTES LATER.
WHERE'D HE--THEY--COME FROM?
WE AREN'T THE ONLY ONES ASKING. LOOK AT THE MAP.
SAME SITUATION. DISCOVERED MINE MINUTES AGO IN WHAT IS ESSENTIALLY--GIVEN BATCAVE SECURITY MEASURES--A LOCKED ROOM.
OVER THE LAST HALF HOUR, SIXTY-TWO OTHER CORPSES FITTING THIS DESCRIPTION RIGHT DOWN TO THE FINGERPRINTS HAVE BEEN FOUND ALL OVER EARTH.
ONE WAS AT THE DAILY PLANET. ANOTHER WAS IN ATLANTIS. STILL ANOTHER WAS AT THE FLASH MUSEUM. AND SO FORTH. THE PATTERN'S OBVIOUS.
THEY WERE SPYING ON SUPER-HEROES.
OR ATTEMPTING TO FIND SOME, AT LEAST, BEFORE BEING GUNNED DOWN.
BY SIXTY-FOUR IDENTICAL BULLETS?
BY ONE. WATCH CLOSELY.
WHATEVER WOUNDS ONE BODY...
...WOUNDS ALL OF THEM.

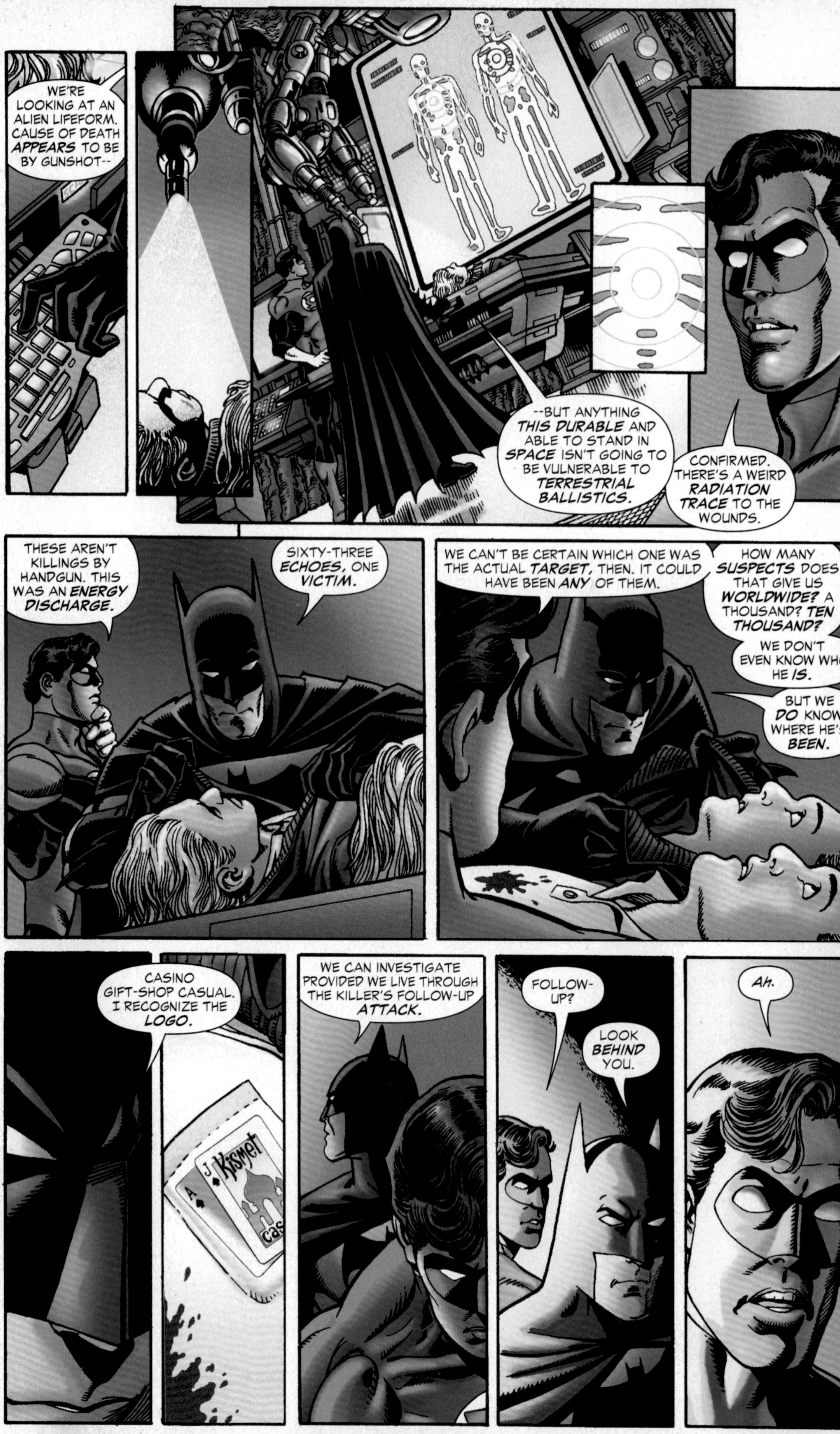

WE'RE LOOKING AT AN ALIEN LIFEFORM. CAUSE OF DEATH APPEARS TO BE BY GUNSHOT--
--BUT ANYTHING THIS DURABLE AND ABLE TO STAND IN SPACE ISN'T GOING TO BE VULNERABLE TO TERRESTRIAL BALLISTICS.
CONFIRMED. THERE'S A WEIRD RADIATION TRACE TO THE WOUNDS.
THESE AREN'T KILLINGS BY HANDGUN. THIS WAS AN ENERGY DISCHARGE.
SIXTY-THREE ECHOES, ONE VICTIM.
WE CAN'T BE CERTAIN WHICH ONE WAS THE ACTUAL TARGET, THEN. IT COULD HAVE BEEN ANY OF THEM.
HOW MANY SUSPECTS DOES THAT GIVE US WORLDWIDE? A THOUSAND? TEN THOUSAND?
WE DON'T EVEN KNOW WHO HE IS.
BUT WE DO KNOW WHERE HE'S BEEN.
CASINO GIFT-SHOP CASUAL. I RECOGNIZE THE LOGO.
Kismet
WE CAN INVESTIGATE PROVIDED WE LIVE THROUGH THE KILLER'S FOLLOW-UP ATTACK.
FOLLOW-UP?
LOOK BEHIND YOU.
Ah.

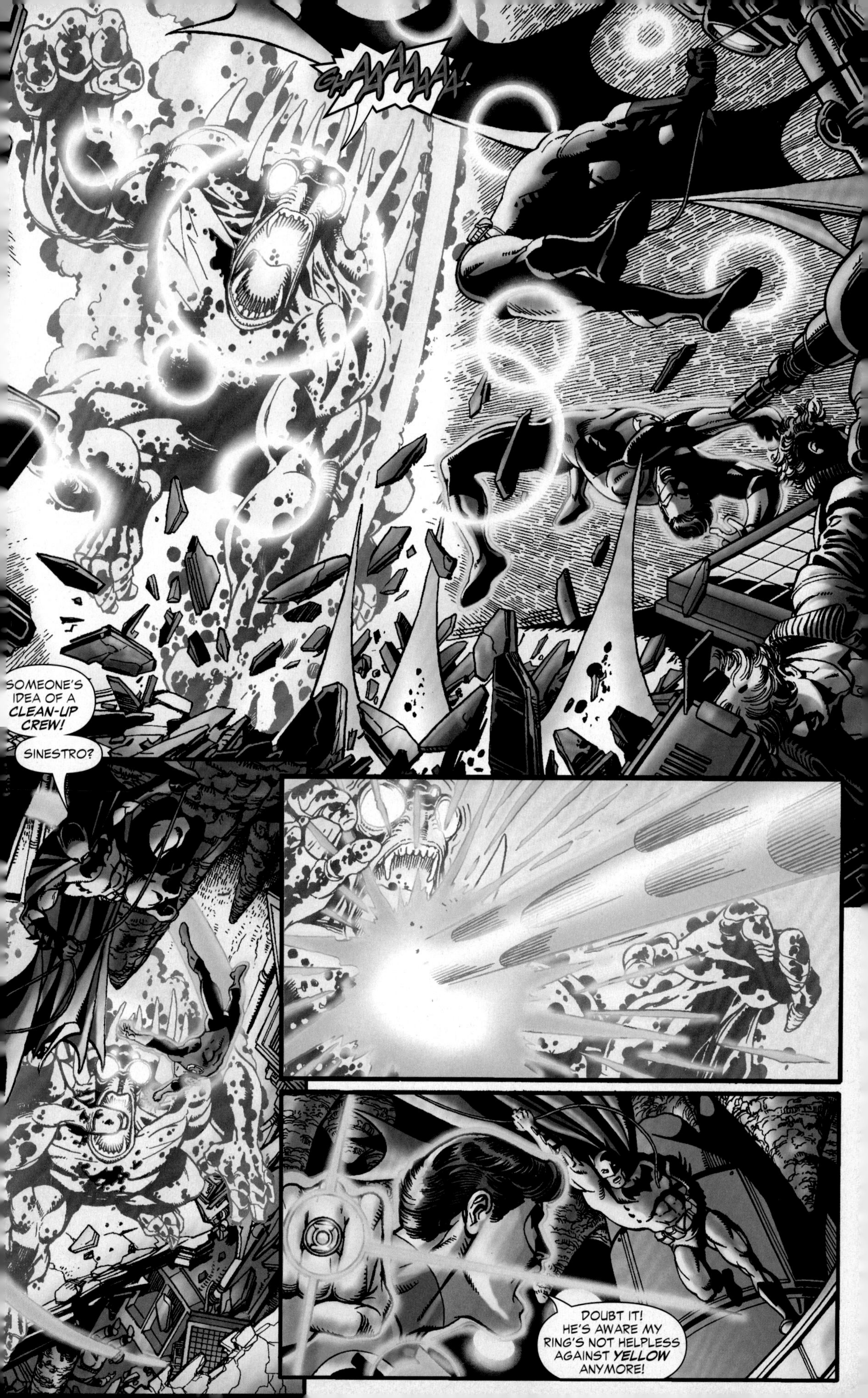
GHAAAAAAA!
SOMEONE'S IDEA OF A CLEAN-UP CREW!
SINESTRO?
DOUBT IT! HE'S AWARE MY RING'S NOT HELPLESS AGAINST YELLOW ANYMORE!

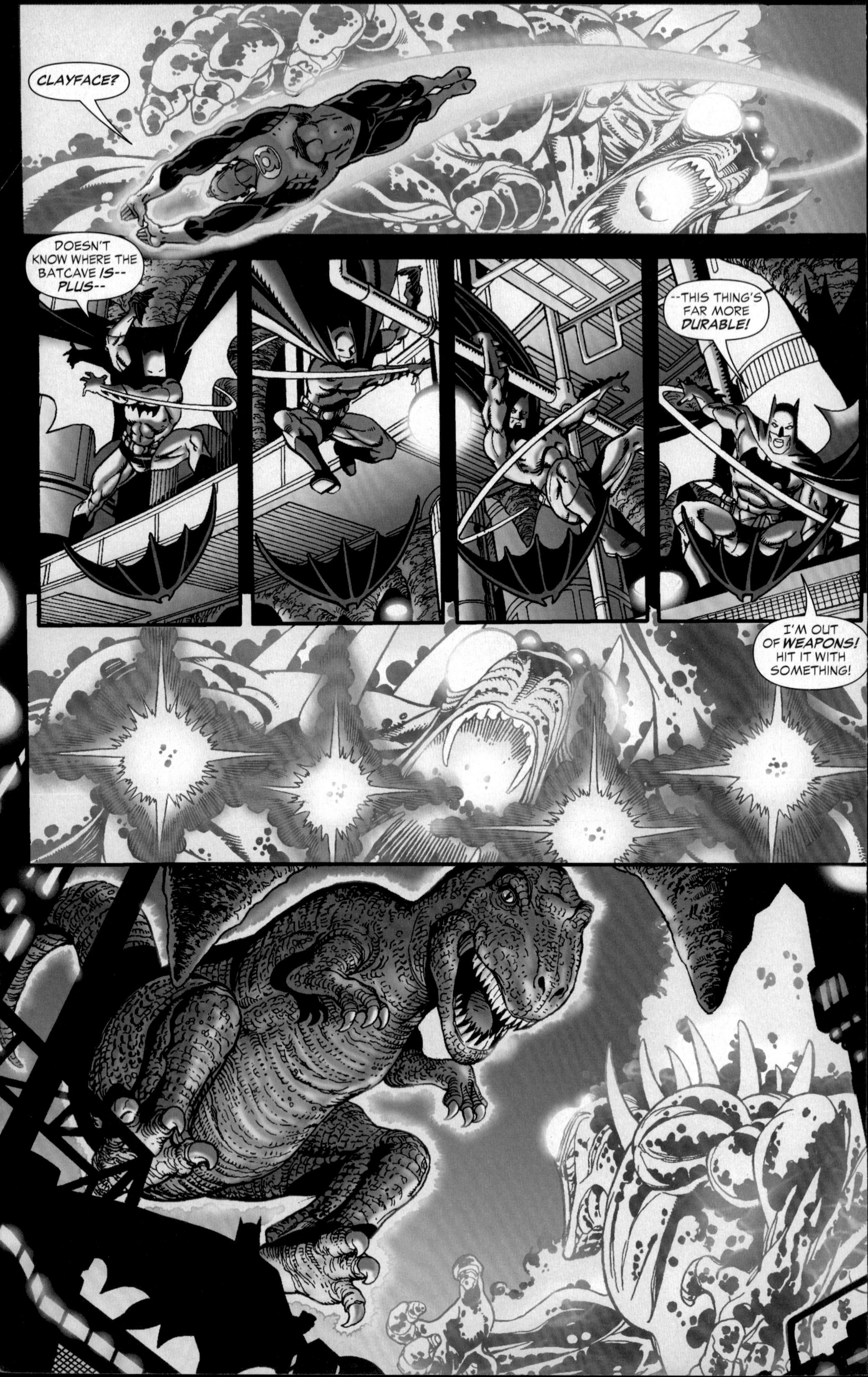
CLAYFACE?
DOESN'T KNOW WHERE THE BATCAVE *IS*-- *PLUS*--
--THIS THING'S FAR MORE *DURABLE!*
I'M OUT OF *WEAPONS!* HIT IT WITH SOMETHING!

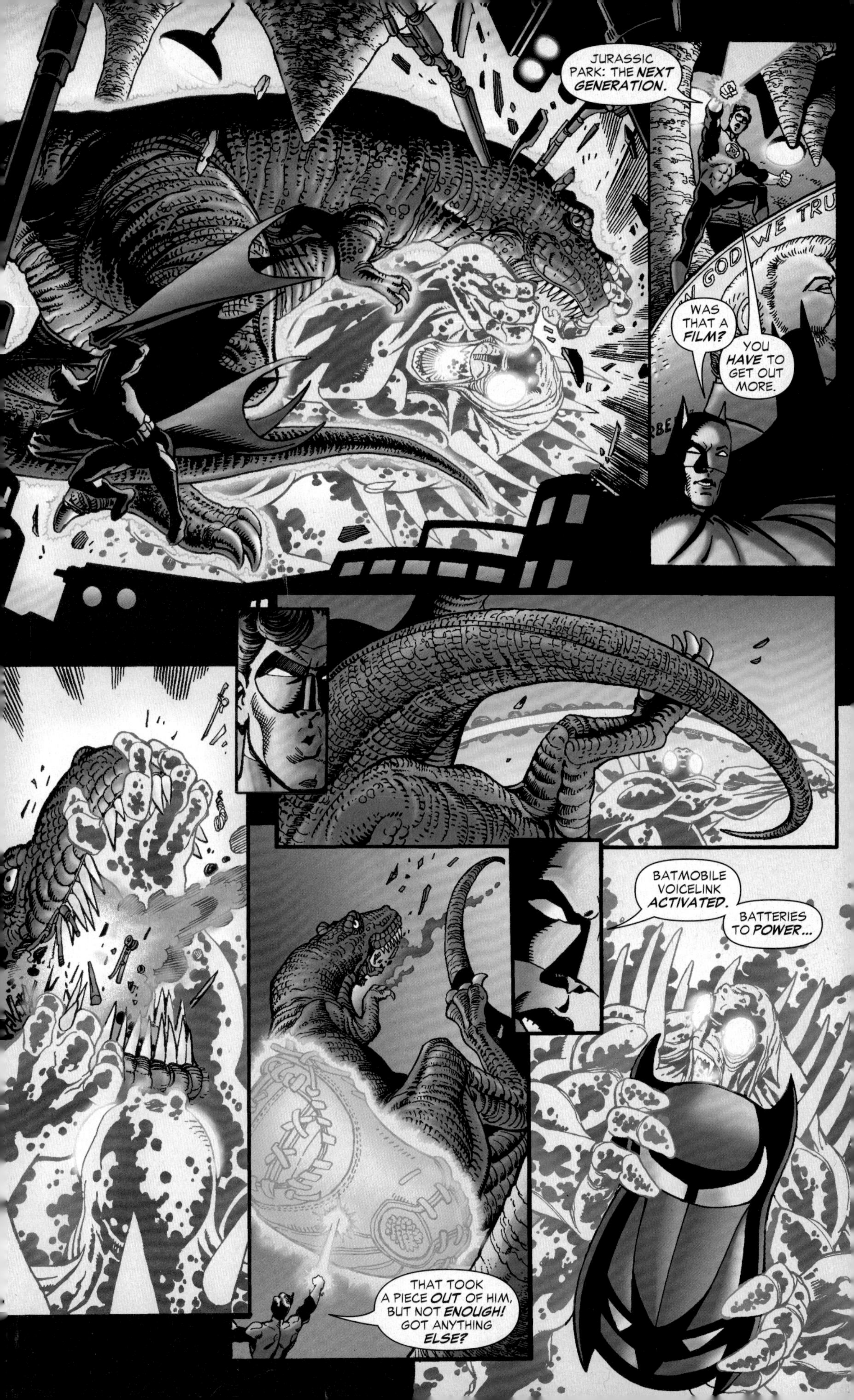
JURASSIC PARK: THE NEXT GENERATION.
IN GOD WE TRU
WAS THAT A FILM?
YOU HAVE TO GET OUT MORE.
BATMOBILE VOICELINK ACTIVATED.
BATTERIES TO POWER...
THAT TOOK A PIECE OUT OF HIM, BUT NOT ENOUGH! GOT ANYTHING ELSE?

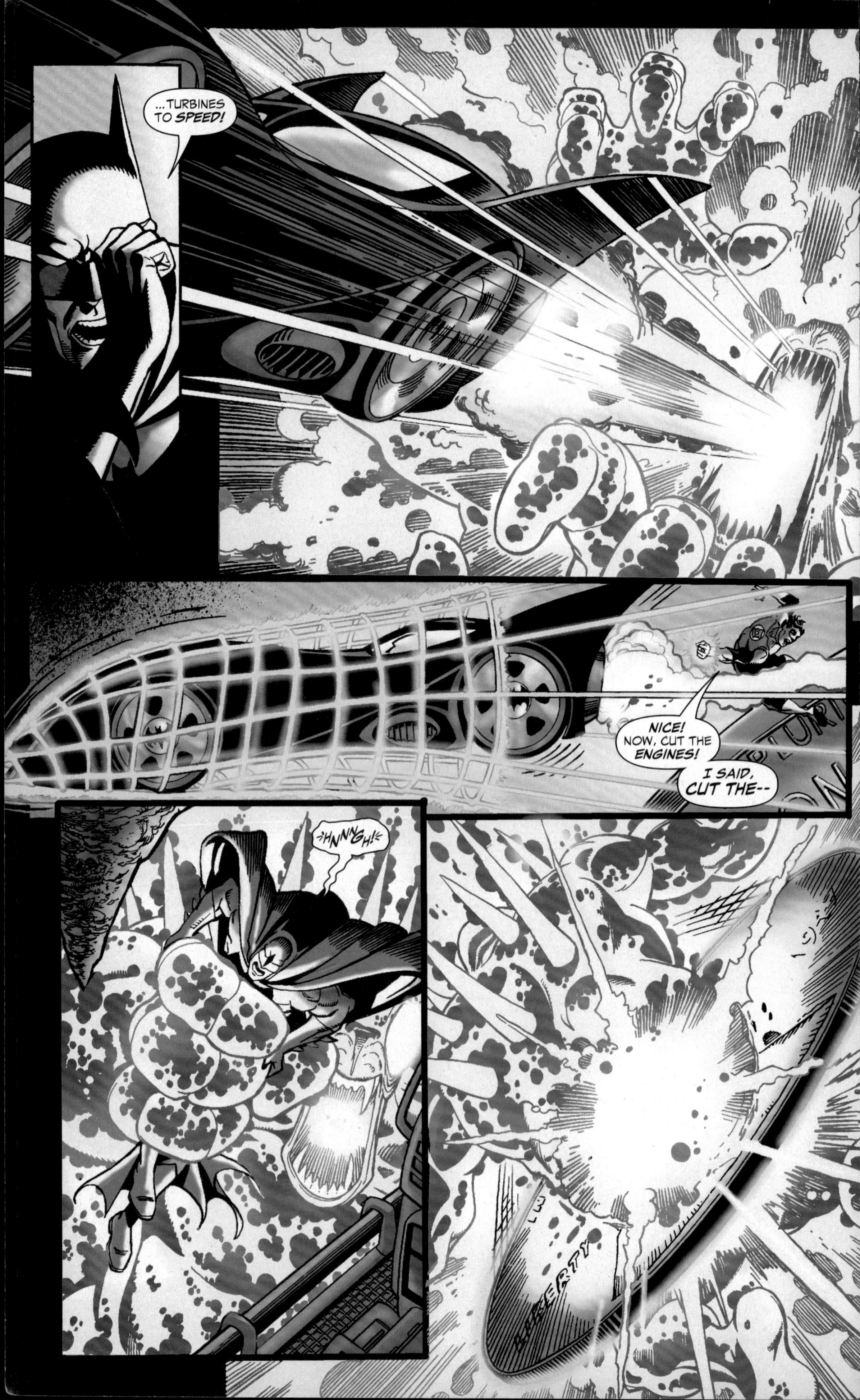
...TURBINES TO SPEED!
NICE! NOW, CUT THE ENGINES!
I SAID, CUT THE--
HNNNGH!

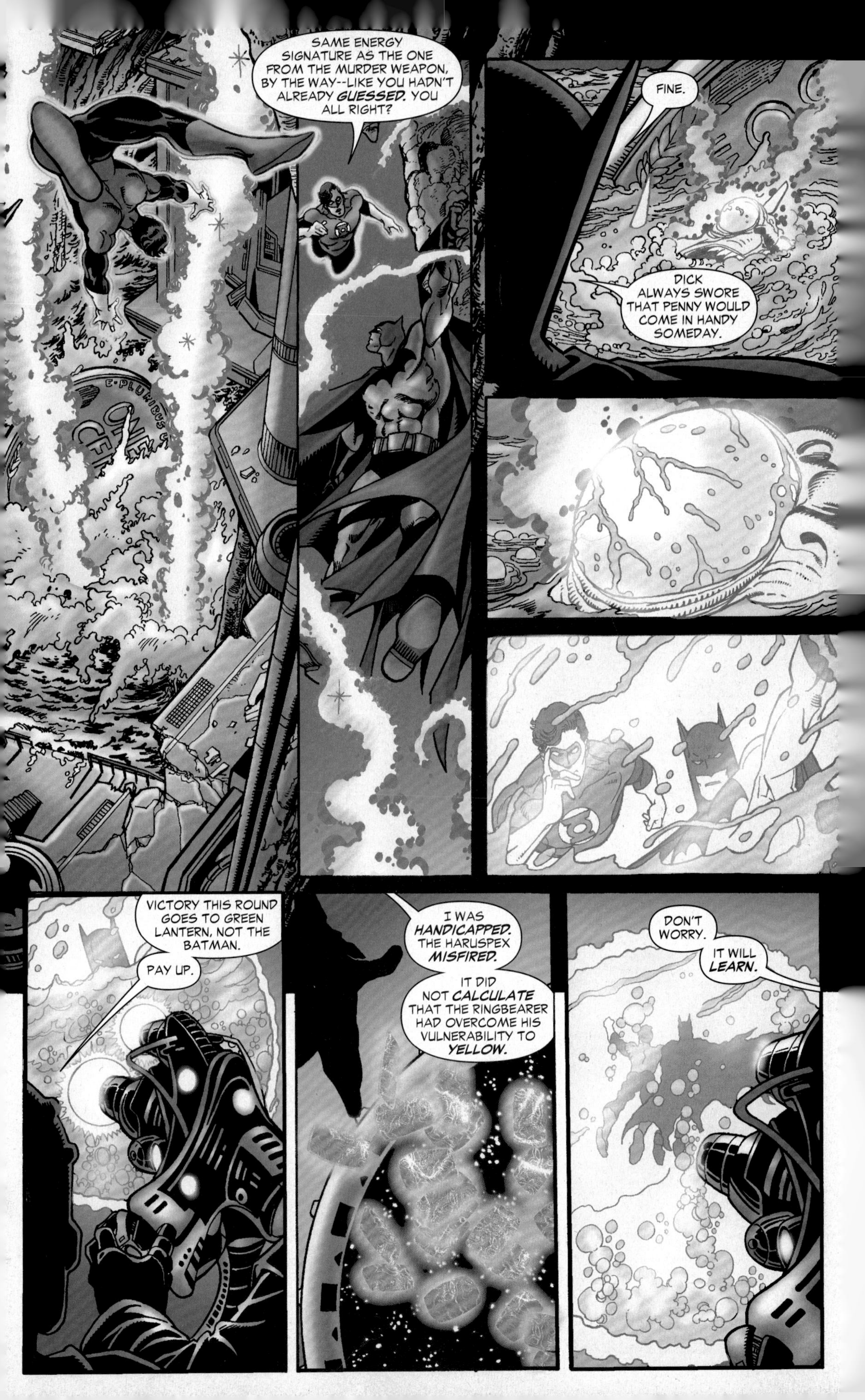
SAME ENERGY SIGNATURE AS THE ONE FROM THE MURDER WEAPON, BY THE WAY--LIKE YOU HADN'T ALREADY GUESSED. YOU ALL RIGHT?
FINE.
DICK ALWAYS SWORE THAT PENNY WOULD COME IN HANDY SOMEDAY.
E PLURIBUS
ONE CENT
VICTORY THIS ROUND GOES TO GREEN LANTERN, NOT THE BATMAN.
PAY UP.
I WAS HANDICAPPED. THE HARUSPEX MISFIRED.
IT DID NOT CALCULATE THAT THE RINGBEARER HAD OVERCOME HIS VULNERABILITY TO YELLOW.
DON'T WORRY.
IT WILL LEARN.

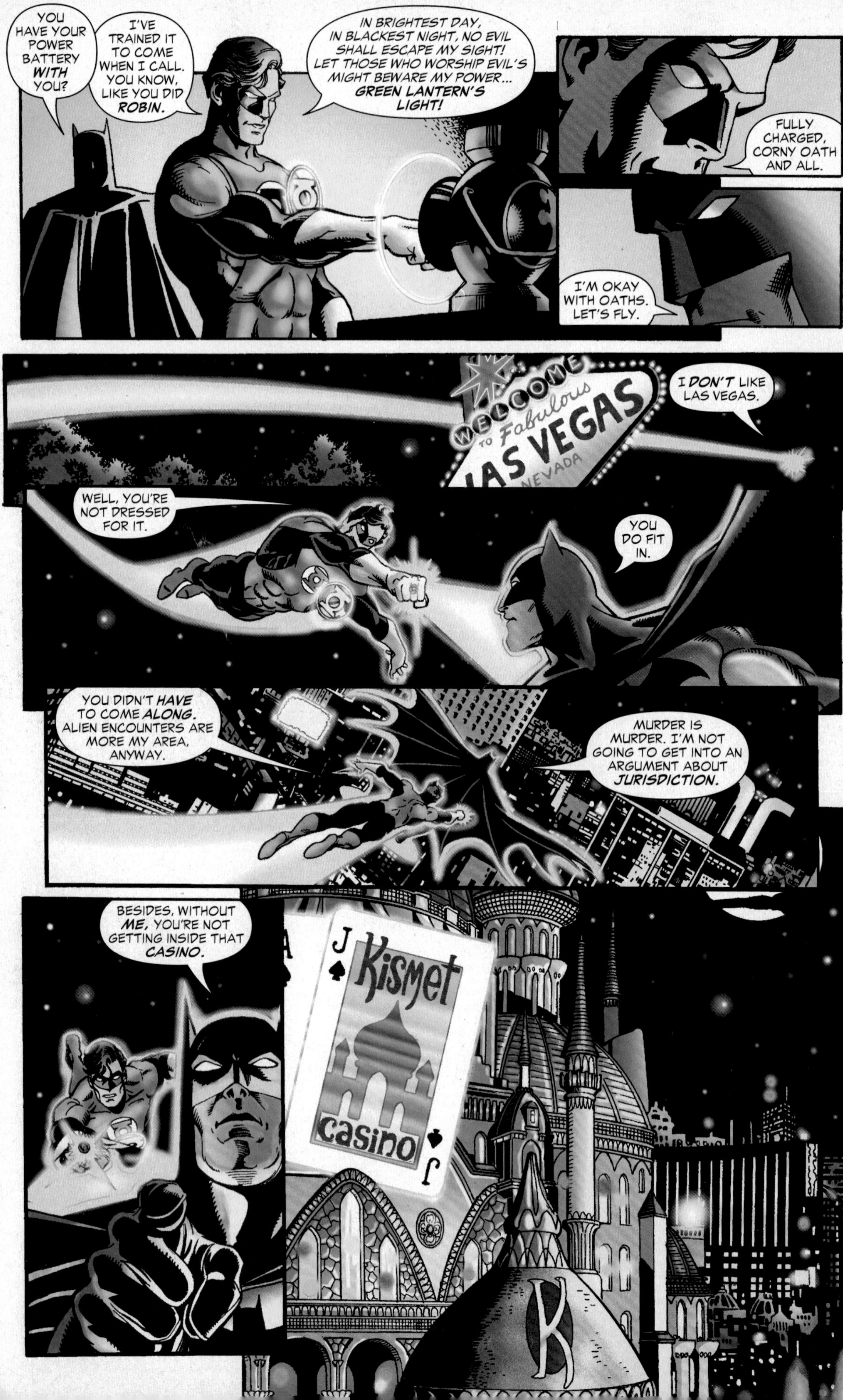
YOU HAVE YOUR POWER BATTERY WITH YOU?
I'VE TRAINED IT TO COME WHEN I CALL. YOU KNOW, LIKE YOU DID ROBIN.
IN BRIGHTEST DAY, IN BLACKEST NIGHT, NO EVIL SHALL ESCAPE MY SIGHT! LET THOSE WHO WORSHIP EVIL'S MIGHT BEWARE MY POWER... GREEN LANTERN'S LIGHT!
FULLY CHARGED, CORNY OATH AND ALL.
I'M OKAY WITH OATHS. LET'S FLY.
WELCOME to Fabulous LAS VEGAS NEVADA
I DON'T LIKE LAS VEGAS.
WELL, YOU'RE NOT DRESSED FOR IT.
YOU DO FIT IN.
YOU DIDN'T HAVE TO COME ALONG. ALIEN ENCOUNTERS ARE MORE MY AREA, ANYWAY.
MURDER IS MURDER. I'M NOT GOING TO GET INTO AN ARGUMENT ABOUT JURISDICTION.
BESIDES, WITHOUT ME, YOU'RE NOT GETTING INSIDE THAT CASINO.
Kismet casino

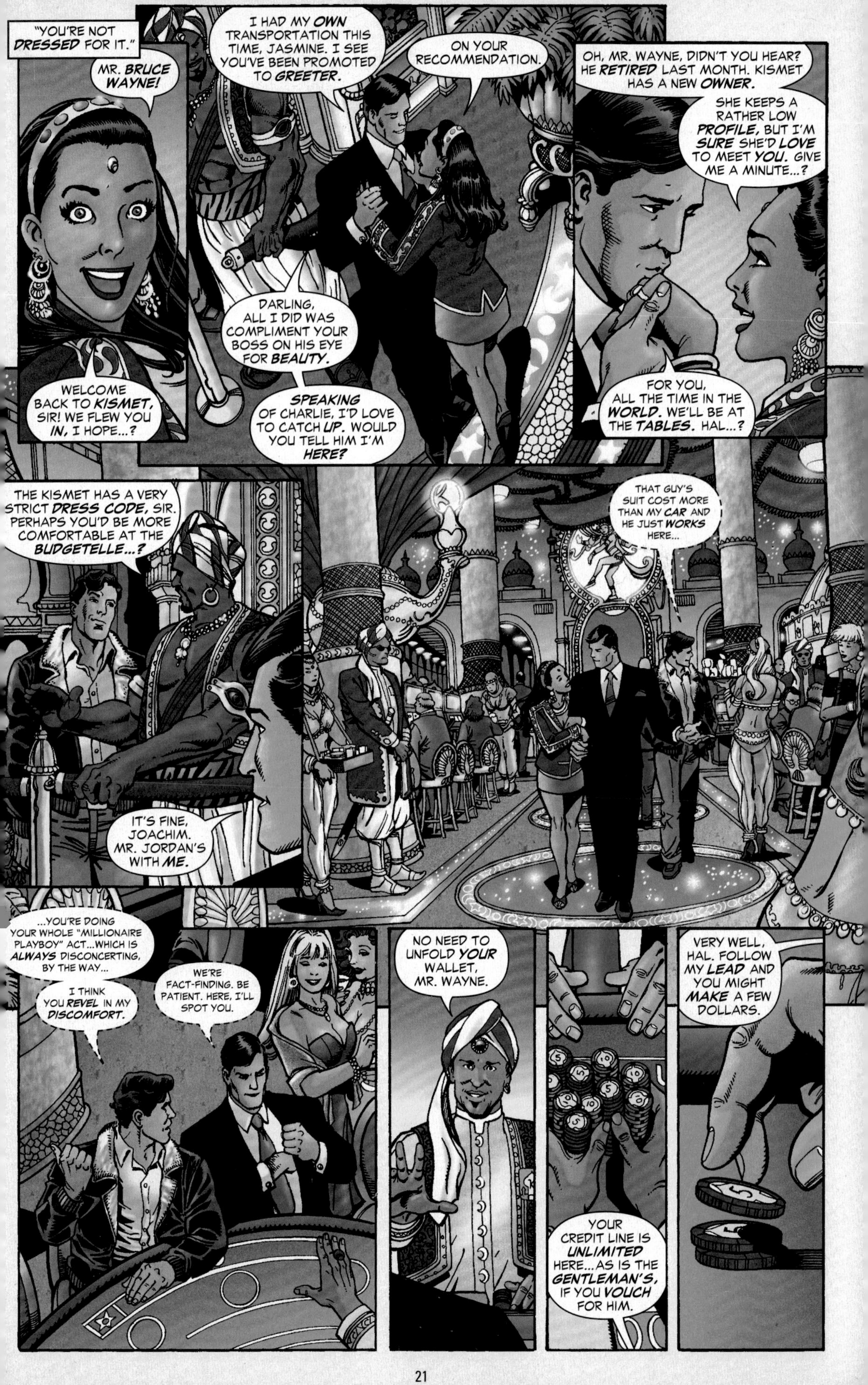

"YOU'RE NOT DRESSED FOR IT."
MR. BRUCE WAYNE!
WELCOME BACK TO KISMET, SIR! WE FLEW YOU IN, I HOPE...?
I HAD MY OWN TRANSPORTATION THIS TIME, JASMINE. I SEE YOU'VE BEEN PROMOTED TO GREETER.
ON YOUR RECOMMENDATION.
DARLING, ALL I DID WAS COMPLIMENT YOUR BOSS ON HIS EYE FOR BEAUTY.
SPEAKING OF CHARLIE, I'D LOVE TO CATCH UP. WOULD YOU TELL HIM I'M HERE?
OH, MR. WAYNE, DIDN'T YOU HEAR? HE RETIRED LAST MONTH. KISMET HAS A NEW OWNER.
SHE KEEPS A RATHER LOW PROFILE, BUT I'M SURE SHE'D LOVE TO MEET YOU. GIVE ME A MINUTE...?
FOR YOU, ALL THE TIME IN THE WORLD. WE'LL BE AT THE TABLES. HAL...?
THE KISMET HAS A VERY STRICT DRESS CODE, SIR. PERHAPS YOU'D BE MORE COMFORTABLE AT THE BUDGETELLE...?
IT'S FINE, JOACHIM. MR. JORDAN'S WITH ME.
THAT GUY'S SUIT COST MORE THAN MY CAR AND HE JUST WORKS HERE...
...YOU'RE DOING YOUR WHOLE "MILLIONAIRE PLAYBOY" ACT...WHICH IS ALWAYS DISCONCERTING, BY THE WAY...
I THINK YOU REVEL IN MY DISCOMFORT.
WE'RE FACT-FINDING. BE PATIENT. HERE, I'LL SPOT YOU.
NO NEED TO UNFOLD YOUR WALLET, MR. WAYNE.
YOUR CREDIT LINE IS UNLIMITED HERE...AS IS THE GENTLEMAN'S, IF YOU VOUCH FOR HIM.
VERY WELL, HAL. FOLLOW MY LEAD AND YOU MIGHT MAKE A FEW DOLLARS.

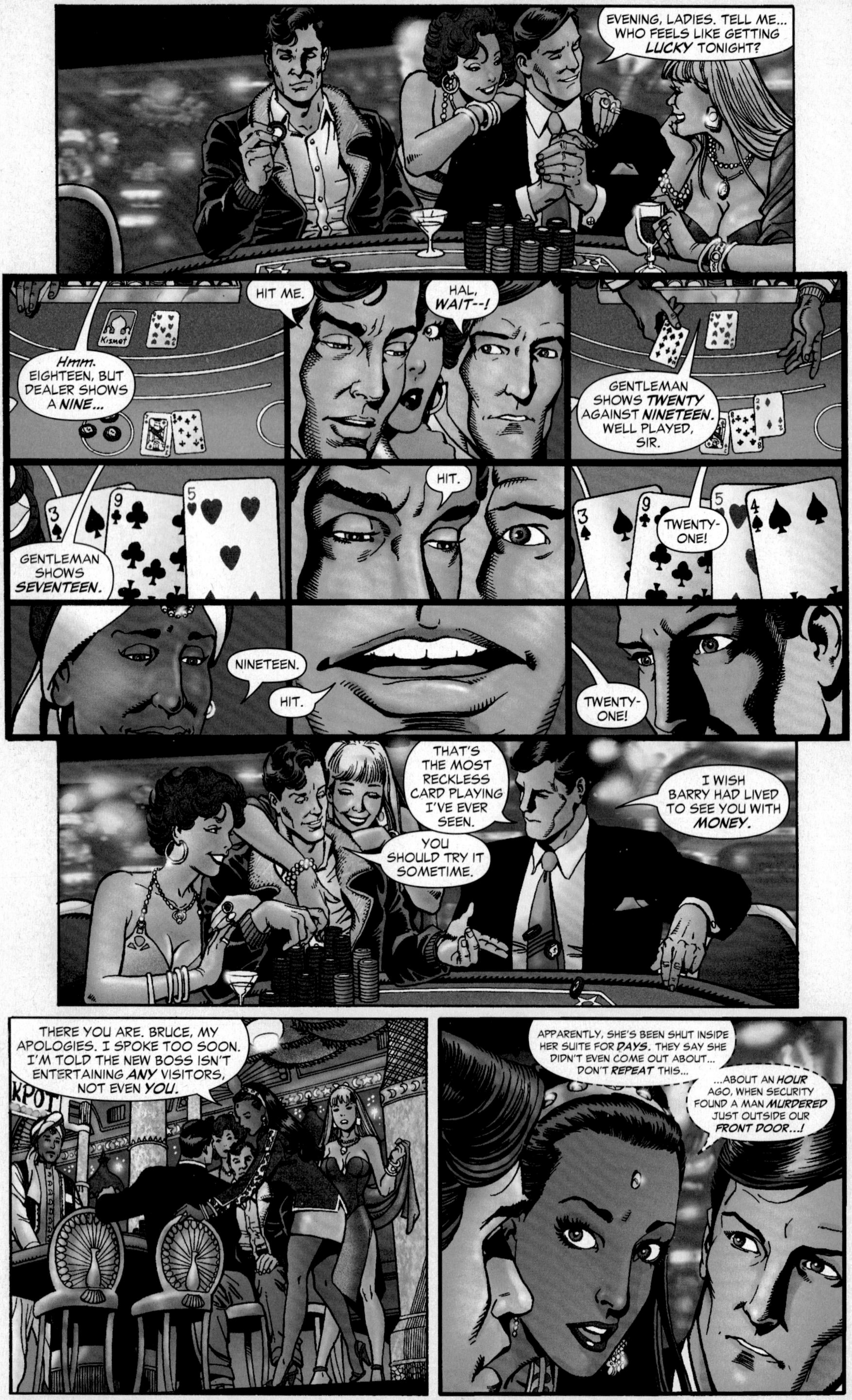

EVENING, LADIES. TELL ME... WHO FEELS LIKE GETTING LUCKY TONIGHT?
Kismet
Hmm. EIGHTEEN, BUT DEALER SHOWS A NINE...
HIT ME.
HAL, WAIT--!
GENTLEMAN SHOWS TWENTY AGAINST NINETEEN. WELL PLAYED, SIR.
GENTLEMAN SHOWS SEVENTEEN.
HIT.
TWENTY-ONE!
NINETEEN.
HIT.
TWENTY-ONE!
THAT'S THE MOST RECKLESS CARD PLAYING I'VE EVER SEEN.
YOU SHOULD TRY IT SOMETIME.
I WISH BARRY HAD LIVED TO SEE YOU WITH MONEY.
THERE YOU ARE. BRUCE, MY APOLOGIES. I SPOKE TOO SOON. I'M TOLD THE NEW BOSS ISN'T ENTERTAINING ANY VISITORS, NOT EVEN YOU.
APPARENTLY, SHE'S BEEN SHUT INSIDE HER SUITE FOR DAYS. THEY SAY SHE DIDN'T EVEN COME OUT ABOUT... DON'T REPEAT THIS...
...ABOUT AN HOUR AGO, WHEN SECURITY FOUND A MAN MURDERED JUST OUTSIDE OUR FRONT DOOR...!

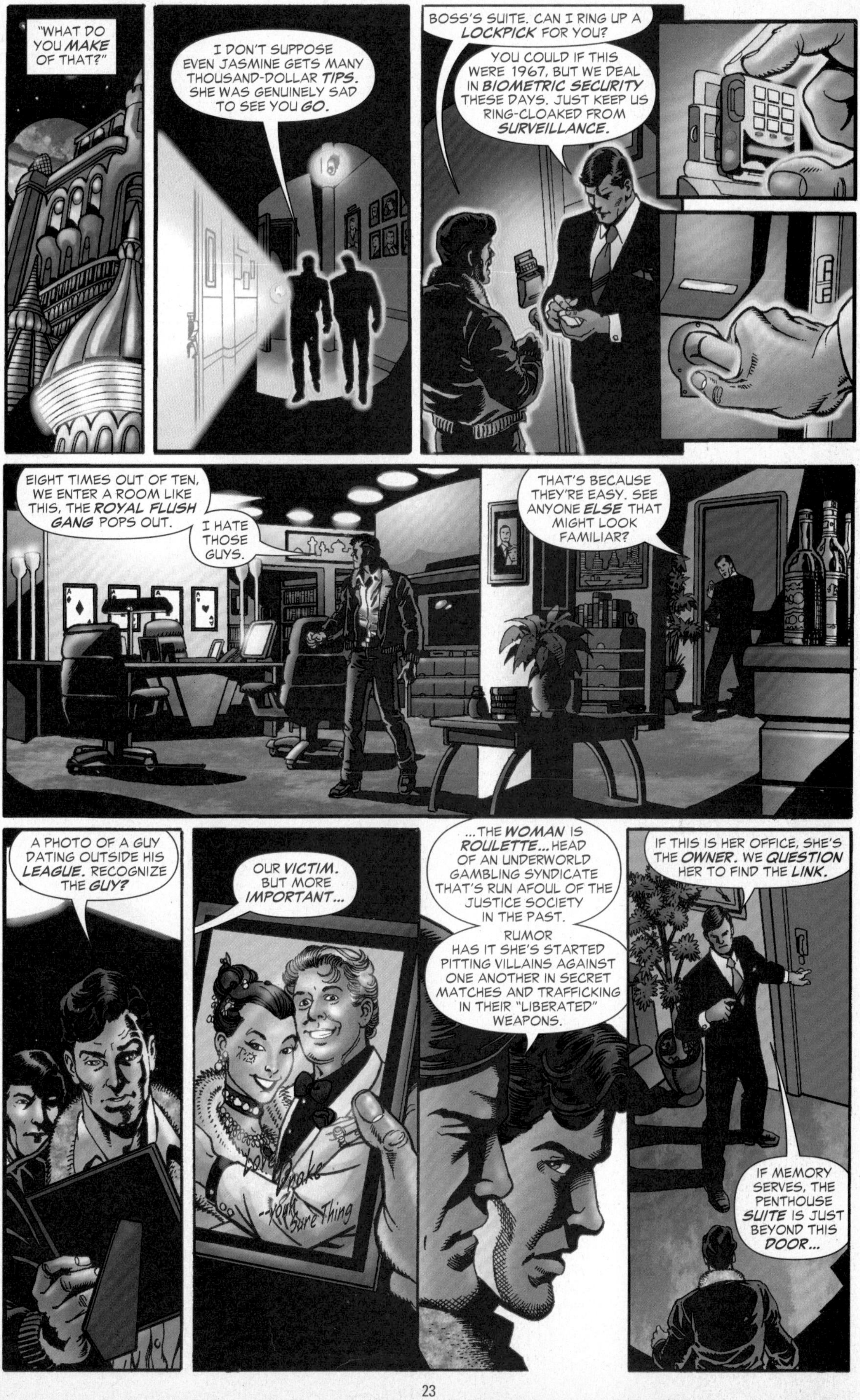
"WHAT DO YOU MAKE OF THAT?"
I DON'T SUPPOSE EVEN JASMINE GETS MANY THOUSAND-DOLLAR TIPS. SHE WAS GENUINELY SAD TO SEE YOU GO.
BOSS'S SUITE. CAN I RING UP A LOCKPICK FOR YOU?
YOU COULD IF THIS WERE 1967, BUT WE DEAL IN BIOMETRIC SECURITY THESE DAYS. JUST KEEP US RING-CLOAKED FROM SURVEILLANCE.
EIGHT TIMES OUT OF TEN, WE ENTER A ROOM LIKE THIS, THE ROYAL FLUSH GANG POPS OUT.
I HATE THOSE GUYS.
THAT'S BECAUSE THEY'RE EASY. SEE ANYONE ELSE THAT MIGHT LOOK FAMILIAR?
A PHOTO OF A GUY DATING OUTSIDE HIS LEAGUE. RECOGNIZE THE GUY?
OUR VICTIM. BUT MORE IMPORTANT...
Love Drake --your Sure Thing
...THE WOMAN IS ROULETTE... HEAD OF AN UNDERWORLD GAMBLING SYNDICATE THAT'S RUN AFOUL OF THE JUSTICE SOCIETY IN THE PAST.
RUMOR HAS IT SHE'S STARTED PITTING VILLAINS AGAINST ONE ANOTHER IN SECRET MATCHES AND TRAFFICKING IN THEIR "LIBERATED" WEAPONS.
IF THIS IS HER OFFICE, SHE'S THE OWNER. WE QUESTION HER TO FIND THE LINK.
IF MEMORY SERVES, THE PENTHOUSE SUITE IS JUST BEYOND THIS DOOR...

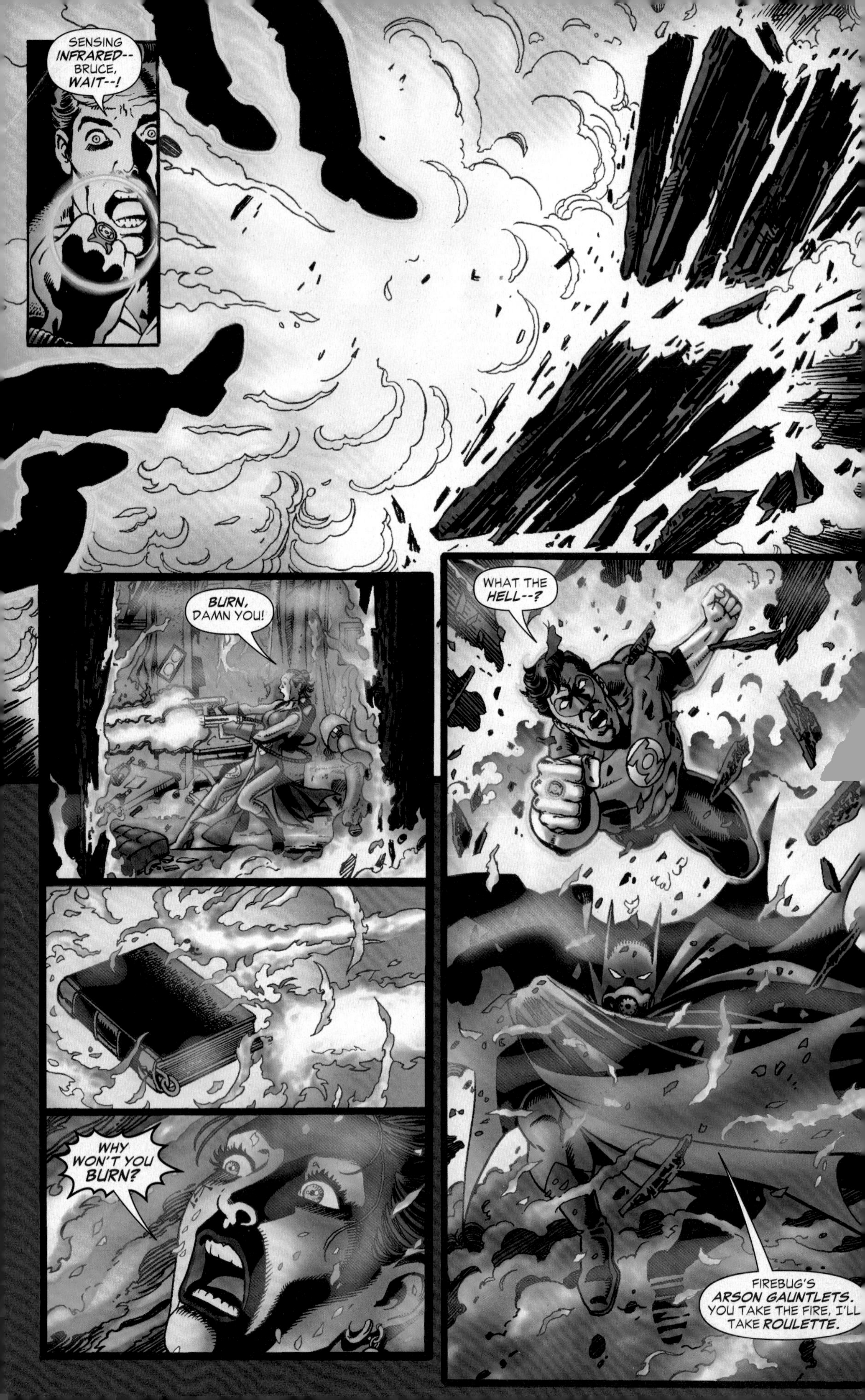
SENSING INFRARED-- BRUCE, WAIT--!
BURN, DAMN YOU!
WHAT THE HELL--?
WHY WON'T YOU BURN?
FIREBUG'S ARSON GAUNTLETS. YOU TAKE THE FIRE, I'LL TAKE ROULETTE.

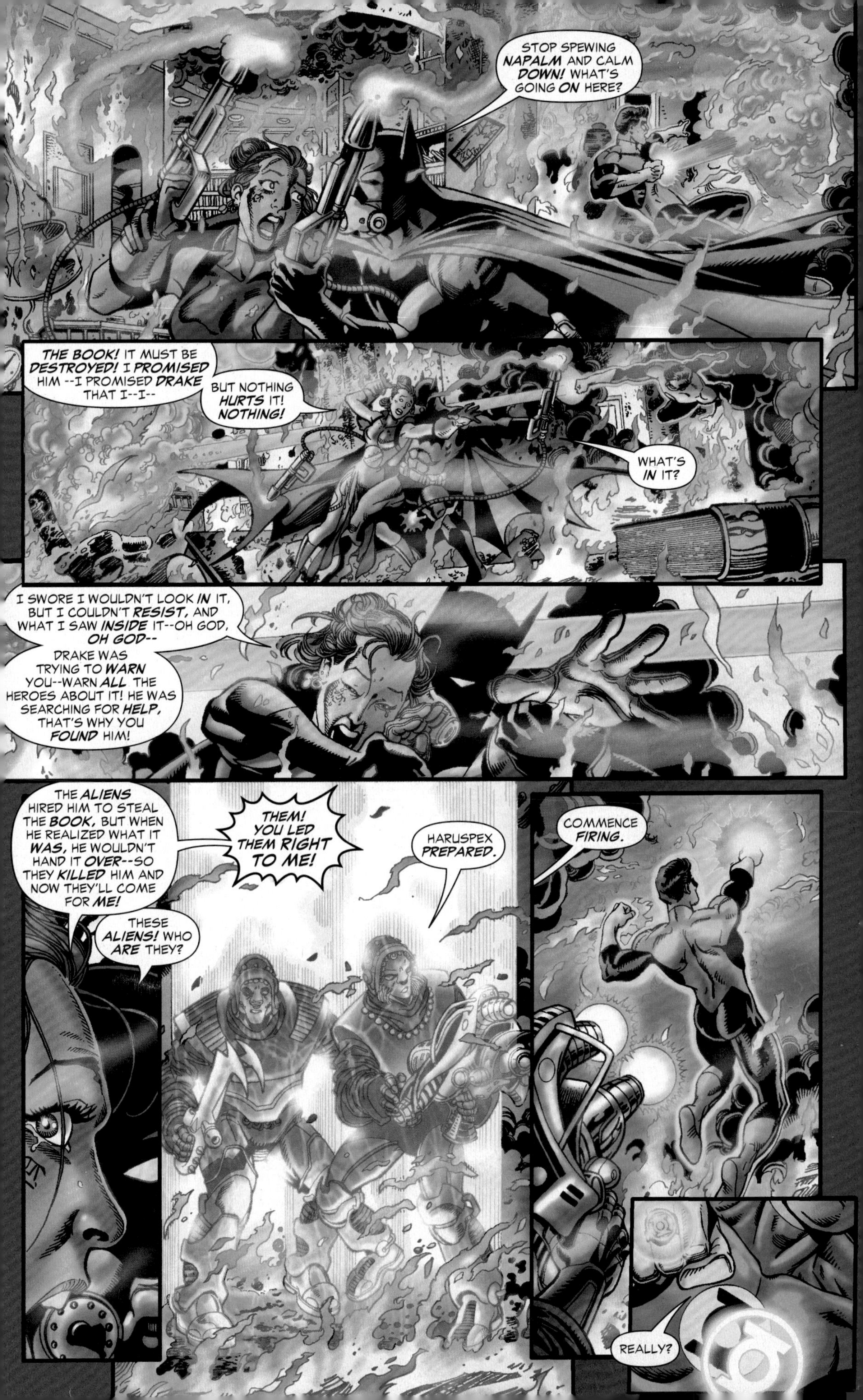

STOP SPEWING NAPALM AND CALM DOWN! WHAT'S GOING ON HERE?
THE BOOK! IT MUST BE DESTROYED! I PROMISED HIM --I PROMISED DRAKE THAT I--I--
BUT NOTHING HURTS IT! NOTHING!
WHAT'S IN IT?
I SWORE I WOULDN'T LOOK IN IT, BUT I COULDN'T RESIST, AND WHAT I SAW INSIDE IT--OH GOD, OH GOD--
DRAKE WAS TRYING TO WARN YOU--WARN ALL THE HEROES ABOUT IT! HE WAS SEARCHING FOR HELP, THAT'S WHY YOU FOUND HIM!
THE ALIENS HIRED HIM TO STEAL THE BOOK, BUT WHEN HE REALIZED WHAT IT WAS, HE WOULDN'T HAND IT OVER--SO THEY KILLED HIM AND NOW THEY'LL COME FOR ME!
THESE ALIENS! WHO ARE THEY?
THEM! YOU LED THEM RIGHT TO ME!
HARUSPEX PREPARED.
COMMENCE FIRING.
REALLY?

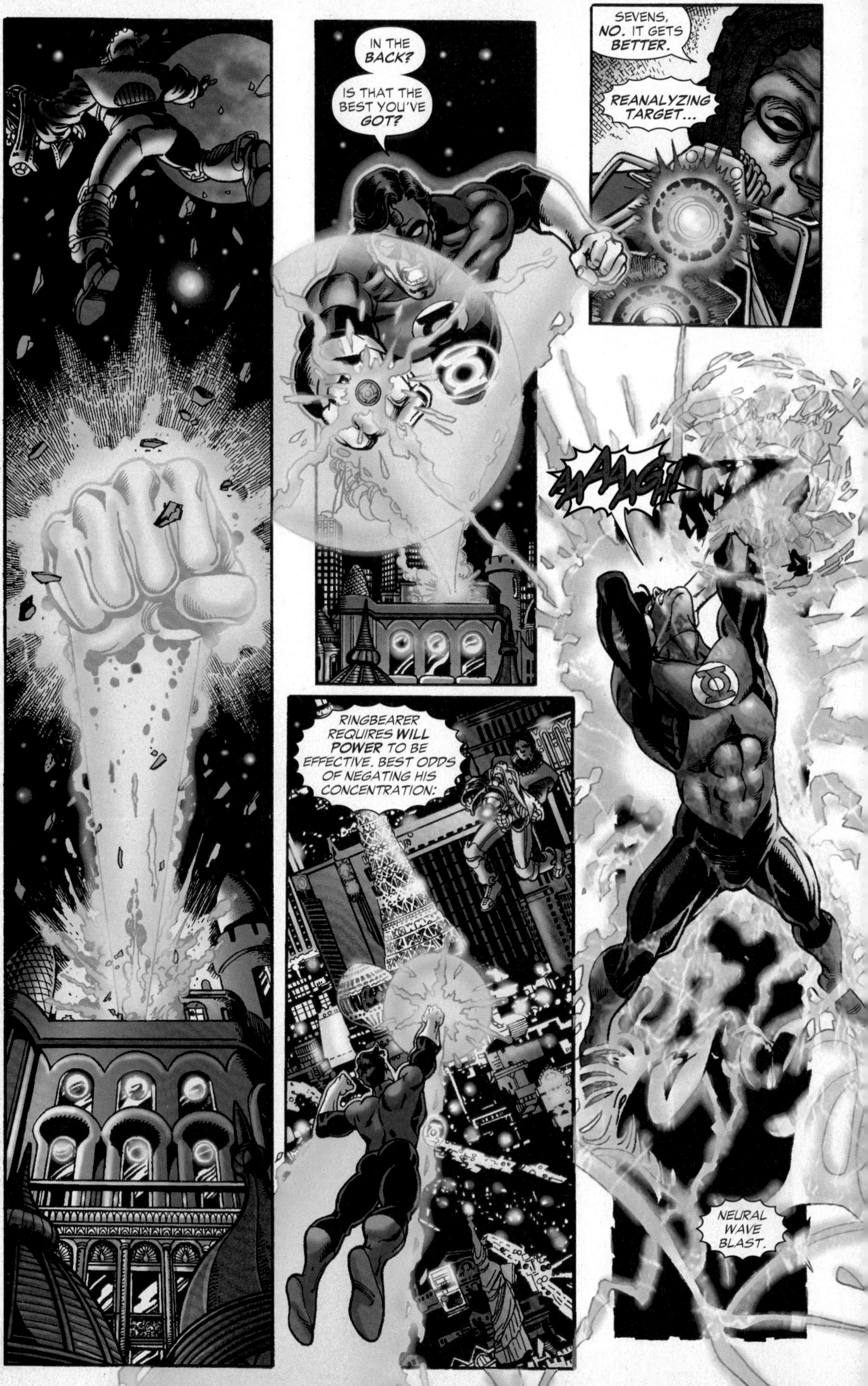
IN THE BACK?
IS THAT THE BEST YOU'VE GOT?
SEVENS, NO. IT GETS BETTER.
REANALYZING TARGET...
RINGBEARER REQUIRES WILL POWER TO BE EFFECTIVE. BEST ODDS OF NEGATING HIS CONCENTRATION:
AAAAAGH!
NEURAL WAVE BLAST.

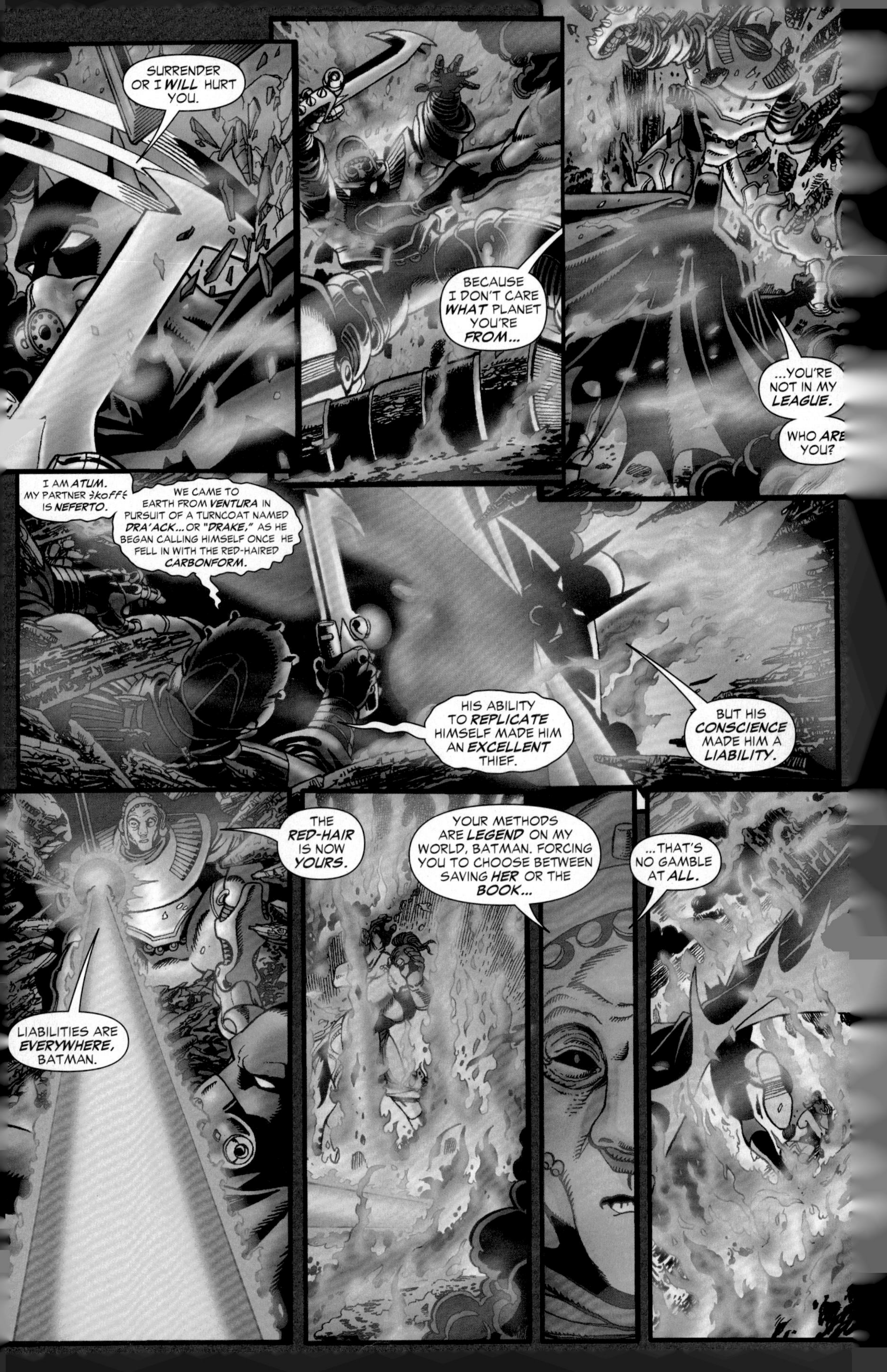
SURRENDER OR I WILL HURT YOU.
BECAUSE I DON'T CARE WHAT PLANET YOU'RE FROM...
...YOU'RE NOT IN MY LEAGUE.
WHO ARE YOU?
I AM ATUM. MY PARTNER ≷koff≶ IS NEFERTO.
WE CAME TO EARTH FROM VENTURA IN PURSUIT OF A TURNCOAT NAMED DRA'ACK...OR "DRAKE," AS HE BEGAN CALLING HIMSELF ONCE HE FELL IN WITH THE RED-HAIRED CARBONFORM.
HIS ABILITY TO REPLICATE HIMSELF MADE HIM AN EXCELLENT THIEF.
BUT HIS CONSCIENCE MADE HIM A LIABILITY.
LIABILITIES ARE EVERYWHERE, BATMAN.
THE RED-HAIR IS NOW YOURS.
YOUR METHODS ARE LEGEND ON MY WORLD, BATMAN. FORCING YOU TO CHOOSE BETWEEN SAVING HER OR THE BOOK...
...THAT'S NO GAMBLE AT ALL.

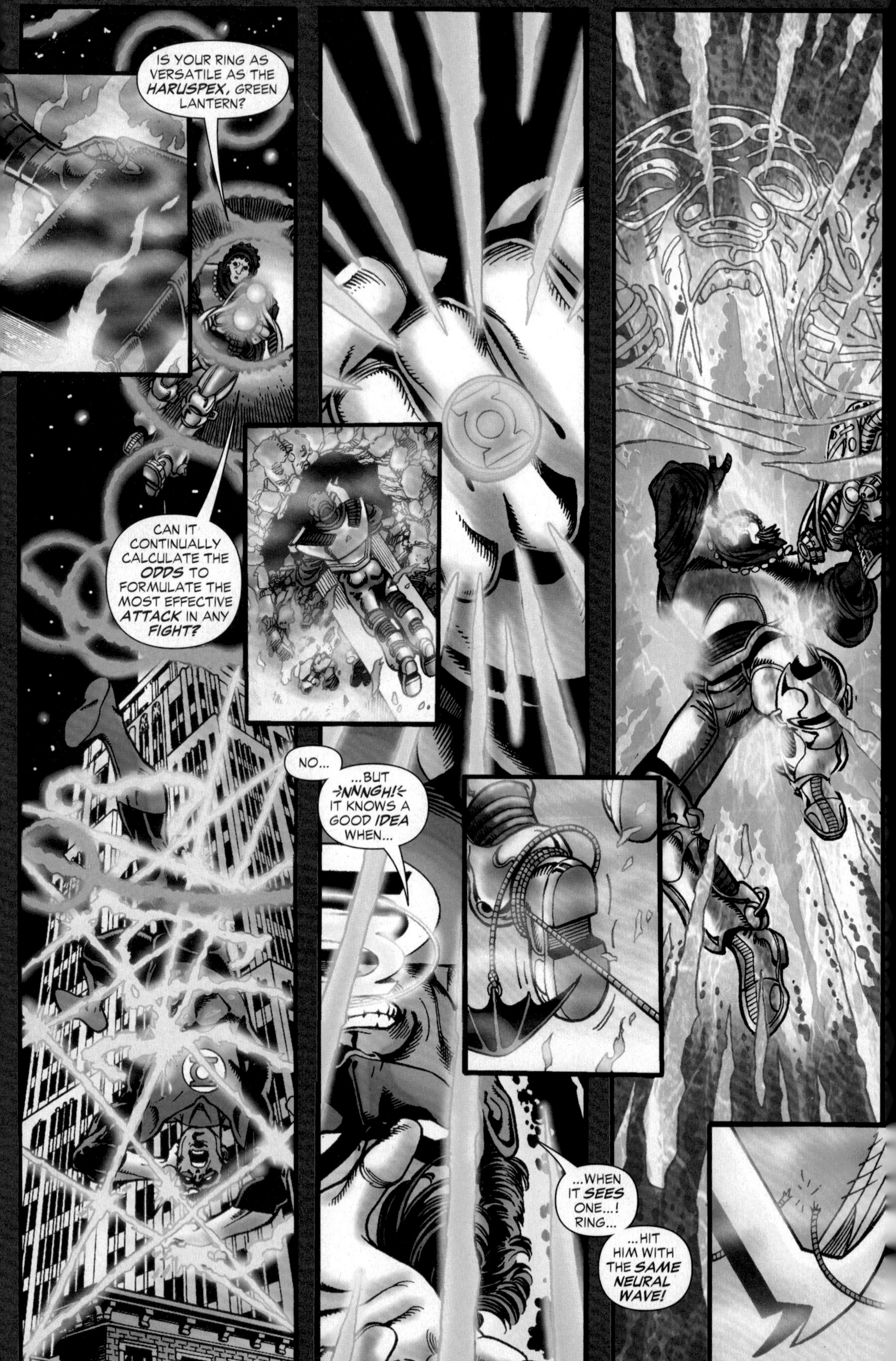
IS YOUR RING AS VERSATILE AS THE HARUSPEX, GREEN LANTERN?
CAN IT CONTINUALLY CALCULATE THE ODDS TO FORMULATE THE MOST EFFECTIVE ATTACK IN ANY FIGHT?
NO...
...BUT NNNGH! IT KNOWS A GOOD IDEA WHEN...
...WHEN IT SEES ONE...! RING...
...HIT HIM WITH THE SAME NEURAL WAVE!

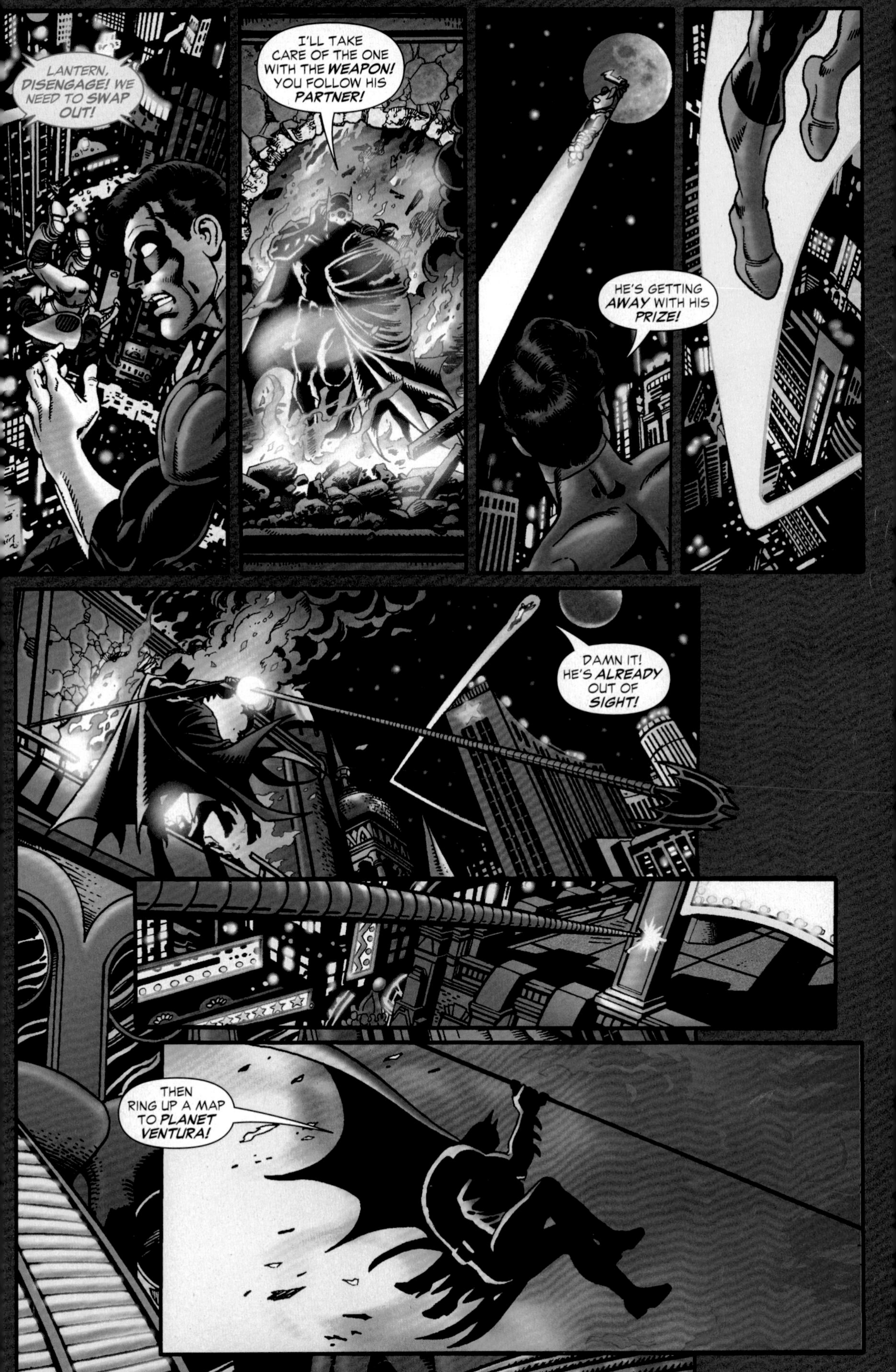
LANTERN, DISENGAGE! WE NEED TO SWAP OUT!
I'LL TAKE CARE OF THE ONE WITH THE WEAPON! YOU FOLLOW HIS PARTNER!
HE'S GETTING AWAY WITH HIS PRIZE!
DAMN IT! HE'S ALREADY OUT OF SIGHT!
THEN RING UP A MAP TO PLANET VENTURA!

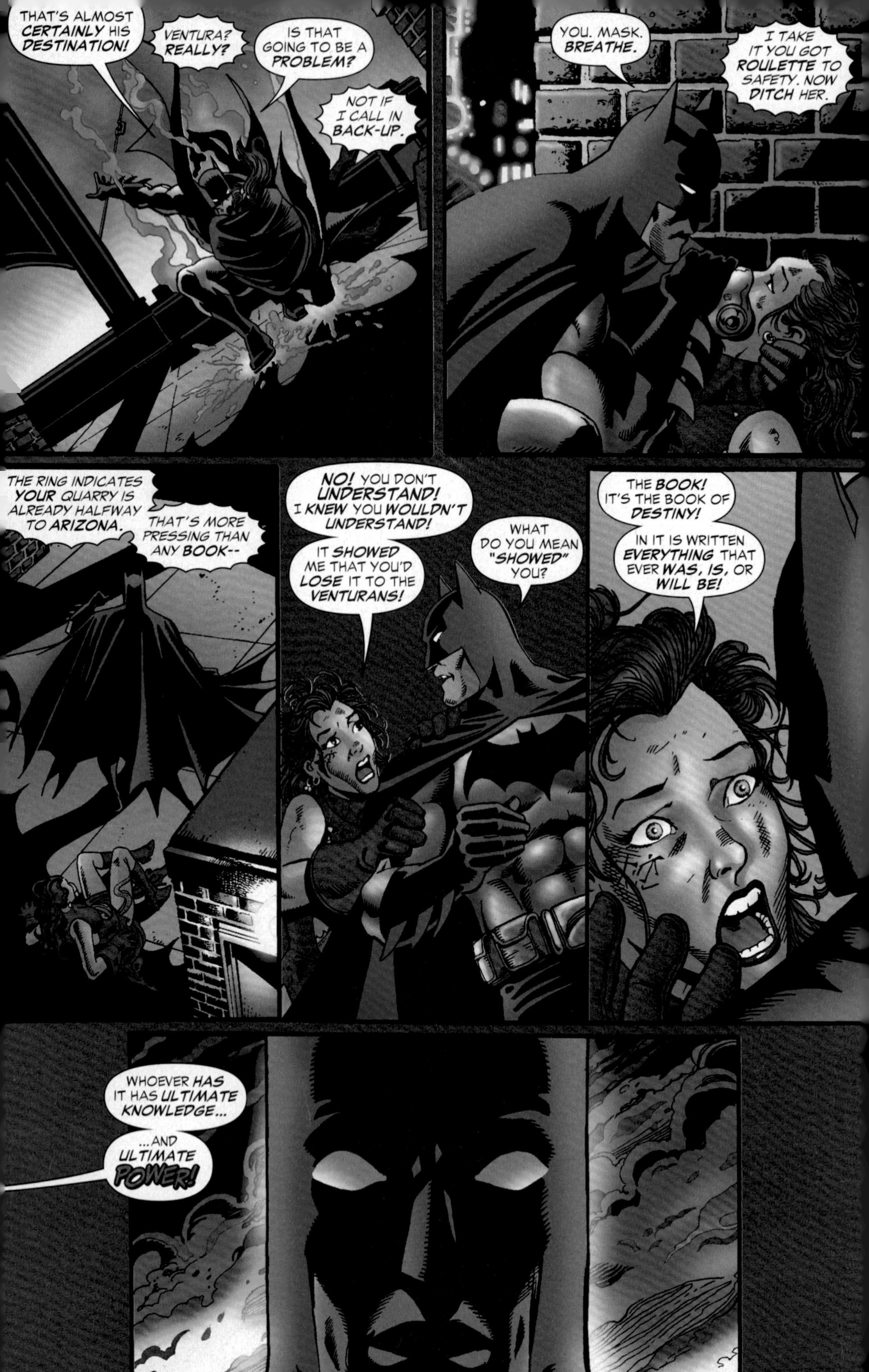
THAT'S ALMOST CERTAINLY HIS DESTINATION!
VENTURA? REALLY?
IS THAT GOING TO BE A PROBLEM?
NOT IF I CALL IN BACK-UP.
YOU. MASK. BREATHE.
I TAKE IT YOU GOT ROULETTE TO SAFETY. NOW DITCH HER.
THE RING INDICATES YOUR QUARRY IS ALREADY HALFWAY TO ARIZONA.
THAT'S MORE PRESSING THAN ANY BOOK--
NO! YOU DON'T UNDERSTAND! I KNEW YOU WOULDN'T UNDERSTAND!
IT SHOWED ME THAT YOU'D LOSE IT TO THE VENTURANS!
WHAT DO YOU MEAN "SHOWED" YOU?
THE BOOK! IT'S THE BOOK OF DESTINY!
IN IT IS WRITTEN EVERYTHING THAT EVER WAS, IS, OR WILL BE!
WHOEVER HAS IT HAS ULTIMATE KNOWLEDGE...
...AND ULTIMATE POWER!

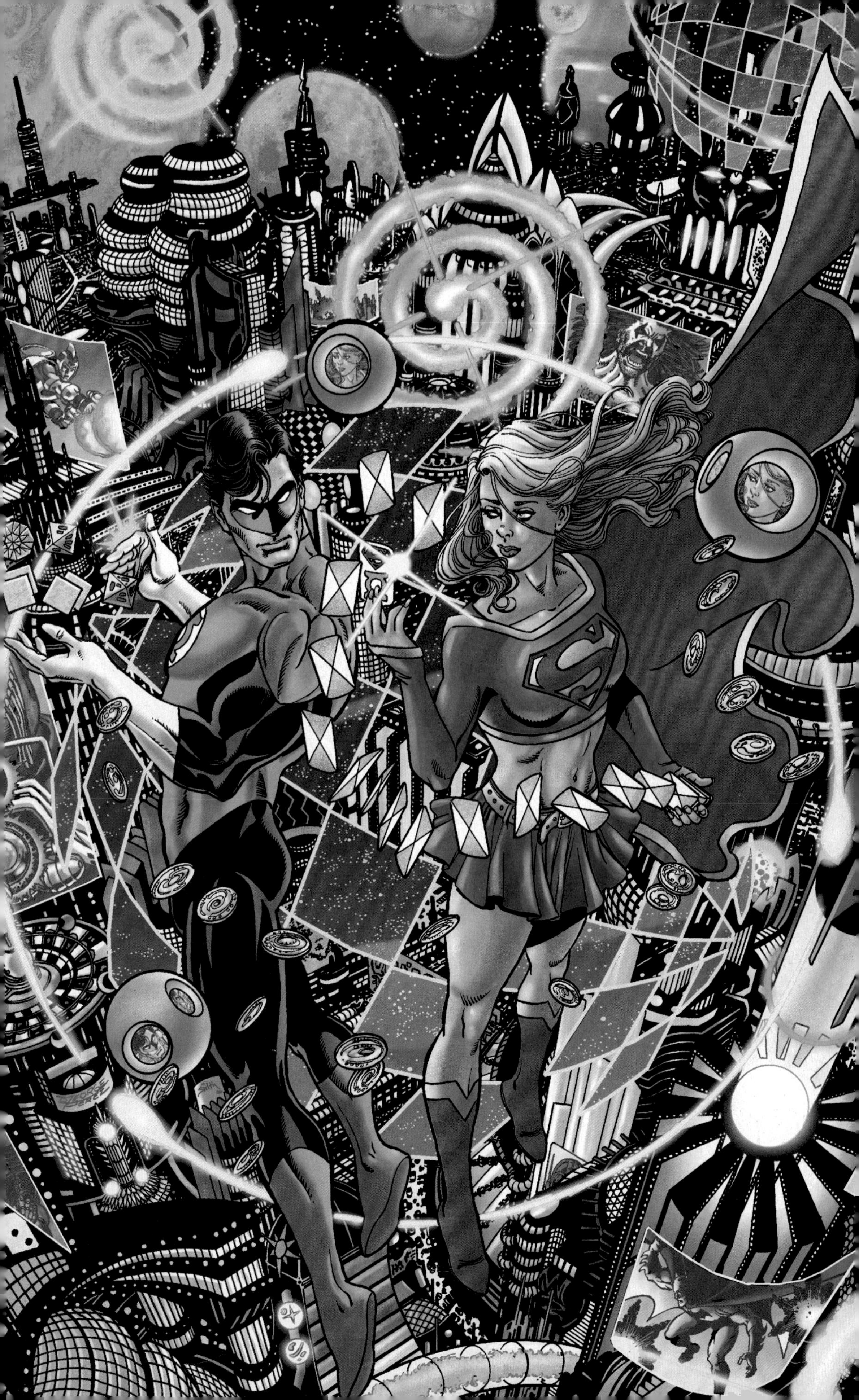

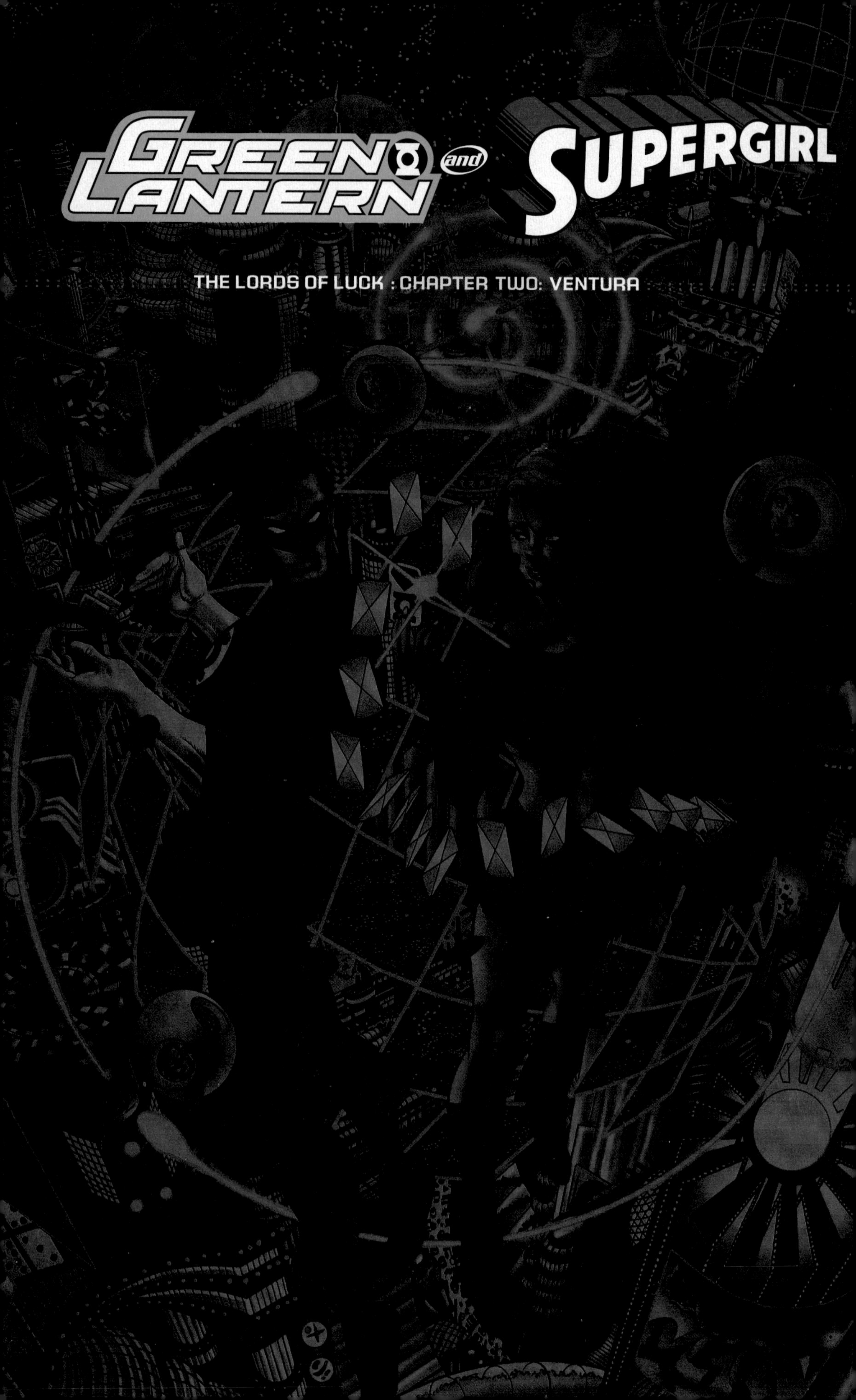
GREEN LANTERN and SUPERGIRL
THE LORDS OF LUCK : CHAPTER TWO: VENTURA

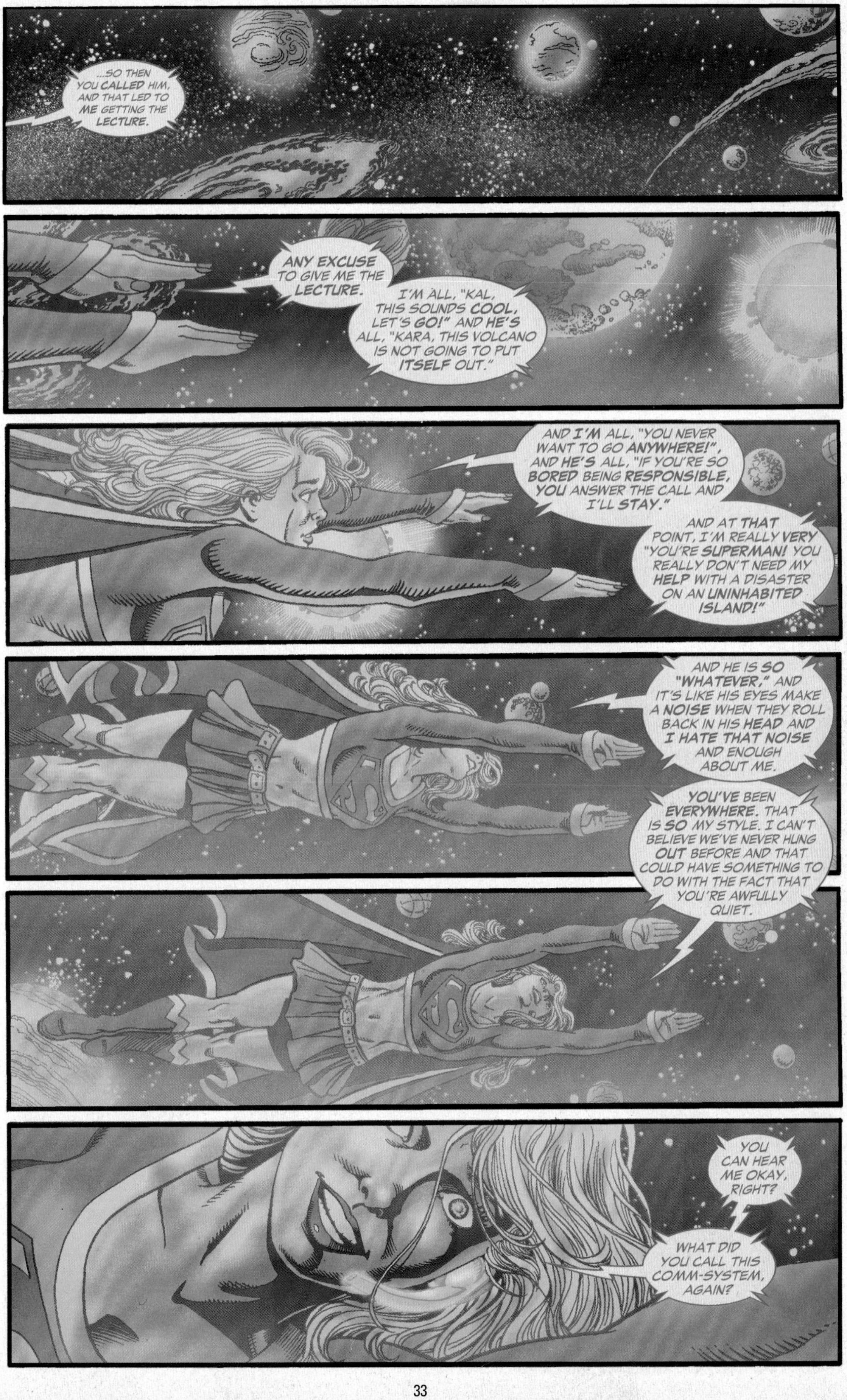
...SO THEN YOU CALLED HIM, AND THAT LED TO ME GETTING THE LECTURE.
ANY EXCUSE TO GIVE ME THE LECTURE.
I'M ALL, "KAL, THIS SOUNDS COOL, LET'S GO!" AND HE'S ALL, "KARA, THIS VOLCANO IS NOT GOING TO PUT ITSELF OUT."
AND I'M ALL, "YOU NEVER WANT TO GO ANYWHERE!", AND HE'S ALL, "IF YOU'RE SO BORED BEING RESPONSIBLE, YOU ANSWER THE CALL AND I'LL STAY."
AND AT THAT POINT, I'M REALLY VERY "YOU'RE SUPERMAN! YOU REALLY DON'T NEED MY HELP WITH A DISASTER ON AN UNINHABITED ISLAND!"
AND HE IS SO "WHATEVER," AND IT'S LIKE HIS EYES MAKE A NOISE WHEN THEY ROLL BACK IN HIS HEAD AND I HATE THAT NOISE AND ENOUGH ABOUT ME.
YOU'VE BEEN EVERYWHERE. THAT IS SO MY STYLE. I CAN'T BELIEVE WE'VE NEVER HUNG OUT BEFORE AND THAT COULD HAVE SOMETHING TO DO WITH THE FACT THAT YOU'RE AWFULLY QUIET.
YOU CAN HEAR ME OKAY, RIGHT?
WHAT DID YOU CALL THIS COMM-SYSTEM, AGAIN?

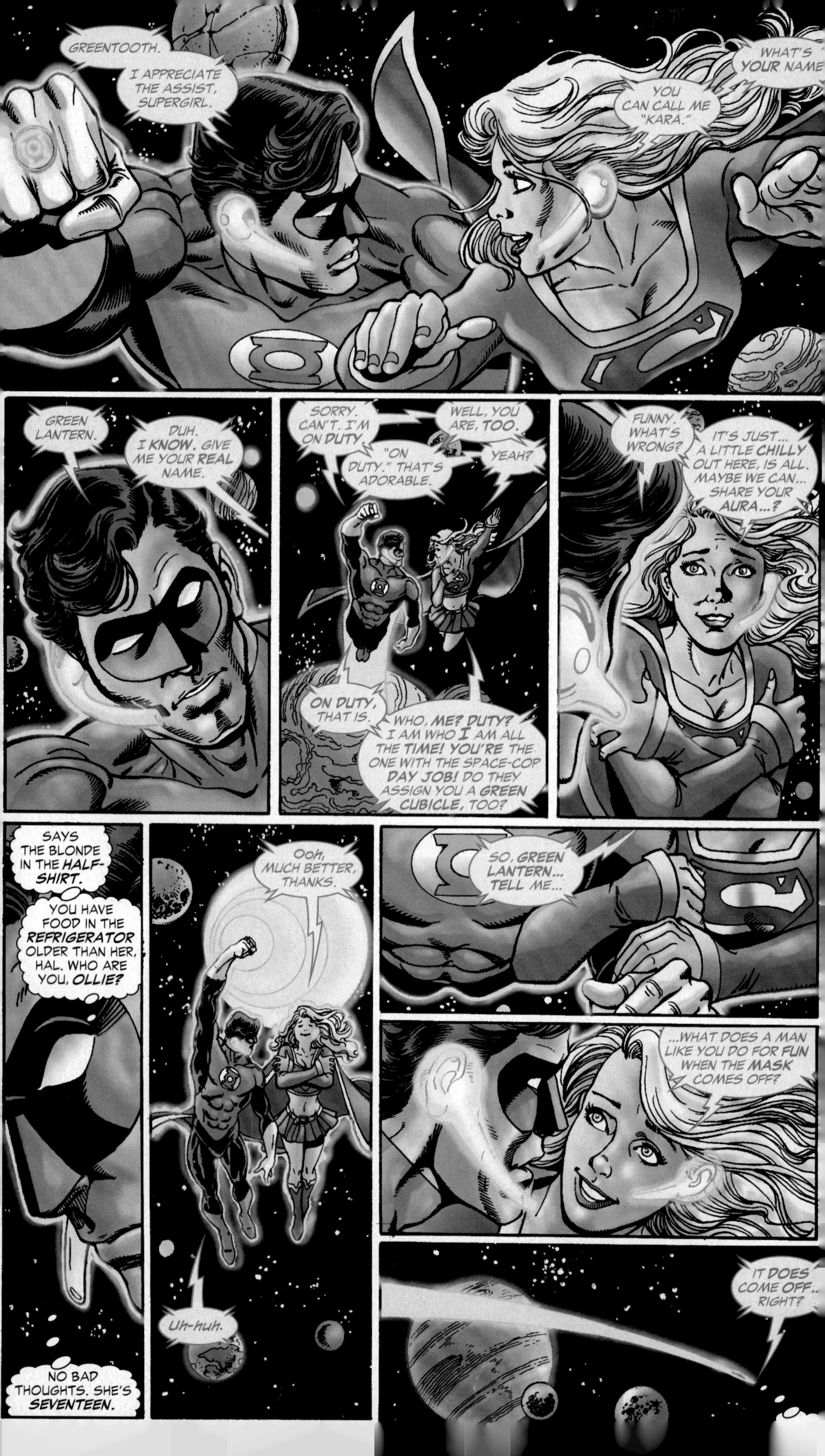
GREENTOOTH.
I APPRECIATE THE ASSIST, SUPERGIRL.
WHAT'S YOUR NAME
YOU CAN CALL ME "KARA."
GREEN LANTERN.
DUH. I KNOW. GIVE ME YOUR REAL NAME.
SORRY. CAN'T. I'M ON DUTY.
WELL, YOU ARE, TOO.
"ON DUTY." THAT'S ADORABLE.
YEAH?
ON DUTY, THAT IS.
WHO, ME? DUTY? I AM WHO I AM ALL THE TIME! YOU'RE THE ONE WITH THE SPACE-COP DAY JOB! DO THEY ASSIGN YOU A GREEN CUBICLE, TOO?
FUNNY. WHAT'S WRONG?
IT'S JUST... A LITTLE CHILLY OUT HERE, IS ALL. MAYBE WE CAN... SHARE YOUR AURA...?
SAYS THE BLONDE IN THE HALF-SHIRT.
YOU HAVE FOOD IN THE REFRIGERATOR OLDER THAN HER, HAL. WHO ARE YOU, OLLIE?
NO BAD THOUGHTS. SHE'S SEVENTEEN.
Ooh, MUCH BETTER, THANKS.
Uh-huh.
SO, GREEN LANTERN... TELL ME...
...WHAT DOES A MAN LIKE YOU DO FOR FUN WHEN THE MASK COMES OFF?
IT DOES COME OFF... RIGHT?

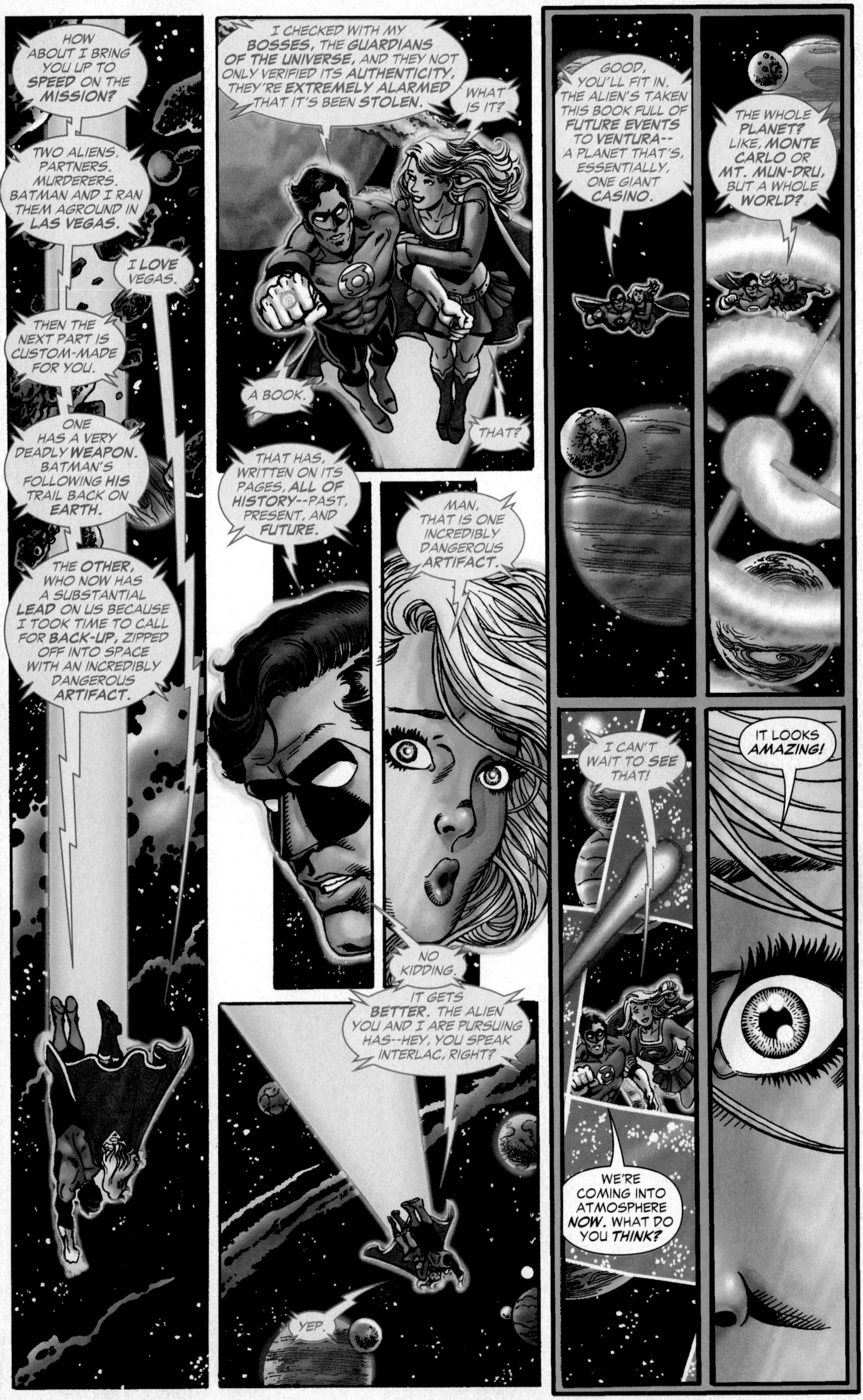
HOW ABOUT I BRING YOU UP TO SPEED ON THE MISSION?
TWO ALIENS. PARTNERS. MURDERERS. BATMAN AND I RAN THEM AGROUND IN LAS VEGAS.
I LOVE VEGAS.
THEN THE NEXT PART IS CUSTOM-MADE FOR YOU.
ONE HAS A VERY DEADLY WEAPON. BATMAN'S FOLLOWING HIS TRAIL BACK ON EARTH.
THE OTHER, WHO NOW HAS A SUBSTANTIAL LEAD ON US BECAUSE I TOOK TIME TO CALL FOR BACK-UP, ZIPPED OFF INTO SPACE WITH AN INCREDIBLY DANGEROUS ARTIFACT.
I CHECKED WITH MY BOSSES, THE GUARDIANS OF THE UNIVERSE, AND THEY NOT ONLY VERIFIED ITS AUTHENTICITY, THEY'RE EXTREMELY ALARMED THAT IT'S BEEN STOLEN.
WHAT IS IT?
A BOOK.
THAT?
THAT HAS, WRITTEN ON ITS PAGES, ALL OF HISTORY--PAST, PRESENT, AND FUTURE.
MAN, THAT IS ONE INCREDIBLY DANGEROUS ARTIFACT.
NO KIDDING.
IT GETS BETTER. THE ALIEN YOU AND I ARE PURSUING HAS--HEY, YOU SPEAK INTERLAC, RIGHT?
YEP.
GOOD, YOU'LL FIT IN. THE ALIEN'S TAKEN THIS BOOK FULL OF FUTURE EVENTS TO VENTURA-- A PLANET THAT'S, ESSENTIALLY, ONE GIANT CASINO.
THE WHOLE PLANET? LIKE, MONTE CARLO OR MT. MUN-DRU, BUT A WHOLE WORLD?
I CAN'T WAIT TO SEE THAT!
WE'RE COMING INTO ATMOSPHERE NOW. WHAT DO YOU THINK?
IT LOOKS AMAZING!

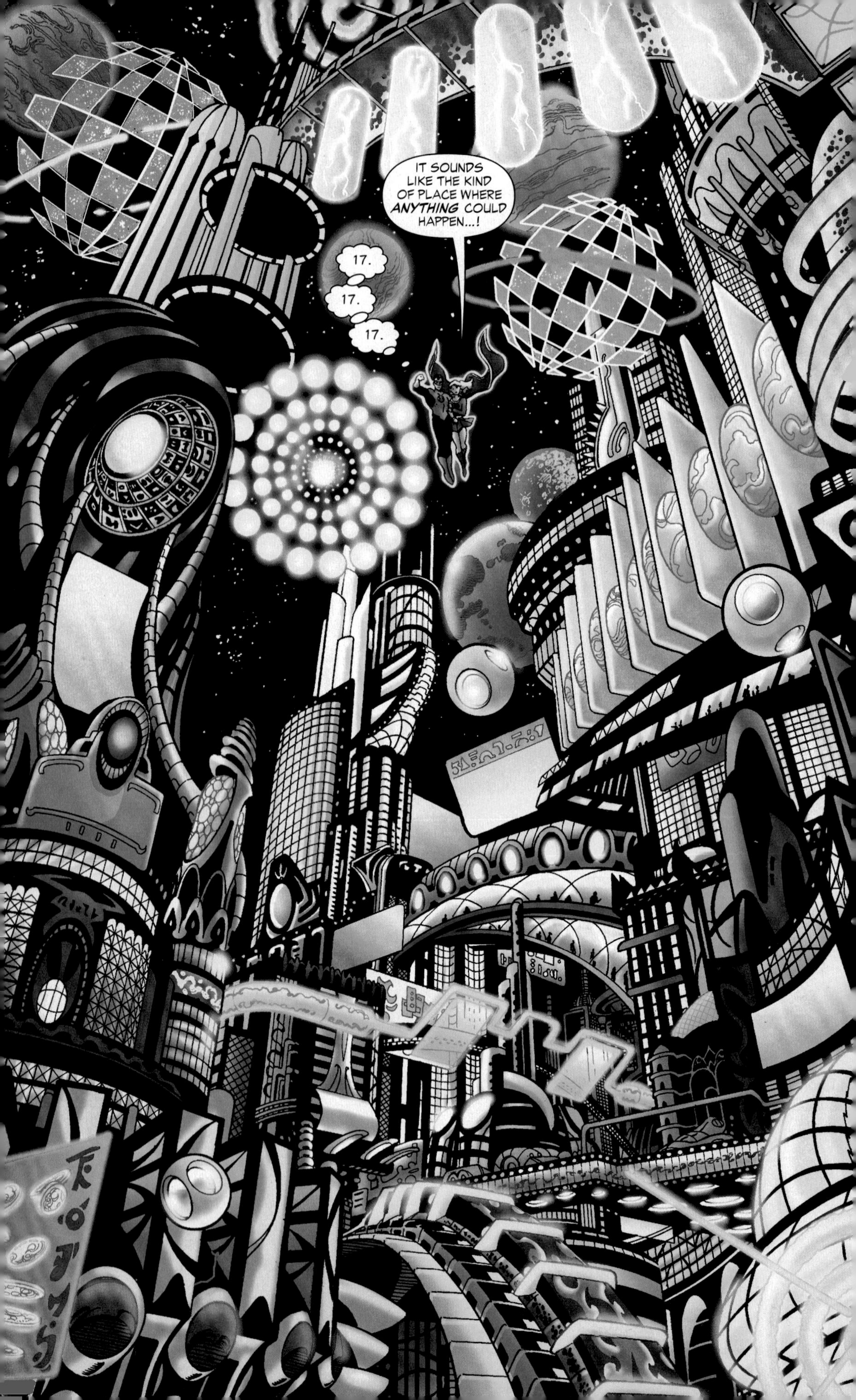
17.
17.
17.
IT SOUNDS LIKE THE KIND OF PLACE WHERE *ANYTHING* COULD HAPPEN...!

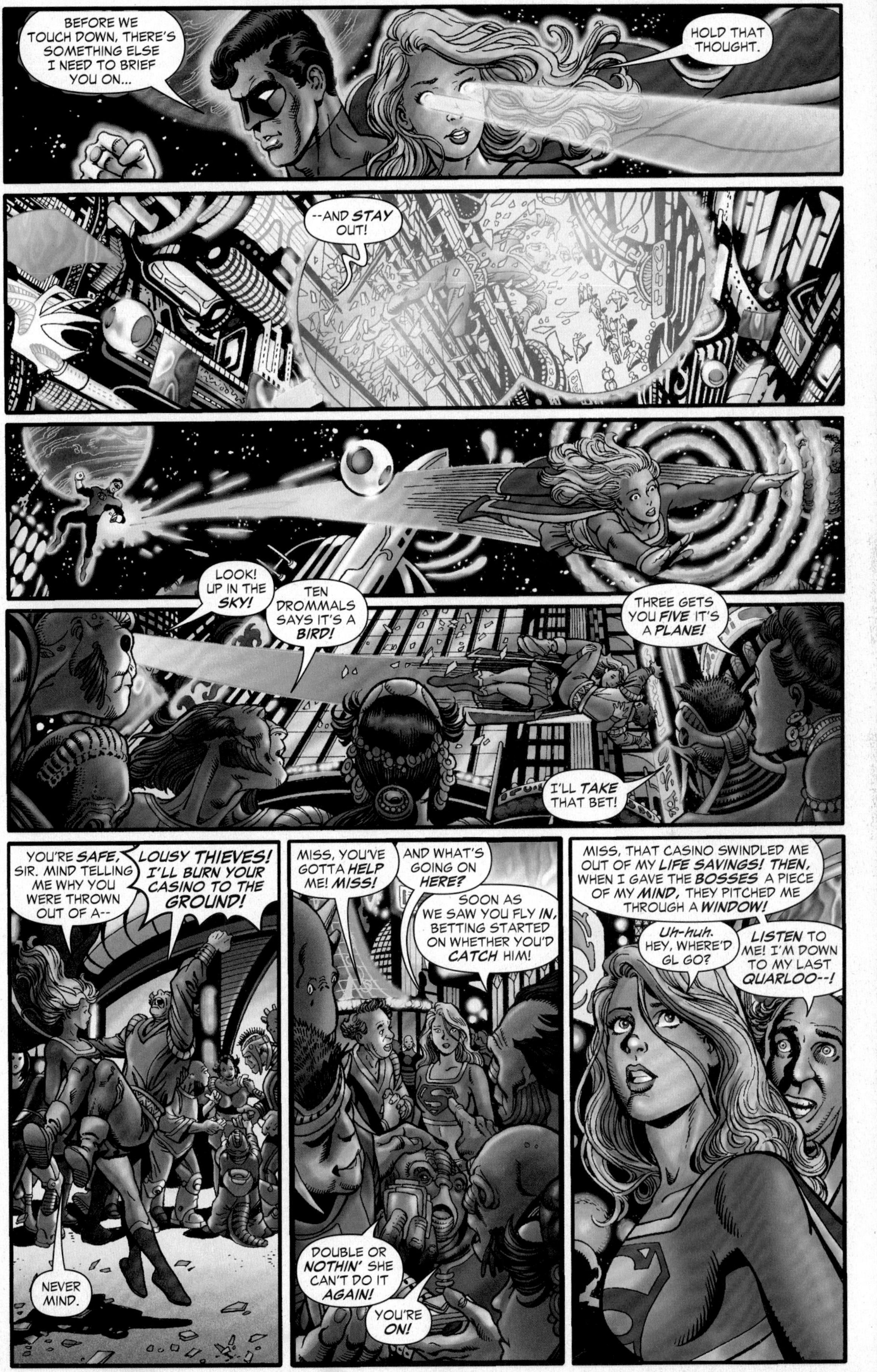
BEFORE WE TOUCH DOWN, THERE'S SOMETHING ELSE I NEED TO BRIEF YOU ON...
HOLD THAT THOUGHT.
--AND STAY OUT!
LOOK! UP IN THE SKY!
TEN DROMMALS SAYS IT'S A BIRD!
THREE GETS YOU FIVE IT'S A PLANE!
I'LL TAKE THAT BET!
YOU'RE SAFE, SIR. MIND TELLING ME WHY YOU WERE THROWN OUT OF A--
LOUSY THIEVES! I'LL BURN YOUR CASINO TO THE GROUND!
NEVER MIND.
MISS, YOU'VE GOTTA HELP ME! MISS!
AND WHAT'S GOING ON HERE?
SOON AS WE SAW YOU FLY IN, BETTING STARTED ON WHETHER YOU'D CATCH HIM!
DOUBLE OR NOTHIN' SHE CAN'T DO IT AGAIN!
YOU'RE ON!
MISS, THAT CASINO SWINDLED ME OUT OF MY LIFE SAVINGS! THEN, WHEN I GAVE THE BOSSES A PIECE OF MY MIND, THEY PITCHED ME THROUGH A WINDOW!
Uh-huh. HEY, WHERE'D GL GO?
LISTEN TO ME! I'M DOWN TO MY LAST QUARLOO--!

SHE CAN'T GET INVOLVED, SIR. MOVE ALONG.

BUT--

I SAID, MOVE ALONG.

GREAT. FIRST I LOSE MY *RIDE*, NOW A *COP* IS ORDERING ME AROUND.

OFFICER, THIS MAN CLAIMS HE WAS *CHEATED*. IS THERE SOMEONE HE CAN TAKE A *GRIEVANCE* TO?

Oh! GL!

HE WASN'T CHEATED. HE WAS JUST *UNLUCKY*.

HOW DO *YOU* KNOW?

BECAUSE THE LAWS HERE APPLY TO GAME *RUNNERS* AS WELL AS GAME *PLAYERS*.

THE ONLY WAY AN ENTIRE PLANETARY ECONOMY CAN SURVIVE ON A FOUNDATION OF GAMBLING IS BY ENFORCING *VERY* STRICT REGULATIONS.

SEE FOR *YOURSELF*.

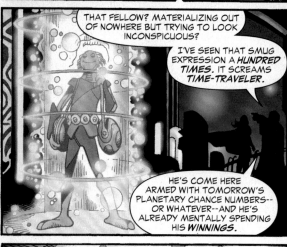

THAT FELLOW? MATERIALIZING OUT OF NOWHERE BUT TRYING TO LOOK INCONSPICUOUS?

I'VE SEEN THAT SMUG EXPRESSION A *HUNDRED TIMES*. IT SCREAMS *TIME-TRAVELER*.

HE'S COME HERE ARMED WITH TOMORROW'S PLANETARY CHANCE NUMBERS-- OR WHATEVER--AND HE'S ALREADY MENTALLY SPENDING HIS *WINNINGS*.

"HE DOESN'T KNOW VENTURA IS *CONTINUALLY PATROLLED* BY THE *HOUNDS OF CHAOS*."

"THEY'RE TRAINED TO SNIFF OUT THE SLIGHTEST *WHIFF* OF *CHRONAL DISTORTION* OR *PROBABILITY STACKING*."

AND THAT'S JUST A *TASTE* OF THE SECURITY MEASURES HERE. VENTURA HAS A *ZERO TOLERANCE POLICY* ON PRECOGS, CHRONONAUTS, SCRYING DEVICES...

HARSH.

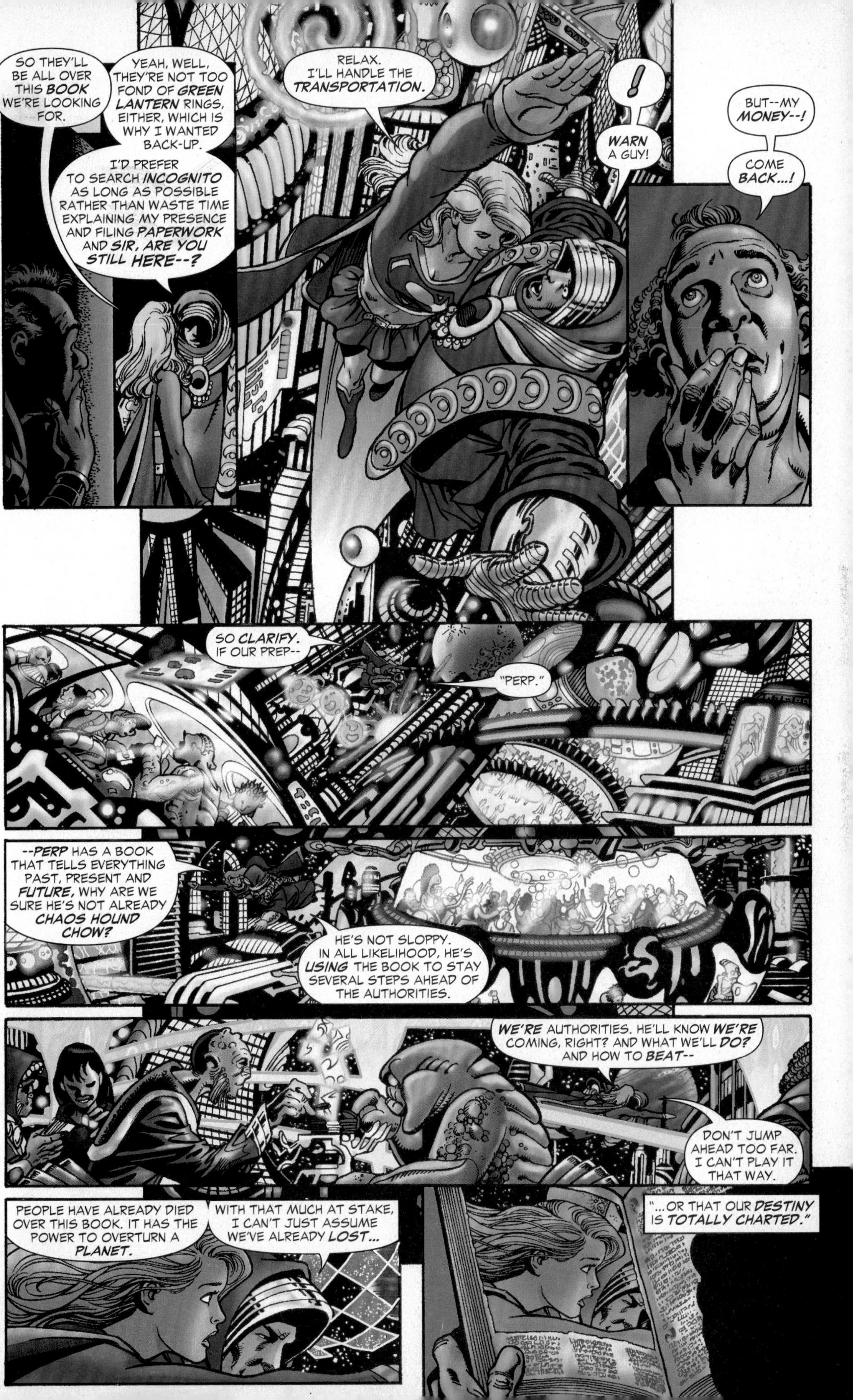

SO THEY'LL BE ALL OVER THIS BOOK WE'RE LOOKING FOR.
YEAH, WELL, THEY'RE NOT TOO FOND OF GREEN LANTERN RINGS, EITHER, WHICH IS WHY I WANTED BACK-UP.
I'D PREFER TO SEARCH INCOGNITO AS LONG AS POSSIBLE RATHER THAN WASTE TIME EXPLAINING MY PRESENCE AND FILING PAPERWORK AND SIR, ARE YOU STILL HERE--?
RELAX. I'LL HANDLE THE TRANSPORTATION.
!
WARN A GUY!
BUT--MY MONEY--!
COME BACK...!
SO CLARIFY. IF OUR PREP--
"PERP."
--PERP HAS A BOOK THAT TELLS EVERYTHING PAST, PRESENT AND FUTURE, WHY ARE WE SURE HE'S NOT ALREADY CHAOS HOUND CHOW?
HE'S NOT SLOPPY. IN ALL LIKELIHOOD, HE'S USING THE BOOK TO STAY SEVERAL STEPS AHEAD OF THE AUTHORITIES.
WE'RE AUTHORITIES. HE'LL KNOW WE'RE COMING, RIGHT? AND WHAT WE'LL DO? AND HOW TO BEAT--
DON'T JUMP AHEAD TOO FAR. I CAN'T PLAY IT THAT WAY.
PEOPLE HAVE ALREADY DIED OVER THIS BOOK. IT HAS THE POWER TO OVERTURN A PLANET.
WITH THAT MUCH AT STAKE, I CAN'T JUST ASSUME WE'VE ALREADY LOST...
"...OR THAT OUR DESTINY IS TOTALLY CHARTED."

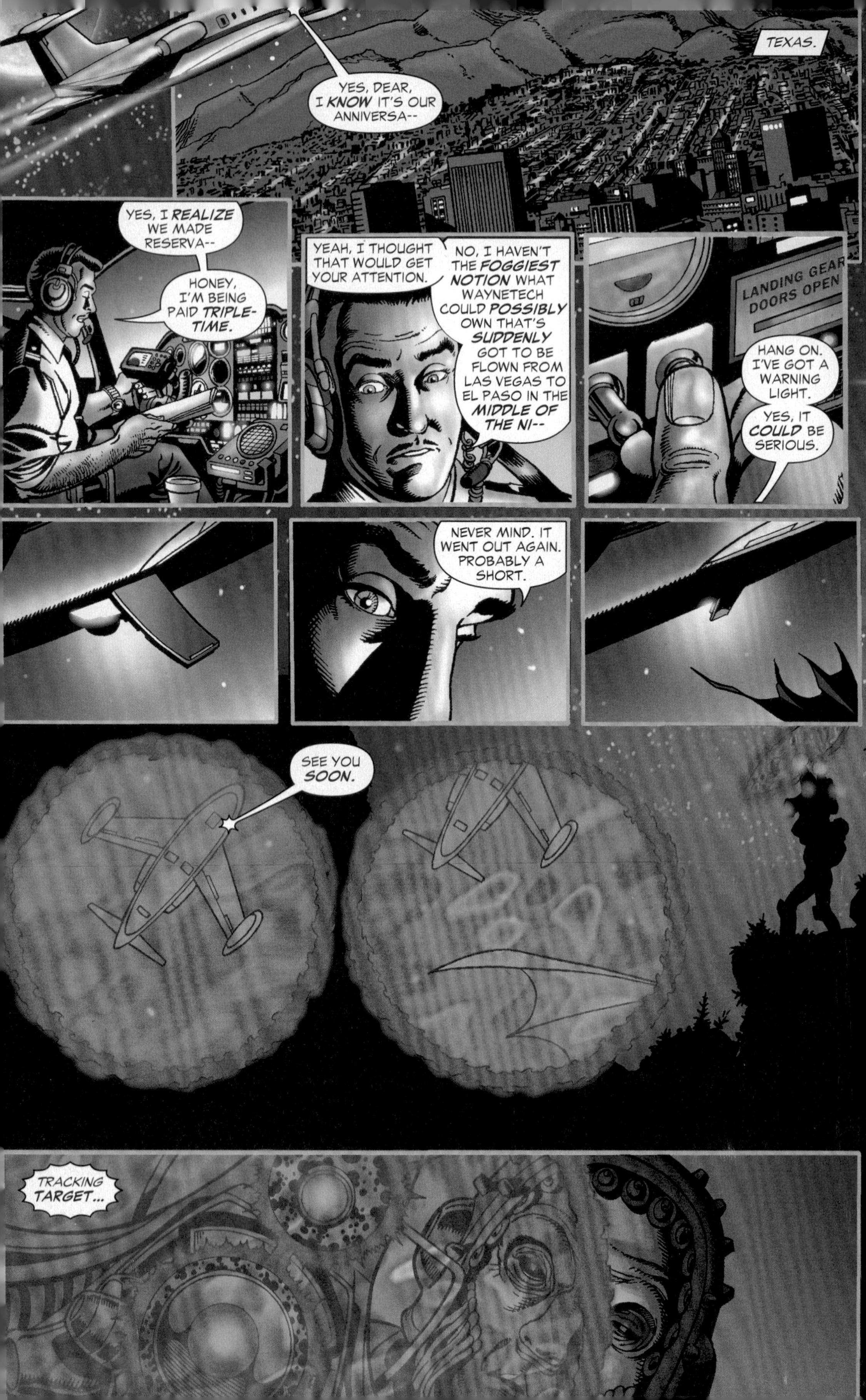
TEXAS.
YES, DEAR, I KNOW IT'S OUR ANNIVERSA--
YES, I REALIZE WE MADE RESERVA--
HONEY, I'M BEING PAID TRIPLE-TIME.
YEAH, I THOUGHT THAT WOULD GET YOUR ATTENTION.
NO, I HAVEN'T THE FOGGIEST NOTION WHAT WAYNETECH COULD POSSIBLY OWN THAT'S SUDDENLY GOT TO BE FLOWN FROM LAS VEGAS TO EL PASO IN THE MIDDLE OF THE NI--
LANDING GEAR DOORS OPEN
HANG ON. I'VE GOT A WARNING LIGHT.
YES, IT COULD BE SERIOUS.
NEVER MIND. IT WENT OUT AGAIN. PROBABLY A SHORT.
SEE YOU SOON.
TRACKING TARGET...

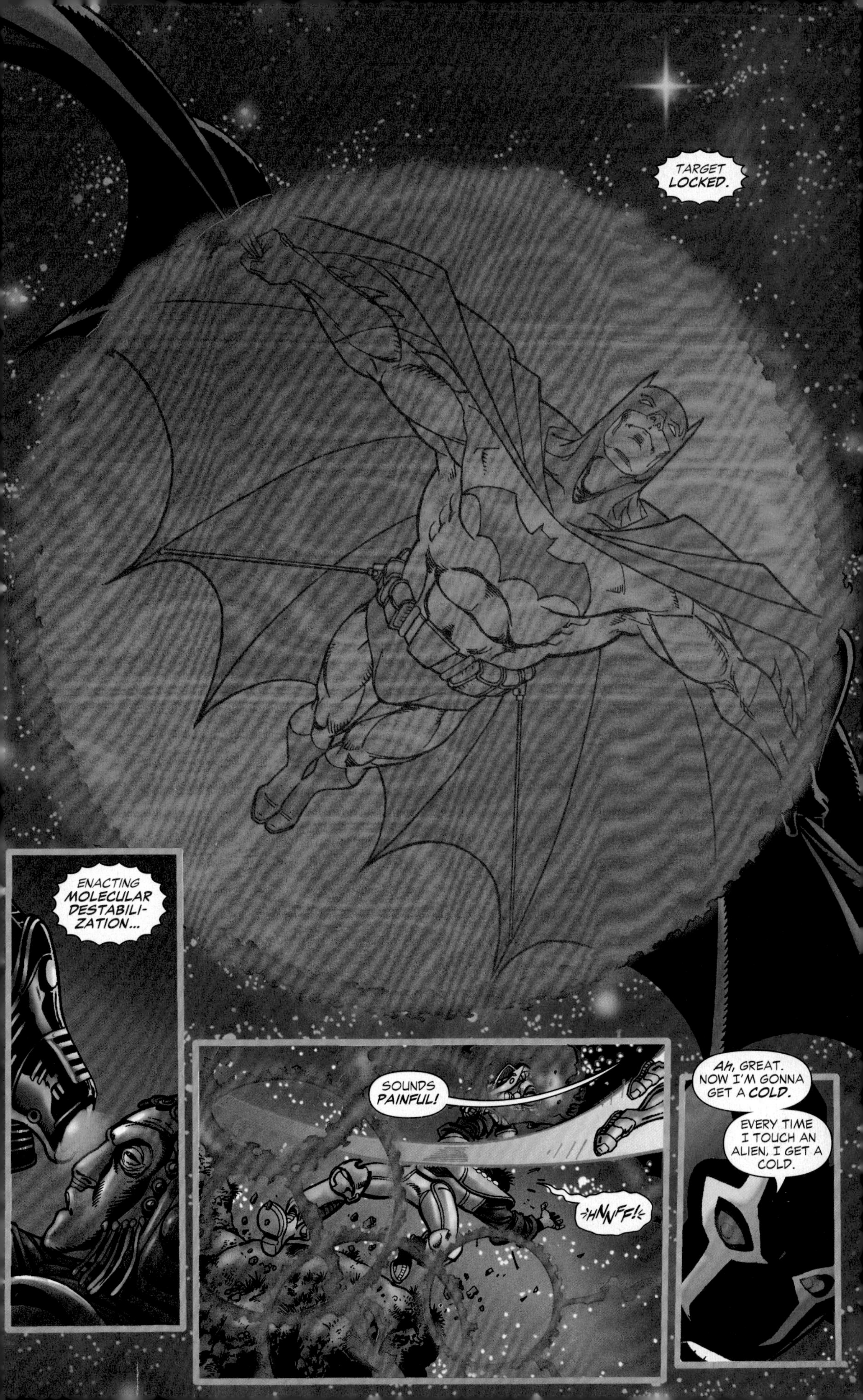
TARGET LOCKED.
ENACTING MOLECULAR DESTABILI-ZATION...
SOUNDS PAINFUL!
HNNFF!
AH, GREAT. NOW I'M GONNA GET A COLD.
EVERY TIME I TOUCH AN ALIEN, I GET A COLD.

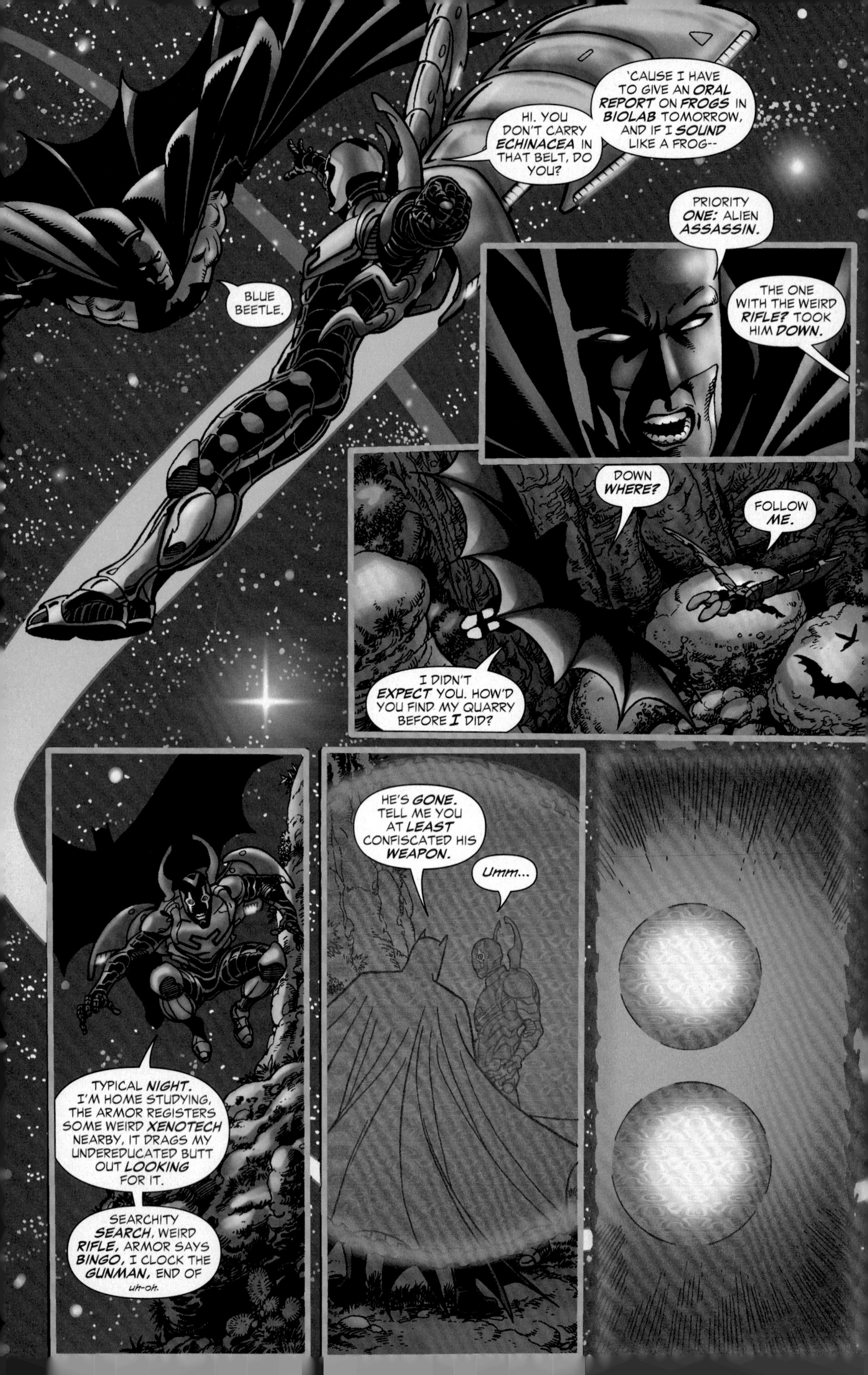
BLUE BEETLE.
HI. YOU DON'T CARRY ECHINACEA IN THAT BELT, DO YOU?
'CAUSE I HAVE TO GIVE AN ORAL REPORT ON FROGS IN BIOLAB TOMORROW, AND IF I SOUND LIKE A FROG--
PRIORITY ONE: ALIEN ASSASSIN.
THE ONE WITH THE WEIRD RIFLE? TOOK HIM DOWN.
DOWN WHERE?
FOLLOW ME.
I DIDN'T EXPECT YOU. HOW'D YOU FIND MY QUARRY BEFORE I DID?
TYPICAL NIGHT. I'M HOME STUDYING, THE ARMOR REGISTERS SOME WEIRD XENOTECH NEARBY, IT DRAGS MY UNDEREDUCATED BUTT OUT LOOKING FOR IT.
SEARCHITY SEARCH, WEIRD RIFLE, ARMOR SAYS BINGO, I CLOCK THE GUNMAN, END OF
uh-oh.
HE'S GONE. TELL ME YOU AT LEAST CONFISCATED HIS WEAPON.
Umm...

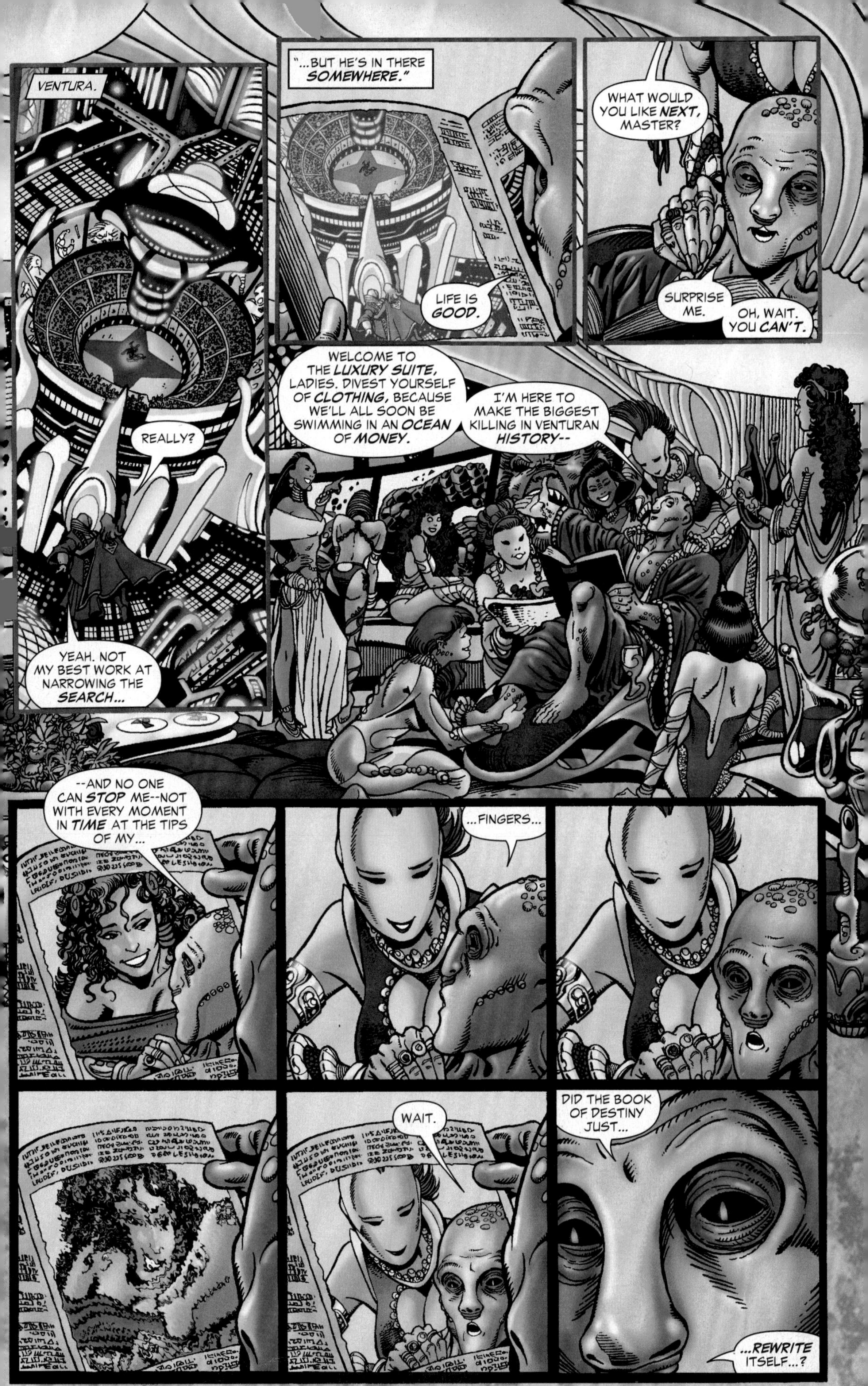
VENTURA.
REALLY?
YEAH. NOT MY BEST WORK AT NARROWING THE SEARCH...
"...BUT HE'S IN THERE SOMEWHERE."
LIFE IS GOOD.
WHAT WOULD YOU LIKE NEXT, MASTER?
SURPRISE ME.
OH, WAIT. YOU CAN'T.
WELCOME TO THE LUXURY SUITE, LADIES. DIVEST YOURSELF OF CLOTHING, BECAUSE WE'LL ALL SOON BE SWIMMING IN AN OCEAN OF MONEY.
I'M HERE TO MAKE THE BIGGEST KILLING IN VENTURAN HISTORY--
--AND NO ONE CAN STOP ME--NOT WITH EVERY MOMENT IN TIME AT THE TIPS OF MY...
...FINGERS...
WAIT.
DID THE BOOK OF DESTINY JUST...
...REWRITE ITSELF...?

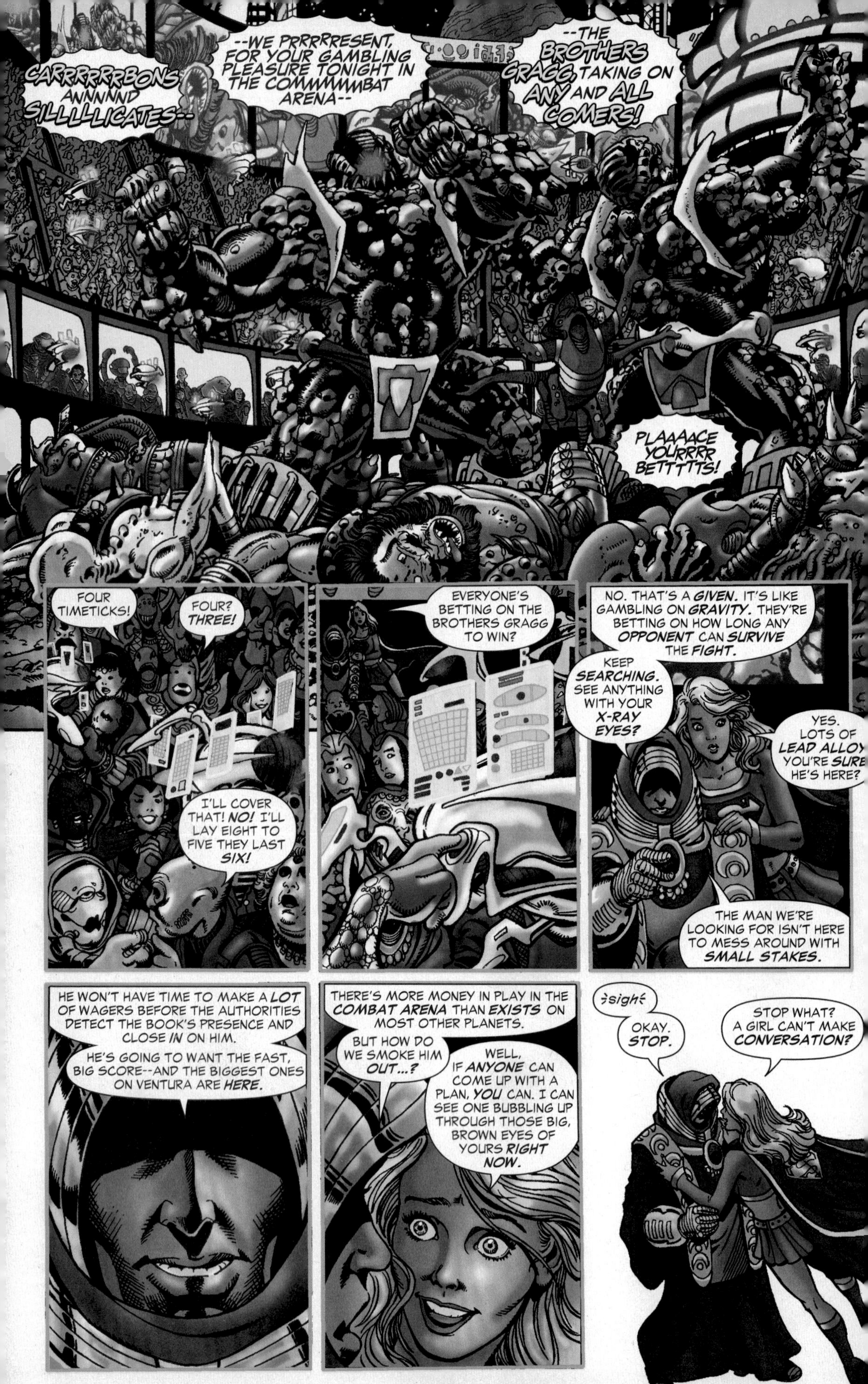
CARRRRRRBONS ANNNNND SILLLLLICATES--
--WE PRRRRRESENT, FOR YOUR GAMBLING PLEASURE TONIGHT IN THE COMMMMMBAT ARENA--
--THE BROTHERS GRAGG, TAKING ON ANY AND ALL COMERS!
PLAAAACE YOURRRR BETTTTTS!
FOUR TIMETICKS!
FOUR? THREE!
I'LL COVER THAT! NO! I'LL LAY EIGHT TO FIVE THEY LAST SIX!
EVERYONE'S BETTING ON THE BROTHERS GRAGG TO WIN?
NO. THAT'S A GIVEN. IT'S LIKE GAMBLING ON GRAVITY. THEY'RE BETTING ON HOW LONG ANY OPPONENT CAN SURVIVE THE FIGHT.
KEEP SEARCHING. SEE ANYTHING WITH YOUR X-RAY EYES?
YES. LOTS OF LEAD ALLOY. YOU'RE SURE HE'S HERE?
THE MAN WE'RE LOOKING FOR ISN'T HERE TO MESS AROUND WITH SMALL STAKES.
HE WON'T HAVE TIME TO MAKE A LOT OF WAGERS BEFORE THE AUTHORITIES DETECT THE BOOK'S PRESENCE AND CLOSE IN ON HIM.
HE'S GOING TO WANT THE FAST, BIG SCORE--AND THE BIGGEST ONES ON VENTURA ARE HERE.
THERE'S MORE MONEY IN PLAY IN THE COMBAT ARENA THAN EXISTS ON MOST OTHER PLANETS.
BUT HOW DO WE SMOKE HIM OUT...?
WELL, IF ANYONE CAN COME UP WITH A PLAN, YOU CAN. I CAN SEE ONE BUBBLING UP THROUGH THOSE BIG, BROWN EYES OF YOURS RIGHT NOW.
sigh
OKAY. STOP.
STOP WHAT? A GIRL CAN'T MAKE CONVERSATION?

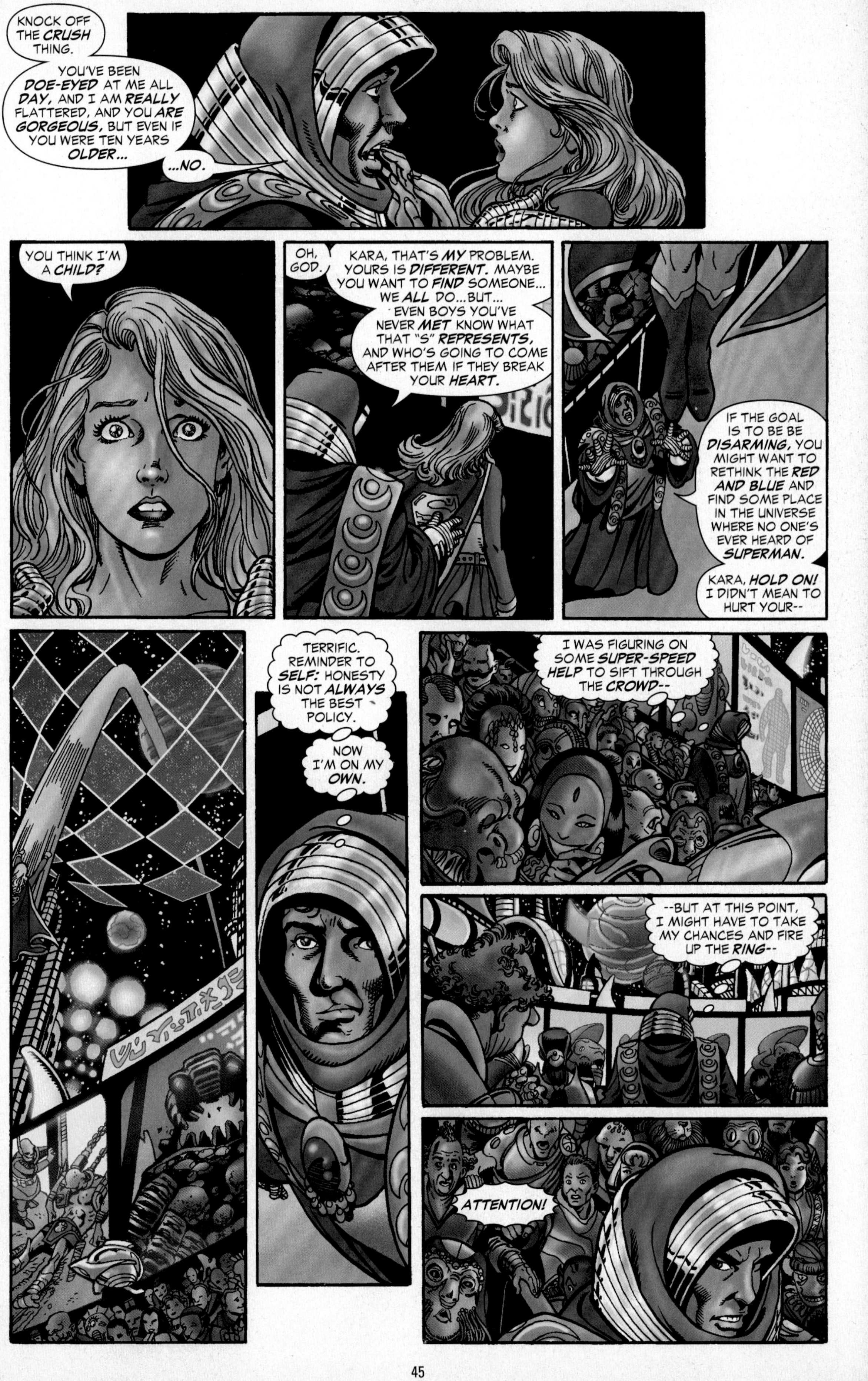

KNOCK OFF THE CRUSH THING.
YOU'VE BEEN DOE-EYED AT ME ALL DAY, AND I AM REALLY FLATTERED, AND YOU ARE GORGEOUS, BUT EVEN IF YOU WERE TEN YEARS OLDER...
...NO.
YOU THINK I'M A CHILD?
OH, GOD.
KARA, THAT'S MY PROBLEM. YOURS IS DIFFERENT. MAYBE YOU WANT TO FIND SOMEONE... WE ALL DO...BUT... EVEN BOYS YOU'VE NEVER MET KNOW WHAT THAT "S" REPRESENTS, AND WHO'S GOING TO COME AFTER THEM IF THEY BREAK YOUR HEART.
IF THE GOAL IS TO BE BE DISARMING, YOU MIGHT WANT TO RETHINK THE RED AND BLUE AND FIND SOME PLACE IN THE UNIVERSE WHERE NO ONE'S EVER HEARD OF SUPERMAN.
KARA, HOLD ON! I DIDN'T MEAN TO HURT YOUR--
TERRIFIC. REMINDER TO SELF: HONESTY IS NOT ALWAYS THE BEST POLICY.
NOW I'M ON MY OWN.
I WAS FIGURING ON SOME SUPER-SPEED HELP TO SIFT THROUGH THE CROWD--
--BUT AT THIS POINT, I MIGHT HAVE TO TAKE MY CHANCES AND FIRE UP THE RING--
ATTENTION!

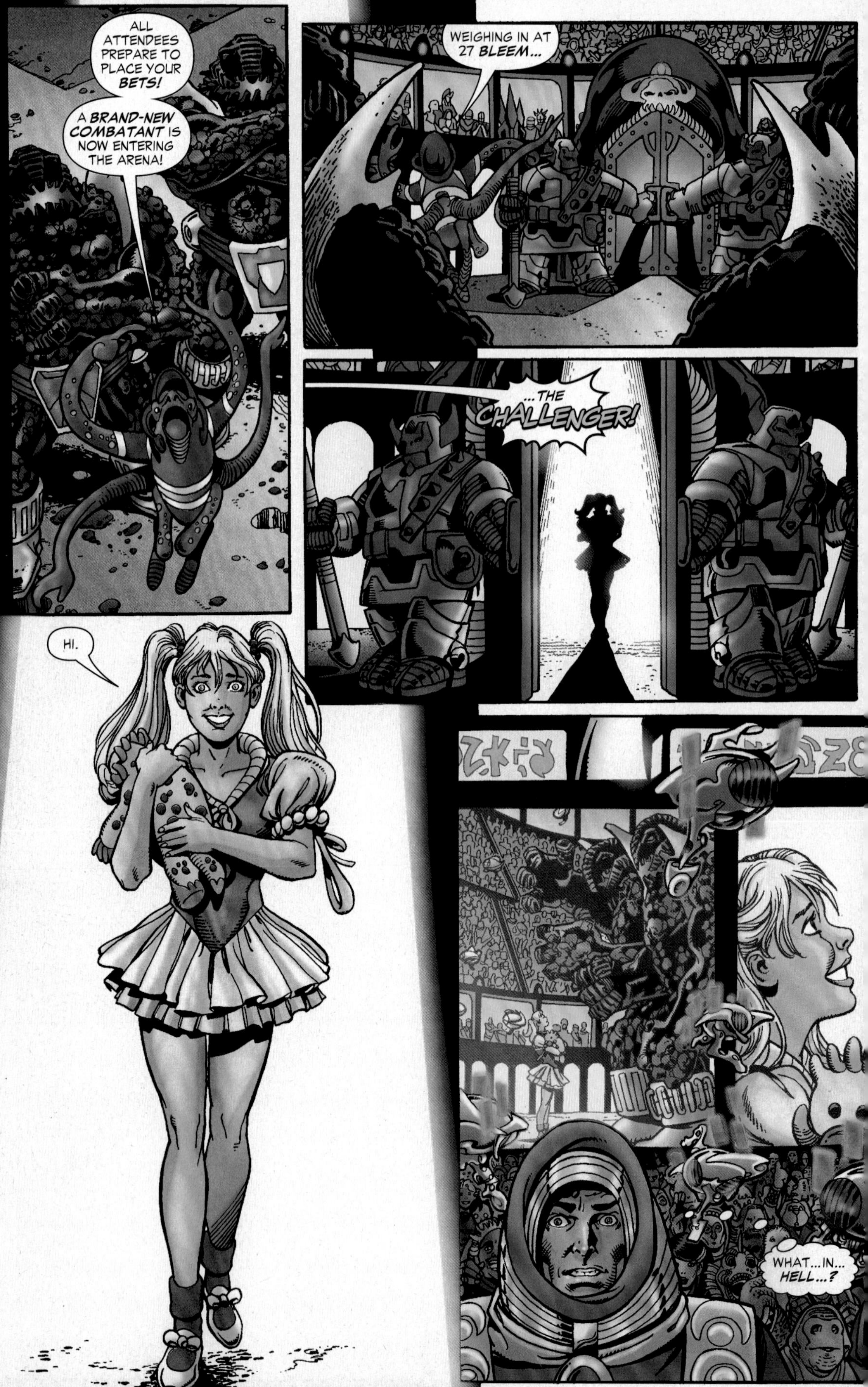
ALL ATTENDEES PREPARE TO PLACE YOUR BETS!
A BRAND-NEW COMBATANT IS NOW ENTERING THE ARENA!
WEIGHING IN AT 27 BLEEM...
...THE CHALLENGER!
HI.
WHAT...IN... HELL...?

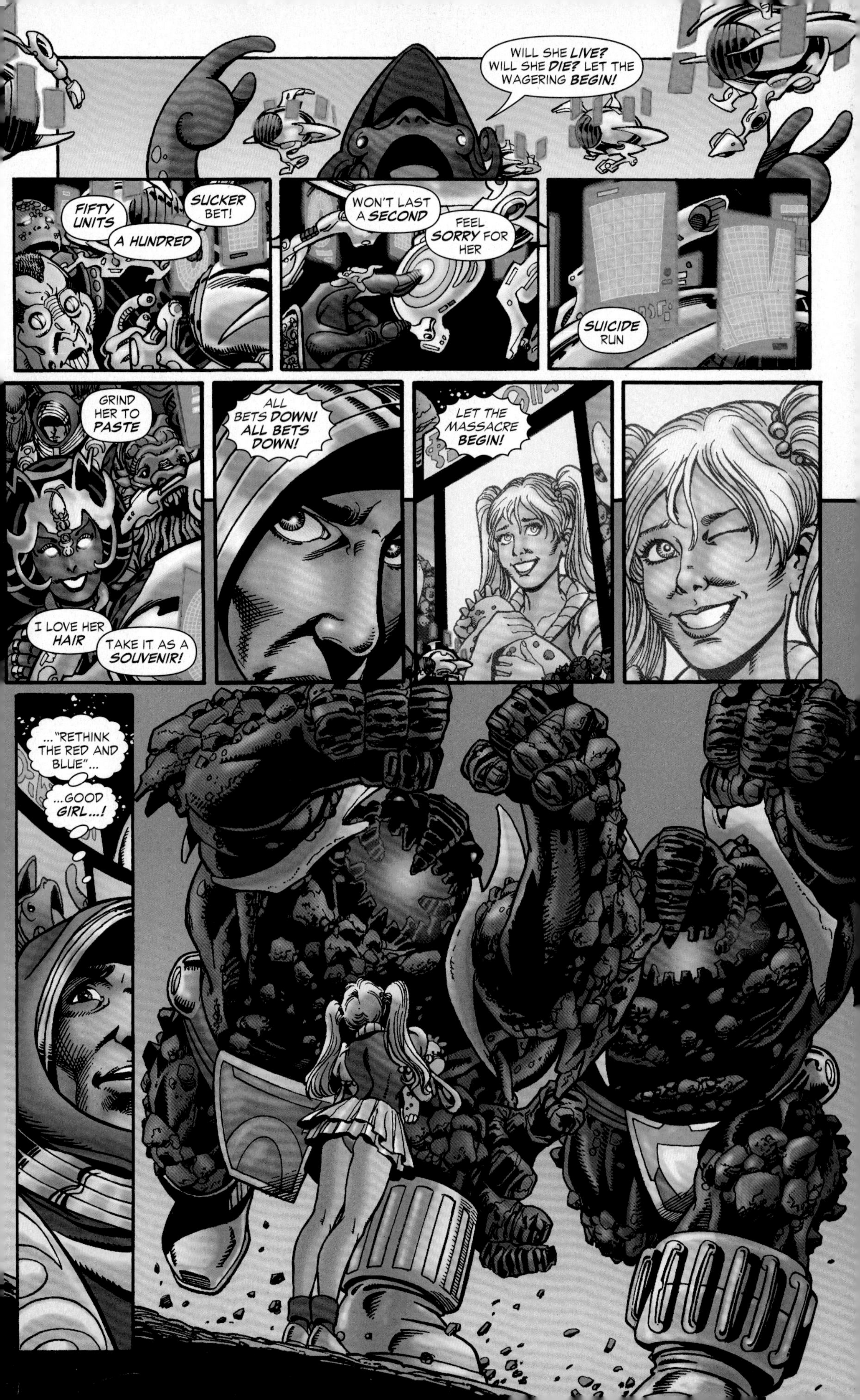
WILL SHE LIVE? WILL SHE DIE? LET THE WAGERING BEGIN!
FIFTY UNITS
SUCKER BET!
A HUNDRED
WON'T LAST A SECOND
FEEL SORRY FOR HER
SUICIDE RUN
GRIND HER TO PASTE
I LOVE HER HAIR
TAKE IT AS A SOUVENIR!
ALL BETS DOWN! ALL BETS DOWN!
LET THE MASSACRE BEGIN!
..."RETHINK THE RED AND BLUE"...
...GOOD GIRL...!

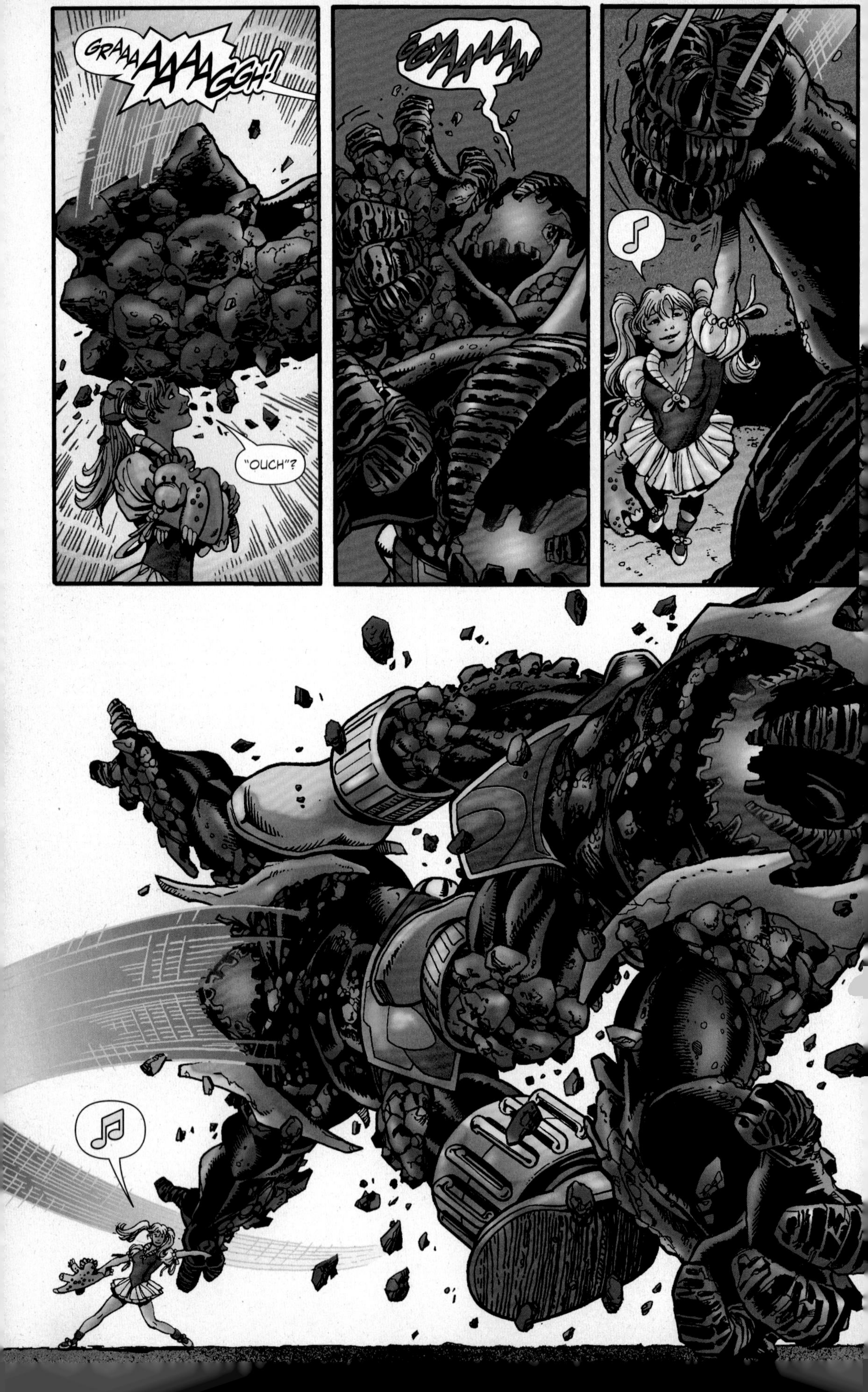
GRAAAAAAAGGH!
GGYAAAAAA!
"OUCH"?

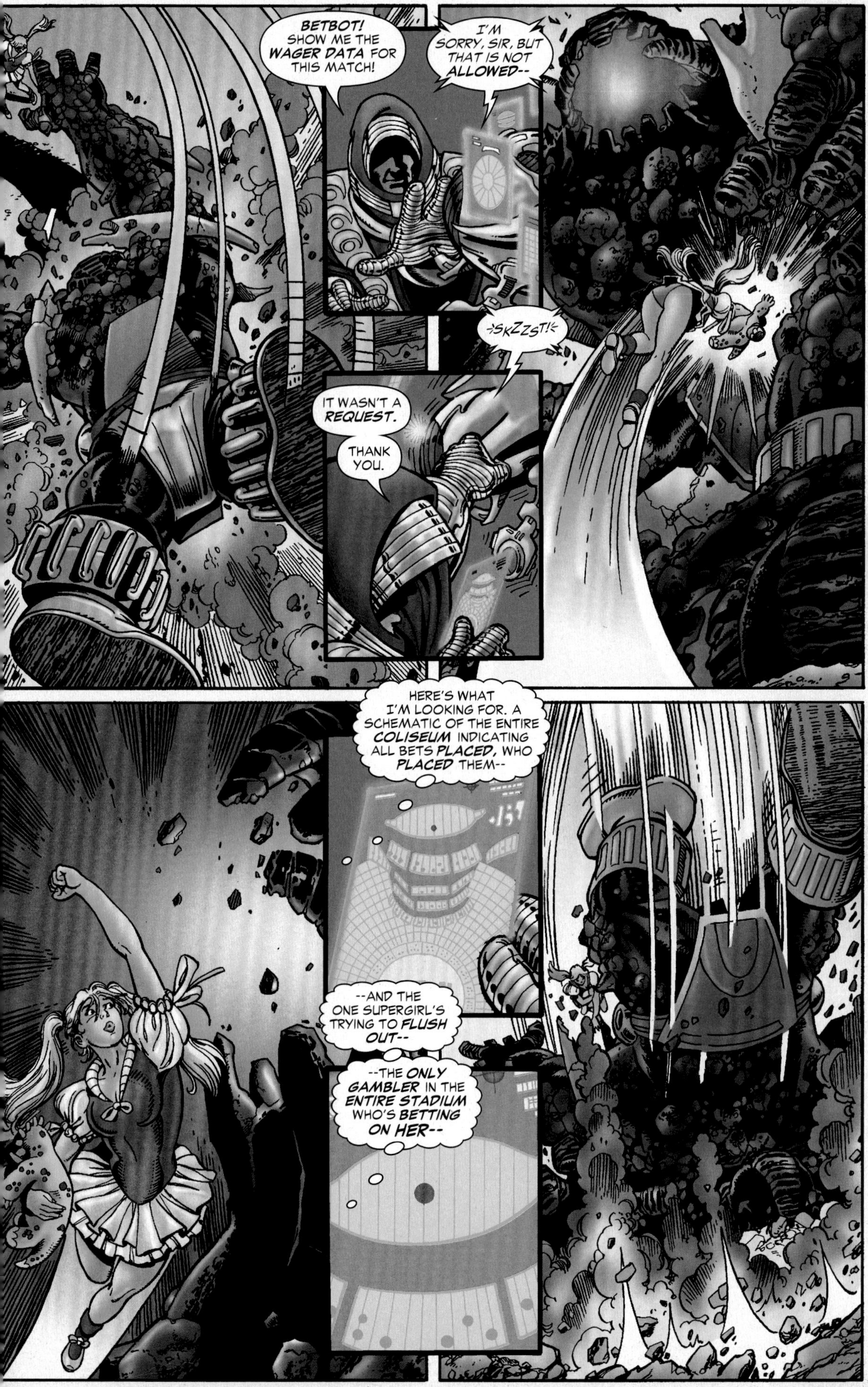
BETBOT! SHOW ME THE WAGER DATA FOR THIS MATCH!
I'M SORRY, SIR, BUT THAT IS NOT ALLOWED--
SKZZST!
IT WASN'T A REQUEST.
THANK YOU.
HERE'S WHAT I'M LOOKING FOR. A SCHEMATIC OF THE ENTIRE COLISEUM INDICATING ALL BETS PLACED, WHO PLACED THEM--
--AND THE ONE SUPERGIRL'S TRYING TO FLUSH OUT--
--THE ONLY GAMBLER IN THE ENTIRE STADIUM WHO'S BETTING ON HER--

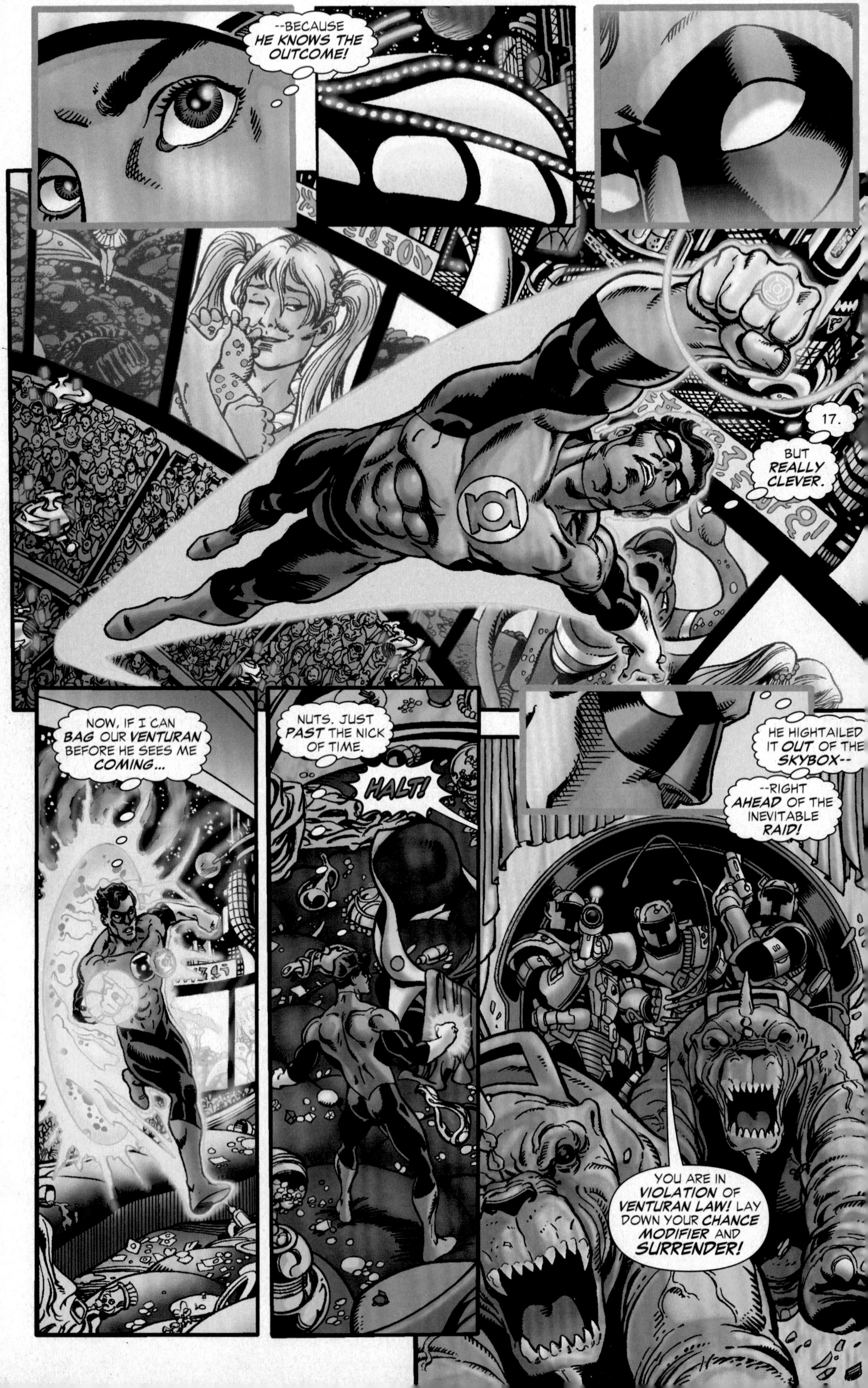
--BECAUSE HE KNOWS THE OUTCOME!
17.
BUT REALLY CLEVER.
NOW, IF I CAN BAG OUR VENTURAN BEFORE HE SEES ME COMING...
NUTS. JUST PAST THE NICK OF TIME.
HALT!
HE HIGHTAILED IT OUT OF THE SKYBOX--
--RIGHT AHEAD OF THE INEVITABLE RAID!
YOU ARE IN VIOLATION OF VENTURAN LAW! LAY DOWN YOUR CHANCE MODIFIER AND SURRENDER!

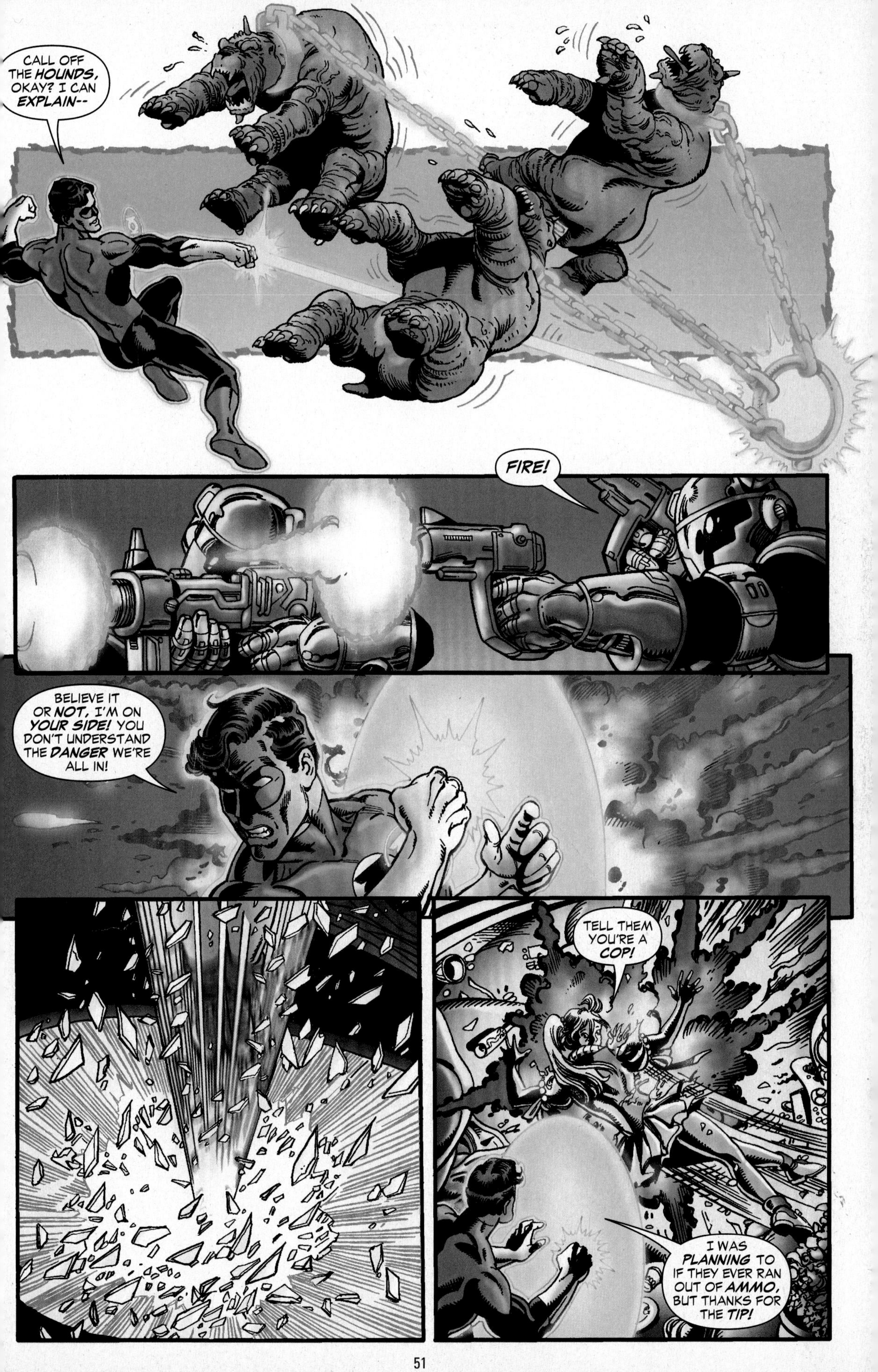
CALL OFF THE HOUNDS, OKAY? I CAN EXPLAIN--
FIRE!
BELIEVE IT OR NOT, I'M ON YOUR SIDE! YOU DON'T UNDERSTAND THE DANGER WE'RE ALL IN!
TELL THEM YOU'RE A COP!
I WAS PLANNING TO IF THEY EVER RAN OUT OF AMMO, BUT THANKS FOR THE TIP!

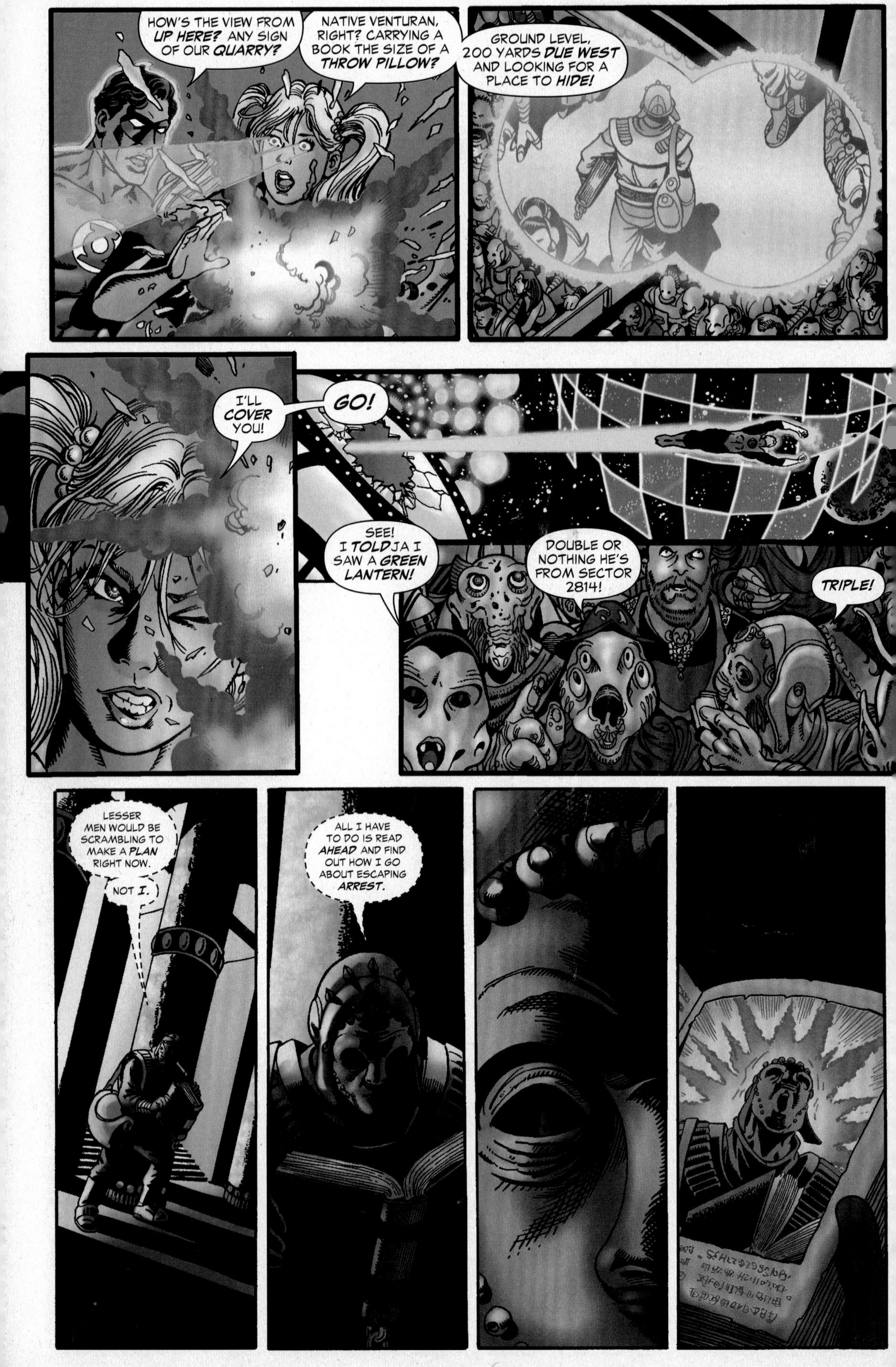
HOW'S THE VIEW FROM UP HERE? ANY SIGN OF OUR QUARRY?
NATIVE VENTURAN, RIGHT? CARRYING A BOOK THE SIZE OF A THROW PILLOW?
GROUND LEVEL, 200 YARDS DUE WEST AND LOOKING FOR A PLACE TO HIDE!
I'LL COVER YOU!
GO!
SEE! I TOLDJA I SAW A GREEN LANTERN!
DOUBLE OR NOTHING HE'S FROM SECTOR 2814!
TRIPLE!
LESSER MEN WOULD BE SCRAMBLING TO MAKE A PLAN RIGHT NOW.
NOT I.
ALL I HAVE TO DO IS READ AHEAD AND FIND OUT HOW I GO ABOUT ESCAPING ARREST.

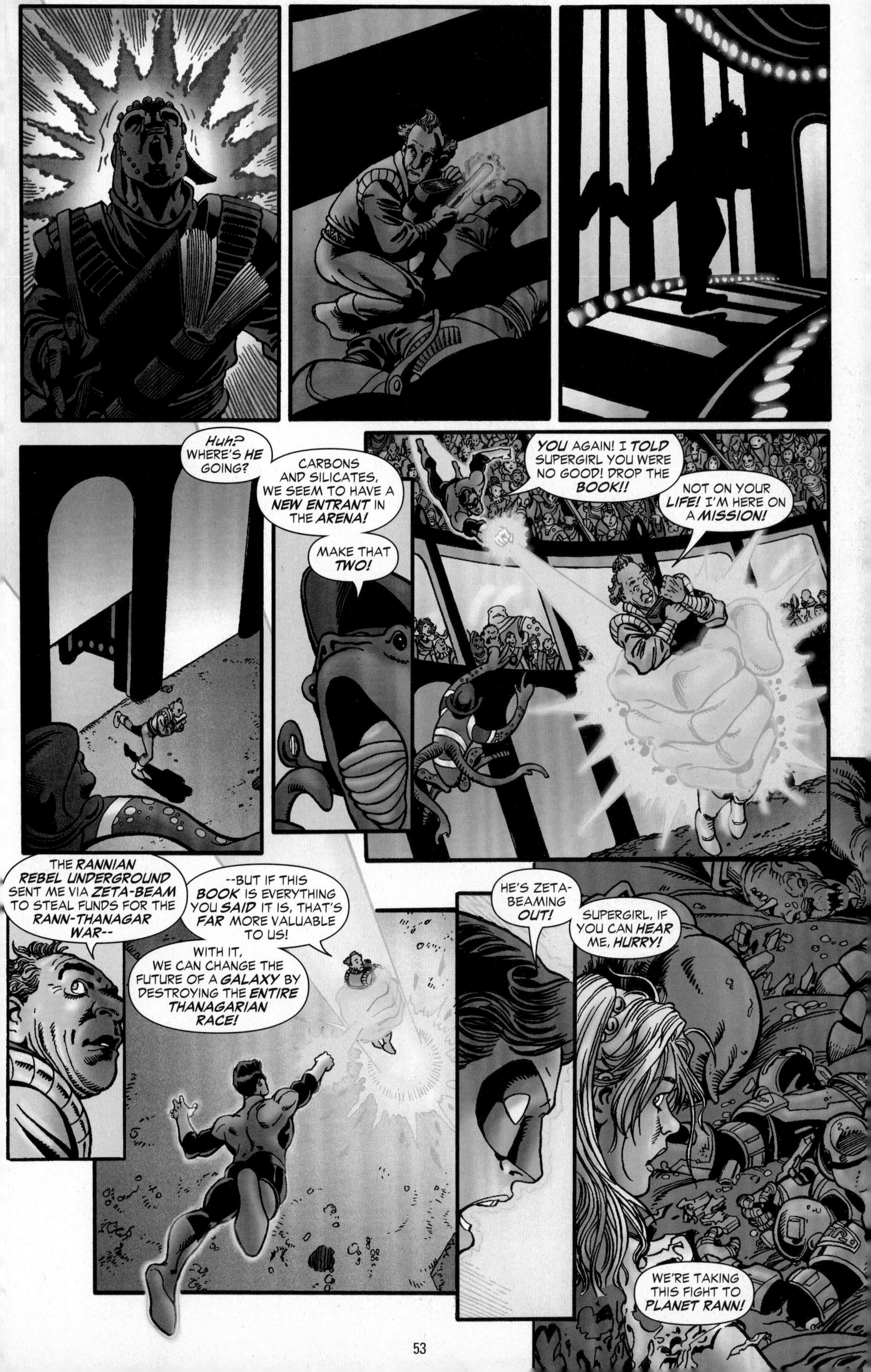
Huh? WHERE'S HE GOING?
CARBONS AND SILICATES, WE SEEM TO HAVE A NEW ENTRANT IN THE ARENA!
MAKE THAT TWO!
YOU AGAIN! I TOLD SUPERGIRL YOU WERE NO GOOD! DROP THE BOOK!!
NOT ON YOUR LIFE! I'M HERE ON A MISSION!
THE RANNIAN REBEL UNDERGROUND SENT ME VIA ZETA-BEAM TO STEAL FUNDS FOR THE RANN-THANAGAR WAR--
--BUT IF THIS BOOK IS EVERYTHING YOU SAID IT IS, THAT'S FAR MORE VALUABLE TO US!
WITH IT, WE CAN CHANGE THE FUTURE OF A GALAXY BY DESTROYING THE ENTIRE THANAGARIAN RACE!
HE'S ZETA-BEAMING OUT!
SUPERGIRL, IF YOU CAN HEAR ME, HURRY!
WE'RE TAKING THIS FIGHT TO PLANET RANN!

GRAB *HOLD* OF ME BEFORE IT'S *TOO LA*

IS THAT THE--? IT *IS!* IT'S *YELLOWHAIR* THE *GRAGG-CRUNCHER* BACK FOR *ANOTHER ROUND!*

YOW! THAT'S *GOTTA* HURT!

WAIT...SHE'S DRAGGING HERSELF OUT OF THE *RUBBLE*...

GL!

GL, I DON'T KNOW WHERE RANN *IS* FROM HERE!

OR, ALSO, *EARTH!*

I COULD BE IN *TROUBLE* HERE...

≥Gasp≤

LOOK!

THE *SYMBOL!* THE FABLED *SYMBOL!*

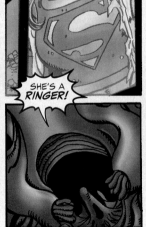

SHE'S A *RINGER!*

YEAH.

DEFINITELY TROUBLE.

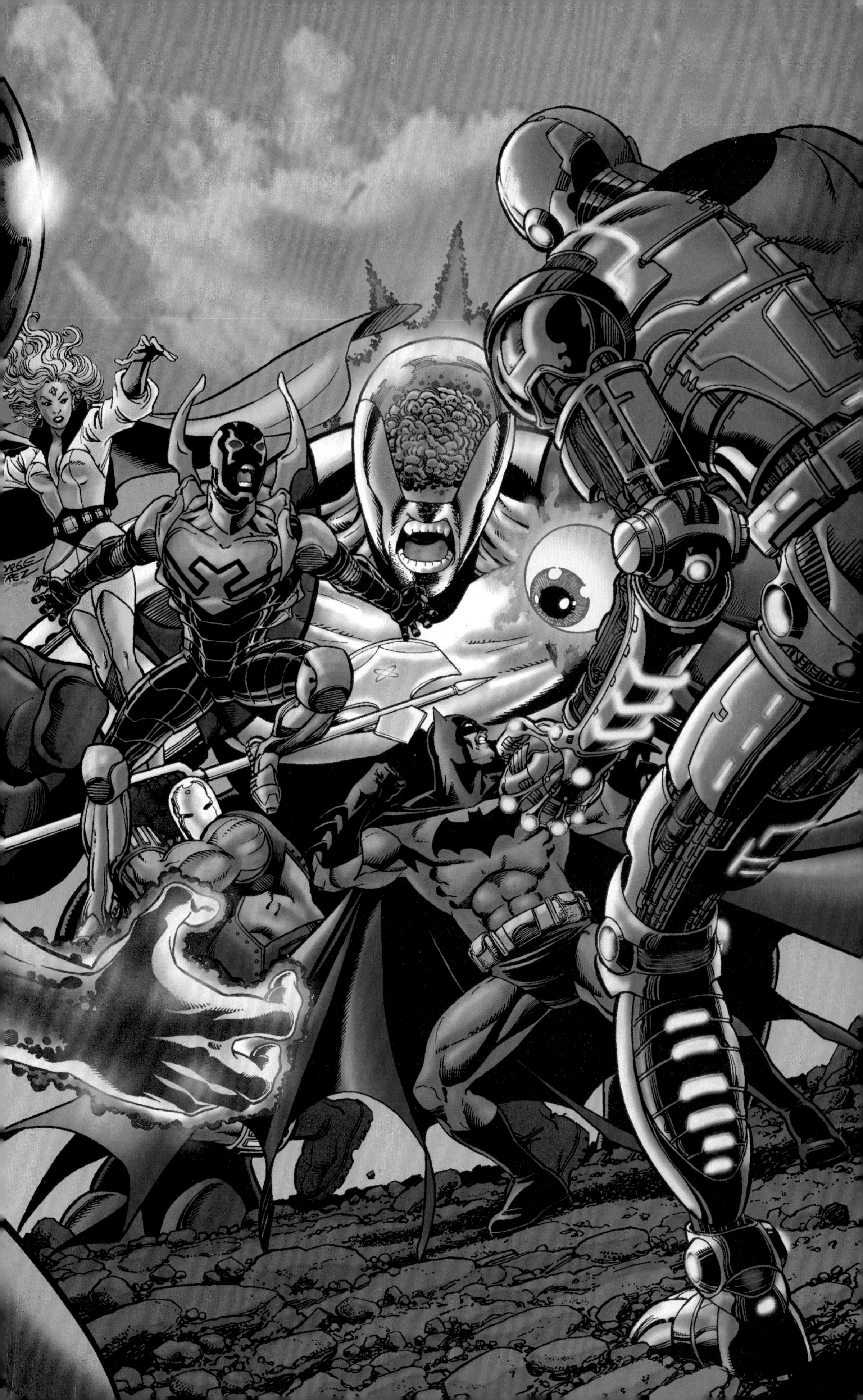

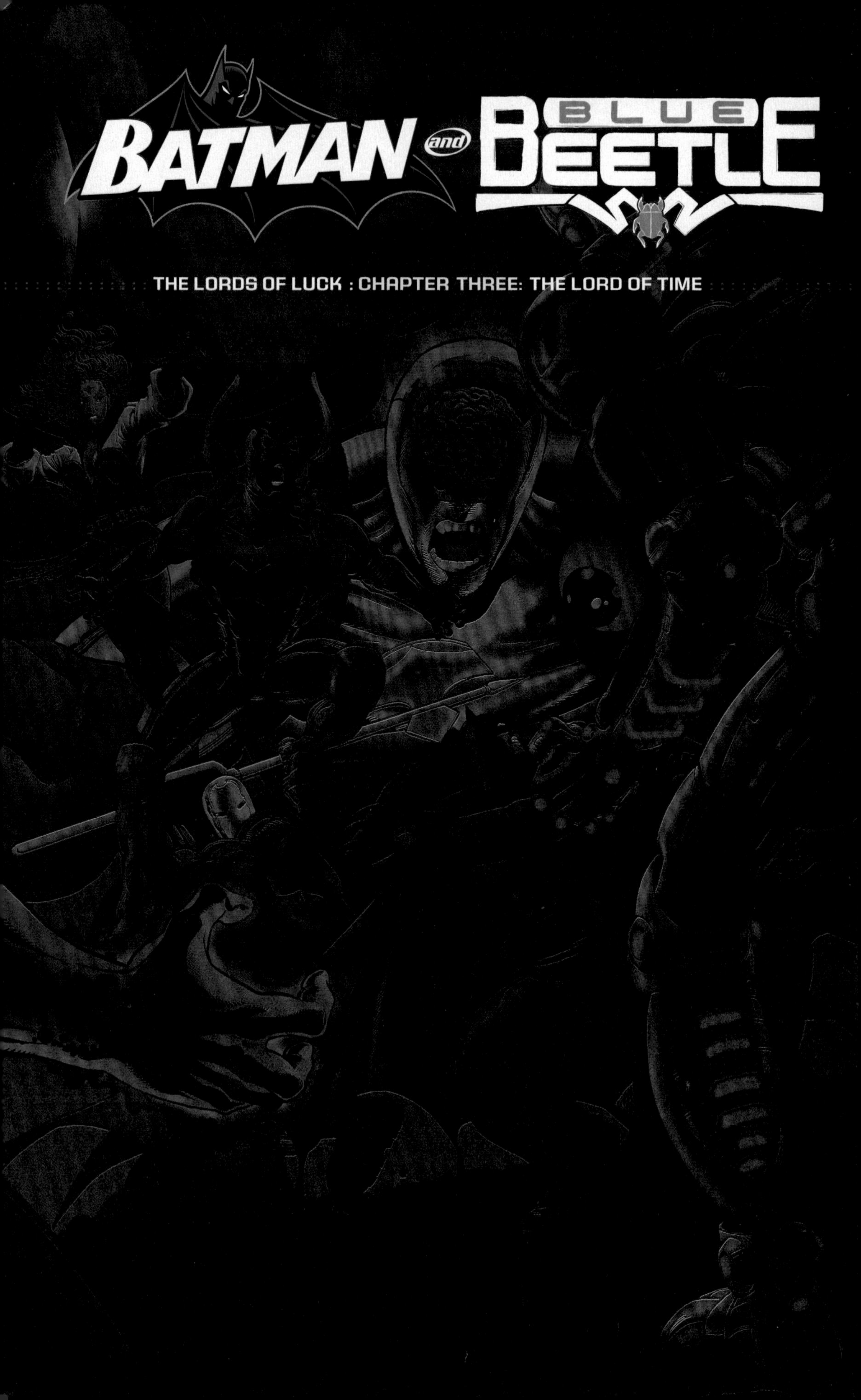
BATMAN and BLUE BEETLE
THE LORDS OF LUCK : CHAPTER THREE: THE LORD OF TIME

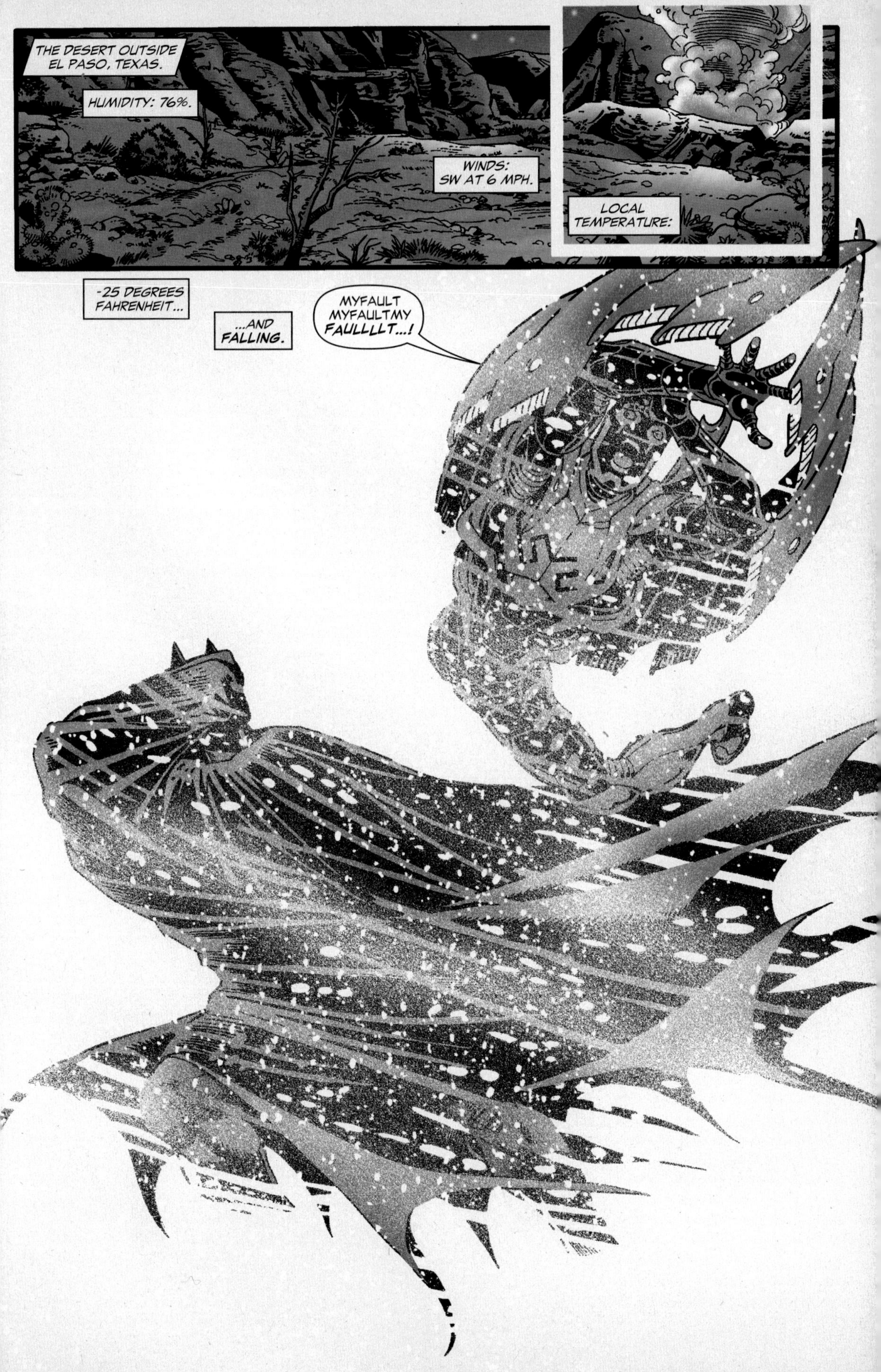
THE DESERT OUTSIDE EL PASO, TEXAS.
HUMIDITY: 76%.
WINDS: SW AT 6 MPH.
LOCAL TEMPERATURE:
-25 DEGREES FAHRENHEIT...
...AND FALLING.
MYFAULT MYFAULTMY FAULLLLT...!

WHERE ARE WE...

WE'RE S-STILL ON THAT B-BUTTE! AMB--

--AMBUSH! NEFER TO HIT US WITH--LOCALIZED BUH-BLIZZARD--!

NO! NOT WITHOUT *HIM*!

WHAT?

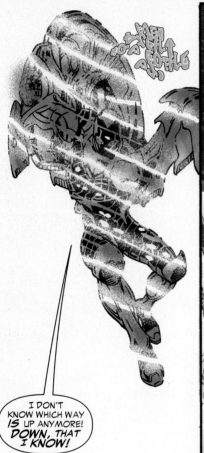

I DON'T KNOW WHICH WAY *IS* UP ANYMORE! *DOWN, THAT I KNOW*!

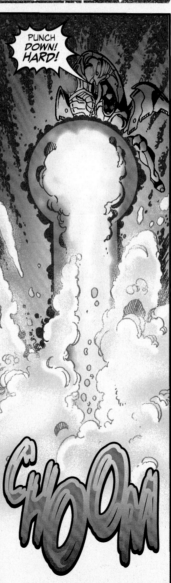

PUNCH *DOWN! HARD!*

SHOOM

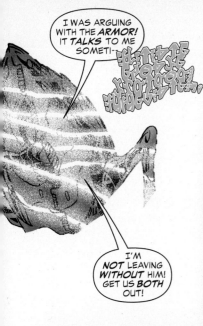

I WAS ARGUING WITH THE *ARMOR!* IT *TALKS* TO ME SOMETI—

I'M *NOT* LEAVING *WITHOUT* HIM! GET US *BOTH* OUT!

DO NOT LET ME LOSE *SIGHT* OF HIM!

BATMAN!

BATMAN? ARE YOU *ALL* RIGHT? CAN YOU *HEAR* ME?

BATMAN!

OH, THANK GOD.

CHFF

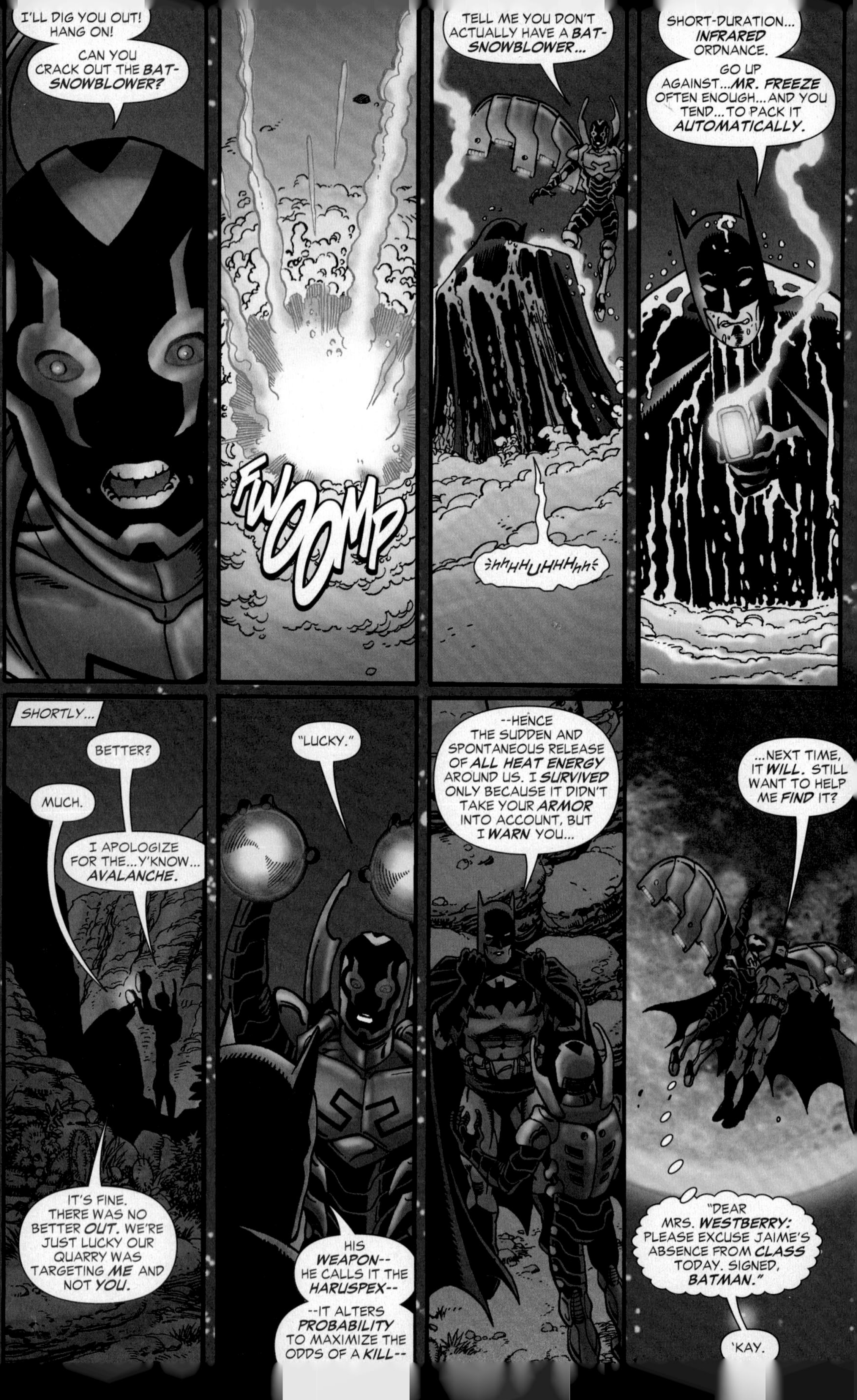
I'LL DIG YOU OUT! HANG ON!
CAN YOU CRACK OUT THE BAT-SNOWBLOWER?
FWOOOMP
TELL ME YOU DON'T ACTUALLY HAVE A BAT-SNOWBLOWER...
hhhHHUHHHhh
SHORT-DURATION... INFRARED ORDNANCE.
GO UP AGAINST...MR. FREEZE OFTEN ENOUGH...AND YOU TEND...TO PACK IT AUTOMATICALLY.
SHORTLY...
BETTER?
MUCH.
I APOLOGIZE FOR THE...Y'KNOW... AVALANCHE.
IT'S FINE. THERE WAS NO BETTER OUT. WE'RE JUST LUCKY OUR QUARRY WAS TARGETING ME AND NOT YOU.
"LUCKY."
HIS WEAPON-- HE CALLS IT THE HARUSPEX--
--IT ALTERS PROBABILITY TO MAXIMIZE THE ODDS OF A KILL--
--HENCE THE SUDDEN AND SPONTANEOUS RELEASE OF ALL HEAT ENERGY AROUND US. I SURVIVED ONLY BECAUSE IT DIDN'T TAKE YOUR ARMOR INTO ACCOUNT, BUT I WARN YOU...
...NEXT TIME, IT WILL. STILL WANT TO HELP ME FIND IT?
"DEAR MRS. WESTBERRY: PLEASE EXCUSE JAIME'S ABSENCE FROM CLASS TODAY. SIGNED, BATMAN."
'KAY.

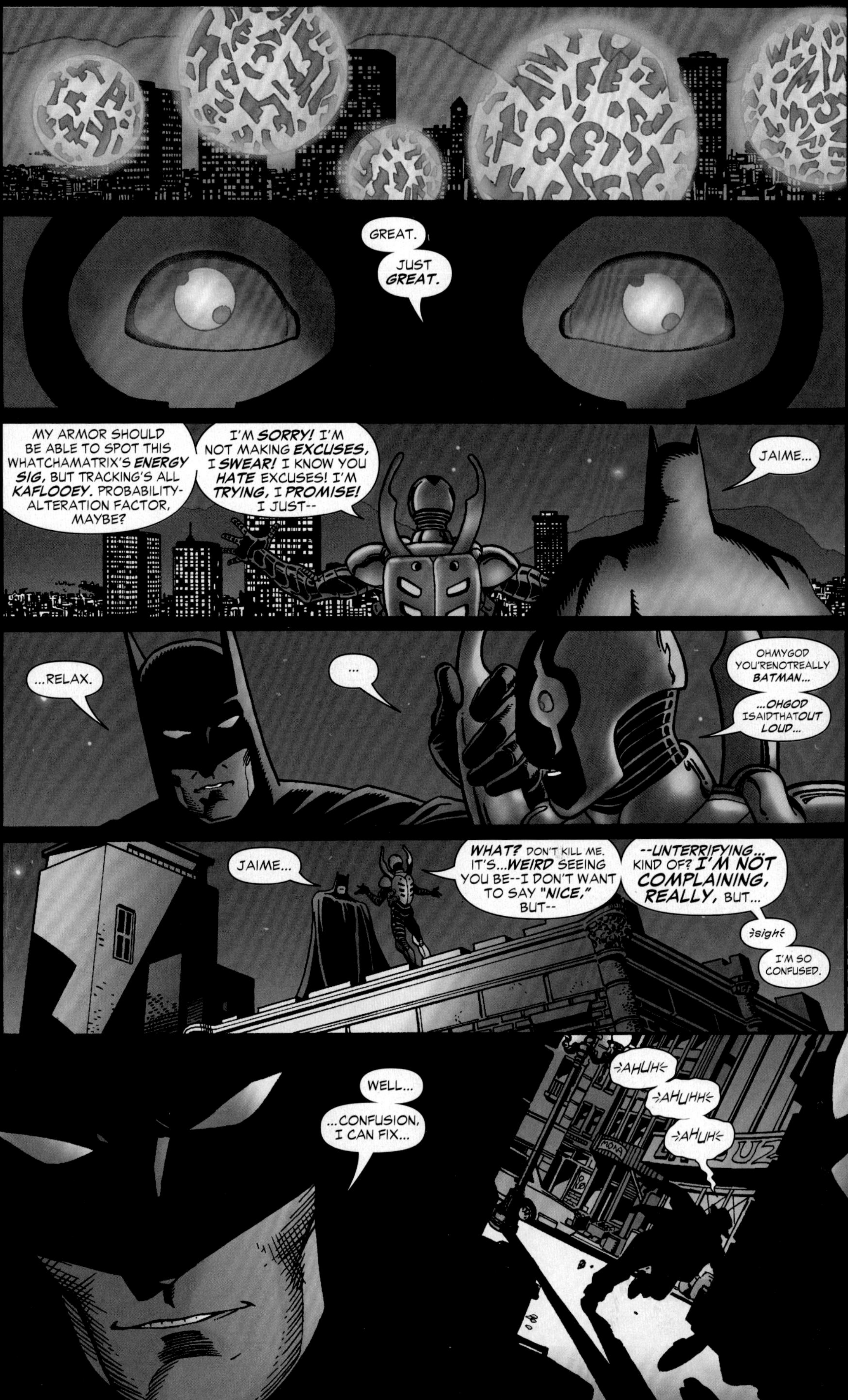
GREAT.
JUST GREAT.
MY ARMOR SHOULD BE ABLE TO SPOT THIS WHATCHAMATRIX'S ENERGY SIG, BUT TRACKING'S ALL KAFLOOEY. PROBABILITY-ALTERATION FACTOR, MAYBE?
I'M SORRY! I'M NOT MAKING EXCUSES, I SWEAR! I KNOW YOU HATE EXCUSES! I'M TRYING, I PROMISE! I JUST--
JAIME...
...RELAX.
...
OHMYGOD YOU'RENOTREALLY BATMAN...
...OHGOD ISAIDTHATOUT LOUD...
JAIME...
WHAT? DON'T KILL ME. IT'S...WEIRD SEEING YOU BE--I DON'T WANT TO SAY "NICE," BUT--
--UNTERRIFYING... KIND OF? I'M NOT COMPLAINING, REALLY, BUT...
sigh
I'M SO CONFUSED.
WELL...
...CONFUSION, I CAN FIX...
AHUH
AHUHH
AHUH

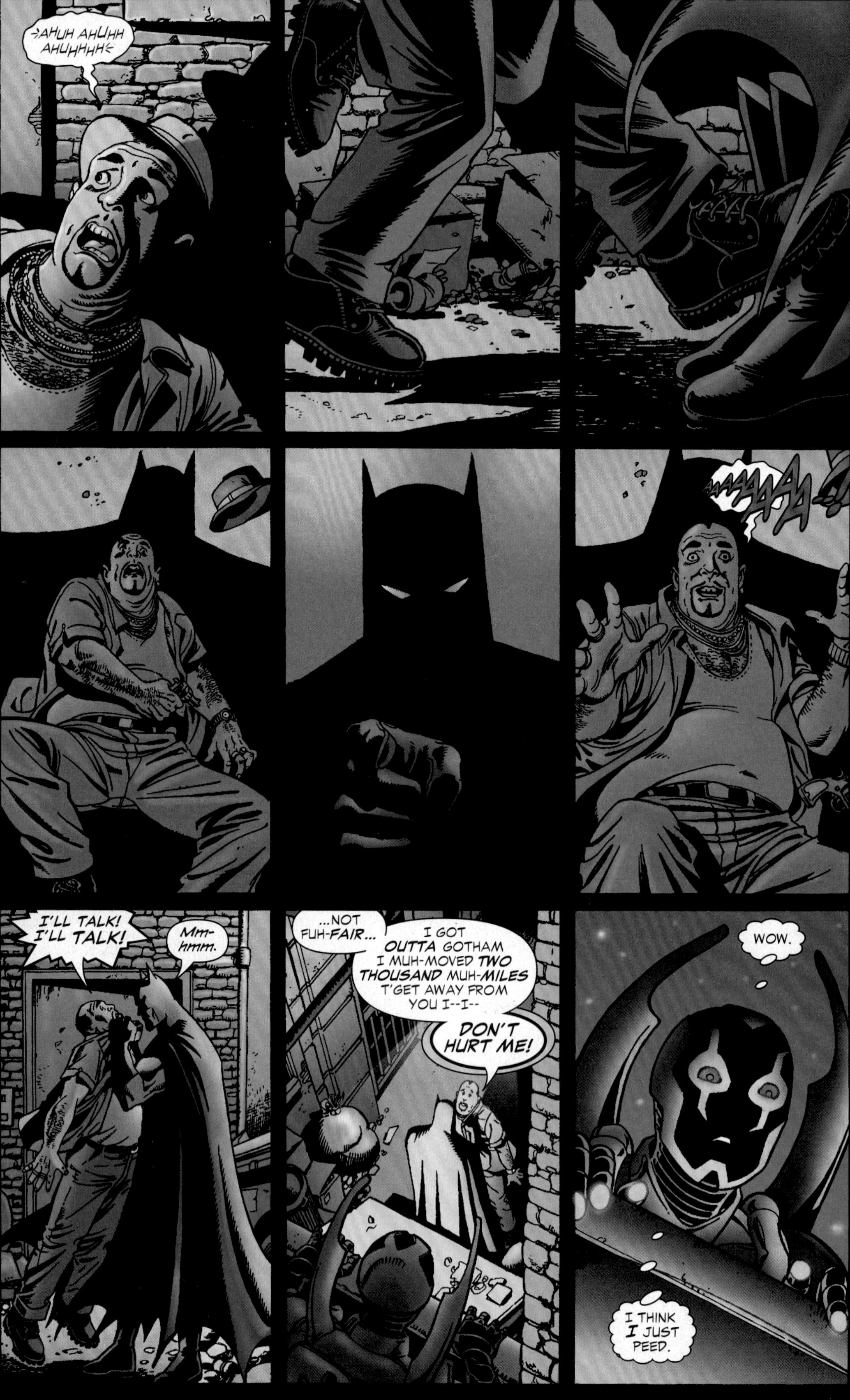
AHUH AHUHH AHUHHHH
AAAAAAAA
I'LL TALK! I'LL TALK!
Mm-hmm.
...NOT FUH-FAIR...
I GOT OUTTA GOTHAM I MUH-MOVED TWO THOUSAND MUH-MILES T'GET AWAY FROM YOU I--I--
DON'T HURT ME!
WOW.
I THINK I JUST PEED.

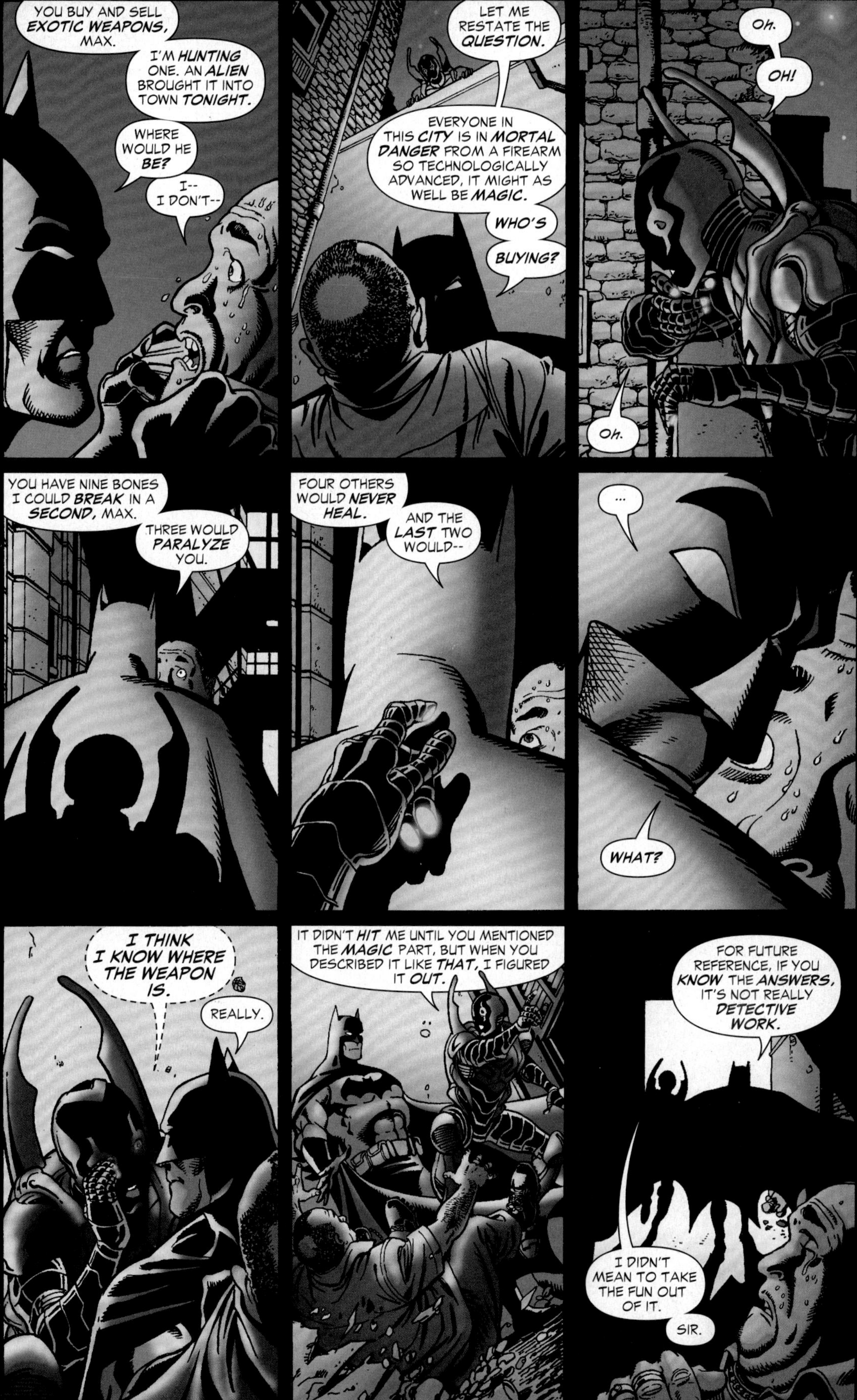
YOU BUY AND SELL EXOTIC WEAPONS, MAX.
I'M HUNTING ONE. AN ALIEN BROUGHT IT INTO TOWN TONIGHT.
WHERE WOULD HE BE?
I-- I DON'T--
LET ME RESTATE THE QUESTION.
EVERYONE IN THIS CITY IS IN MORTAL DANGER FROM A FIREARM SO TECHNOLOGICALLY ADVANCED, IT MIGHT AS WELL BE MAGIC.
WHO'S
BUYING?
Oh.
OH!
Oh.
YOU HAVE NINE BONES I COULD BREAK IN A SECOND, MAX.
THREE WOULD PARALYZE YOU.
FOUR OTHERS WOULD NEVER HEAL.
AND THE LAST TWO WOULD--
...
WHAT?
I THINK I KNOW WHERE THE WEAPON IS.
REALLY.
IT DIDN'T HIT ME UNTIL YOU MENTIONED THE MAGIC PART, BUT WHEN YOU DESCRIBED IT LIKE THAT, I FIGURED IT OUT.
FOR FUTURE REFERENCE, IF YOU KNOW THE ANSWERS, IT'S NOT REALLY DETECTIVE WORK.
I DIDN'T MEAN TO TAKE THE FUN OUT OF IT.
SIR.

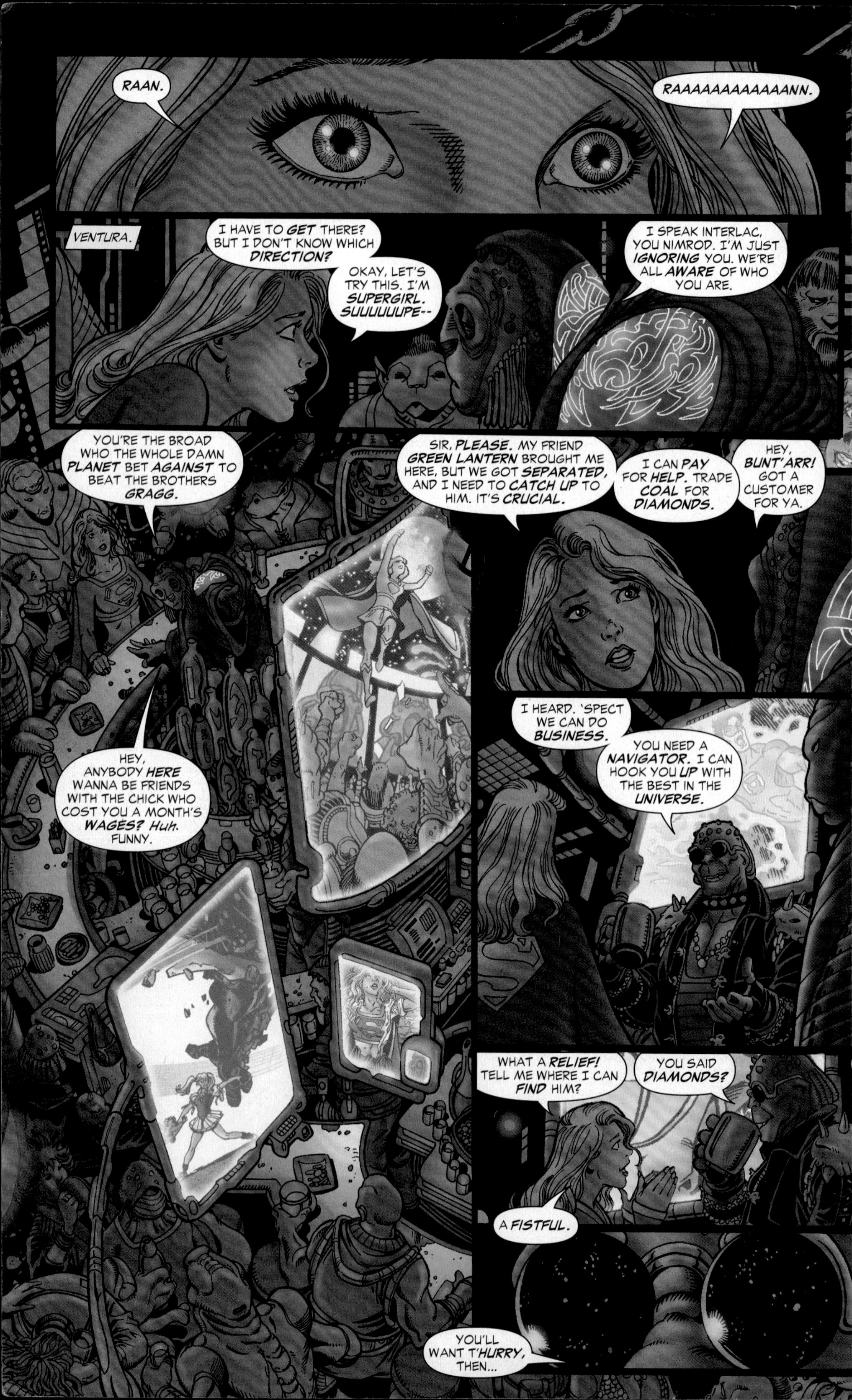
RAAN.
RAAAAAAAAAAAANN.
VENTURA.
I HAVE TO GET THERE? BUT I DON'T KNOW WHICH DIRECTION?
OKAY, LET'S TRY THIS. I'M SUPERGIRL. SUUUUUUPE--
I SPEAK INTERLAC, YOU NIMROD. I'M JUST IGNORING YOU. WE'RE ALL AWARE OF WHO YOU ARE.
YOU'RE THE BROAD WHO THE WHOLE DAMN PLANET BET AGAINST TO BEAT THE BROTHERS GRAGG.
HEY, ANYBODY HERE WANNA BE FRIENDS WITH THE CHICK WHO COST YOU A MONTH'S WAGES? Huh. FUNNY.
SIR, PLEASE. MY FRIEND GREEN LANTERN BROUGHT ME HERE, BUT WE GOT SEPARATED, AND I NEED TO CATCH UP TO HIM. IT'S CRUCIAL.
I CAN PAY FOR HELP. TRADE COAL FOR DIAMONDS.
HEY, BUNT'ARR! GOT A CUSTOMER FOR YA.
I HEARD. 'SPECT WE CAN DO BUSINESS.
YOU NEED A NAVIGATOR. I CAN HOOK YOU UP WITH THE BEST IN THE UNIVERSE.
WHAT A RELIEF! TELL ME WHERE I CAN FIND HIM?
YOU SAID DIAMONDS?
A FISTFUL.
YOU'LL WANT T'HURRY, THEN...

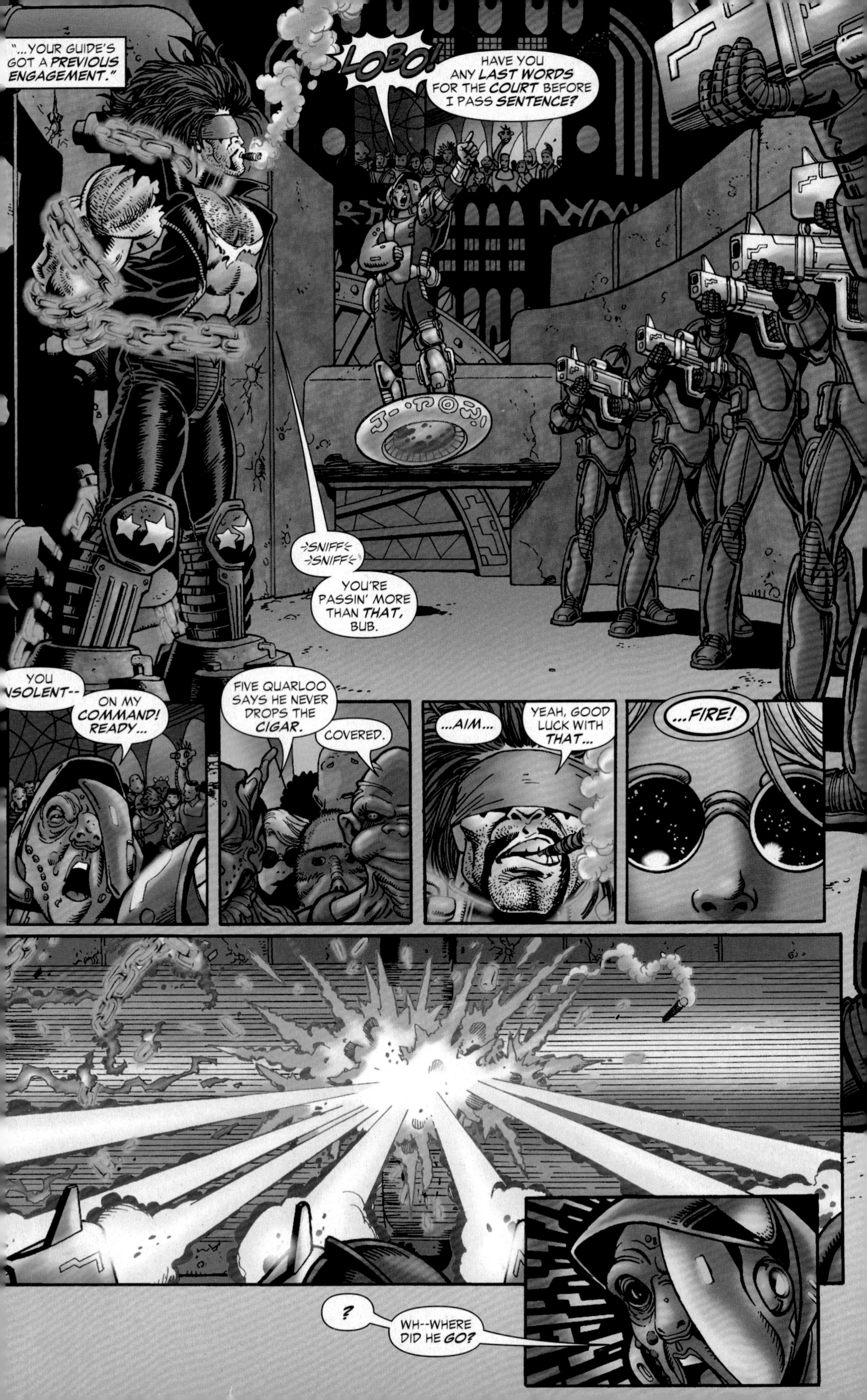
"...YOUR GUIDE'S GOT A PREVIOUS ENGAGEMENT."
LOBO!
HAVE YOU ANY LAST WORDS FOR THE COURT BEFORE I PASS SENTENCE?
J-TOW!
SNIFF SNIFF
YOU'RE PASSIN' MORE THAN THAT, BUB.
YOU NSOLENT--
ON MY COMMAND! READY...
FIVE QUARLOO SAYS HE NEVER DROPS THE CIGAR.
COVERED.
...AIM...
YEAH, GOOD LUCK WITH THAT...
...FIRE!
?
WH--WHERE DID HE GO?

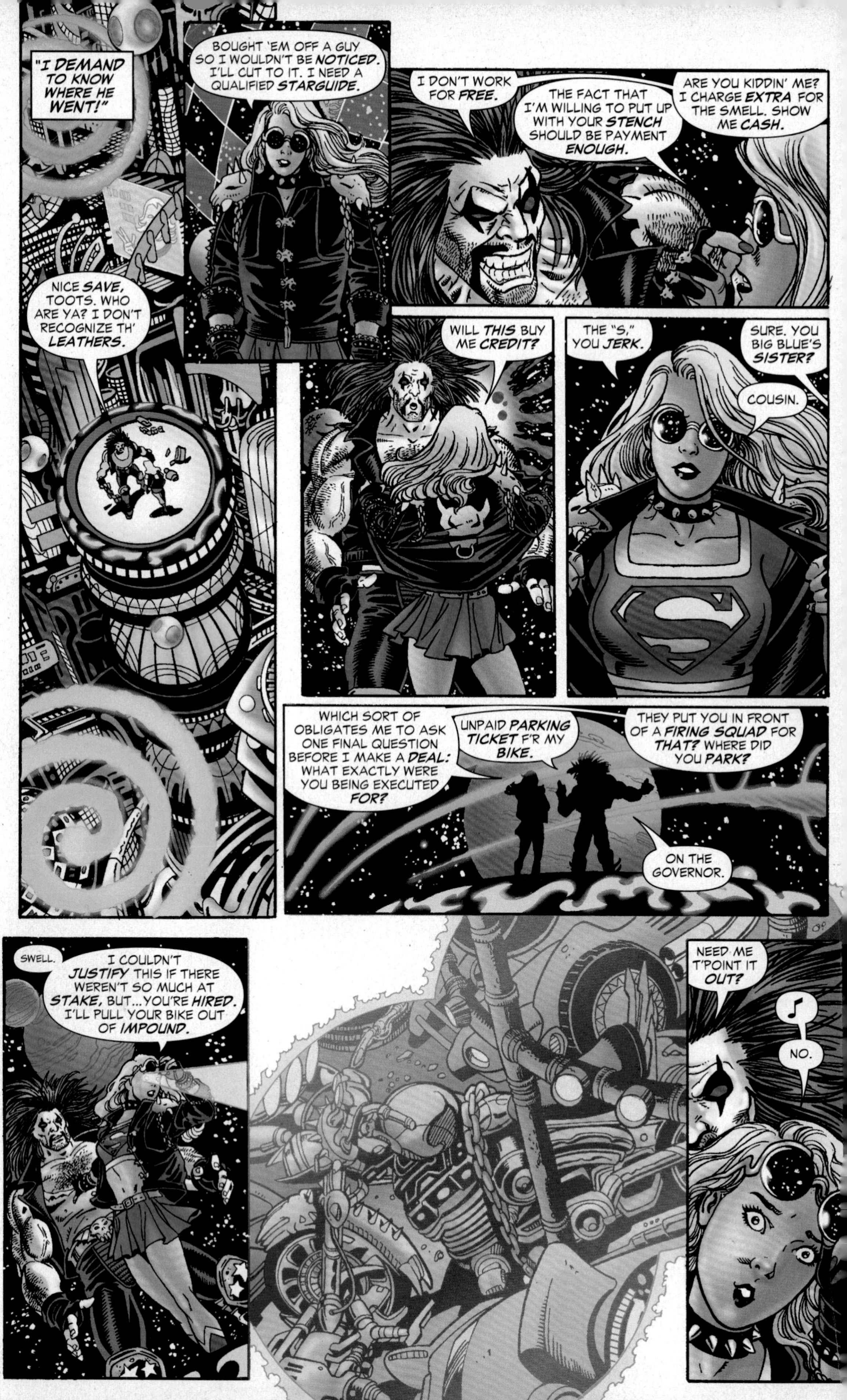
"I DEMAND TO KNOW WHERE HE WENT!"
BOUGHT 'EM OFF A GUY SO I WOULDN'T BE NOTICED. I'LL CUT TO IT. I NEED A QUALIFIED STARGUIDE.
I DON'T WORK FOR FREE.
THE FACT THAT I'M WILLING TO PUT UP WITH YOUR STENCH SHOULD BE PAYMENT ENOUGH.
ARE YOU KIDDIN' ME? I CHARGE EXTRA FOR THE SMELL. SHOW ME CASH.
NICE SAVE, TOOTS. WHO ARE YA? I DON'T RECOGNIZE TH' LEATHERS.
WILL THIS BUY ME CREDIT?
THE "S," YOU JERK.
SURE. YOU BIG BLUE'S SISTER?
COUSIN.
WHICH SORT OF OBLIGATES ME TO ASK ONE FINAL QUESTION BEFORE I MAKE A DEAL: WHAT EXACTLY WERE YOU BEING EXECUTED FOR?
UNPAID PARKING TICKET F'R MY BIKE.
THEY PUT YOU IN FRONT OF A FIRING SQUAD FOR THAT? WHERE DID YOU PARK?
ON THE GOVERNOR.
SWELL.
I COULDN'T JUSTIFY THIS IF THERE WEREN'T SO MUCH AT STAKE, BUT...YOU'RE HIRED. I'LL PULL YOUR BIKE OUT OF IMPOUND.
NEED ME T'POINT IT OUT?
♪
NO.

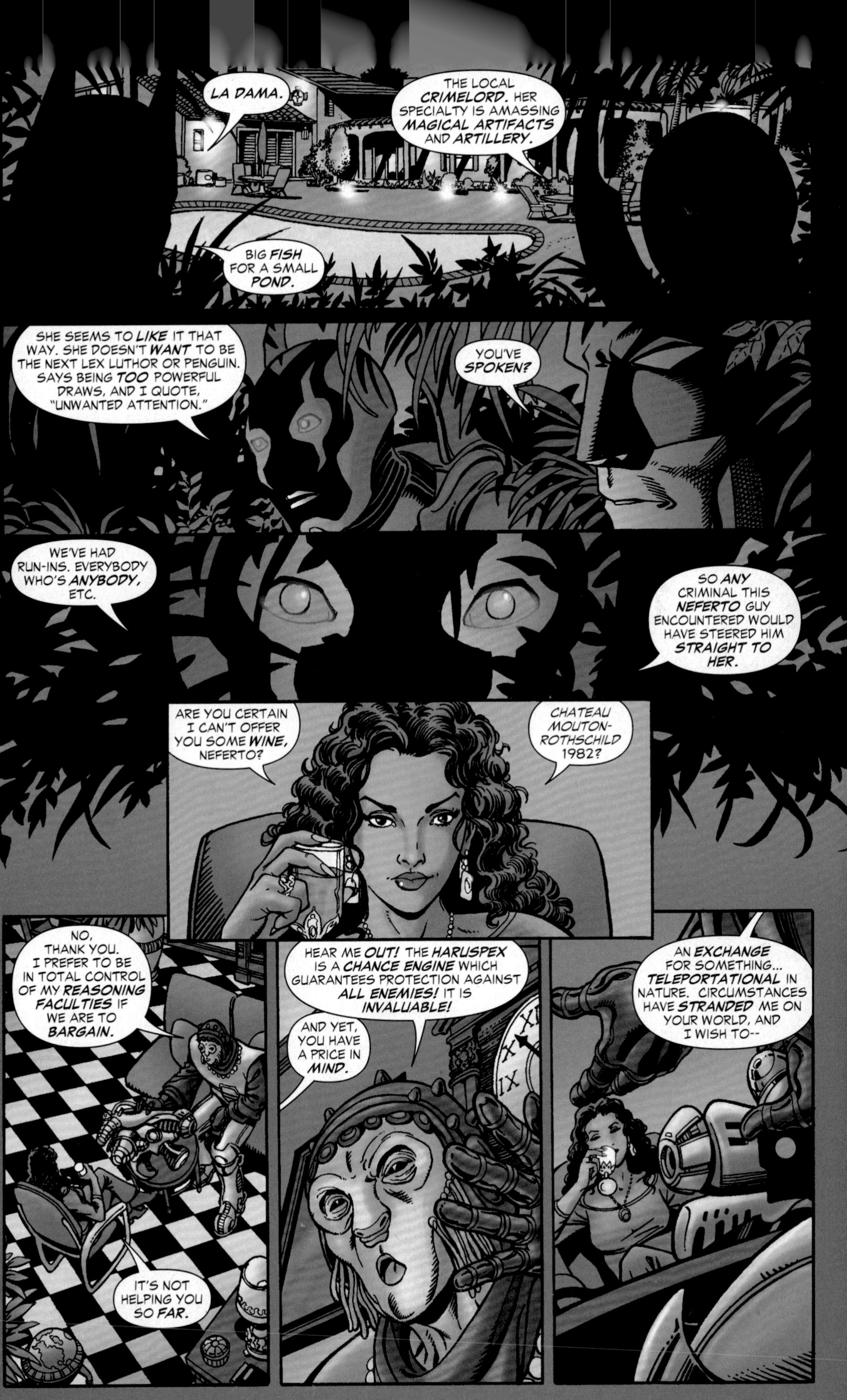
LA DAMA.
THE LOCAL CRIMELORD. HER SPECIALTY IS AMASSING MAGICAL ARTIFACTS AND ARTILLERY.
BIG FISH FOR A SMALL POND.
SHE SEEMS TO LIKE IT THAT WAY. SHE DOESN'T WANT TO BE THE NEXT LEX LUTHOR OR PENGUIN. SAYS BEING TOO POWERFUL DRAWS, AND I QUOTE, "UNWANTED ATTENTION."
YOU'VE SPOKEN?
WE'VE HAD RUN-INS. EVERYBODY WHO'S ANYBODY, ETC.
SO ANY CRIMINAL THIS NEFERTO GUY ENCOUNTERED WOULD HAVE STEERED HIM STRAIGHT TO HER.
ARE YOU CERTAIN I CAN'T OFFER YOU SOME WINE, NEFERTO?
CHATEAU MOUTON-ROTHSCHILD 1982?
NO, THANK YOU. I PREFER TO BE IN TOTAL CONTROL OF MY REASONING FACULTIES IF WE ARE TO BARGAIN.
IT'S NOT HELPING YOU SO FAR.
HEAR ME OUT! THE HARUSPEX IS A CHANCE ENGINE WHICH GUARANTEES PROTECTION AGAINST ALL ENEMIES! IT IS INVALUABLE!
AND YET, YOU HAVE A PRICE IN MIND.
AN EXCHANGE FOR SOMETHING... TELEPORTATIONAL IN NATURE. CIRCUMSTANCES HAVE STRANDED ME ON YOUR WORLD, AND I WISH TO--

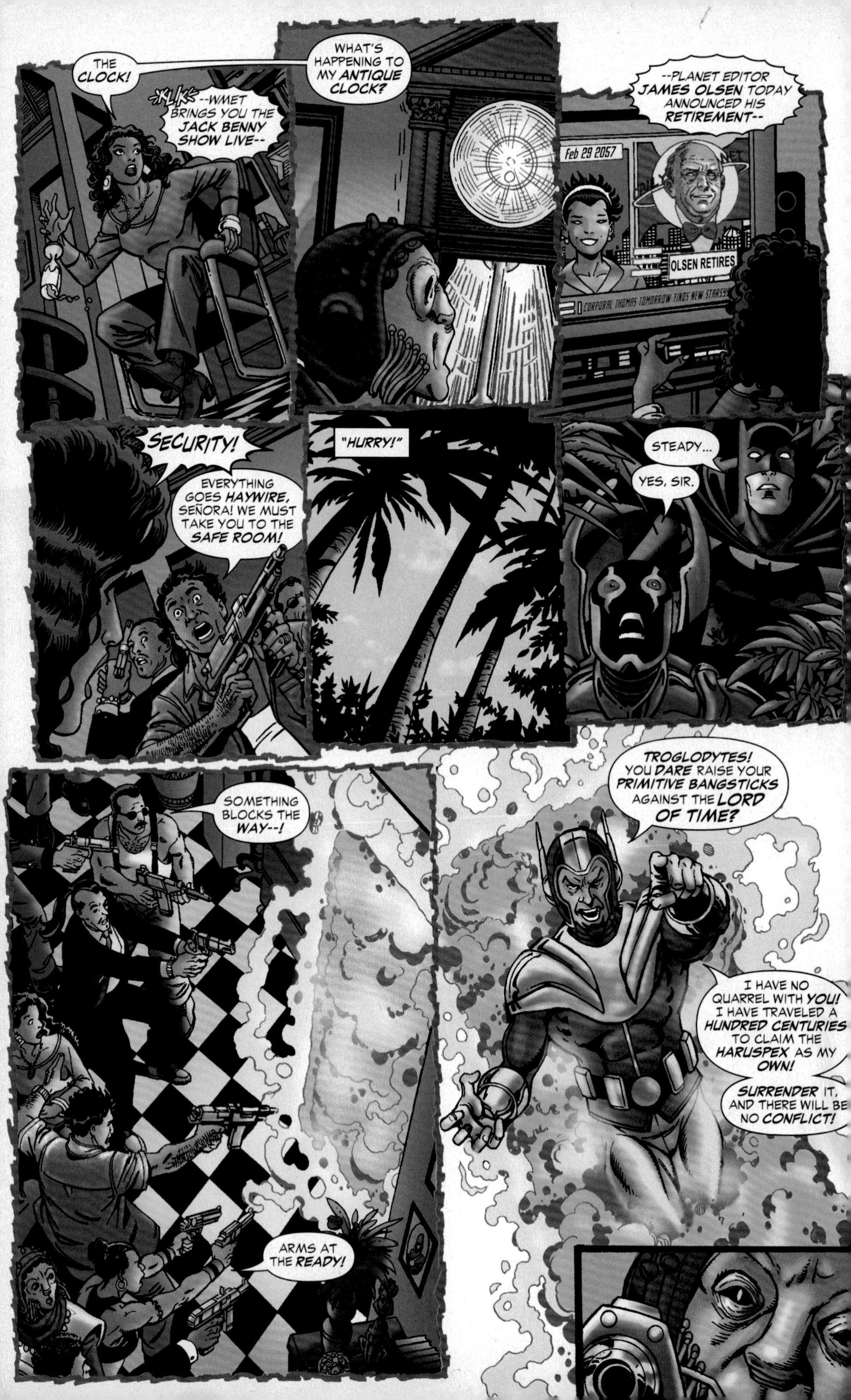
THE CLOCK!
KLIK --WMET BRINGS YOU THE JACK BENNY SHOW LIVE--
WHAT'S HAPPENING TO MY ANTIQUE CLOCK?
--PLANET EDITOR JAMES OLSEN TODAY ANNOUNCED HIS RETIREMENT--
Feb 29 2057
OLSEN RETIRES
CORPORAL THOMAS TOMORROW FINDS NEW STARS
SECURITY!
EVERYTHING GOES HAYWIRE, SEÑORA! WE MUST TAKE YOU TO THE SAFE ROOM!
"HURRY!"
STEADY...
YES, SIR.
SOMETHING BLOCKS THE WAY--!
TROGLODYTES! YOU DARE RAISE YOUR PRIMITIVE BANGSTICKS AGAINST THE LORD OF TIME?
I HAVE NO QUARREL WITH YOU! I HAVE TRAVELED A HUNDRED CENTURIES TO CLAIM THE HARUSPEX AS MY OWN!
SURRENDER IT, AND THERE WILL BE NO CONFLICT!
ARMS AT THE READY!

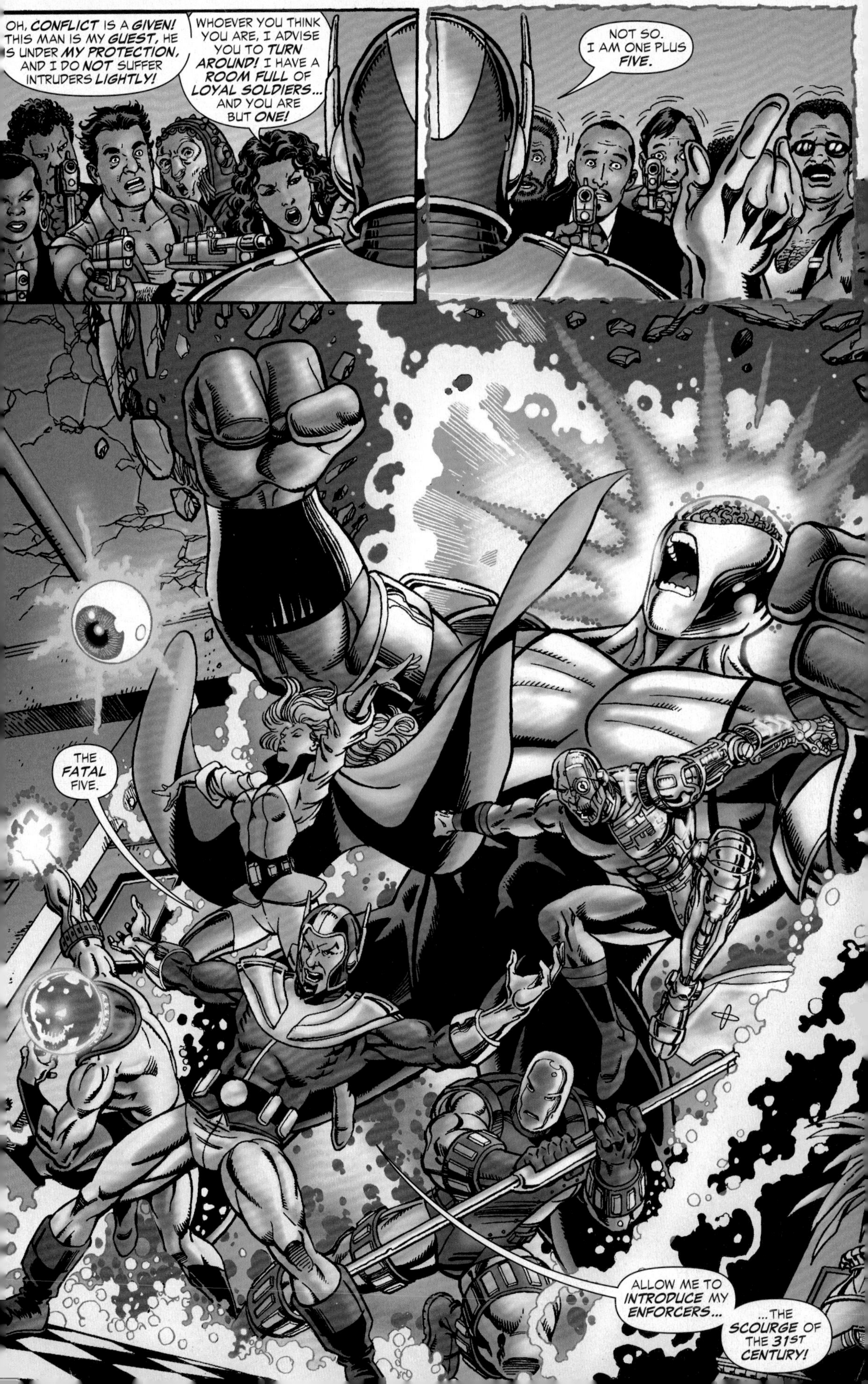
OH, CONFLICT IS A GIVEN! THIS MAN IS MY GUEST, HE IS UNDER MY PROTECTION, AND I DO NOT SUFFER INTRUDERS LIGHTLY!
WHOEVER YOU THINK YOU ARE, I ADVISE YOU TO TURN AROUND! I HAVE A ROOM FULL OF LOYAL SOLDIERS... AND YOU ARE BUT ONE!
NOT SO. I AM ONE PLUS FIVE.
THE FATAL FIVE.
ALLOW ME TO INTRODUCE MY ENFORCERS...
...THE SCOURGE OF THE 31ST CENTURY!

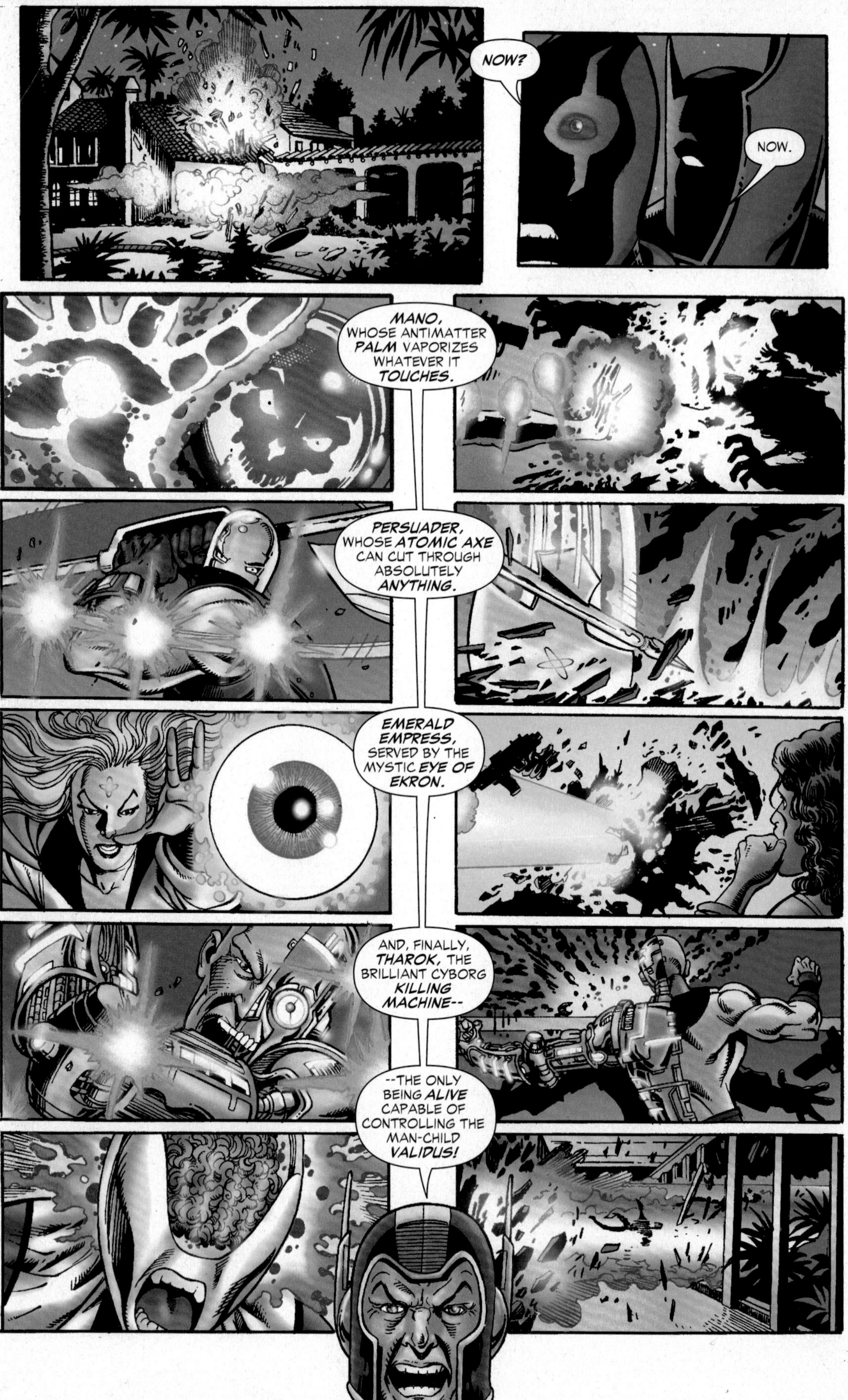
NOW?
NOW.
MANO, WHOSE ANTIMATTER PALM VAPORIZES WHATEVER IT TOUCHES.
PERSUADER, WHOSE ATOMIC AXE CAN CUT THROUGH ABSOLUTELY ANYTHING.
EMERALD EMPRESS, SERVED BY THE MYSTIC EYE OF EKRON.
AND, FINALLY, THAROK, THE BRILLIANT CYBORG KILLING MACHINE--
--THE ONLY BEING ALIVE CAPABLE OF CONTROLLING THE MAN-CHILD VALIDUS!

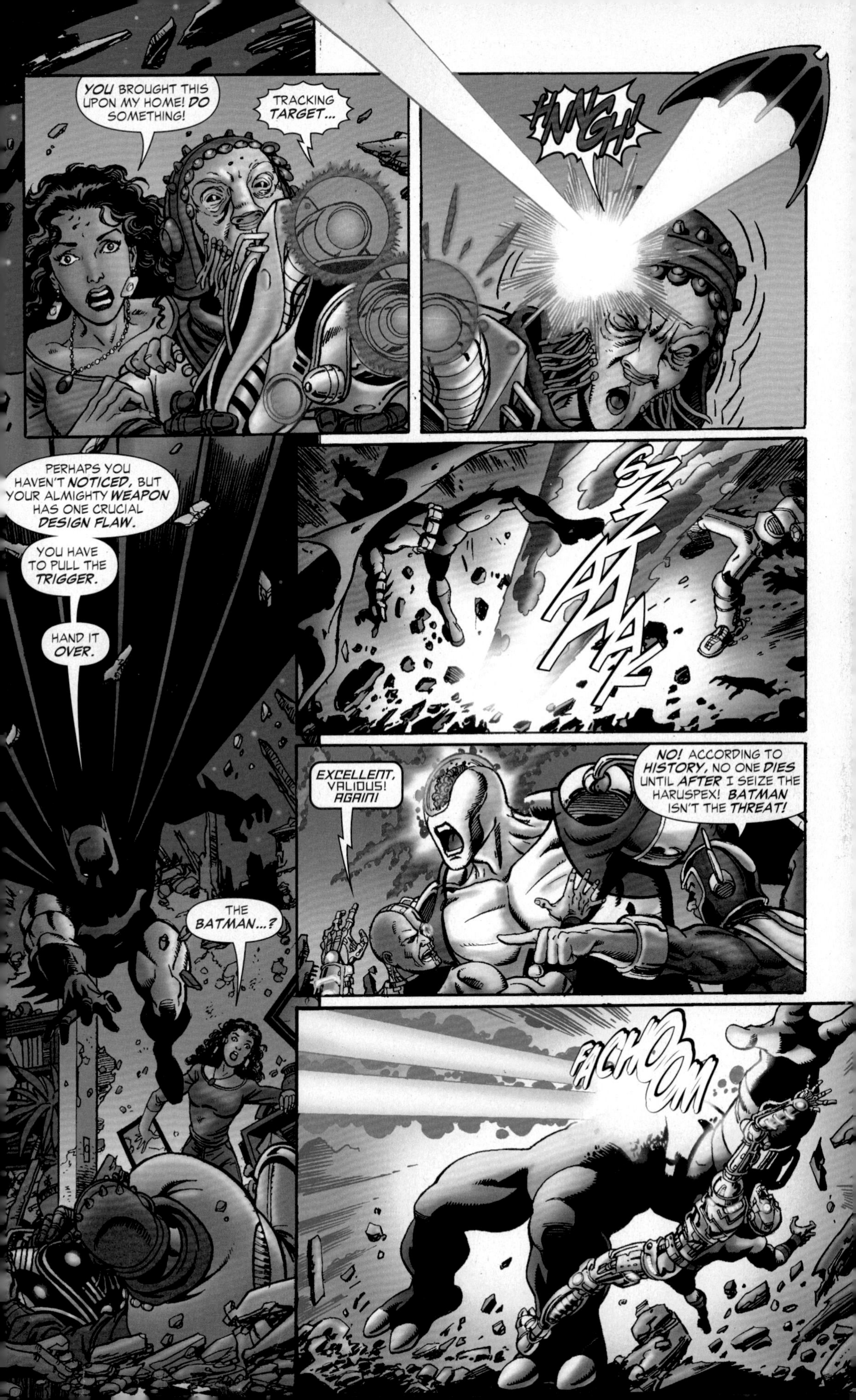
YOU BROUGHT THIS UPON MY HOME! DO SOMETHING!
TRACKING TARGET...
HNNGH!
PERHAPS YOU HAVEN'T NOTICED, BUT YOUR ALMIGHTY WEAPON HAS ONE CRUCIAL DESIGN FLAW.
YOU HAVE TO PULL THE TRIGGER.
HAND IT OVER.
THE BATMAN...?
SMAAAK
EXCELLENT, VALIDUS! AGAIN!
NO! ACCORDING TO HISTORY, NO ONE DIES UNTIL AFTER I SEIZE THE HARUSPEX! BATMAN ISN'T THE THREAT!
FACHOOM

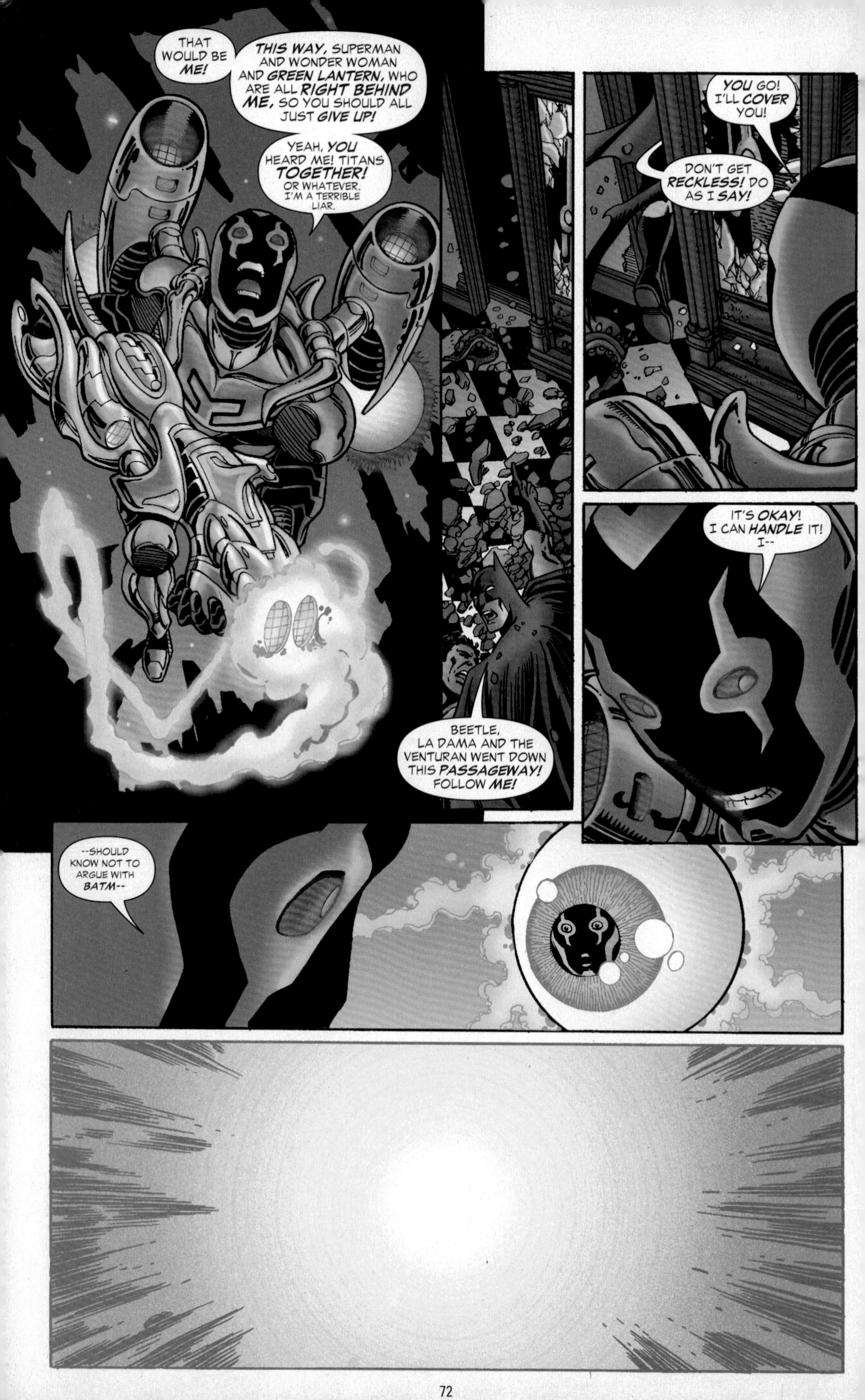

THAT WOULD BE ME!
THIS WAY, SUPERMAN AND WONDER WOMAN AND GREEN LANTERN, WHO ARE ALL RIGHT BEHIND ME, SO YOU SHOULD ALL JUST GIVE UP!
YEAH, YOU HEARD ME! TITANS TOGETHER! OR WHATEVER. I'M A TERRIBLE LIAR.
BEETLE, LA DAMA AND THE VENTURAN WENT DOWN THIS PASSAGEWAY! FOLLOW ME!
YOU GO! I'LL COVER YOU!
DON'T GET RECKLESS! DO AS I SAY!
IT'S OKAY! I CAN HANDLE IT! I--
--SHOULD KNOW NOT TO ARGUE WITH BATM--

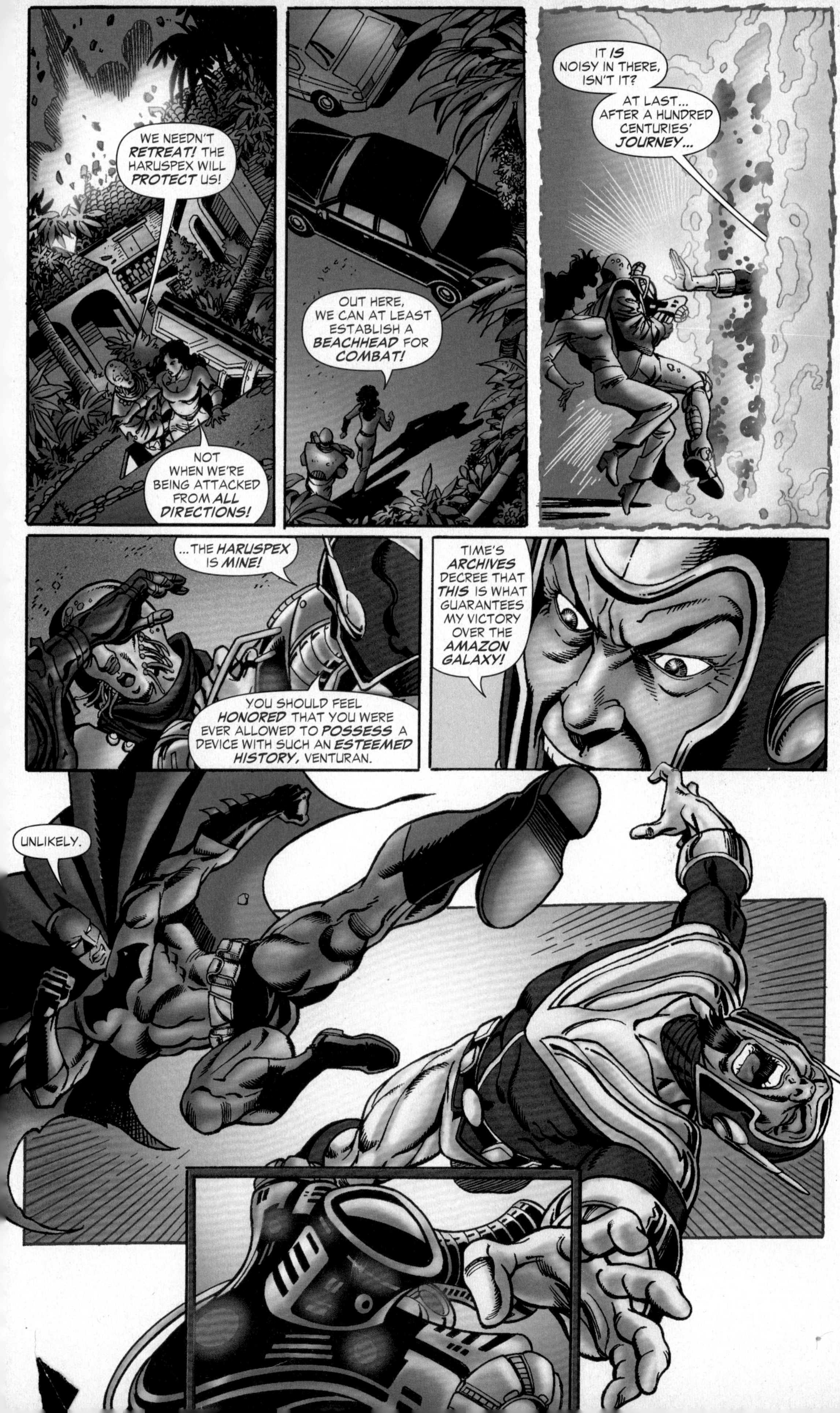

WE NEEDN'T RETREAT! THE HARUSPEX WILL PROTECT US!
NOT WHEN WE'RE BEING ATTACKED FROM ALL DIRECTIONS!
OUT HERE, WE CAN AT LEAST ESTABLISH A BEACHHEAD FOR COMBAT!
IT IS NOISY IN THERE, ISN'T IT?
AT LAST... AFTER A HUNDRED CENTURIES' JOURNEY...
...THE HARUSPEX IS MINE!
YOU SHOULD FEEL HONORED THAT YOU WERE EVER ALLOWED TO POSSESS A DEVICE WITH SUCH AN ESTEEMED HISTORY, VENTURAN.
TIME'S ARCHIVES DECREE THAT THIS IS WHAT GUARANTEES MY VICTORY OVER THE AMAZON GALAXY!
UNLIKELY.

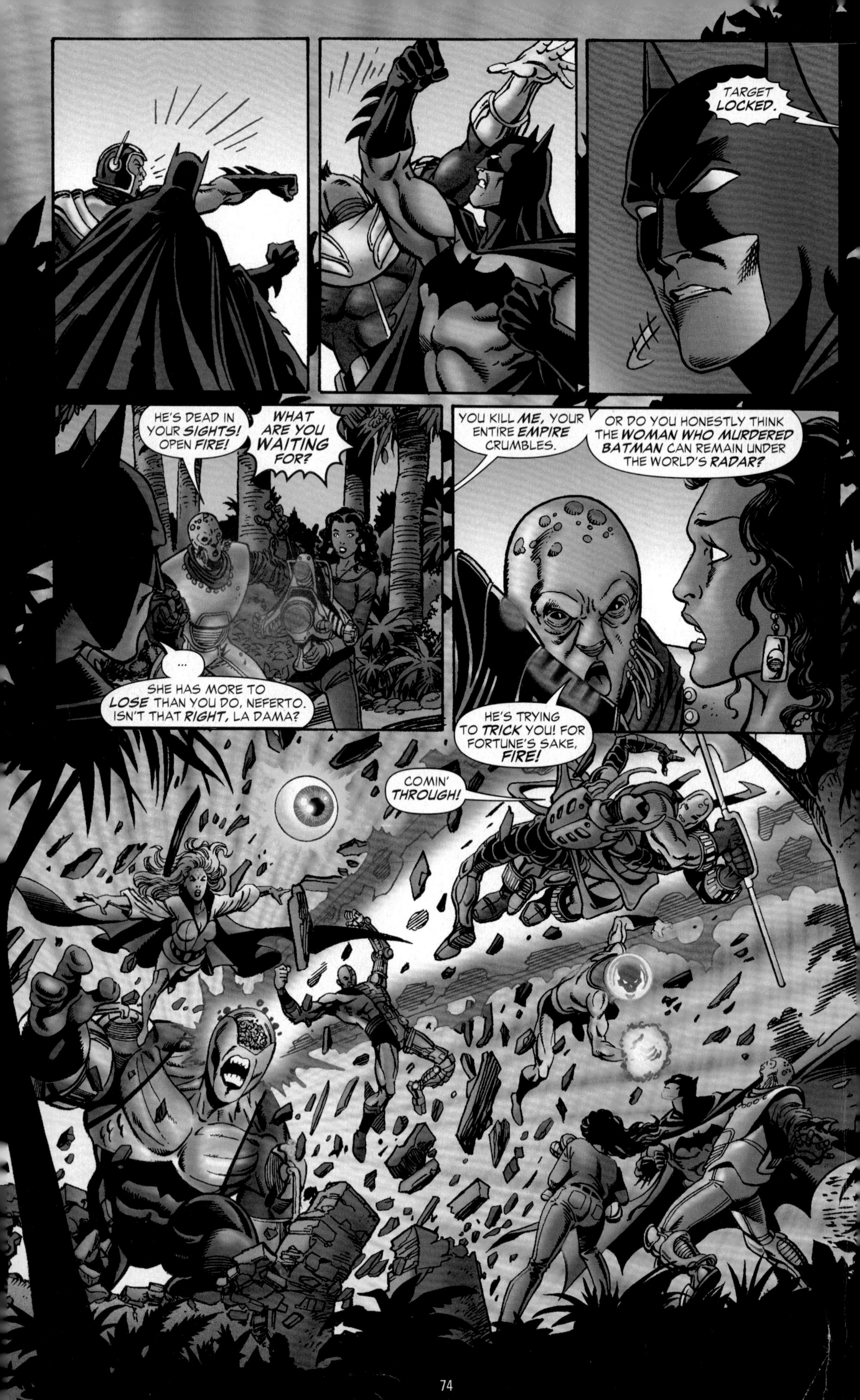
TARGET LOCKED.
HE'S DEAD IN YOUR SIGHTS! OPEN FIRE!
WHAT ARE YOU WAITING FOR?
...
SHE HAS MORE TO LOSE THAN YOU DO, NEFERTO. ISN'T THAT RIGHT, LA DAMA?
YOU KILL ME, YOUR ENTIRE EMPIRE CRUMBLES.
OR DO YOU HONESTLY THINK THE WOMAN WHO MURDERED BATMAN CAN REMAIN UNDER THE WORLD'S RADAR?
HE'S TRYING TO TRICK YOU! FOR FORTUNE'S SAKE, FIRE!
COMIN' THROUGH!

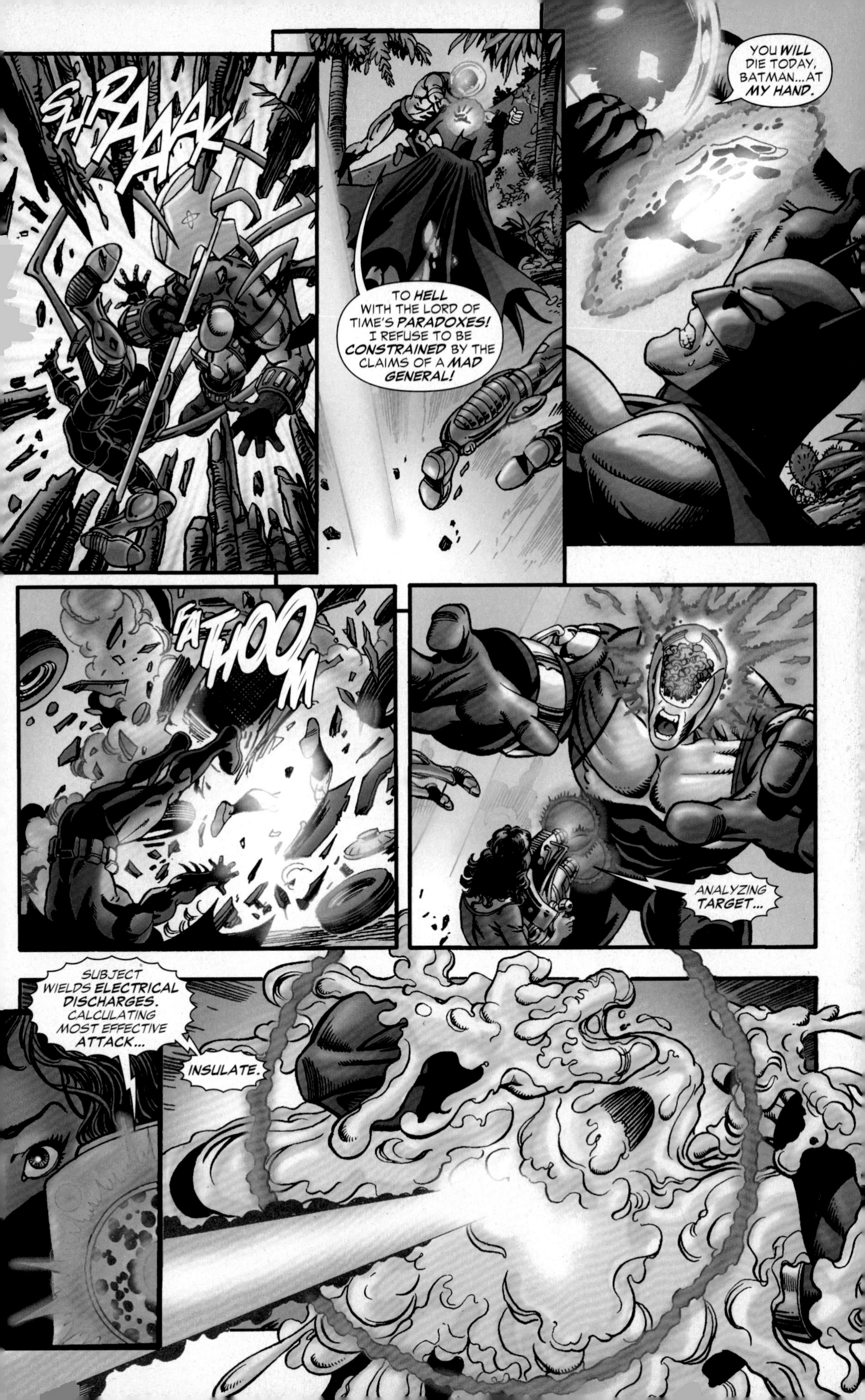
SHRAAAK
TO HELL WITH THE LORD OF TIME'S PARADOXES! I REFUSE TO BE CONSTRAINED BY THE CLAIMS OF A MAD GENERAL!
YOU WILL DIE TODAY, BATMAN...AT MY HAND.
FATHOOOM
ANALYZING TARGET...
SUBJECT WIELDS ELECTRICAL DISCHARGES. CALCULATING MOST EFFECTIVE ATTACK...
INSULATE.

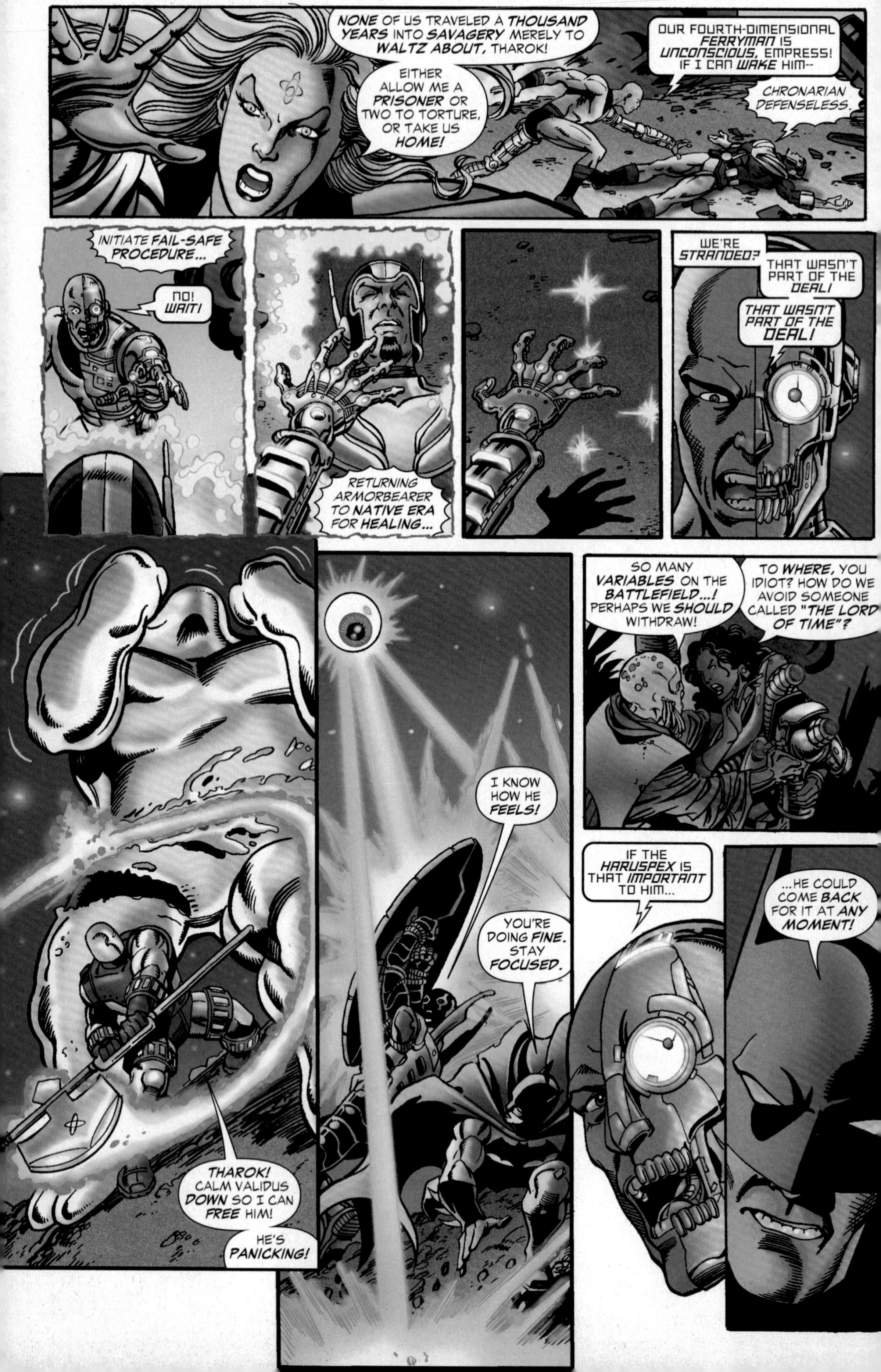
NONE OF US TRAVELED A THOUSAND YEARS INTO SAVAGERY MERELY TO WALTZ ABOUT, THAROK!
EITHER ALLOW ME A PRISONER OR TWO TO TORTURE, OR TAKE US HOME!
OUR FOURTH-DIMENSIONAL FERRYMAN IS UNCONSCIOUS, EMPRESS! IF I CAN WAKE HIM--
CHRONARIAN DEFENSELESS.
INITIATE FAIL-SAFE PROCEDURE...
NO! WAIT!
RETURNING ARMORBEARER TO NATIVE ERA FOR HEALING...
WE'RE STRANDED?
THAT WASN'T PART OF THE DEAL!
THAT WASN'T PART OF THE DEAL!
THAROK! CALM VALIDUS DOWN SO I CAN FREE HIM!
HE'S PANICKING!
I KNOW HOW HE FEELS!
YOU'RE DOING FINE. STAY FOCUSED.
SO MANY VARIABLES ON THE BATTLEFIELD...! PERHAPS WE SHOULD WITHDRAW!
TO WHERE, YOU IDIOT? HOW DO WE AVOID SOMEONE CALLED "THE LORD OF TIME"?
IF THE HARUSPEX IS THAT IMPORTANT TO HIM...
...HE COULD COME BACK FOR IT AT ANY MOMENT!

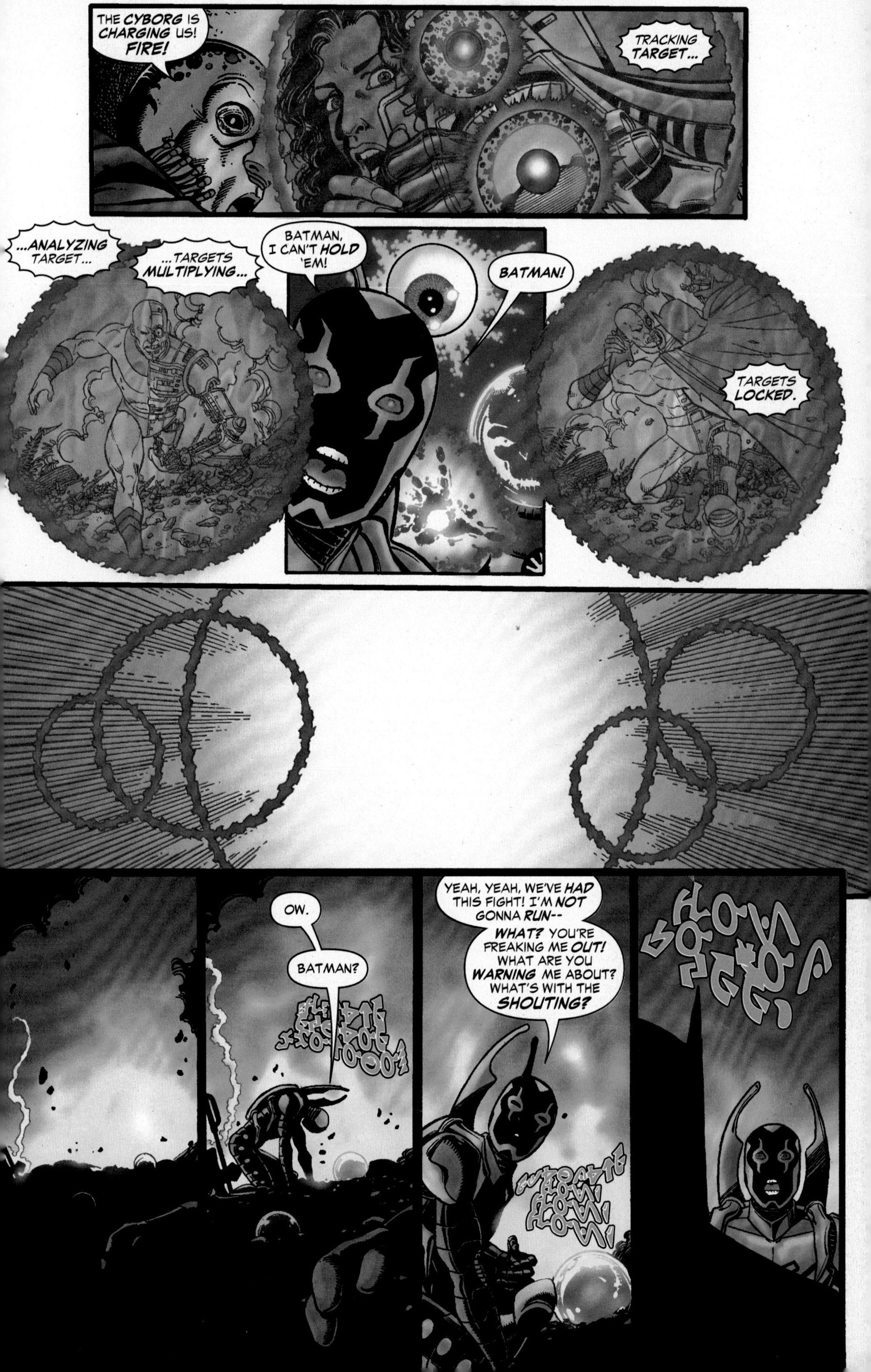
THE CYBORG IS CHARGING US! FIRE!
TRACKING TARGET...
...ANALYZING TARGET...
...TARGETS MULTIPLYING...
BATMAN, I CAN'T HOLD 'EM!
BATMAN!
TARGETS LOCKED.
OW.
BATMAN?
YEAH, YEAH, WE'VE HAD THIS FIGHT! I'M NOT GONNA RUN--
WHAT? YOU'RE FREAKING ME OUT! WHAT ARE YOU WARNING ME ABOUT? WHAT'S WITH THE SHOUTING?

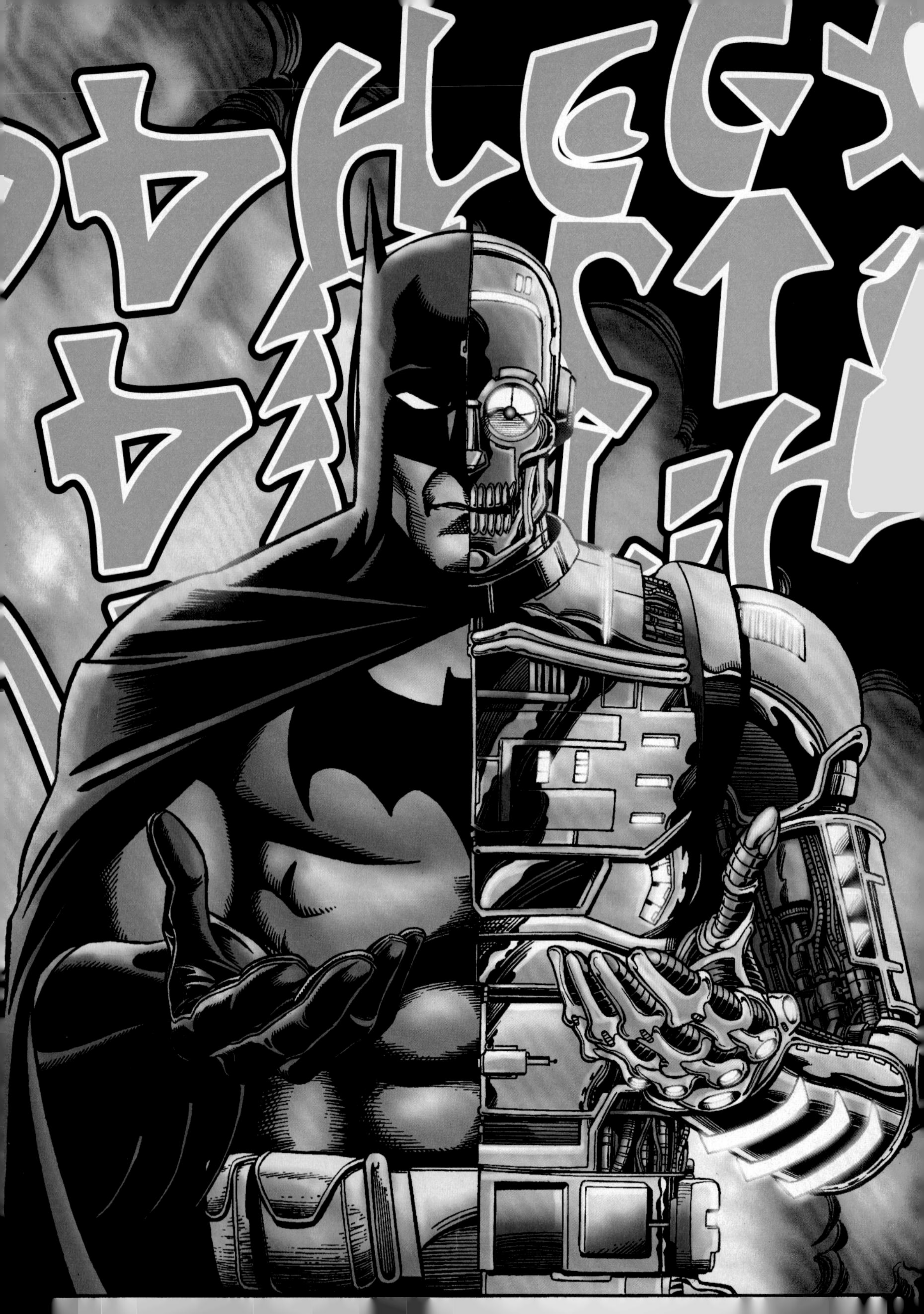

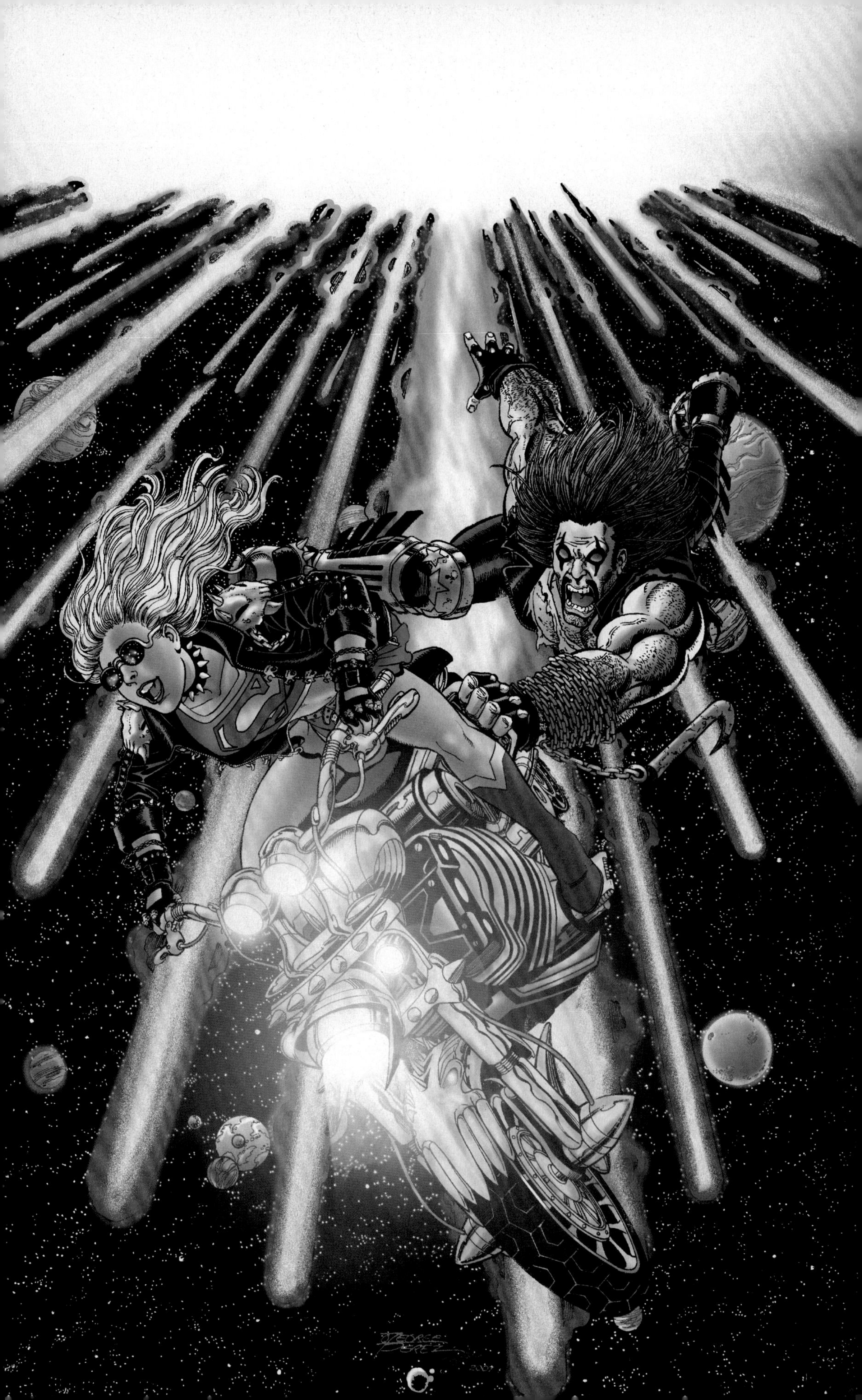

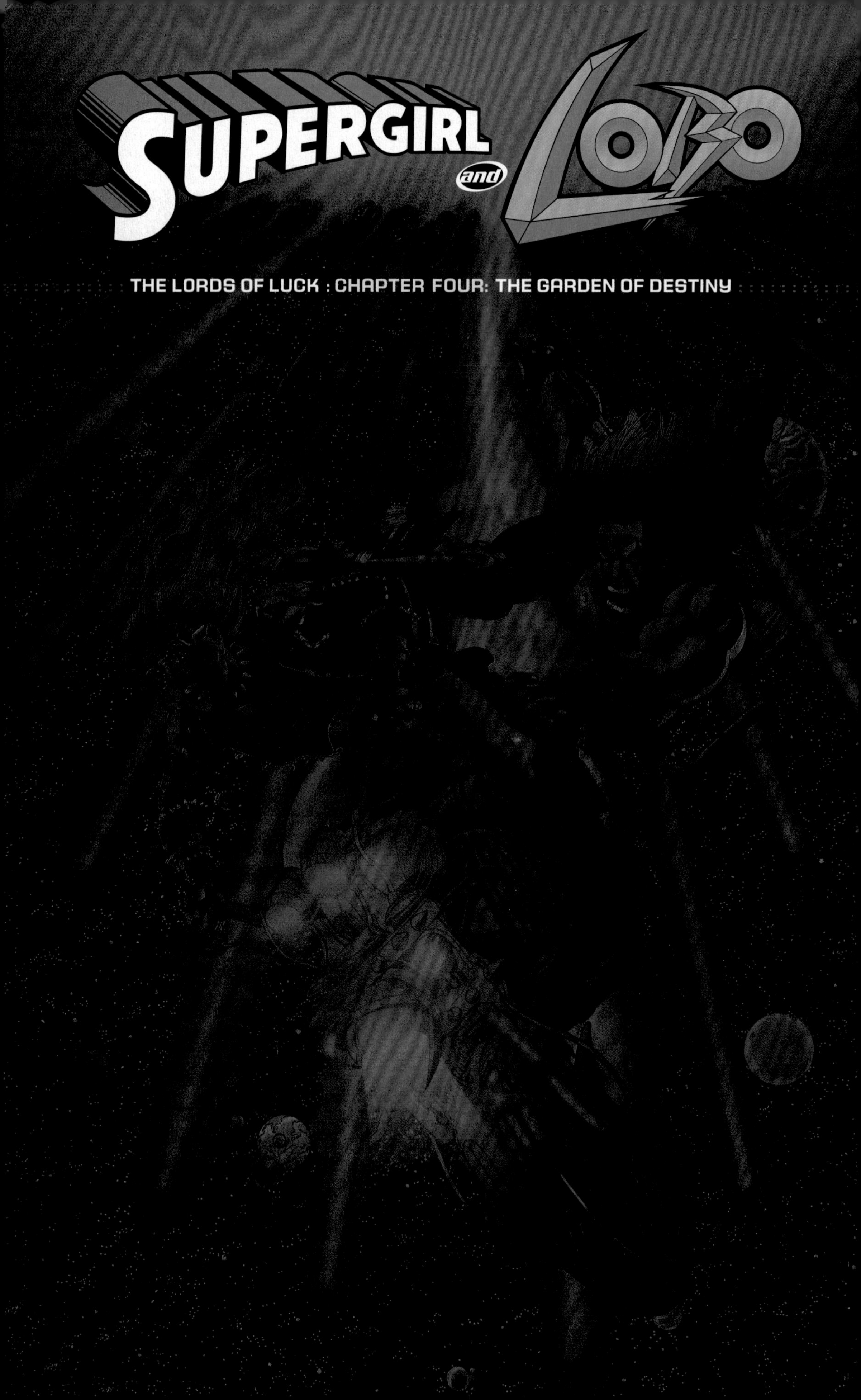
SUPERGIRL and LOBO
THE LORDS OF LUCK : CHAPTER FOUR: THE GARDEN OF DESTINY

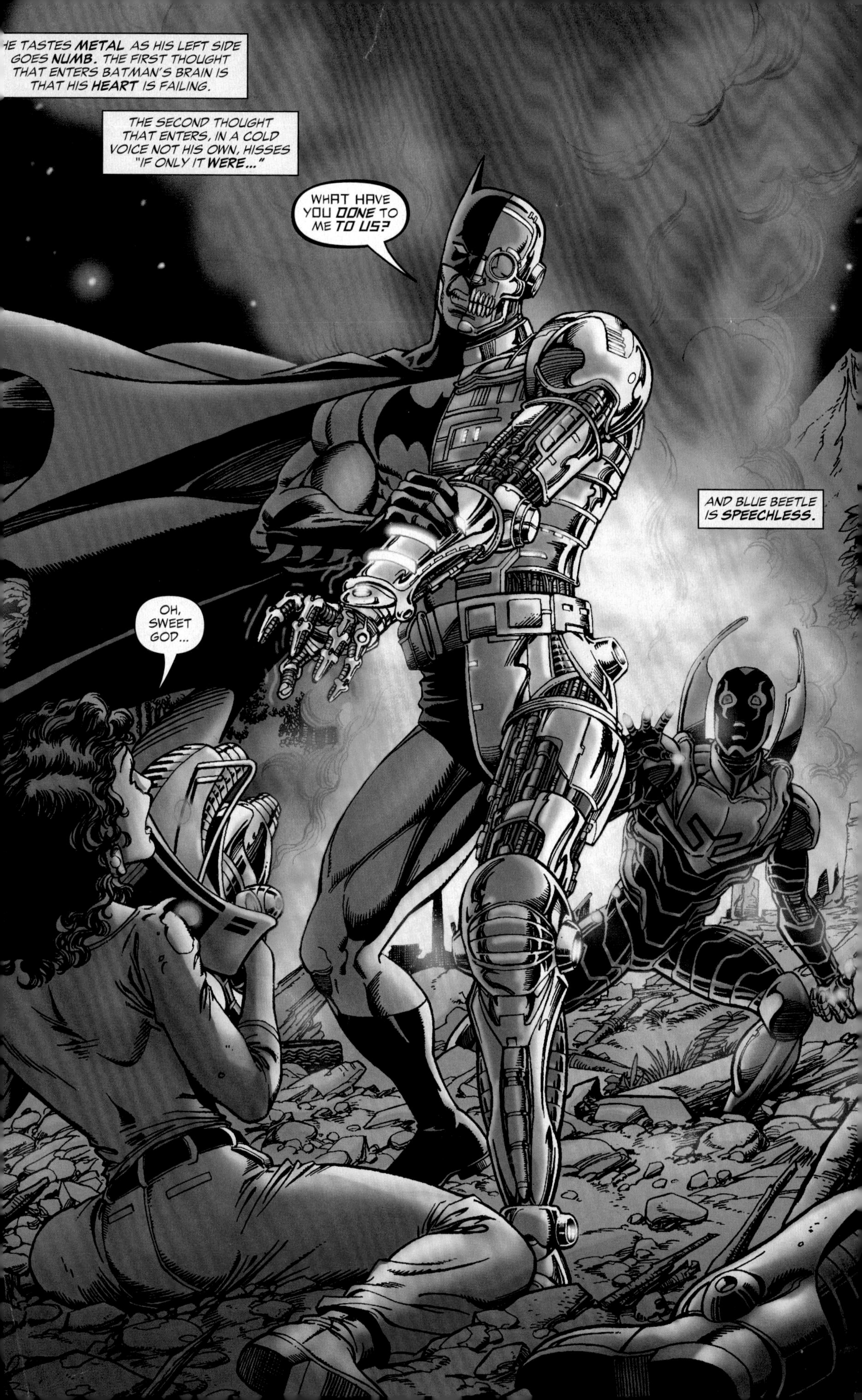
HE TASTES METAL AS HIS LEFT SIDE GOES NUMB. THE FIRST THOUGHT THAT ENTERS BATMAN'S BRAIN IS THAT HIS HEART IS FAILING.
THE SECOND THOUGHT THAT ENTERS, IN A COLD VOICE NOT HIS OWN, HISSES "IF ONLY IT WERE..."
WHAT HAVE YOU DONE TO ME TO US?
AND BLUE BEETLE IS SPEECHLESS.
OH, SWEET GOD...

ARROGANT *PRIMITIVE*...

...FIRING A WEAPON YOU DON'T UNDER-STAND...

LA DAMA, *RUN!* I'M-- HOLDING *BACK,* BUT--

--THE FLESH IS *WEAK,* YOU *APE?*

HANG ON, *BATMAN!* I'LL...

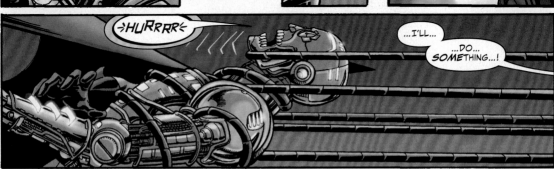

>HURRRR<

...I'LL...

...DO... SOMETHING...!

>HNNNGH!<

ARMOR! *ANALYZE!* TELL ME HOW MR. CLANKY'S *ROBOT* HALF GOT STUCK TO *BAT--*

YES, I *KNOW* HIS NAME IS *THAROK!* JUST *SCAN!*

WHAT DO YOU MEAN, THEY'RE "*BOTH PRESENT*"? I ONLY SEE *HALF* OF *BATMAN!* THAT'S *IMPOSSIBLE!*

THE... *HARUSPEX* WEAPON... ...*DOES* THE *IMPOSSIBLE,* BOY. KEEP *SCANNING...!*

NO! *BEETLE*... ...*BEHIND* YOU...

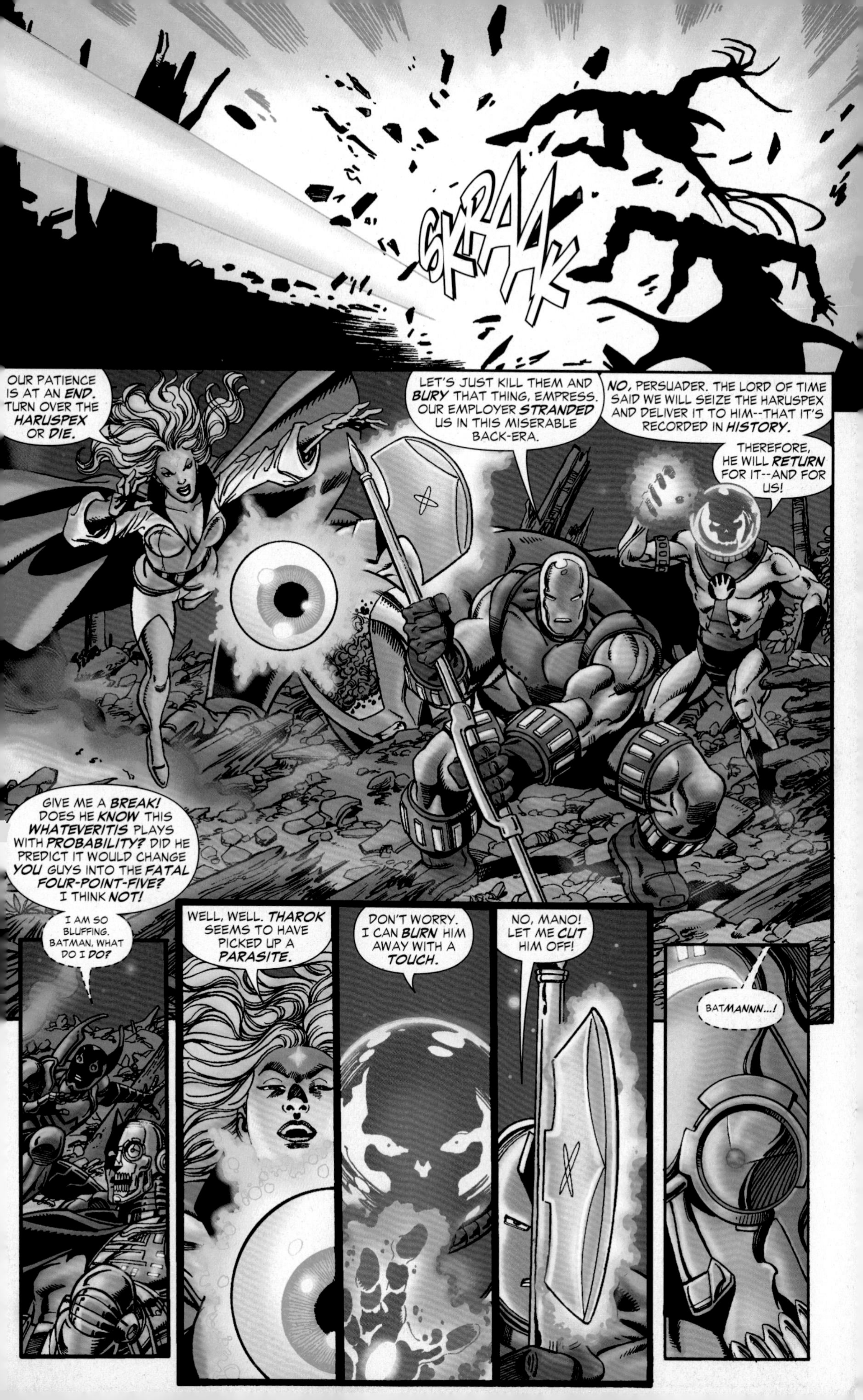
SKRAAAK
OUR PATIENCE IS AT AN END. TURN OVER THE HARUSPEX OR DIE.
LET'S JUST KILL THEM AND BURY THAT THING, EMPRESS. OUR EMPLOYER STRANDED US IN THIS MISERABLE BACK-ERA.
NO, PERSUADER. THE LORD OF TIME SAID WE WILL SEIZE THE HARUSPEX AND DELIVER IT TO HIM--THAT IT'S RECORDED IN HISTORY.
THEREFORE, HE WILL RETURN FOR IT--AND FOR US!
GIVE ME A BREAK! DOES HE KNOW THIS WHATEVERITIS PLAYS WITH PROBABILITY? DID HE PREDICT IT WOULD CHANGE YOU GUYS INTO THE FATAL FOUR-POINT-FIVE? I THINK NOT!
I AM SO BLUFFING. BATMAN, WHAT DO I DO?
WELL, WELL. THAROK SEEMS TO HAVE PICKED UP A PARASITE.
DON'T WORRY. I CAN BURN HIM AWAY WITH A TOUCH.
NO, MANO! LET ME CUT HIM OFF!
BATMANNN...!

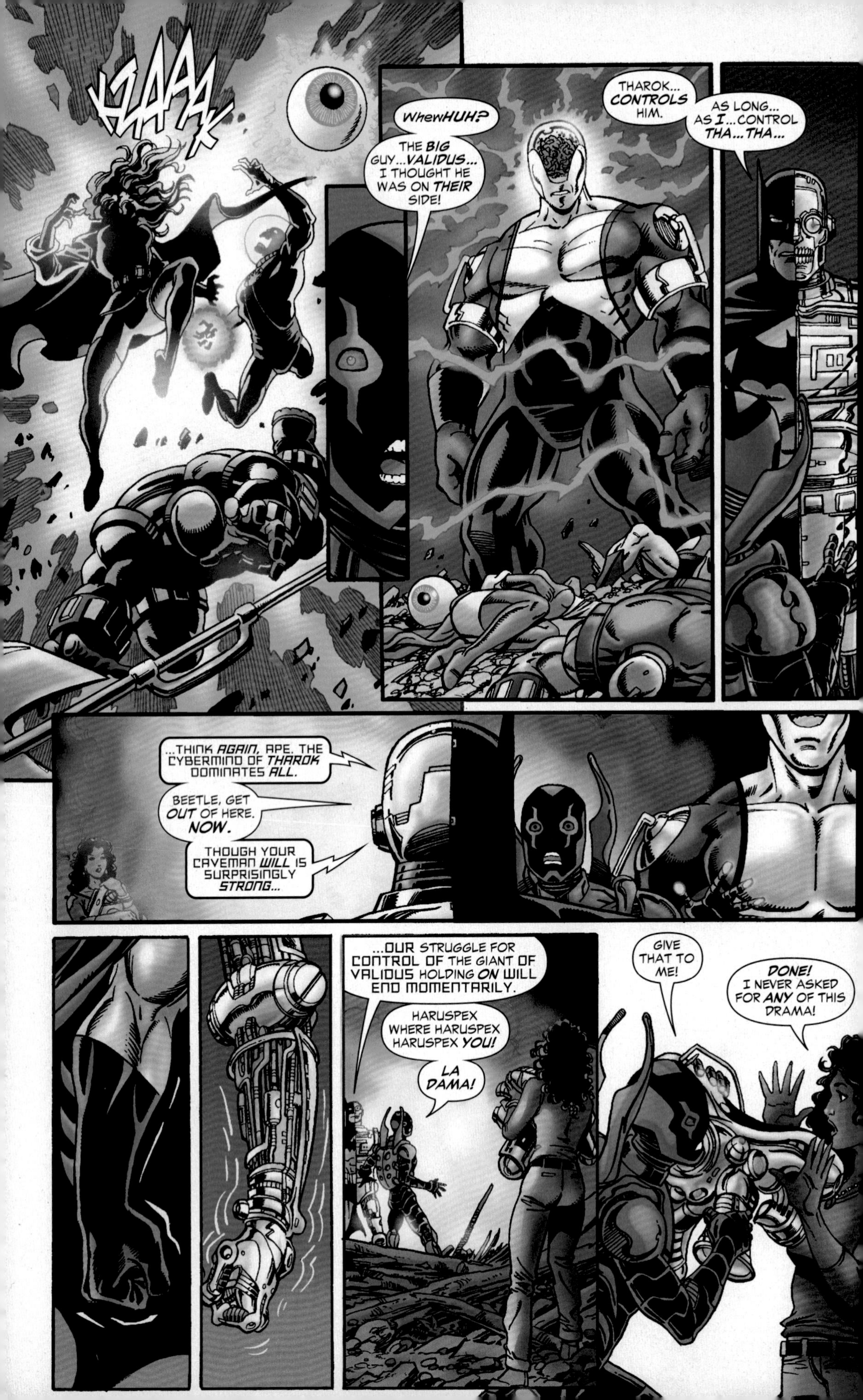
KZAAAK
WhewHUH?
THE BIG GUY...VALIDUS... I THOUGHT HE WAS ON THEIR SIDE!
THAROK... CONTROLS HIM.
AS LONG... AS I...CONTROL THA...THA...
...THINK AGAIN, APE. THE CYBERMIND OF THAROK DOMINATES ALL.
BEETLE, GET OUT OF HERE. NOW.
THOUGH YOUR CAVEMAN WILL IS SURPRISINGLY STRONG...
...OUR STRUGGLE FOR CONTROL OF THE GIANT OF VALIDUS HOLDING ON WILL END MOMENTARILY.
HARUSPEX WHERE HARUSPEX HARUSPEX YOU!
LA DAMA!
GIVE THAT TO ME!
DONE! I NEVER ASKED FOR ANY OF THIS DRAMA!

ARMOR, *HELP!* FIND A *REWIND* BUTTON ON THIS THING! *SOMETHING!*

NO "*UNDO*"? THERE *HAS* TO BE A *FAIL-SAFE!* COME ON!

BATMAN IS GETTING 'BORGED, I HAVE A *GIANT* ON MY *BUTT* WITH A *THUNDERCLOUD* FOR A *BRAIN,* AND WE ARE ABOUT TO *DIE* BY *LIGHTNING!*

YES.

THAROK?

LET GO OF THE *WEAPON.*

NO! WHAT ARE YOU *DOING?*

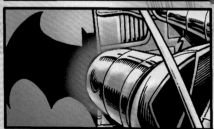

SAVING YOU.

KLIK

GONE... HARUSPEX AND *ALL...*

...THEY'RE *ALL...GONE...*

IT'S QUITE THE *MOMENT* FOR YOU.

JOKER. SCARECROW. RA'S AL GHUL. ALL THE GREAT ONES *TRIED* IT.

BUT YOU *DID* IT.

YOU KILLED THE *BATMAN...*

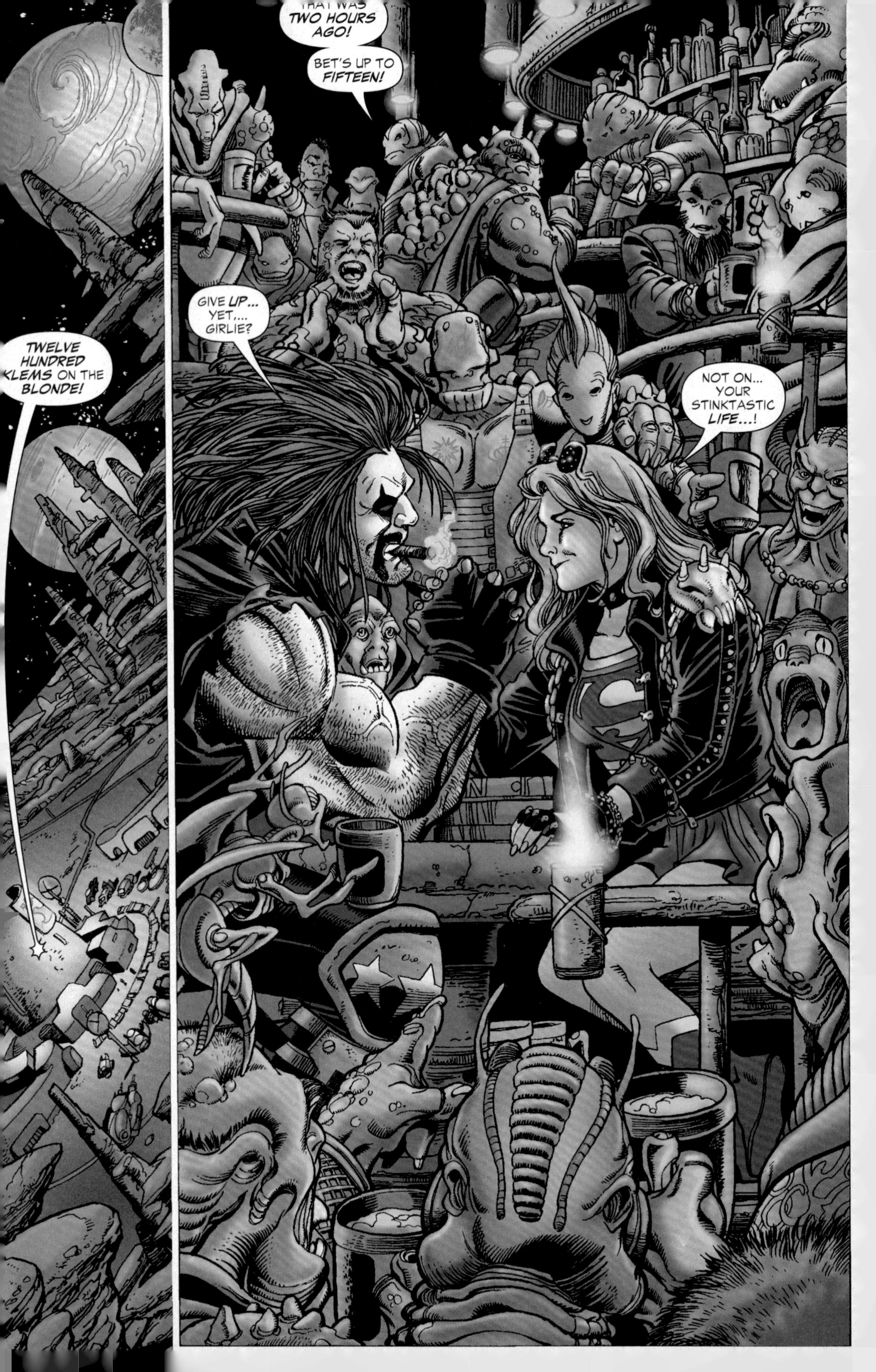
TWELVE HUNDRED KLEMS ON THE BLONDE!
THAT WAS TWO HOURS AGO!
BET'S UP TO FIFTEEN!
GIVE UP... YET,... GIRLIE?
NOT ON... YOUR STINKTASTIC LIFE...!

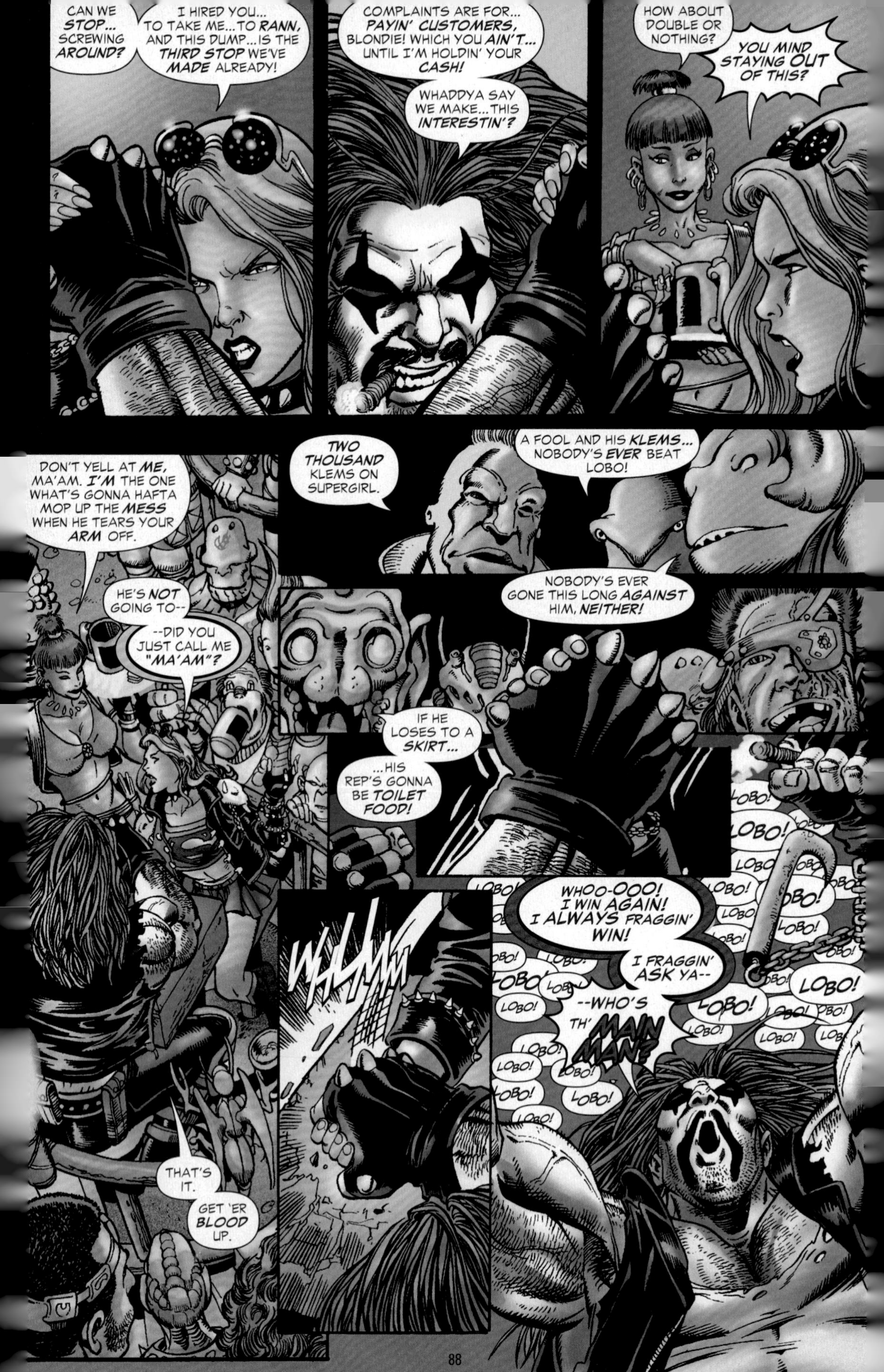
CAN WE STOP... SCREWING AROUND?
I HIRED YOU... TO TAKE ME... TO RANN, AND THIS DUMP... IS THE THIRD STOP WE'VE MADE ALREADY!
COMPLAINTS ARE FOR... PAYIN' CUSTOMERS, BLONDIE! WHICH YOU AIN'T... UNTIL I'M HOLDIN' YOUR CASH!
WHADDYA SAY WE MAKE... THIS INTERESTIN'?
HOW ABOUT DOUBLE OR NOTHING?
YOU MIND STAYING OUT OF THIS?
DON'T YELL AT ME, MA'AM. I'M THE ONE WHAT'S GONNA HAFTA MOP UP THE MESS WHEN HE TEARS YOUR ARM OFF.
HE'S NOT GOING TO--
--DID YOU JUST CALL ME "MA'AM"?
TWO THOUSAND KLEMS ON SUPERGIRL.
A FOOL AND HIS KLEMS... NOBODY'S EVER BEAT LOBO!
NOBODY'S EVER GONE THIS LONG AGAINST HIM, NEITHER!
IF HE LOSES TO A SKIRT...
...HIS REP'S GONNA BE TOILET FOOD!
THAT'S IT.
GET 'ER BLOOD UP.
WHUMM
WHOO-OOO! I WIN AGAIN! I ALWAYS FRAGGIN' WIN!
I FRAGGIN' ASK YA--
--WHO'S TH' MAIN MAN?
LOBO!

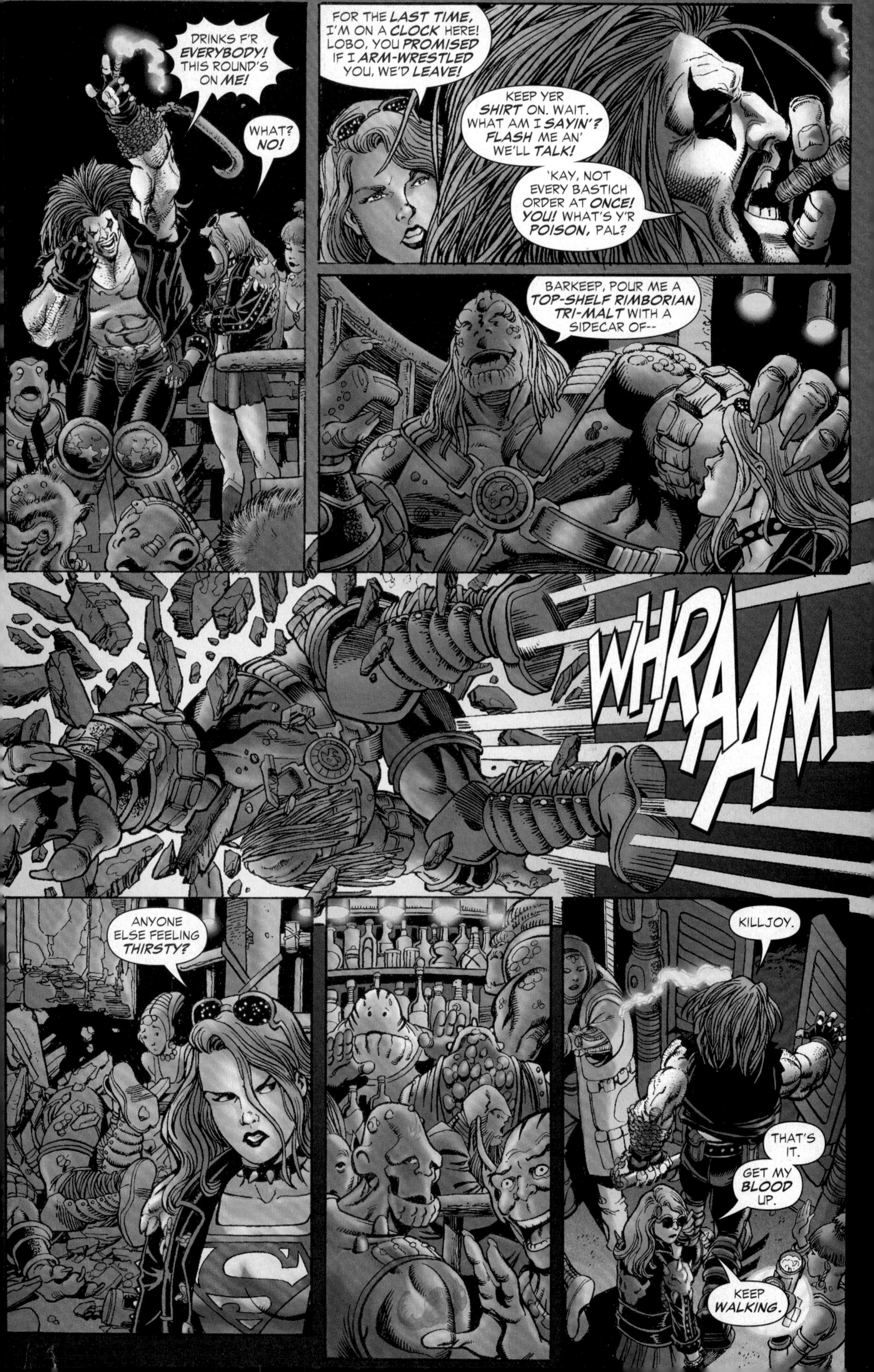
DRINKS F'R EVERYBODY! THIS ROUND'S ON ME!
WHAT? NO!
FOR THE LAST TIME, I'M ON A CLOCK HERE! LOBO, YOU PROMISED IF I ARM-WRESTLED YOU, WE'D LEAVE!
KEEP YER SHIRT ON. WAIT. WHAT AM I SAYIN'? FLASH ME AN' WE'LL TALK!
'KAY, NOT EVERY BASTICH ORDER AT ONCE! YOU! WHAT'S Y'R POISON, PAL?
BARKEEP, POUR ME A TOP-SHELF RIMBORIAN TRI-MALT WITH A SIDECAR OF--
WHRAAAM
ANYONE ELSE FEELING THIRSTY?
KILLJOY.
THAT'S IT.
GET MY BLOOD UP.
KEEP WALKING.

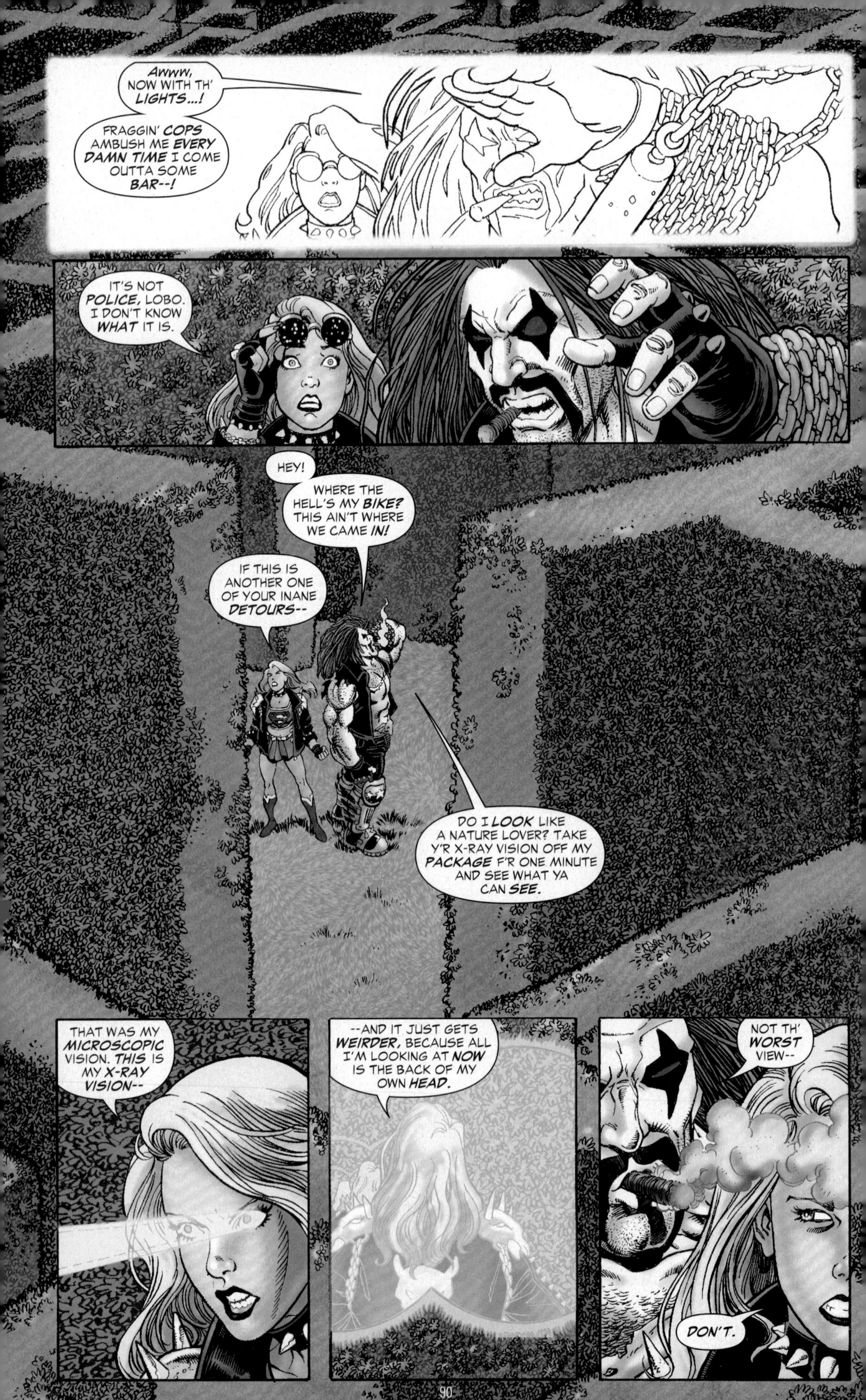
AWWW, NOW WITH TH' LIGHTS...!
FRAGGIN' COPS AMBUSH ME EVERY DAMN TIME I COME OUTTA SOME BAR--!
IT'S NOT POLICE, LOBO. I DON'T KNOW WHAT IT IS.
HEY!
WHERE THE HELL'S MY BIKE? THIS AIN'T WHERE WE CAME IN!
IF THIS IS ANOTHER ONE OF YOUR INANE DETOURS--
DO I LOOK LIKE A NATURE LOVER? TAKE Y'R X-RAY VISION OFF MY PACKAGE F'R ONE MINUTE AND SEE WHAT YA CAN SEE.
THAT WAS MY MICROSCOPIC VISION. THIS IS MY X-RAY VISION--
--AND IT JUST GETS WEIRDER, BECAUSE ALL I'M LOOKING AT NOW IS THE BACK OF MY OWN HEAD.
NOT TH' WORST VIEW--
DON'T.

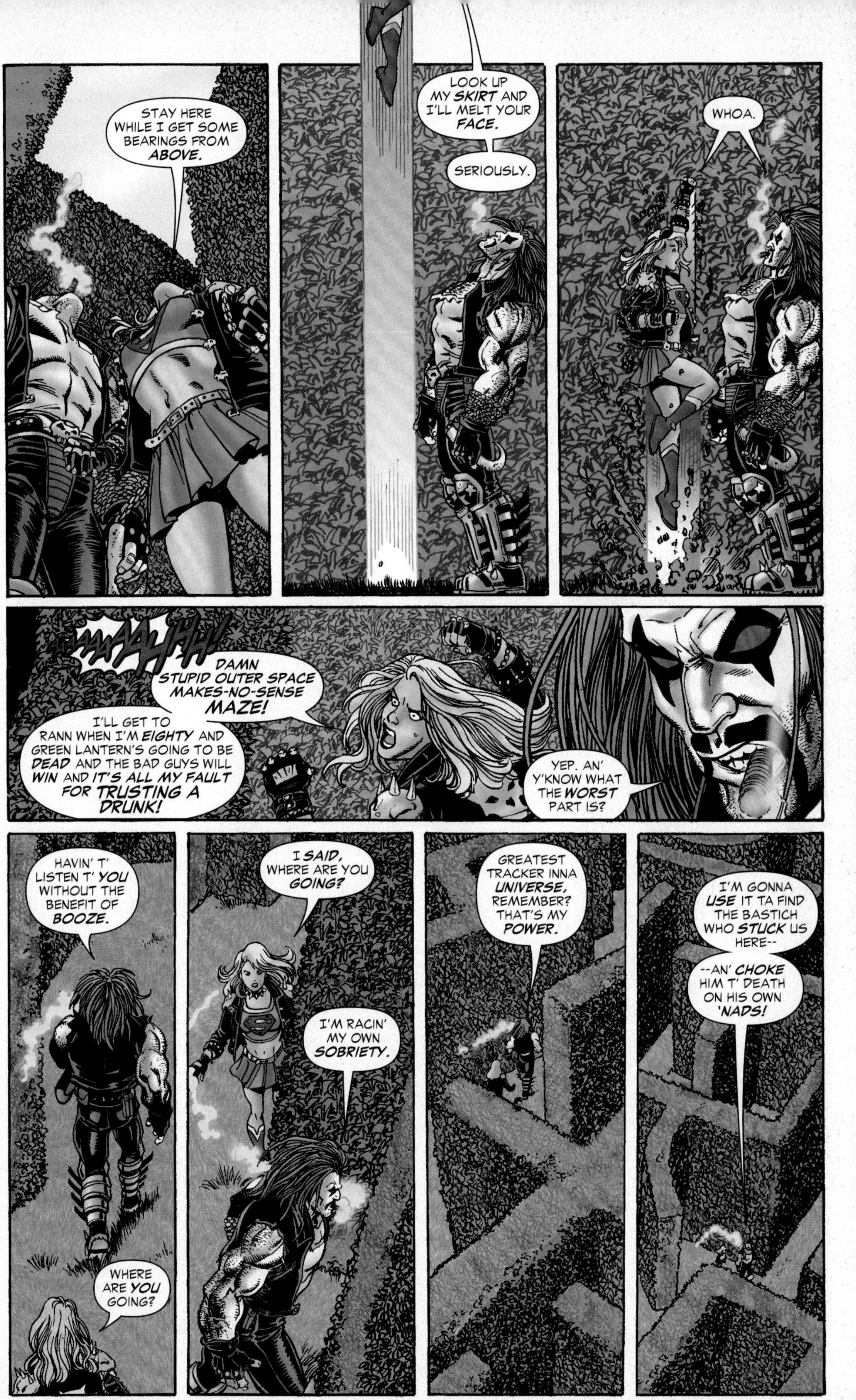

STAY HERE WHILE I GET SOME BEARINGS FROM ABOVE.
LOOK UP MY SKIRT AND I'LL MELT YOUR FACE.
SERIOUSLY.
WHOA.
AAAAAAAHHH!
DAMN STUPID OUTER SPACE MAKES-NO-SENSE MAZE!
I'LL GET TO RANN WHEN I'M EIGHTY AND GREEN LANTERN'S GOING TO BE DEAD AND THE BAD GUYS WILL WIN AND IT'S ALL MY FAULT FOR TRUSTING A DRUNK!
YEP. AN' Y'KNOW WHAT THE WORST PART IS?
HAVIN' T' LISTEN T' YOU WITHOUT THE BENEFIT OF BOOZE.
WHERE ARE YOU GOING?
I SAID, WHERE ARE YOU GOING?
I'M RACIN' MY OWN SOBRIETY.
GREATEST TRACKER INNA UNIVERSE, REMEMBER? THAT'S MY POWER.
I'M GONNA USE IT TA FIND THE BASTICH WHO STUCK US HERE--
--AN' CHOKE HIM T' DEATH ON HIS OWN 'NADS!

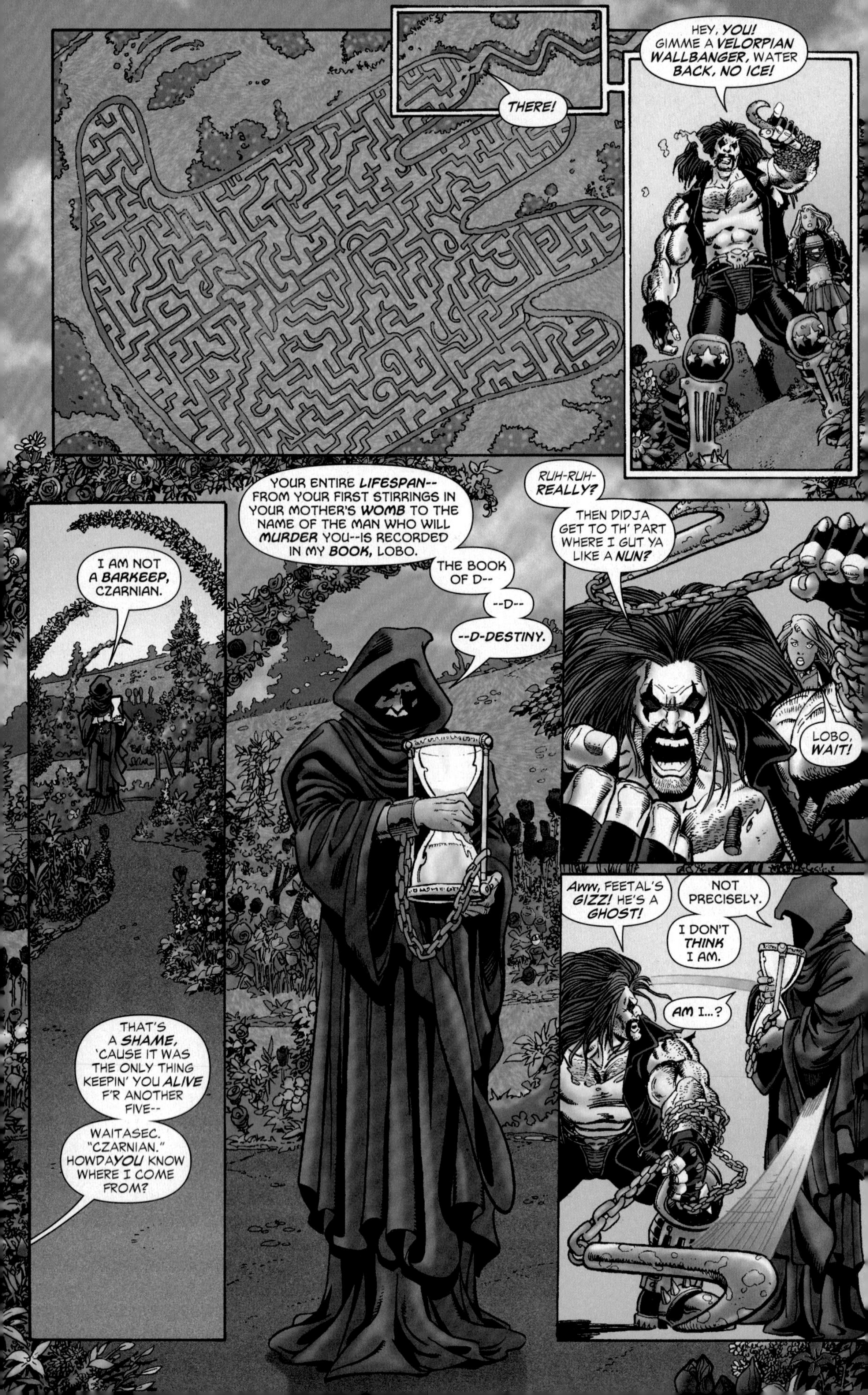
THERE!
HEY, YOU! GIMME A VELORPIAN WALLBANGER, WATER BACK, NO ICE!
I AM NOT A BARKEEP, CZARNIAN.
THAT'S A SHAME, 'CAUSE IT WAS THE ONLY THING KEEPIN' YOU ALIVE F'R ANOTHER FIVE--
WAITASEC. "CZARNIAN." HOWDAYOU KNOW WHERE I COME FROM?
YOUR ENTIRE LIFESPAN-- FROM YOUR FIRST STIRRINGS IN YOUR MOTHER'S WOMB TO THE NAME OF THE MAN WHO WILL MURDER YOU--IS RECORDED IN MY BOOK, LOBO.
THE BOOK OF D--
--D--
--D-DESTINY.
RUH-RUH-REALLY?
THEN DIDJA GET TO TH' PART WHERE I GUT YA LIKE A NUN?
LOBO, WAIT!
AWW, FEETAL'S GIZZ! HE'S A GHOST!
NOT PRECISELY.
I DON'T THINK I AM.
AM I...?

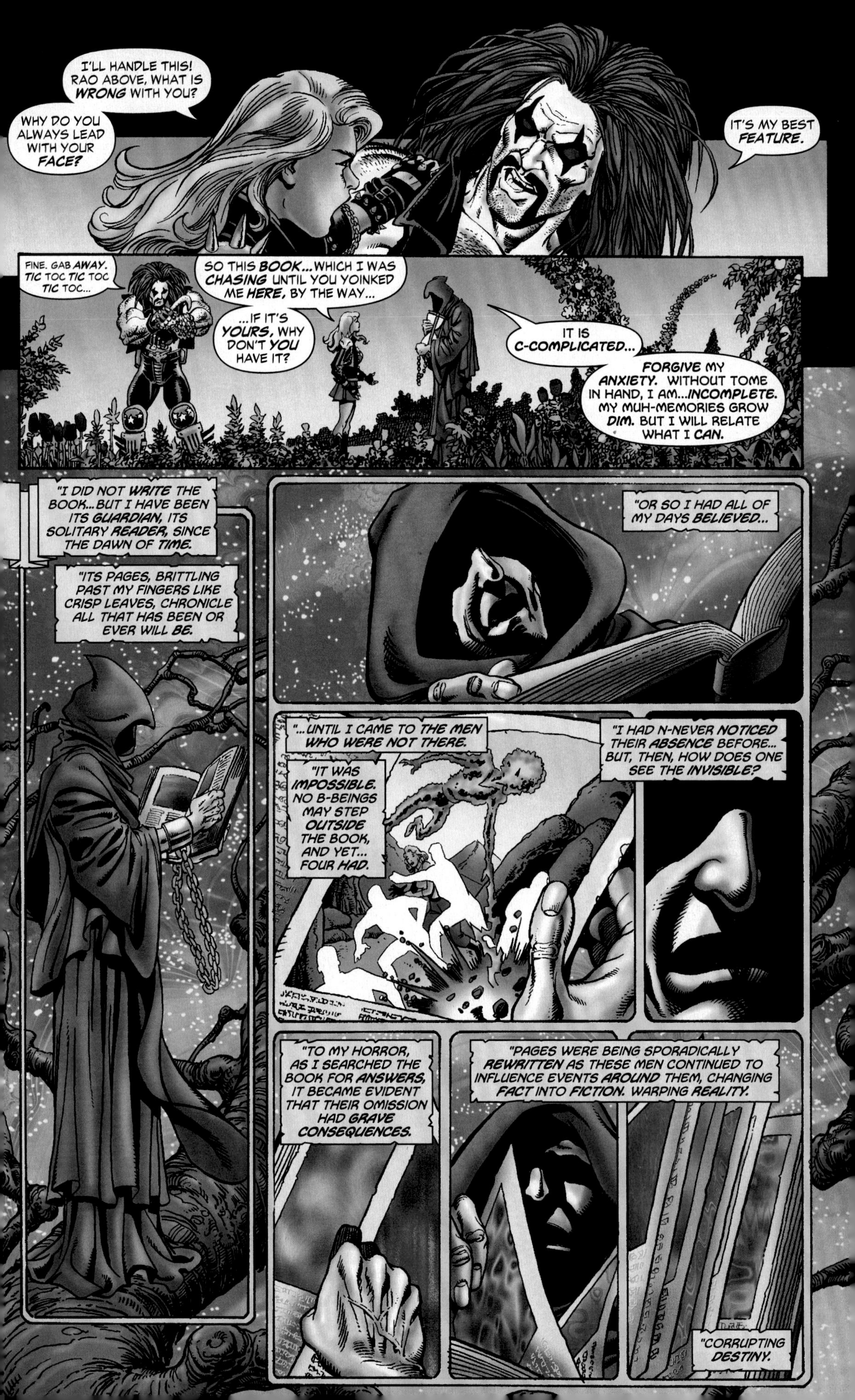
I'LL HANDLE THIS! RAO ABOVE, WHAT IS WRONG WITH YOU?
WHY DO YOU ALWAYS LEAD WITH YOUR FACE?
IT'S MY BEST FEATURE.
FINE. GAB AWAY. TIC TOC TIC TOC TIC TOC...
SO THIS BOOK... WHICH I WAS CHASING UNTIL YOU YOINKED ME HERE, BY THE WAY...
...IF IT'S YOURS, WHY DON'T YOU HAVE IT?
IT IS C-COMPLICATED...
FORGIVE MY ANXIETY. WITHOUT TOME IN HAND, I AM...INCOMPLETE. MY MUH-MEMORIES GROW DIM. BUT I WILL RELATE WHAT I CAN.
"I DID NOT WRITE THE BOOK...BUT I HAVE BEEN ITS GUARDIAN, ITS SOLITARY READER, SINCE THE DAWN OF TIME.
"ITS PAGES, BRITTLING PAST MY FINGERS LIKE CRISP LEAVES, CHRONICLE ALL THAT HAS BEEN OR EVER WILL BE.
"OR SO I HAD ALL OF MY DAYS BELIEVED...
"...UNTIL I CAME TO THE MEN WHO WERE NOT THERE.
"IT WAS IMPOSSIBLE. NO B-BEINGS MAY STEP OUTSIDE THE BOOK, AND YET... FOUR HAD.
"I HAD N-NEVER NOTICED THEIR ABSENCE BEFORE... BUT, THEN, HOW DOES ONE SEE THE INVISIBLE?
"TO MY HORROR, AS I SEARCHED THE BOOK FOR ANSWERS, IT BECAME EVIDENT THAT THEIR OMISSION HAD GRAVE CONSEQUENCES.
"PAGES WERE BEING SPORADICALLY REWRITTEN AS THESE MEN CONTINUED TO INFLUENCE EVENTS AROUND THEM, CHANGING FACT INTO FICTION. WARPING REALITY.
"CORRUPTING DESTINY.

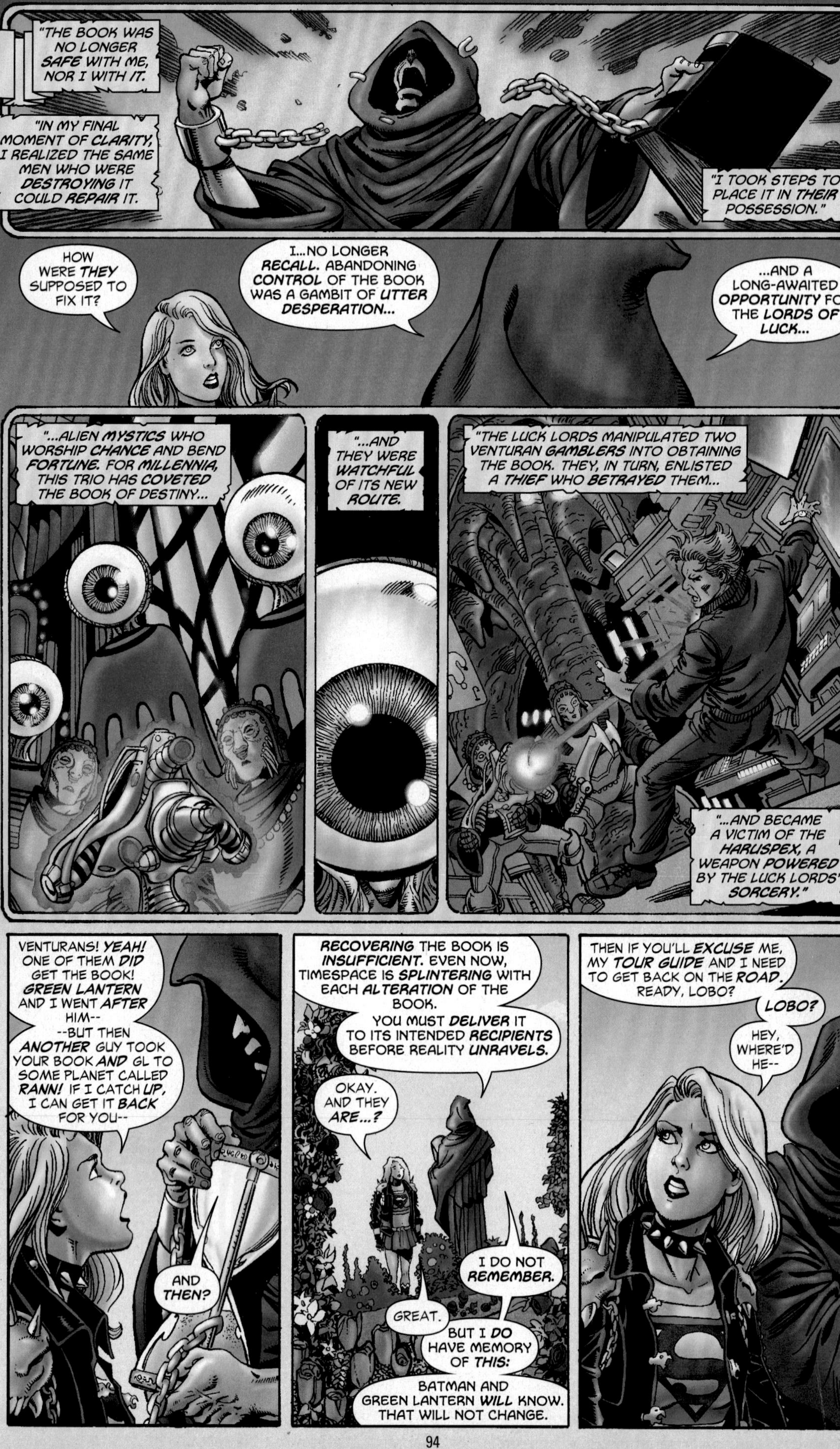

"THE BOOK WAS NO LONGER SAFE WITH ME, NOR I WITH IT.
"IN MY FINAL MOMENT OF CLARITY, I REALIZED THE SAME MEN WHO WERE DESTROYING IT COULD REPAIR IT.
"I TOOK STEPS TO PLACE IT IN THEIR POSSESSION."
HOW WERE THEY SUPPOSED TO FIX IT?
I...NO LONGER RECALL. ABANDONING CONTROL OF THE BOOK WAS A GAMBIT OF UTTER DESPERATION...
...AND A LONG-AWAITED OPPORTUNITY FOR THE LORDS OF LUCK...
"...ALIEN MYSTICS WHO WORSHIP CHANCE AND BEND FORTUNE. FOR MILLENNIA, THIS TRIO HAS COVETED THE BOOK OF DESTINY...
"...AND THEY WERE WATCHFUL OF ITS NEW ROUTE.
"THE LUCK LORDS MANIPULATED TWO VENTURAN GAMBLERS INTO OBTAINING THE BOOK. THEY, IN TURN, ENLISTED A THIEF WHO BETRAYED THEM...
"...AND BECAME A VICTIM OF THE HARUSPEX, A WEAPON POWERED BY THE LUCK LORDS' SORCERY."
VENTURANS! YEAH! ONE OF THEM DID GET THE BOOK! GREEN LANTERN AND I WENT AFTER HIM--
--BUT THEN ANOTHER GUY TOOK YOUR BOOK AND GL TO SOME PLANET CALLED RANN! IF I CATCH UP, I CAN GET IT BACK FOR YOU--
AND THEN?
RECOVERING THE BOOK IS INSUFFICIENT. EVEN NOW, TIMESPACE IS SPLINTERING WITH EACH ALTERATION OF THE BOOK.
YOU MUST DELIVER IT TO ITS INTENDED RECIPIENTS BEFORE REALITY UNRAVELS.
OKAY. AND THEY ARE...?
I DO NOT REMEMBER.
GREAT.
BUT I DO HAVE MEMORY OF THIS:
BATMAN AND GREEN LANTERN WILL KNOW. THAT WILL NOT CHANGE.
THEN IF YOU'LL EXCUSE ME, MY TOUR GUIDE AND I NEED TO GET BACK ON THE ROAD. READY, LOBO?
LOBO?
HEY, WHERE'D HE--

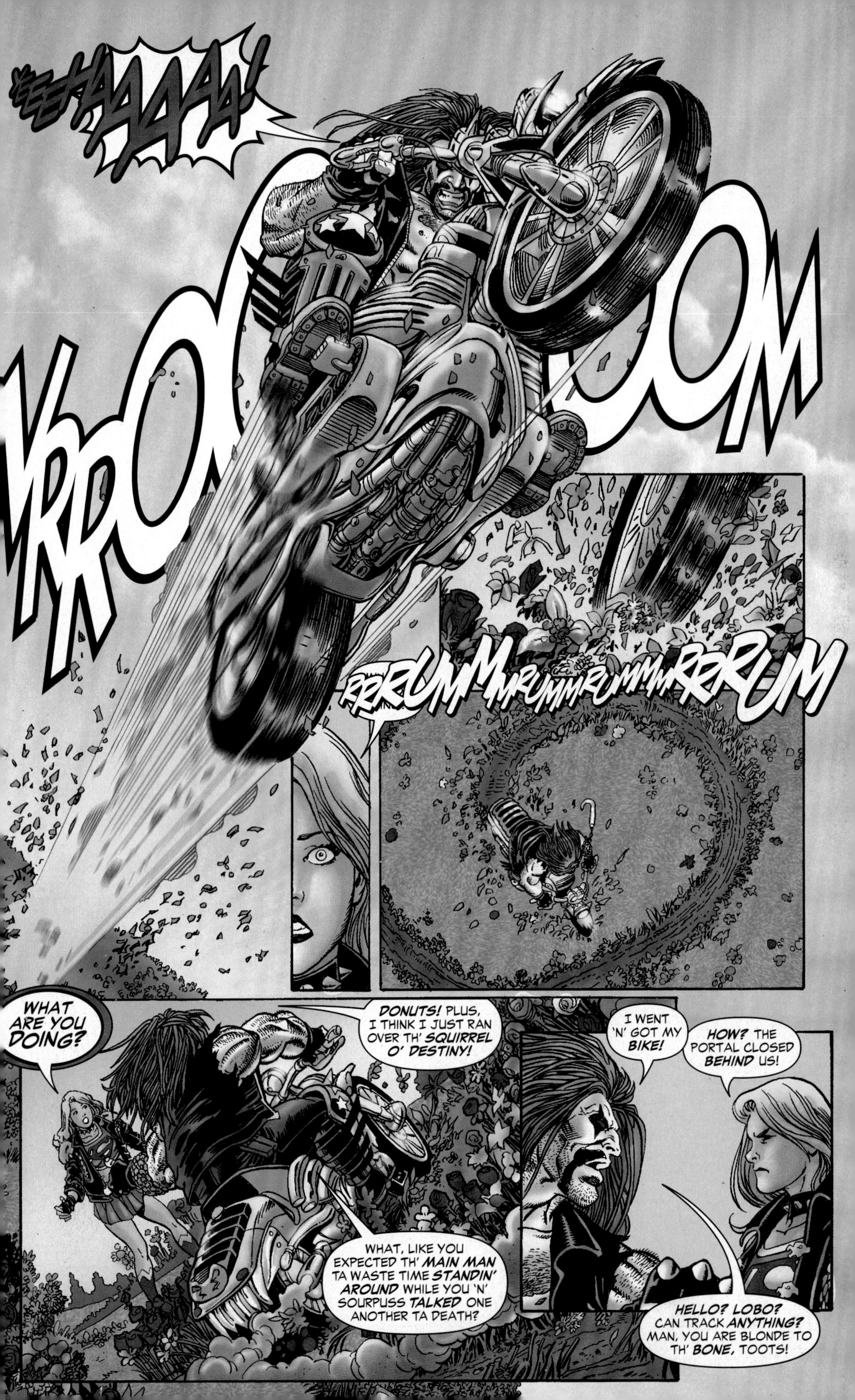

YEEEHAAAAAA!
VRROOOOOOM
RRRUMMMRUMMRUMMMRRRUM
WHAT ARE YOU DOING?
DONUTS! PLUS, I THINK I JUST RAN OVER TH' SQUIRREL O' DESTINY!
WHAT, LIKE YOU EXPECTED TH' MAIN MAN TA WASTE TIME STANDIN' AROUND WHILE YOU 'N' SOURPUSS TALKED ONE ANOTHER TA DEATH?
I WENT 'N' GOT MY BIKE!
HOW? THE PORTAL CLOSED BEHIND US!
HELLO? LOBO? CAN TRACK ANYTHING? MAN, YOU ARE BLONDE TO TH' BONE, TOOTS!

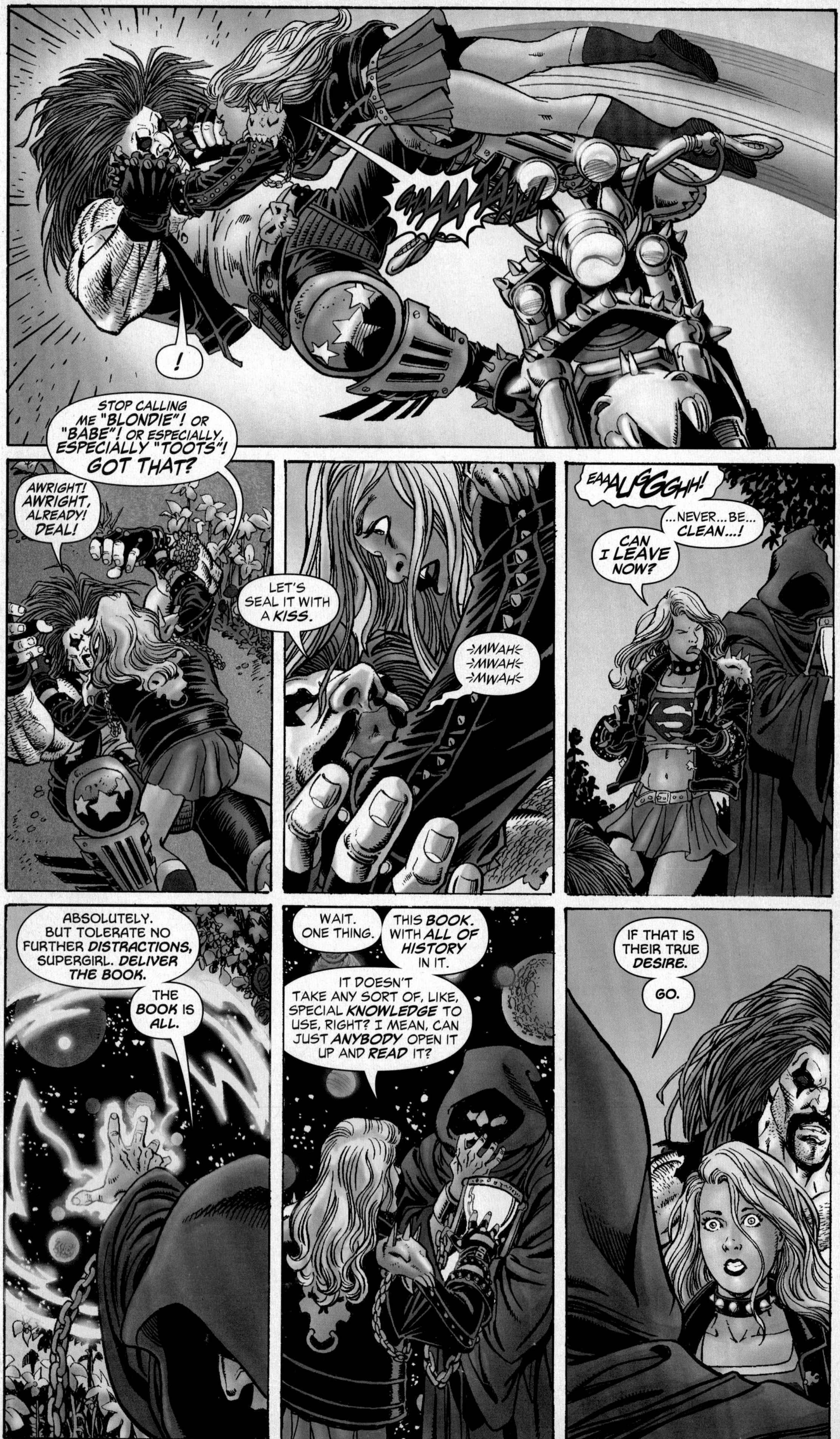
GWAAAAAAH!
!
STOP CALLING ME "BLONDIE"! OR "BABE"! OR ESPECIALLY, ESPECIALLY "TOOTS"! GOT THAT?
AWRIGHT! AWRIGHT, ALREADY! DEAL!
LET'S SEAL IT WITH A KISS.
MWAH MWAH MWAH
EAAAUGGGHH!
...NEVER...BE... CLEAN...!
CAN I LEAVE NOW?
ABSOLUTELY. BUT TOLERATE NO FURTHER DISTRACTIONS, SUPERGIRL. DELIVER THE BOOK.
THE BOOK IS ALL.
WAIT. ONE THING.
THIS BOOK. WITH ALL OF HISTORY IN IT.
IT DOESN'T TAKE ANY SORT OF, LIKE, SPECIAL KNOWLEDGE TO USE, RIGHT? I MEAN, CAN JUST ANYBODY OPEN IT UP AND READ IT?
IF THAT IS THEIR TRUE DESIRE.
GO.

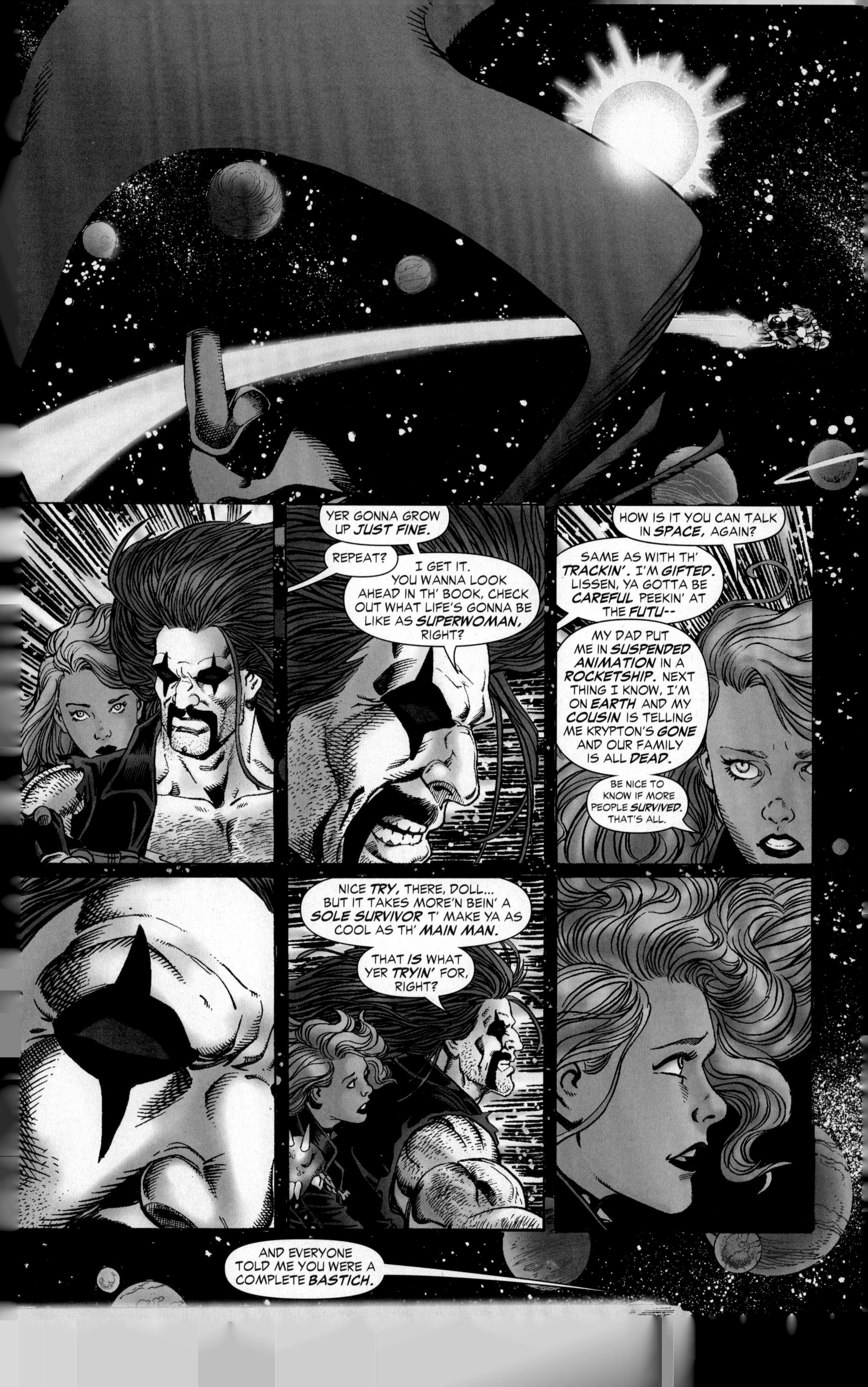
YER GONNA GROW UP JUST FINE.
REPEAT?
I GET IT. YOU WANNA LOOK AHEAD IN TH' BOOK, CHECK OUT WHAT LIFE'S GONNA BE LIKE AS SUPERWOMAN, RIGHT?
HOW IS IT YOU CAN TALK IN SPACE, AGAIN?
SAME AS WITH TH' TRACKIN'. I'M GIFTED. LISSEN, YA GOTTA BE CAREFUL PEEKIN' AT THE FUTU--
MY DAD PUT ME IN SUSPENDED ANIMATION IN A ROCKETSHIP. NEXT THING I KNOW, I'M ON EARTH AND MY COUSIN IS TELLING ME KRYPTON'S GONE AND OUR FAMILY IS ALL DEAD.
BE NICE TO KNOW IF MORE PEOPLE SURVIVED. THAT'S ALL.
NICE TRY, THERE, DOLL... BUT IT TAKES MORE'N BEIN' A SOLE SURVIVOR T' MAKE YA AS COOL AS TH' MAIN MAN.
THAT IS WHAT YER TRYIN' FOR, RIGHT?
AND EVERYONE TOLD ME YOU WERE A COMPLETE BASTICH.

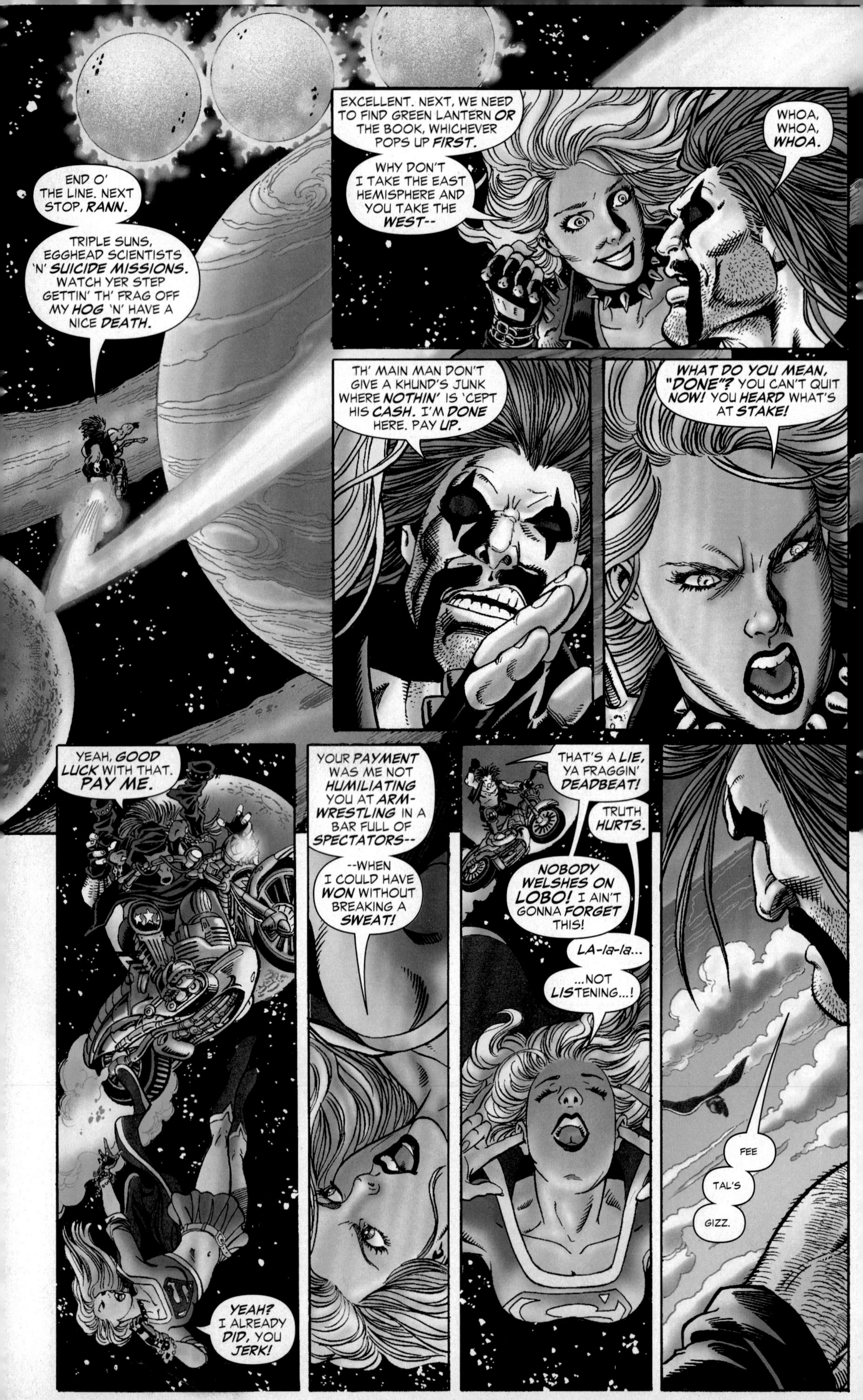
END O' THE LINE. NEXT STOP, RANN.
TRIPLE SUNS, EGGHEAD SCIENTISTS 'N' SUICIDE MISSIONS. WATCH YER STEP GETTIN' TH' FRAG OFF MY HOG 'N' HAVE A NICE DEATH.
EXCELLENT. NEXT, WE NEED TO FIND GREEN LANTERN OR THE BOOK, WHICHEVER POPS UP FIRST.
WHY DON'T I TAKE THE EAST HEMISPHERE AND YOU TAKE THE WEST--
WHOA, WHOA, WHOA.
TH' MAIN MAN DON'T GIVE A KHUND'S JUNK WHERE NOTHIN' IS 'CEPT HIS CASH. I'M DONE HERE. PAY UP.
WHAT DO YOU MEAN, "DONE"? YOU CAN'T QUIT NOW! YOU HEARD WHAT'S AT STAKE!
YEAH, GOOD LUCK WITH THAT. PAY ME.
YOUR PAYMENT WAS ME NOT HUMILIATING YOU AT ARM-WRESTLING IN A BAR FULL OF SPECTATORS--
--WHEN I COULD HAVE WON WITHOUT BREAKING A SWEAT!
YEAH? I ALREADY DID, YOU JERK!
THAT'S A LIE, YA FRAGGIN' DEADBEAT!
TRUTH HURTS.
NOBODY WELSHES ON LOBO! I AIN'T GONNA FORGET THIS!
LA-la-la...
...NOT LISTENING...!
FEE
TAL'S
GIZZ.

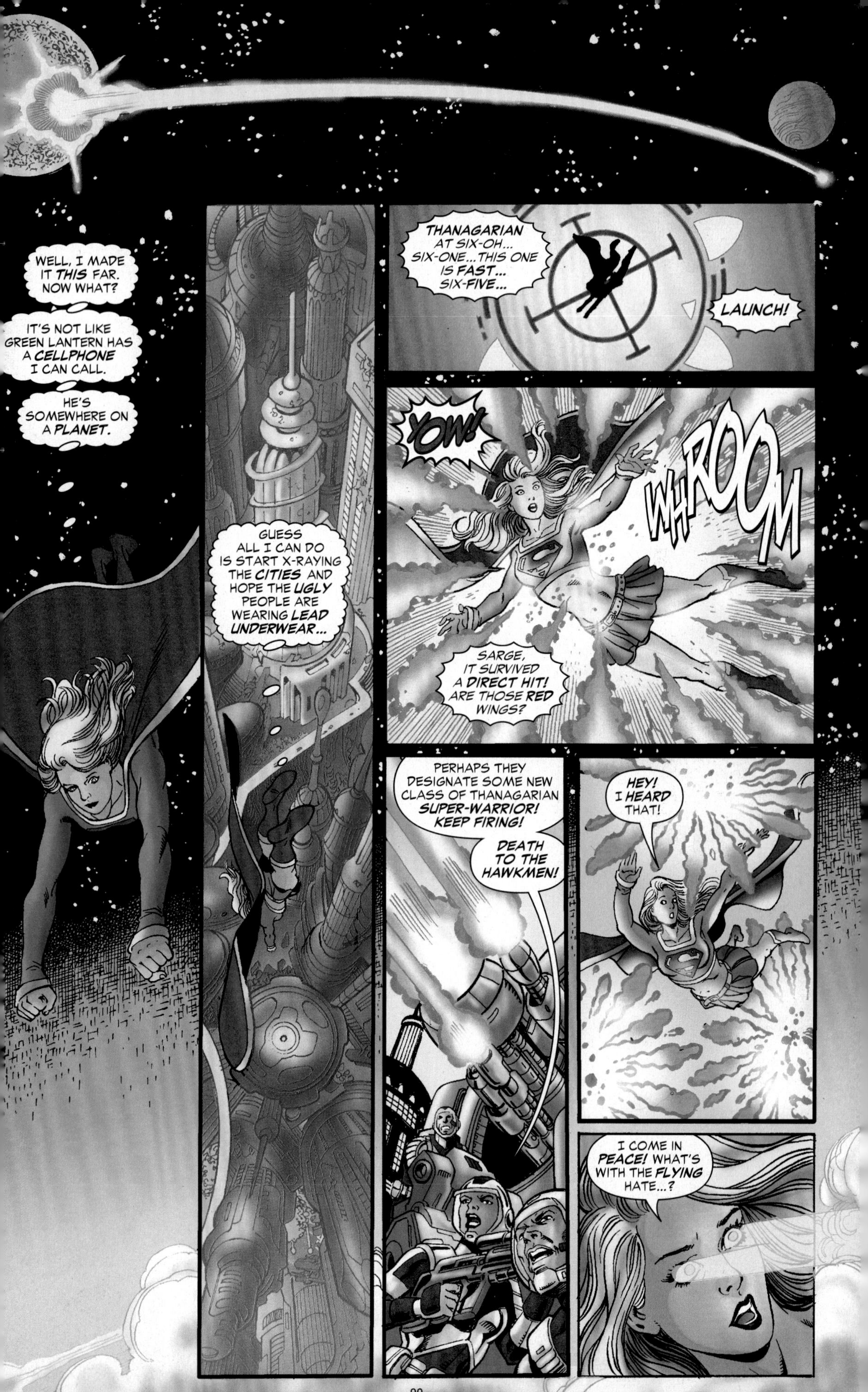
WELL, I MADE IT THIS FAR. NOW WHAT?
IT'S NOT LIKE GREEN LANTERN HAS A CELLPHONE I CAN CALL.
HE'S SOMEWHERE ON A PLANET.
GUESS ALL I CAN DO IS START X-RAYING THE CITIES AND HOPE THE UGLY PEOPLE ARE WEARING LEAD UNDERWEAR...
THANAGARIAN AT SIX-OH... SIX-ONE... THIS ONE IS FAST... SIX-FIVE...
LAUNCH!
YOW!
WHROOM
SARGE, IT SURVIVED A DIRECT HIT! ARE THOSE RED WINGS?
PERHAPS THEY DESIGNATE SOME NEW CLASS OF THANAGARIAN SUPER-WARRIOR! KEEP FIRING!
DEATH TO THE HAWKMEN!
HEY! I HEARD THAT!
I COME IN PEACE! WHAT'S WITH THE FLYING HATE...?

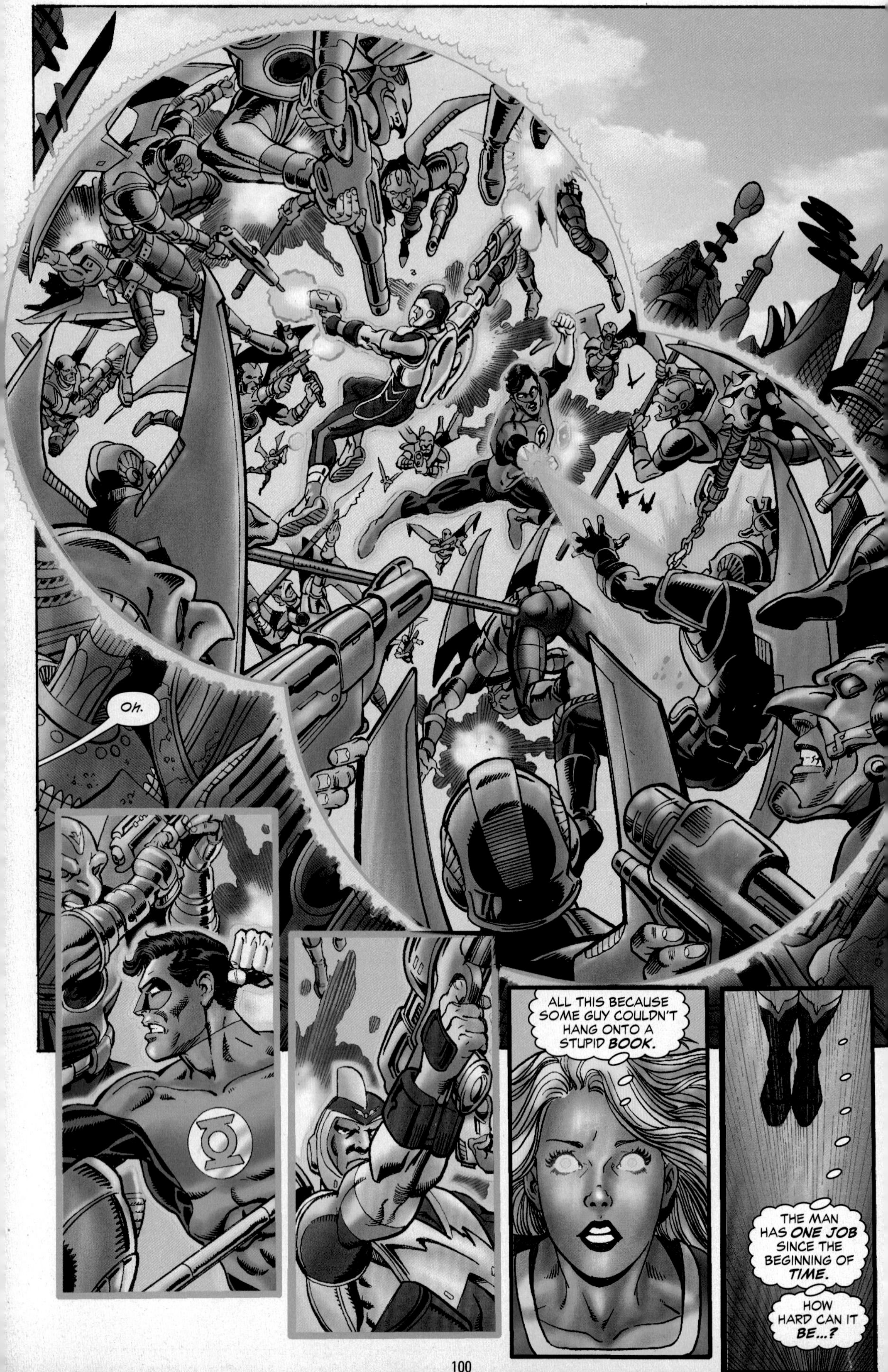
Oh.
ALL THIS BECAUSE SOME GUY COULDN'T HANG ONTO A STUPID BOOK.
THE MAN HAS ONE JOB SINCE THE BEGINNING OF TIME.
HOW HARD CAN IT BE...?

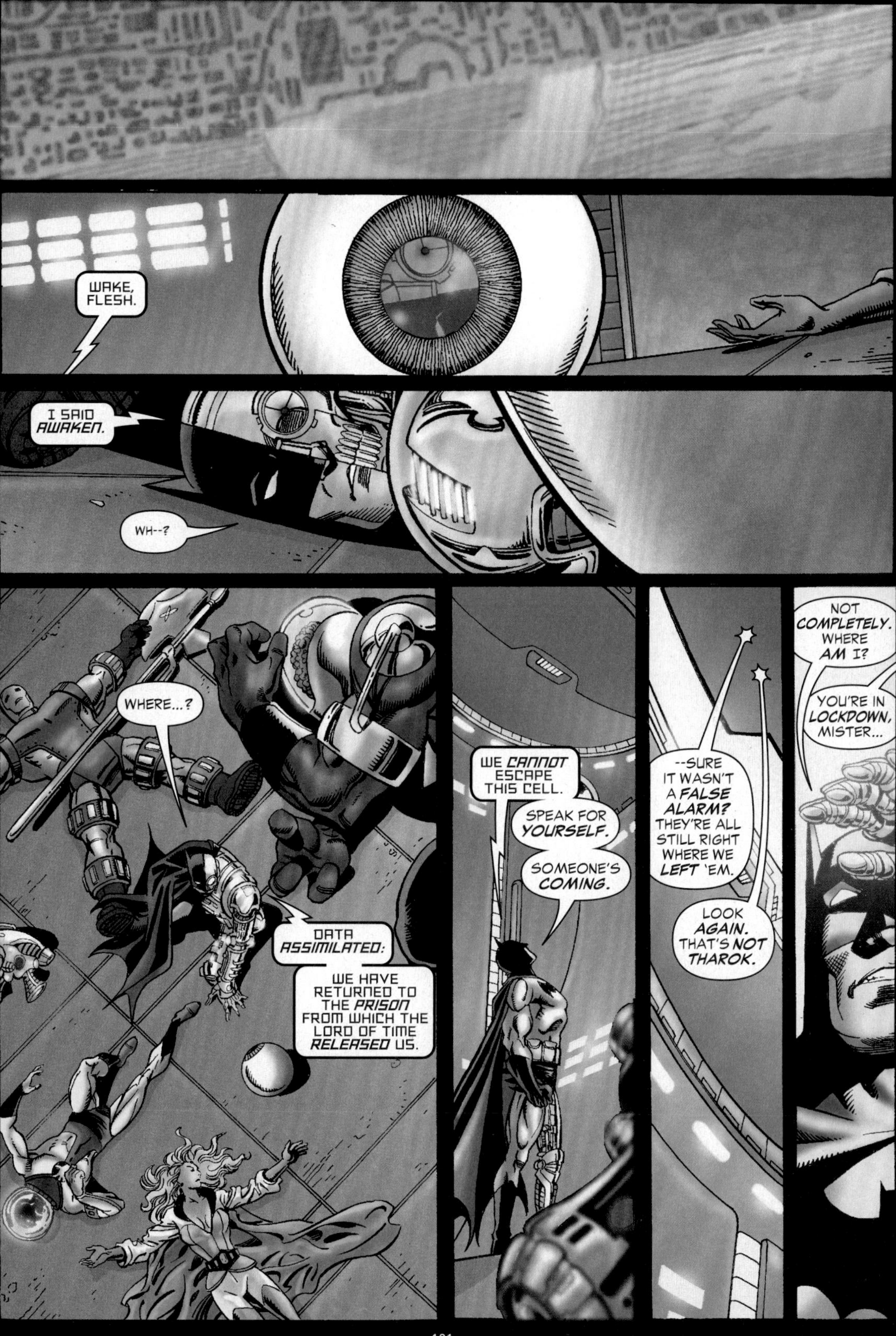

WAKE, FLESH.
I SAID AWAKEN.
WH--?
WHERE...?
DATA ASSIMILATED:
WE HAVE RETURNED TO THE PRISON FROM WHICH THE LORD OF TIME RELEASED US.
WE CANNOT ESCAPE THIS CELL.
SPEAK FOR YOURSELF.
SOMEONE'S COMING.
--SURE IT WASN'T A FALSE ALARM? THEY'RE ALL STILL RIGHT WHERE WE LEFT 'EM.
LOOK AGAIN. THAT'S NOT THAROK.
NOT COMPLETELY. WHERE AM I?
YOU'RE IN LOCKDOWN, MISTER...

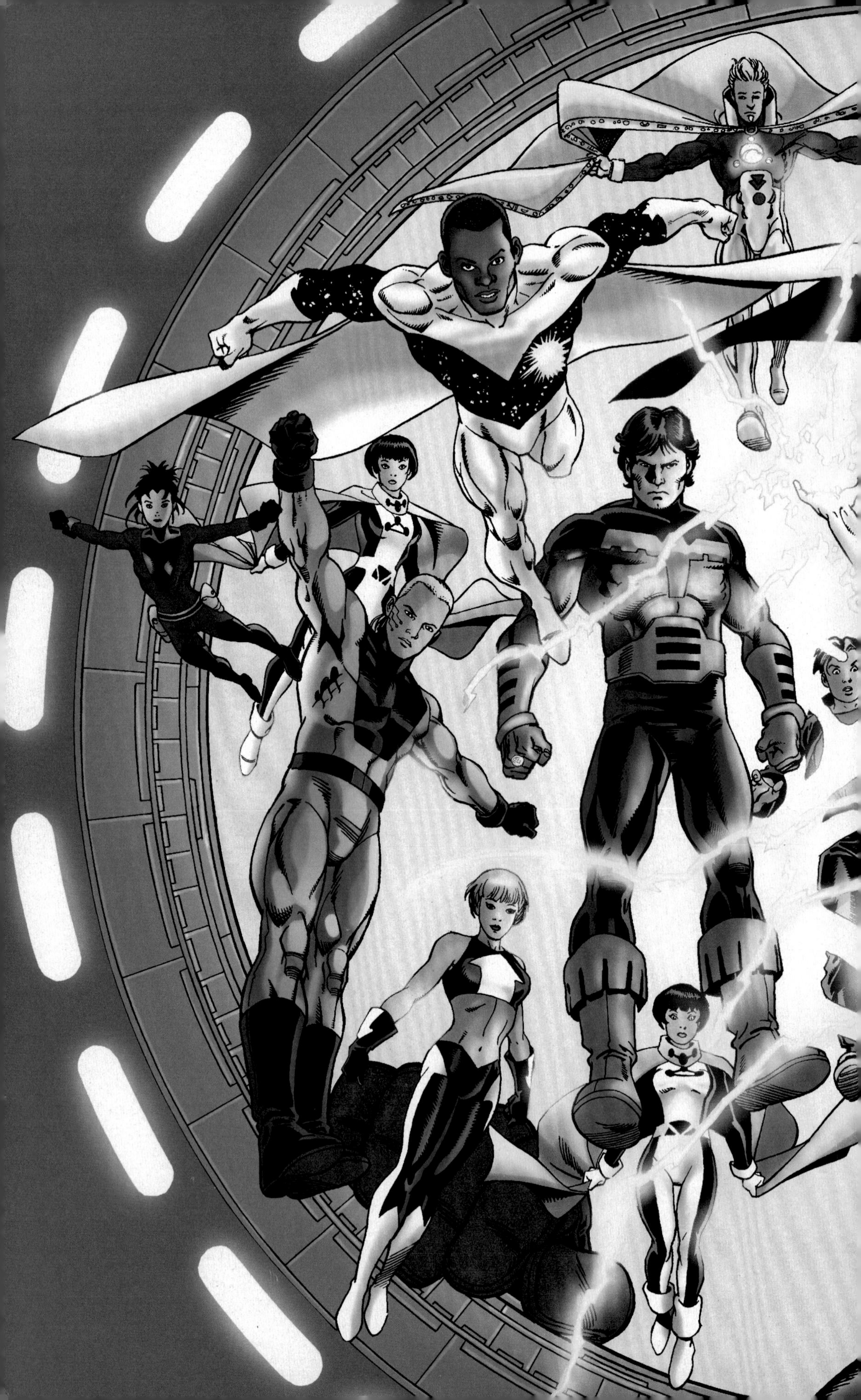

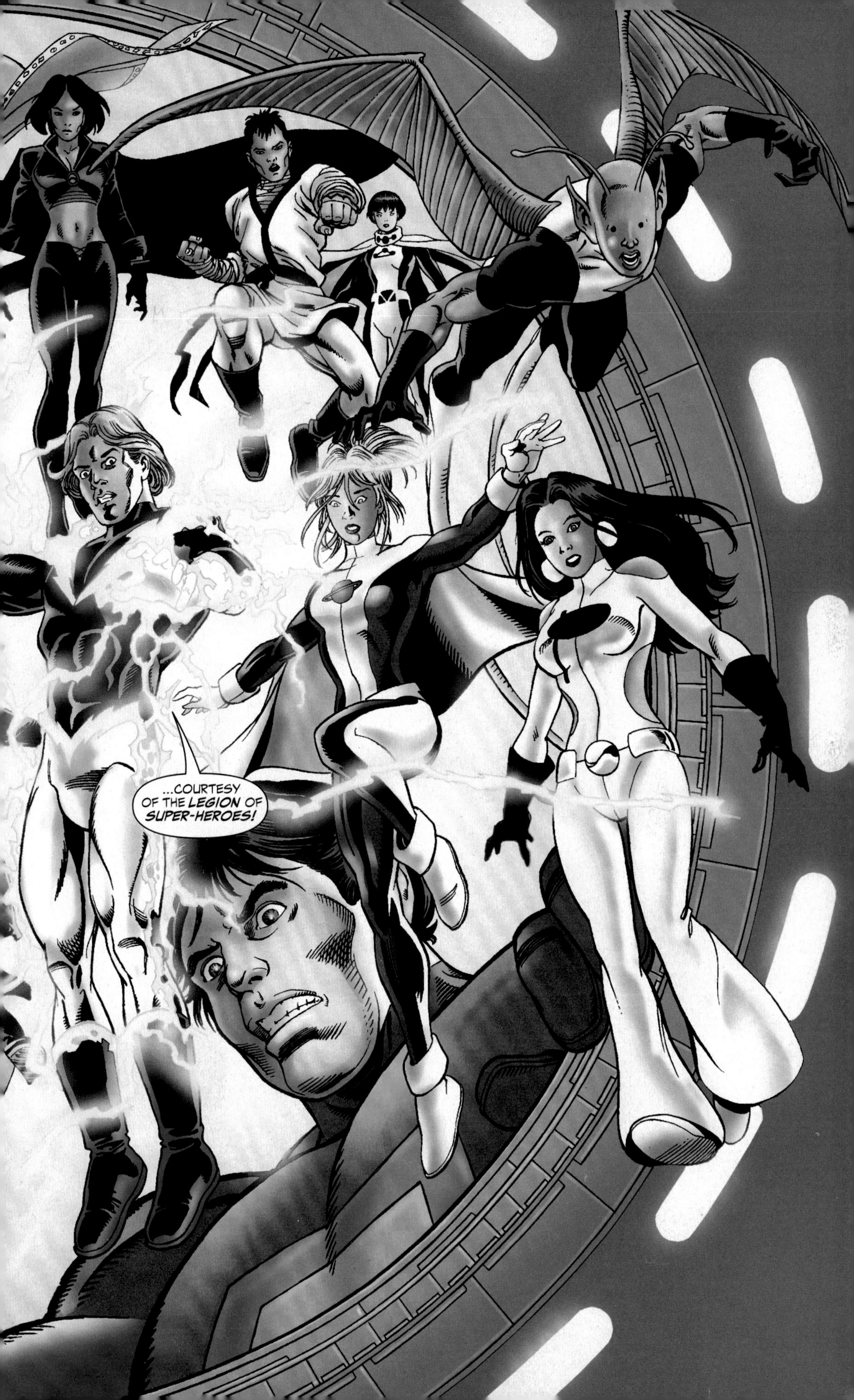
...COURTESY OF THE LEGION OF SUPER-HEROES!

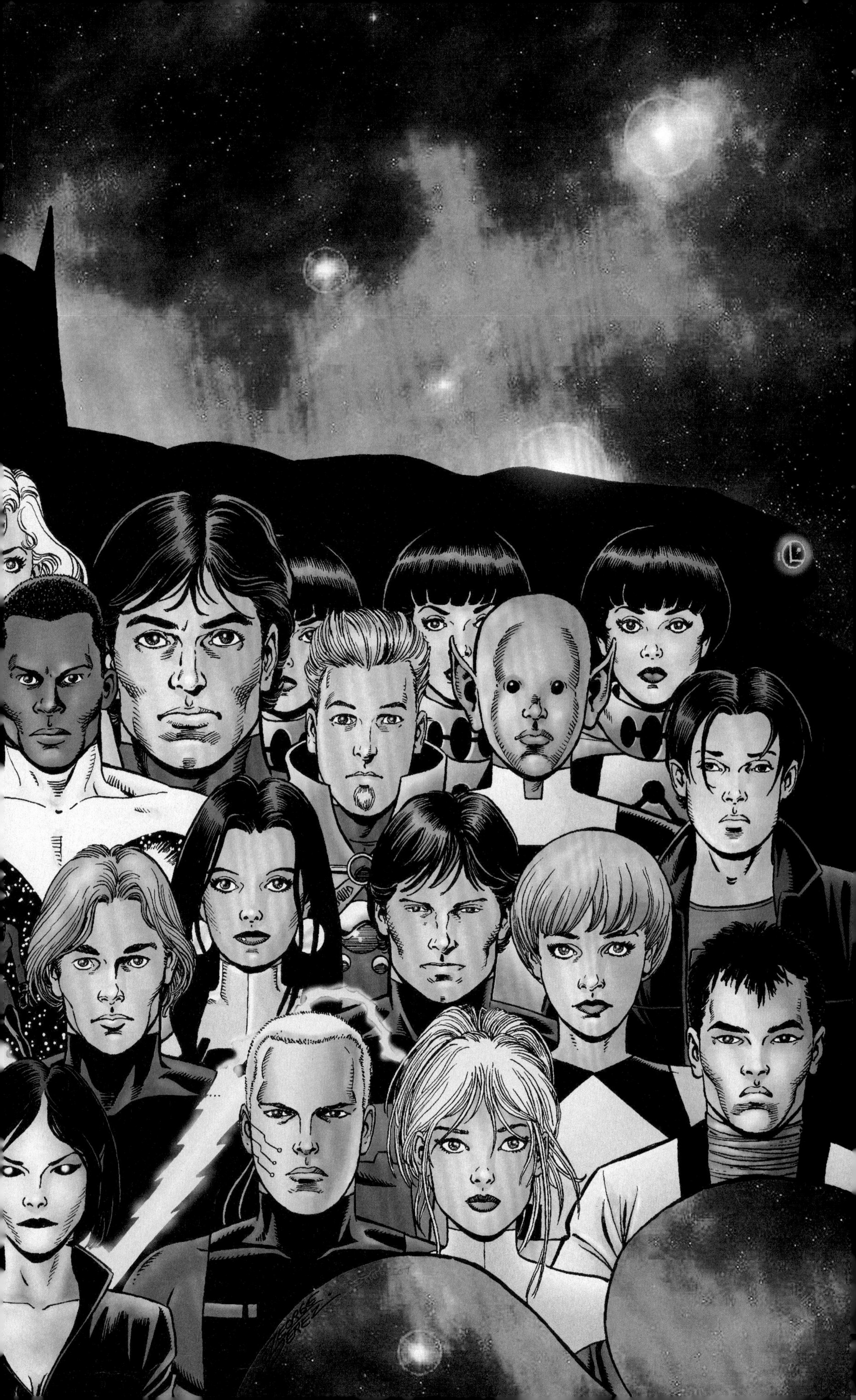

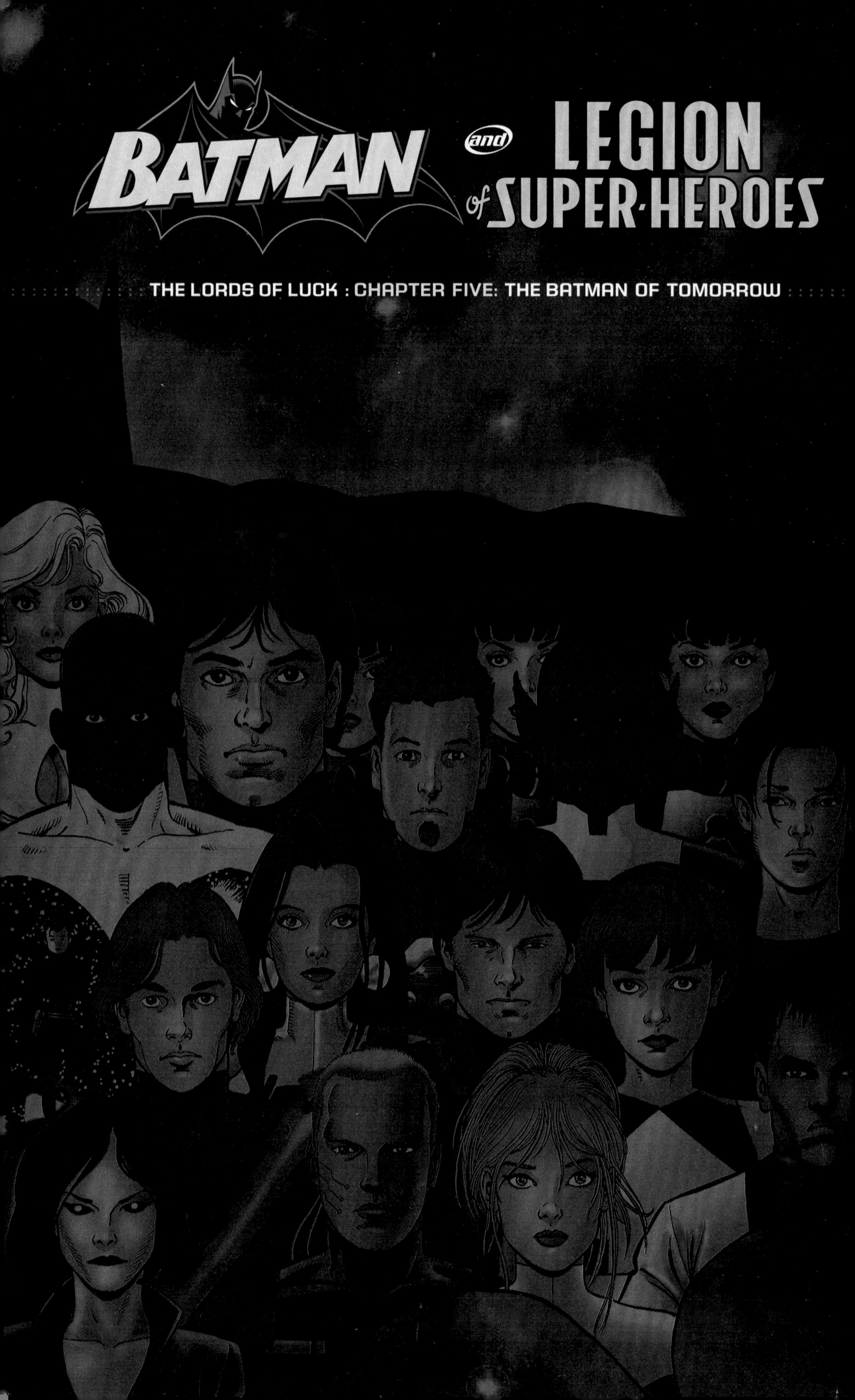
BATMAN and LEGION of SUPER-HEROES
THE LORDS OF LUCK : CHAPTER FIVE: THE BATMAN OF TOMORROW

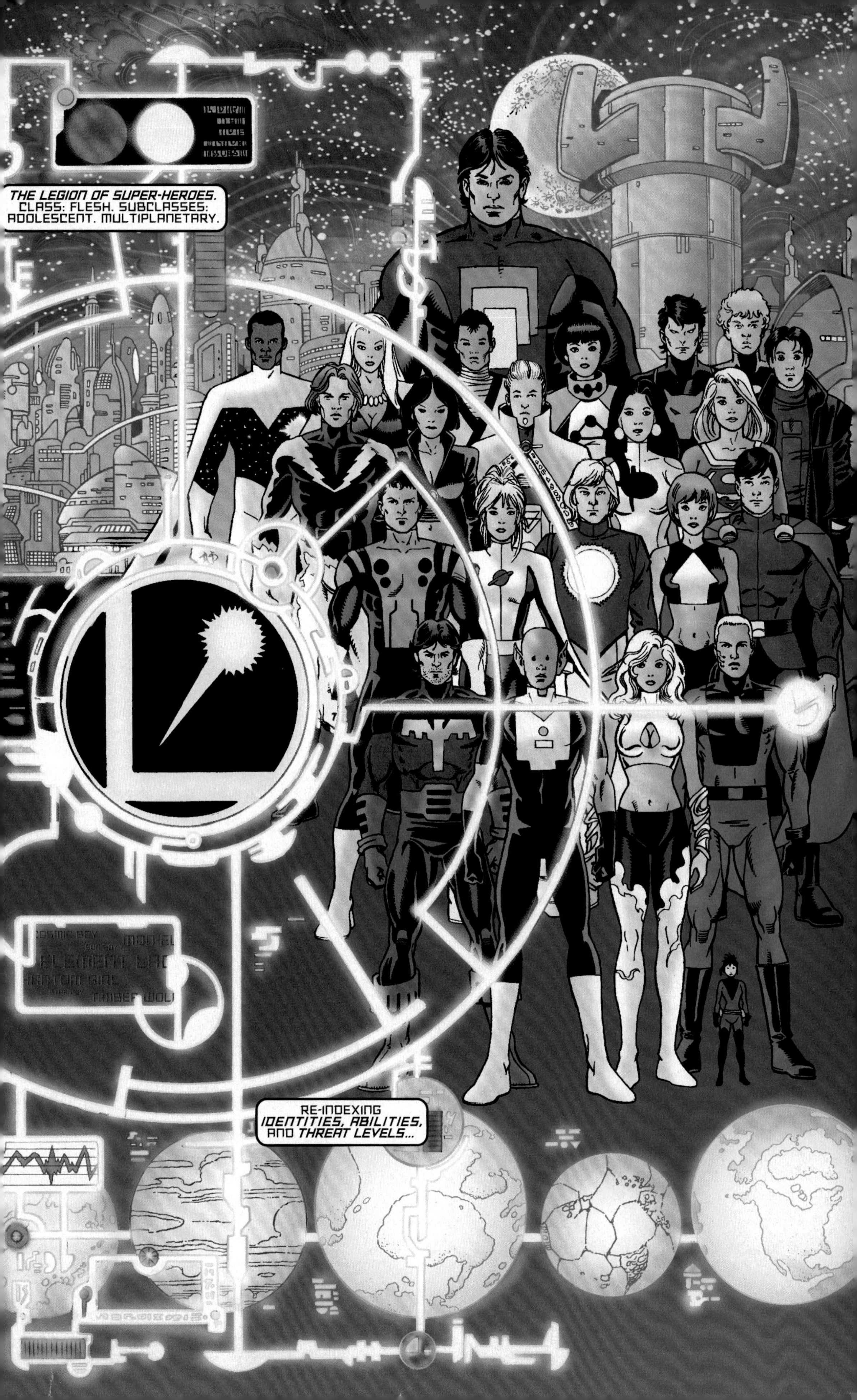
THE LEGION OF SUPER-HEROES. CLASS: FLESH. SUBCLASSES: ADOLESCENT. MULTIPLANETARY.
RE-INDEXING IDENTITIES, ABILITIES, AND THREAT LEVELS...

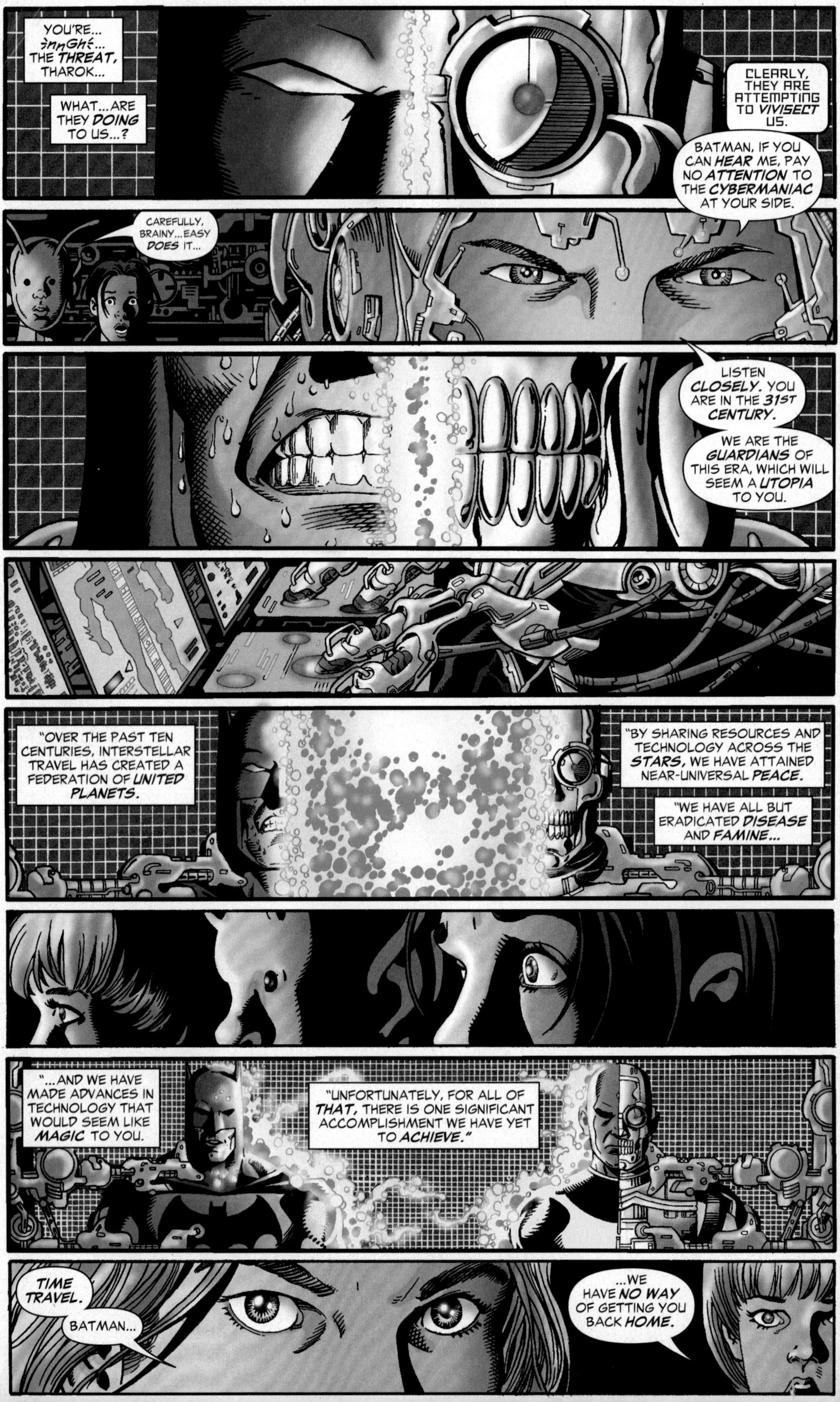
YOU'RE... ƎnnGhƐ... THE THREAT, THAROK...
WHAT...ARE THEY DOING TO US...?
CLEARLY, THEY ARE ATTEMPTING TO VIVISECT US.
BATMAN, IF YOU CAN HEAR ME, PAY NO ATTENTION TO THE CYBERMANIAC AT YOUR SIDE.
CAREFULLY, BRAINY...EASY DOES IT...
LISTEN CLOSELY. YOU ARE IN THE 31ST CENTURY.
WE ARE THE GUARDIANS OF THIS ERA, WHICH WILL SEEM A UTOPIA TO YOU.
"OVER THE PAST TEN CENTURIES, INTERSTELLAR TRAVEL HAS CREATED A FEDERATION OF UNITED PLANETS.
"BY SHARING RESOURCES AND TECHNOLOGY ACROSS THE STARS, WE HAVE ATTAINED NEAR-UNIVERSAL PEACE.
"WE HAVE ALL BUT ERADICATED DISEASE AND FAMINE...
"...AND WE HAVE MADE ADVANCES IN TECHNOLOGY THAT WOULD SEEM LIKE MAGIC TO YOU.
"UNFORTUNATELY, FOR ALL OF THAT, THERE IS ONE SIGNIFICANT ACCOMPLISHMENT WE HAVE YET TO ACHIEVE."
TIME TRAVEL.
BATMAN...
...WE HAVE NO WAY OF GETTING YOU BACK HOME.

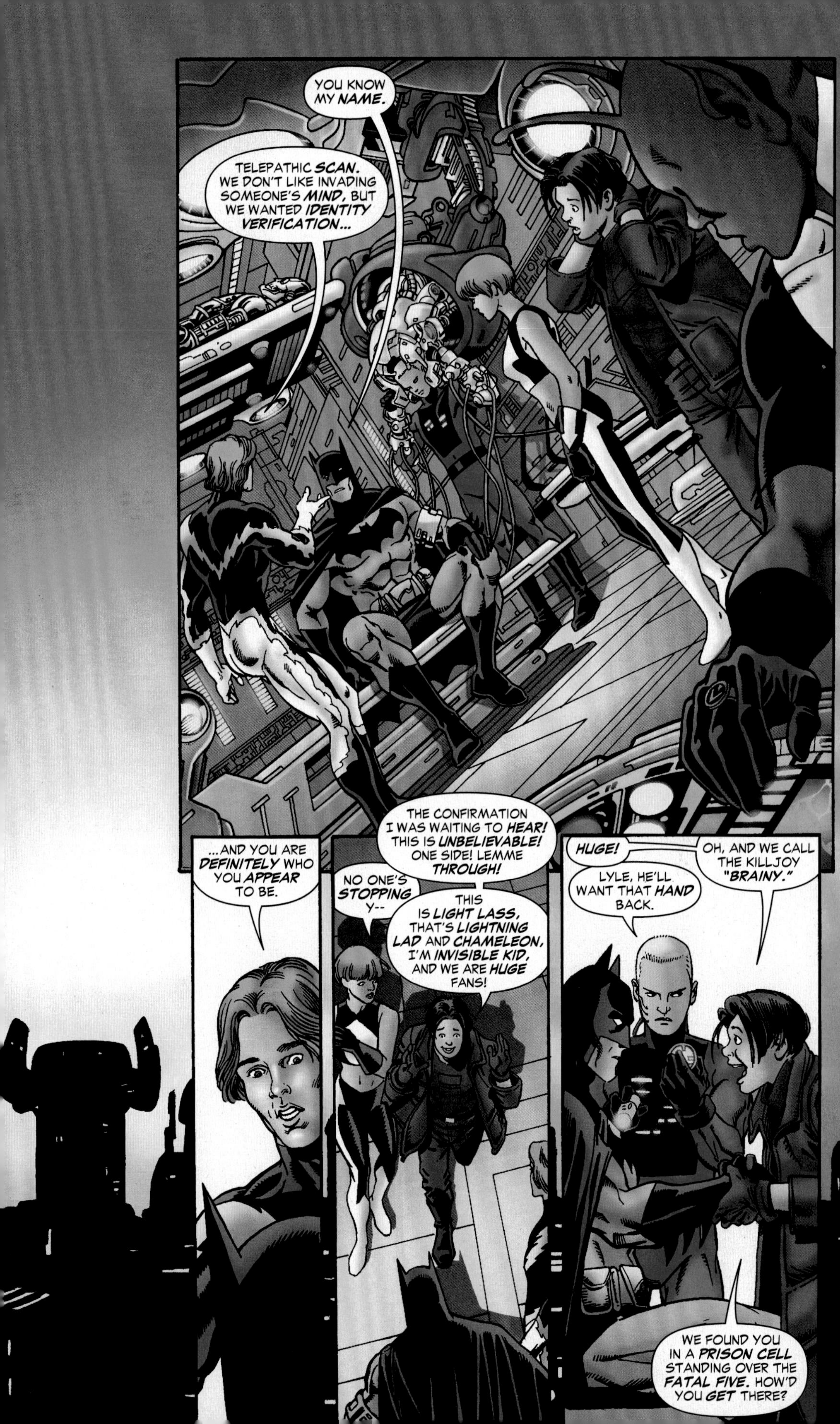
YOU KNOW MY NAME.
TELEPATHIC SCAN. WE DON'T LIKE INVADING SOMEONE'S MIND, BUT WE WANTED IDENTITY VERIFICATION...
...AND YOU ARE DEFINITELY WHO YOU APPEAR TO BE.
THE CONFIRMATION I WAS WAITING TO HEAR! THIS IS UNBELIEVABLE! ONE SIDE! LEMME THROUGH!
NO ONE'S STOPPING Y--
THIS IS LIGHT LASS, THAT'S LIGHTNING LAD AND CHAMELEON, I'M INVISIBLE KID, AND WE ARE HUGE FANS!
HUGE!
LYLE, HE'LL WANT THAT HAND BACK.
OH, AND WE CALL THE KILLJOY "BRAINY."
WE FOUND YOU IN A PRISON CELL STANDING OVER THE FATAL FIVE. HOW'D YOU GET THERE?

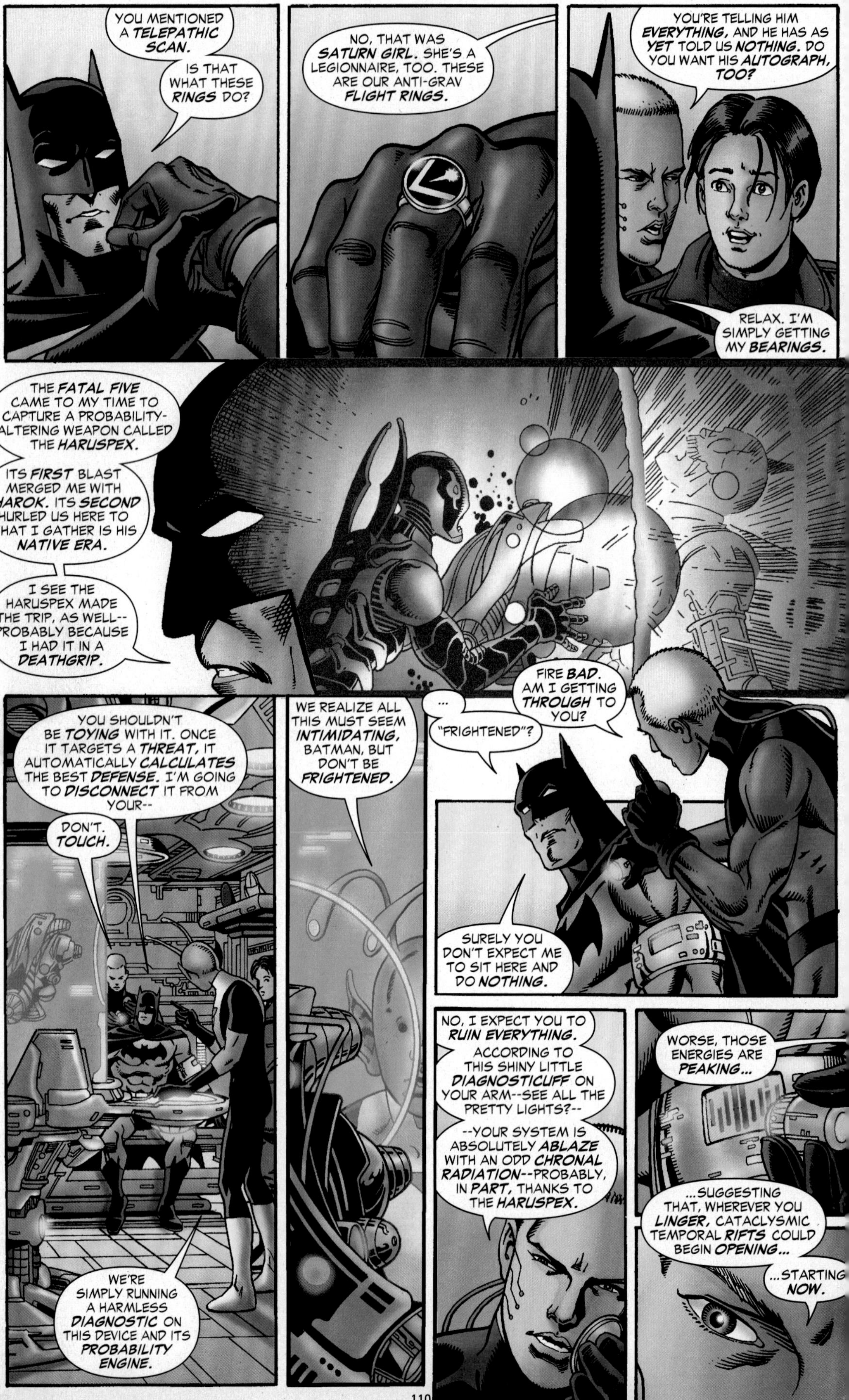

YOU MENTIONED A TELEPATHIC SCAN.
IS THAT WHAT THESE RINGS DO?
NO, THAT WAS SATURN GIRL. SHE'S A LEGIONNAIRE, TOO. THESE ARE OUR ANTI-GRAV FLIGHT RINGS.
YOU'RE TELLING HIM EVERYTHING, AND HE HAS AS YET TOLD US NOTHING. DO YOU WANT HIS AUTOGRAPH, TOO?
RELAX. I'M SIMPLY GETTING MY BEARINGS.
THE FATAL FIVE CAME TO MY TIME TO CAPTURE A PROBABILITY-ALTERING WEAPON CALLED THE HARUSPEX.
ITS FIRST BLAST MERGED ME WITH THAROK. ITS SECOND HURLED US HERE TO WHAT I GATHER IS HIS NATIVE ERA.
I SEE THE HARUSPEX MADE THE TRIP, AS WELL-- PROBABLY BECAUSE I HAD IT IN A DEATHGRIP.
YOU SHOULDN'T BE TOYING WITH IT. ONCE IT TARGETS A THREAT, IT AUTOMATICALLY CALCULATES THE BEST DEFENSE. I'M GOING TO DISCONNECT IT FROM YOUR--
DON'T. TOUCH.
WE'RE SIMPLY RUNNING A HARMLESS DIAGNOSTIC ON THIS DEVICE AND ITS PROBABILITY ENGINE.
WE REALIZE ALL THIS MUST SEEM INTIMIDATING, BATMAN, BUT DON'T BE FRIGHTENED.
...
"FRIGHTENED"?
FIRE BAD. AM I GETTING THROUGH TO YOU?
SURELY YOU DON'T EXPECT ME TO SIT HERE AND DO NOTHING.
NO, I EXPECT YOU TO RUIN EVERYTHING.
ACCORDING TO THIS SHINY LITTLE DIAGNOSTICUFF ON YOUR ARM--SEE ALL THE PRETTY LIGHTS?--
--YOUR SYSTEM IS ABSOLUTELY ABLAZE WITH AN ODD CHRONAL RADIATION--PROBABLY, IN PART, THANKS TO THE HARUSPEX.
WORSE, THOSE ENERGIES ARE PEAKING...
...SUGGESTING THAT, WHEREVER YOU LINGER, CATACLYSMIC TEMPORAL RIFTS COULD BEGIN OPENING...
...STARTING NOW.

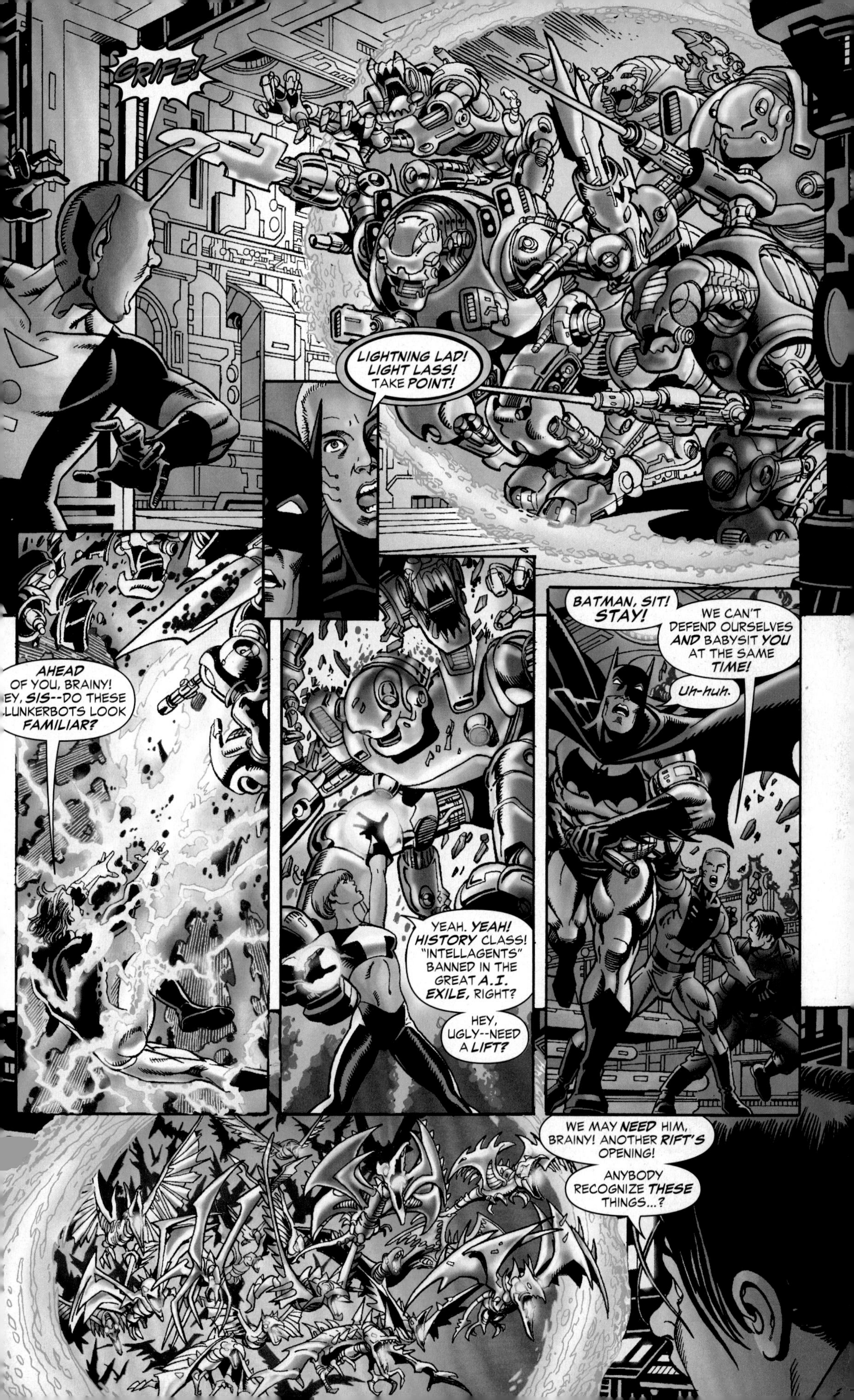
GRIFE!
LIGHTNING LAD! LIGHT LASS! TAKE POINT!
AHEAD OF YOU, BRAINY! EY, SIS--DO THESE LUNKERBOTS LOOK FAMILIAR?
YEAH. YEAH! HISTORY CLASS! "INTELLAGENTS" BANNED IN THE GREAT A.I. EXILE, RIGHT?
HEY, UGLY--NEED A LIFT?
BATMAN, SIT! STAY!
WE CAN'T DEFEND OURSELVES AND BABYSIT YOU AT THE SAME TIME!
Uh-huh.
WE MAY NEED HIM, BRAINY! ANOTHER RIFT'S OPENING!
ANYBODY RECOGNIZE THESE THINGS...?

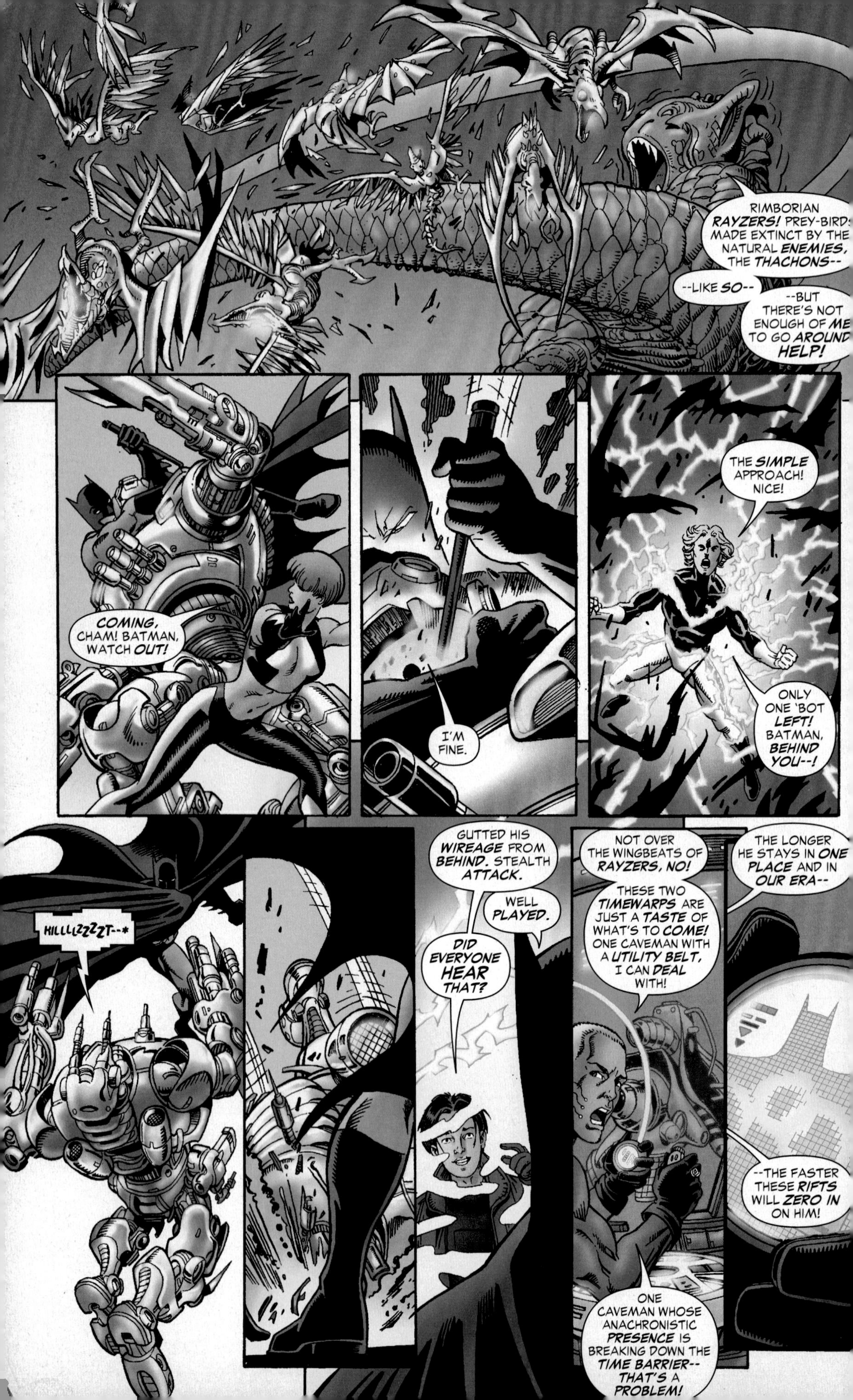

RIMBORIAN RAYZERS! PREY-BIRDS MADE EXTINCT BY THE NATURAL ENEMIES, THE THACHONS--
--LIKE SO--
--BUT THERE'S NOT ENOUGH OF ME TO GO AROUND HELP!
COMING, CHAM! BATMAN, WATCH OUT!
I'M FINE.
THE SIMPLE APPROACH! NICE!
ONLY ONE 'BOT LEFT! BATMAN, BEHIND YOU--!
HILLLLZZZZT--*
GUTTED HIS WIREAGE FROM BEHIND. STEALTH ATTACK.
WELL PLAYED.
DID EVERYONE HEAR THAT?
NOT OVER THE WINGBEATS OF RAYZERS, NO!
THESE TWO TIMEWARPS ARE JUST A TASTE OF WHAT'S TO COME! ONE CAVEMAN WITH A UTILITY BELT, I CAN DEAL WITH!
ONE CAVEMAN WHOSE ANACHRONISTIC PRESENCE IS BREAKING DOWN THE TIME BARRIER-- THAT'S A PROBLEM!
THE LONGER HE STAYS IN ONE PLACE AND IN OUR ERA--
--THE FASTER THESE RIFTS WILL ZERO IN ON HIM!

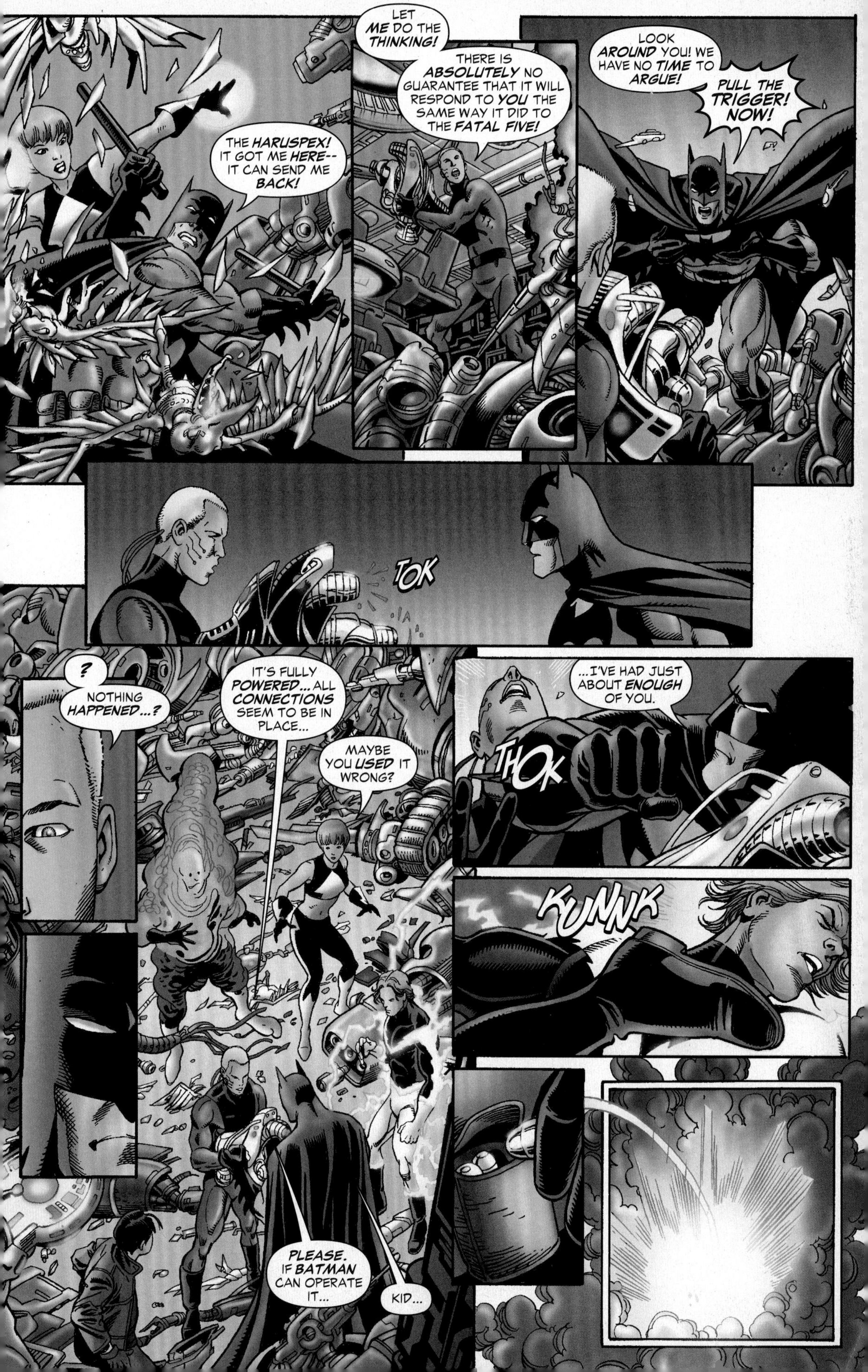
THE HARUSPEX! IT GOT ME HERE-- IT CAN SEND ME BACK!
LET ME DO THE THINKING!
THERE IS ABSOLUTELY NO GUARANTEE THAT IT WILL RESPOND TO YOU THE SAME WAY IT DID TO THE FATAL FIVE!
LOOK AROUND YOU! WE HAVE NO TIME TO ARGUE!
PULL THE TRIGGER! NOW!
TOK
?
NOTHING HAPPENED...?
IT'S FULLY POWERED... ALL CONNECTIONS SEEM TO BE IN PLACE...
MAYBE YOU USED IT WRONG?
PLEASE. IF BATMAN CAN OPERATE IT...
KID...
...I'VE HAD JUST ABOUT ENOUGH OF YOU.
THOK
KUNNK

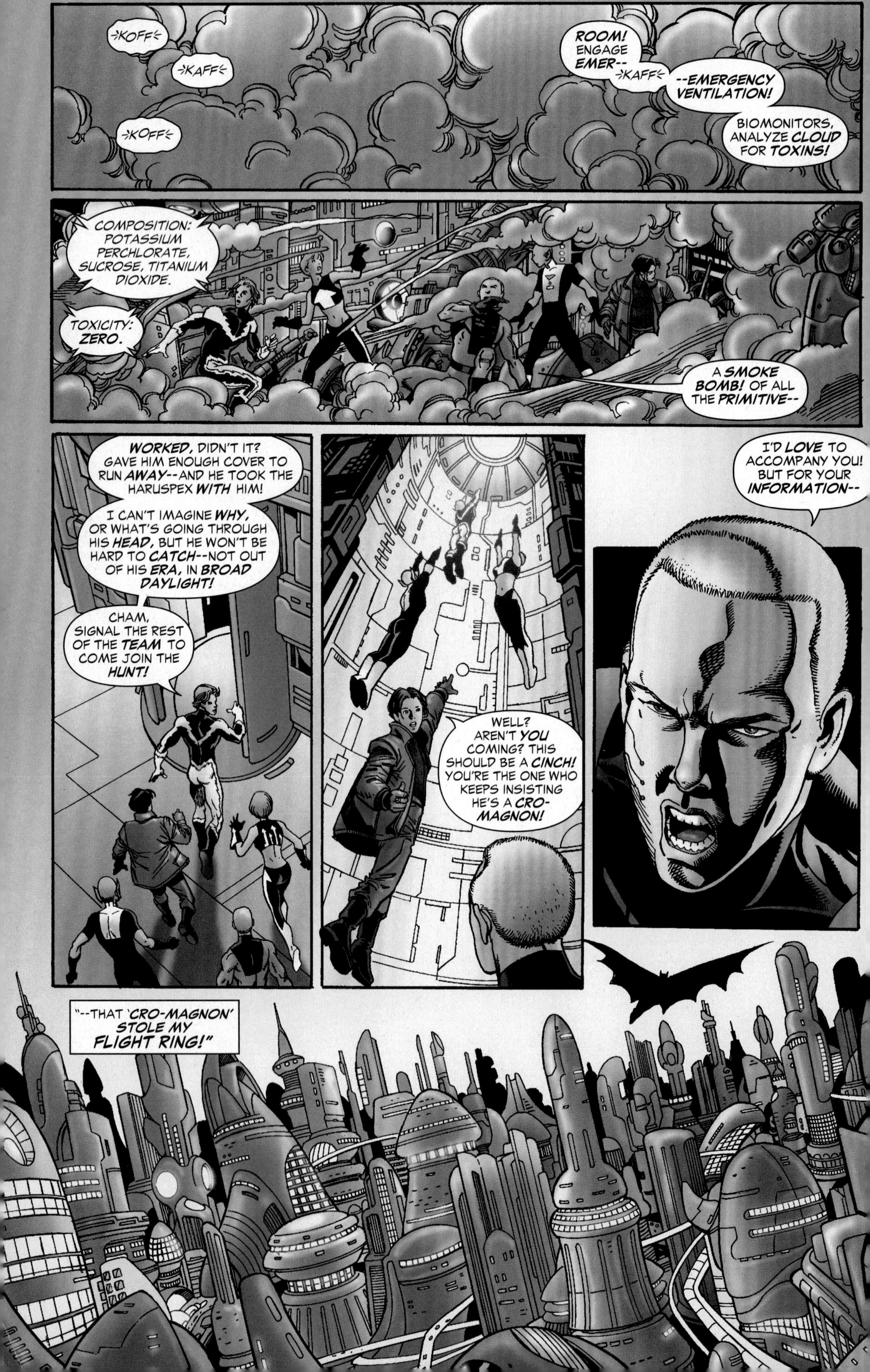

KOFF
KAFF
KOFF
ROOM! ENGAGE EMER-- KAFF
--EMERGENCY VENTILATION!
BIOMONITORS, ANALYZE CLOUD FOR TOXINS!
COMPOSITION: POTASSIUM PERCHLORATE, SUCROSE, TITANIUM DIOXIDE.
TOXICITY: ZERO.
A SMOKE BOMB! OF ALL THE PRIMITIVE--
WORKED, DIDN'T IT? GAVE HIM ENOUGH COVER TO RUN AWAY--AND HE TOOK THE HARUSPEX WITH HIM!
I CAN'T IMAGINE WHY, OR WHAT'S GOING THROUGH HIS HEAD, BUT HE WON'T BE HARD TO CATCH--NOT OUT OF HIS ERA, IN BROAD DAYLIGHT!
CHAM, SIGNAL THE REST OF THE TEAM TO COME JOIN THE HUNT!
WELL? AREN'T YOU COMING? THIS SHOULD BE A CINCH! YOU'RE THE ONE WHO KEEPS INSISTING HE'S A CRO-MAGNON!
I'D LOVE TO ACCOMPANY YOU! BUT FOR YOUR INFORMATION--
"--THAT 'CRO-MAGNON' STOLE MY FLIGHT RING!"

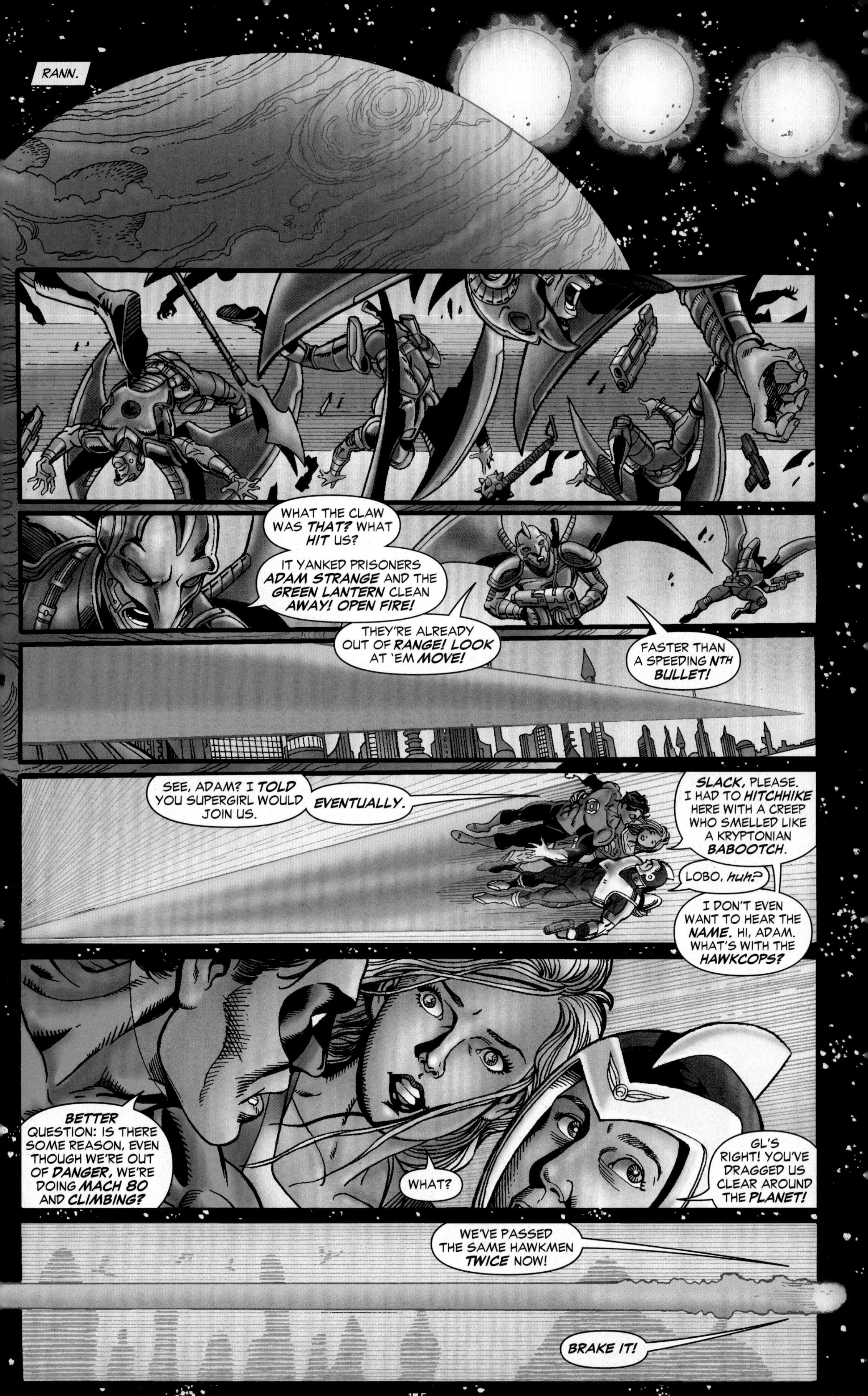
RANN.
WHAT THE CLAW WAS THAT? WHAT HIT US?
IT YANKED PRISONERS ADAM STRANGE AND THE GREEN LANTERN CLEAN AWAY! OPEN FIRE!
THEY'RE ALREADY OUT OF RANGE! LOOK AT 'EM MOVE!
FASTER THAN A SPEEDING NTH BULLET!
SEE, ADAM? I TOLD YOU SUPERGIRL WOULD JOIN US.
EVENTUALLY.
SLACK, PLEASE. I HAD TO HITCHHIKE HERE WITH A CREEP WHO SMELLED LIKE A KRYPTONIAN BABOOTCH.
LOBO, huh?
I DON'T EVEN WANT TO HEAR THE NAME. HI, ADAM. WHAT'S WITH THE HAWKCOPS?
BETTER QUESTION: IS THERE SOME REASON, EVEN THOUGH WE'RE OUT OF DANGER, WE'RE DOING MACH 80 AND CLIMBING?
WHAT?
GL'S RIGHT! YOU'VE DRAGGED US CLEAR AROUND THE PLANET!
WE'VE PASSED THE SAME HAWKMEN TWICE NOW!
BRAKE IT!

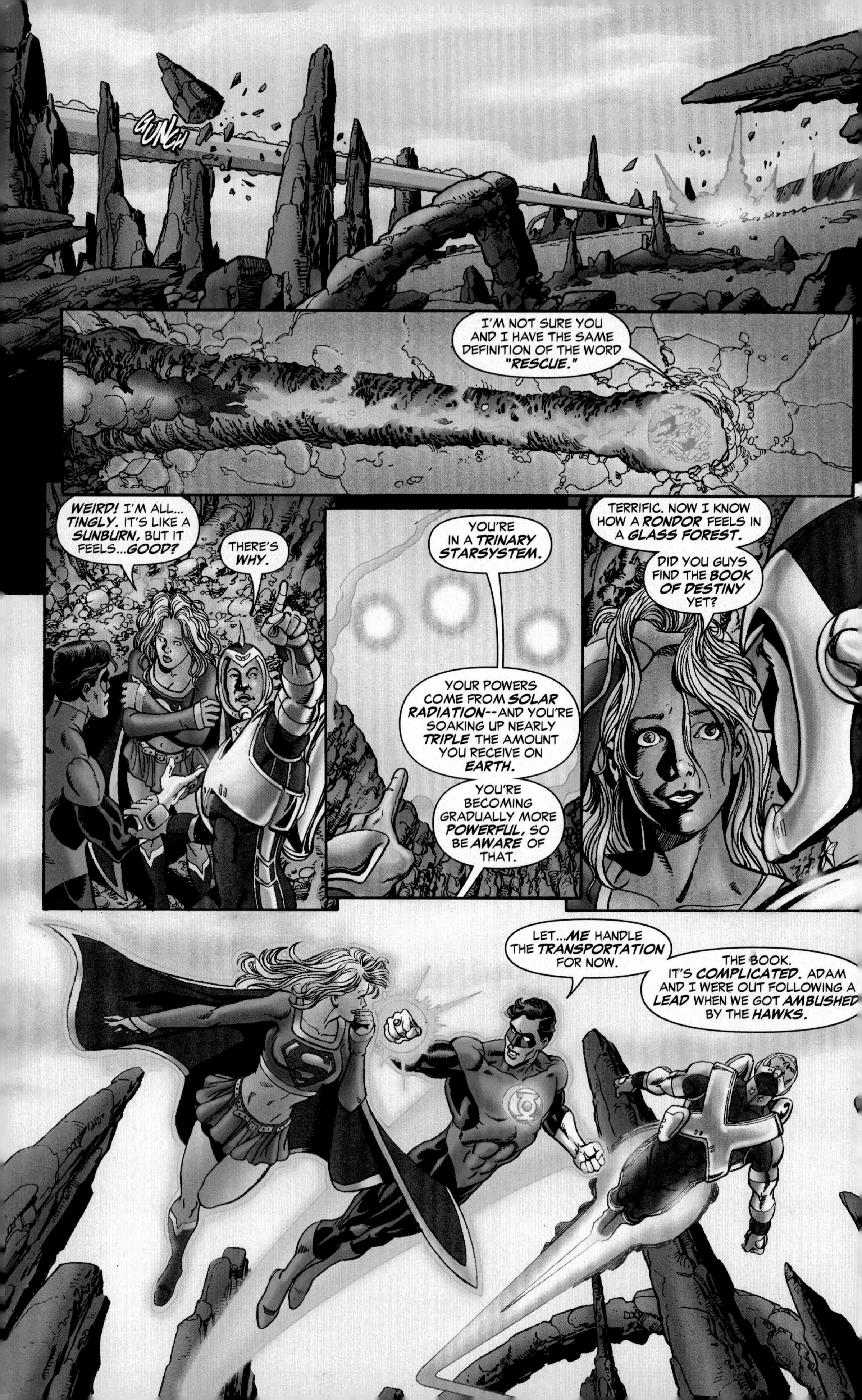
GLINCH
I'M NOT SURE YOU AND I HAVE THE SAME DEFINITION OF THE WORD "RESCUE."
WEIRD! I'M ALL... TINGLY. IT'S LIKE A SUNBURN, BUT IT FEELS...GOOD?
THERE'S WHY.
YOU'RE IN A TRINARY STARSYSTEM.
YOUR POWERS COME FROM SOLAR RADIATION--AND YOU'RE SOAKING UP NEARLY TRIPLE THE AMOUNT YOU RECEIVE ON EARTH.
YOU'RE BECOMING GRADUALLY MORE POWERFUL, SO BE AWARE OF THAT.
TERRIFIC. NOW I KNOW HOW A RONDOR FEELS IN A GLASS FOREST.
DID YOU GUYS FIND THE BOOK OF DESTINY YET?
LET...ME HANDLE THE TRANSPORTATION FOR NOW.
THE BOOK. IT'S COMPLICATED. ADAM AND I WERE OUT FOLLOWING A LEAD WHEN WE GOT AMBUSHED BY THE HAWKS.

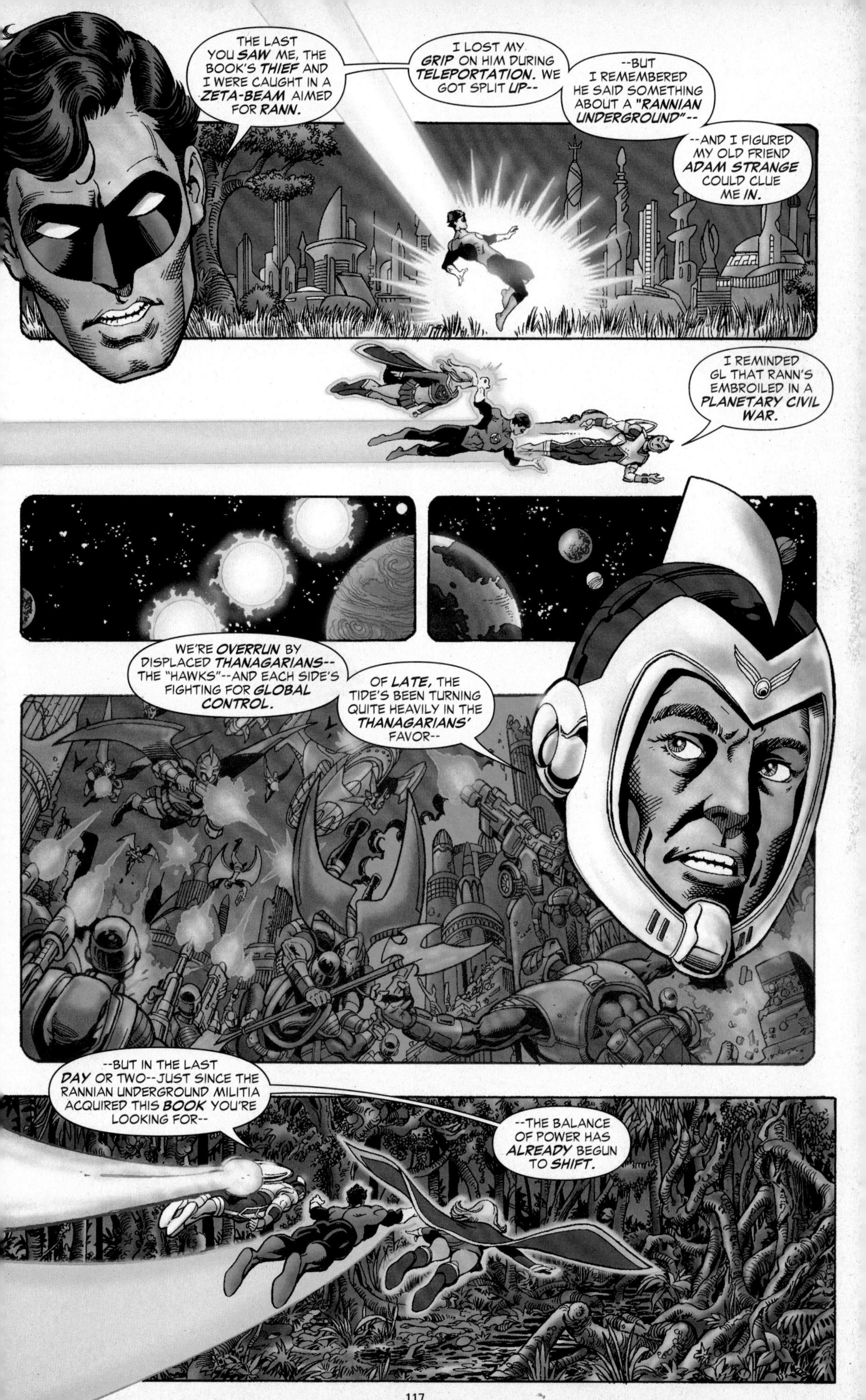
THE LAST YOU SAW ME, THE BOOK'S THIEF AND I WERE CAUGHT IN A ZETA-BEAM AIMED FOR RANN.
I LOST MY GRIP ON HIM DURING TELEPORTATION. WE GOT SPLIT UP--
--BUT I REMEMBERED HE SAID SOMETHING ABOUT A "RANNIAN UNDERGROUND"--
--AND I FIGURED MY OLD FRIEND ADAM STRANGE COULD CLUE ME IN.
I REMINDED GL THAT RANN'S EMBROILED IN A PLANETARY CIVIL WAR.
WE'RE OVERRUN BY DISPLACED THANAGARIANS-- THE "HAWKS"--AND EACH SIDE'S FIGHTING FOR GLOBAL CONTROL.
OF LATE, THE TIDE'S BEEN TURNING QUITE HEAVILY IN THE THANAGARIANS' FAVOR--
--BUT IN THE LAST DAY OR TWO--JUST SINCE THE RANNIAN UNDERGROUND MILITIA ACQUIRED THIS BOOK YOU'RE LOOKING FOR--
--THE BALANCE OF POWER HAS ALREADY BEGUN TO SHIFT.

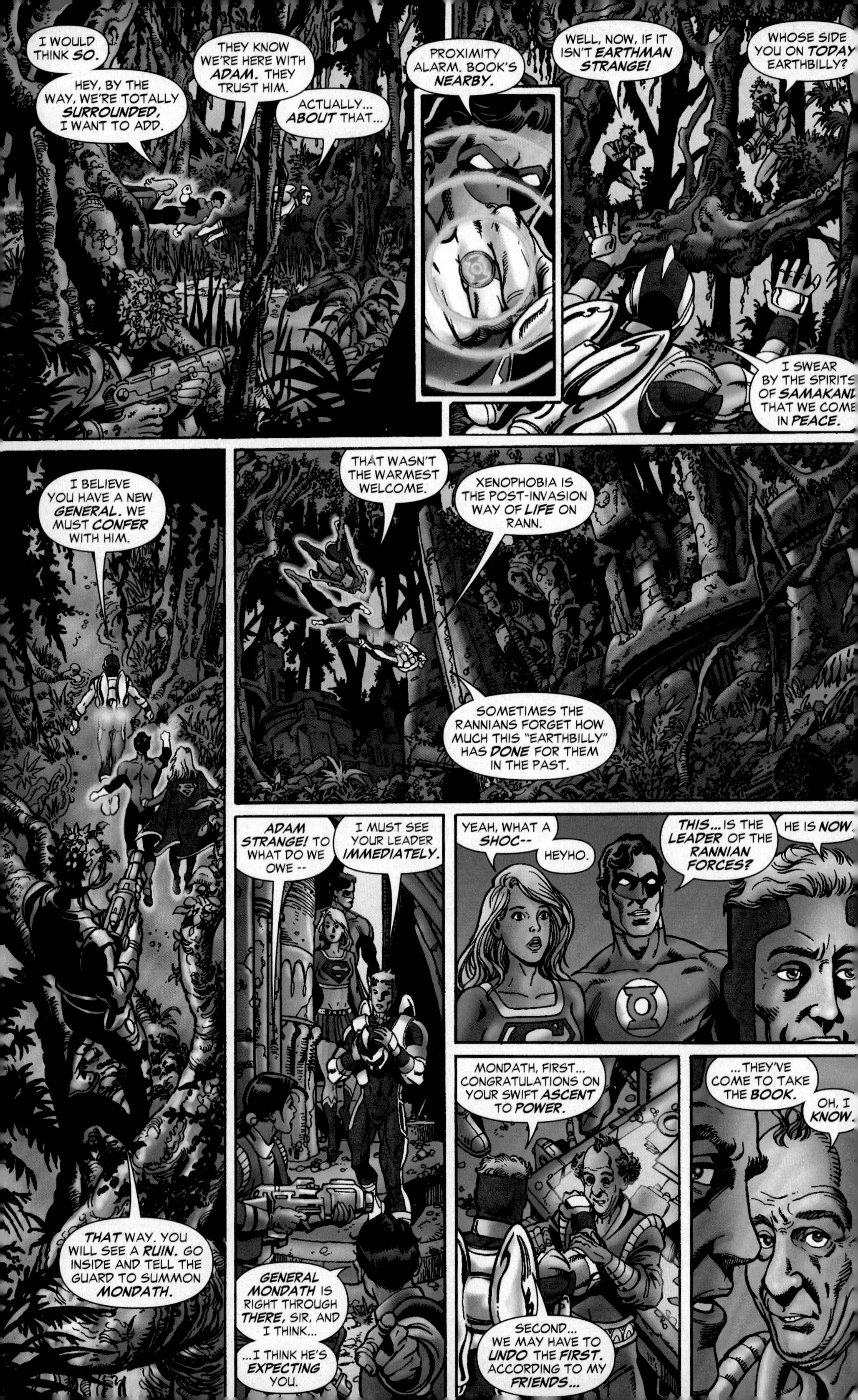
I WOULD THINK SO.
HEY, BY THE WAY, WE'RE TOTALLY SURROUNDED, I WANT TO ADD.
THEY KNOW WE'RE HERE WITH ADAM. THEY TRUST HIM.
ACTUALLY... ABOUT THAT...
PROXIMITY ALARM. BOOK'S NEARBY.
WELL, NOW, IF IT ISN'T EARTHMAN STRANGE!
WHOSE SIDE YOU ON TODAY EARTHBILLY?
I SWEAR BY THE SPIRITS OF SAMAKAND THAT WE COME IN PEACE.
I BELIEVE YOU HAVE A NEW GENERAL. WE MUST CONFER WITH HIM.
THAT WAY. YOU WILL SEE A RUIN. GO INSIDE AND TELL THE GUARD TO SUMMON MONDATH.
THAT WASN'T THE WARMEST WELCOME.
XENOPHOBIA IS THE POST-INVASION WAY OF LIFE ON RANN.
SOMETIMES THE RANNIANS FORGET HOW MUCH THIS "EARTHBILLY" HAS DONE FOR THEM IN THE PAST.
ADAM STRANGE! TO WHAT DO WE OWE --
I MUST SEE YOUR LEADER IMMEDIATELY.
GENERAL MONDATH IS RIGHT THROUGH THERE, SIR, AND I THINK...
...I THINK HE'S EXPECTING YOU.
YEAH, WHAT A SHOC--
HEYHO.
THIS... IS THE LEADER OF THE RANNIAN FORCES?
HE IS NOW.
MONDATH, FIRST... CONGRATULATIONS ON YOUR SWIFT ASCENT TO POWER.
SECOND... WE MAY HAVE TO UNDO THE FIRST. ACCORDING TO MY FRIENDS...
...THEY'VE COME TO TAKE THE BOOK.
OH, I KNOW.

THAT'S *HIM!* THAT'S THE LITTLE *THIEF* WHO SNATCHED THE BOOK BACK ON *VENTURA!*

WATCH THE *LUNGPOWER!* YOU REMEMBER WHAT *WHISPERING* IS LIKE, RIGHT?

STUPID TRINARY *SUN...*

MONDATH, GREEN LANTERN IS CONCERNED THAT THE BOOK OF DESTINY PRESENTS A SPECIFIC *DANGER--*

YES! TO THE *THANAGARIANS!*

THEY HAVE THE *ABSORBASCON,* A CURSED *SPY DEVICE* WHICH SCRIES EVERY SCRAP OF RANNIAN *KNOWLEDGE* AND *PLANNING!* THERE WAS NO FIGHTING *THAT--*

--UNTIL *FATE* DELIVERED TO ME A *BOOK* THAT SHOWS THE *PAST* AND *FUTURE!*

"FATE"? OR "LUCK"?

CAREFUL... KEEP A LID...!

DESTINY *HIMSELF* TOLD ME HOW THAT THING FELL INTO YOUR HANDS THANKS TO SOME SORCERERS CALLED THE *LUCK LORDS!*

WE'VE GOT TO GET IT *BACK* BEFORE THEY SCOOP IT UP *THEMSELVES!* OTHERWISE, ALL TIME AND... AND *WHATEVER--*

SPACE?

--SPACE-- IS *DOOMED!*

LUCK LORDS... LUCK LORDS... *hmmm...*

HERE. THESE *MAGICIANS* YOU'RE SO DESPERATE TO *OUTRACE.* IS THIS *THEM?*

I THINK SO, YEAH. I--

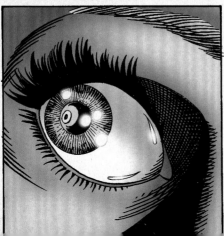

THEN YOU'RE A BIT *LATE.*

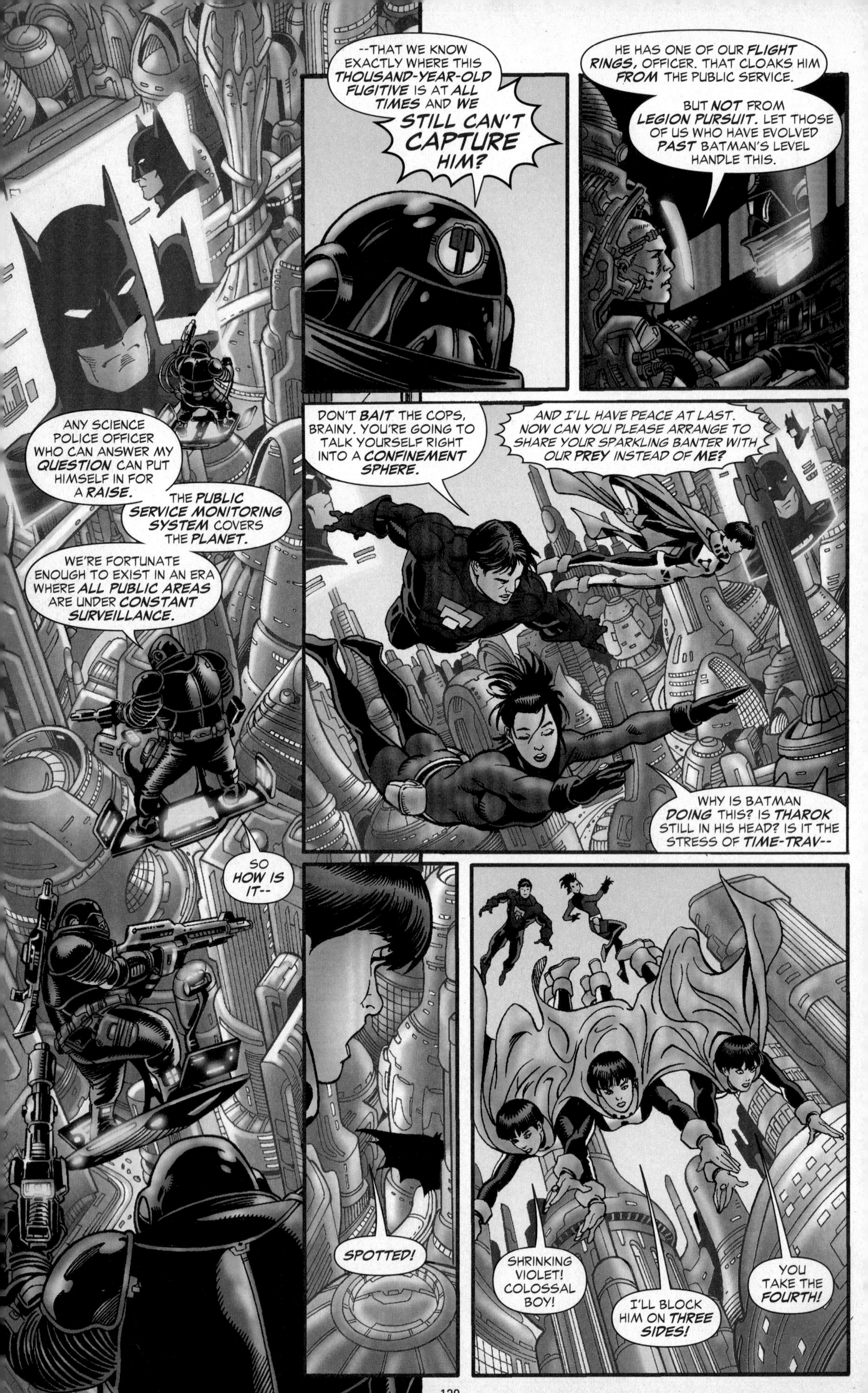
--THAT WE KNOW EXACTLY WHERE THIS THOUSAND-YEAR-OLD FUGITIVE IS AT ALL TIMES AND WE STILL CAN'T CAPTURE HIM?
HE HAS ONE OF OUR FLIGHT RINGS, OFFICER. THAT CLOAKS HIM FROM THE PUBLIC SERVICE.
BUT NOT FROM LEGION PURSUIT. LET THOSE OF US WHO HAVE EVOLVED PAST BATMAN'S LEVEL HANDLE THIS.
ANY SCIENCE POLICE OFFICER WHO CAN ANSWER MY QUESTION CAN PUT HIMSELF IN FOR A RAISE.
THE PUBLIC SERVICE MONITORING SYSTEM COVERS THE PLANET.
WE'RE FORTUNATE ENOUGH TO EXIST IN AN ERA WHERE ALL PUBLIC AREAS ARE UNDER CONSTANT SURVEILLANCE.
DON'T BAIT THE COPS, BRAINY. YOU'RE GOING TO TALK YOURSELF RIGHT INTO A CONFINEMENT SPHERE.
AND I'LL HAVE PEACE AT LAST. NOW CAN YOU PLEASE ARRANGE TO SHARE YOUR SPARKLING BANTER WITH OUR PREY INSTEAD OF ME?
WHY IS BATMAN DOING THIS? IS THAROK STILL IN HIS HEAD? IS IT THE STRESS OF TIME-TRAV--
SO HOW IS IT--
SPOTTED!
SHRINKING VIOLET! COLOSSAL BOY!
I'LL BLOCK HIM ON THREE SIDES!
YOU TAKE THE FOURTH!

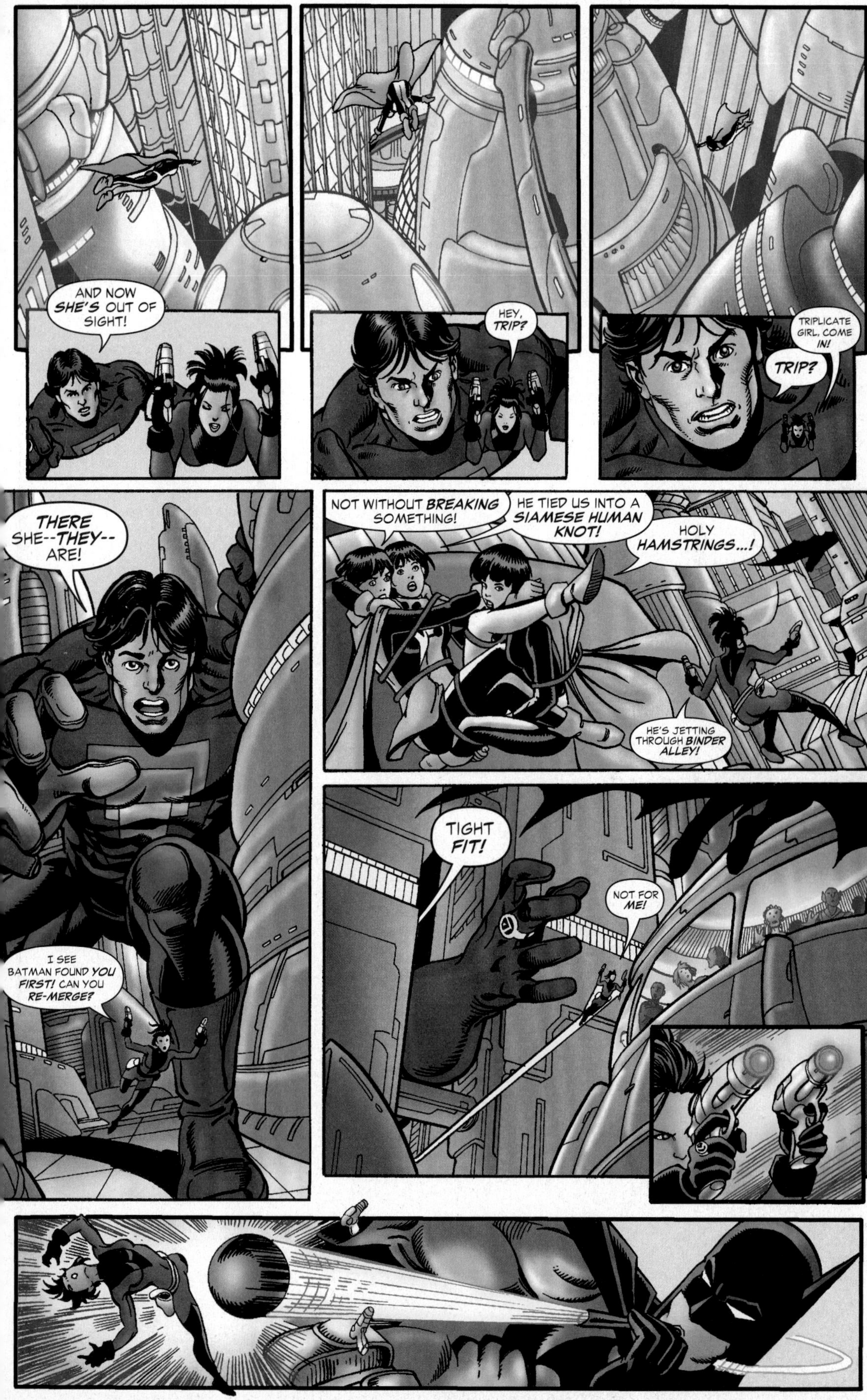
AND NOW SHE'S OUT OF SIGHT!
HEY, TRIP?
TRIPLICATE GIRL, COME IN!
TRIP?
THERE SHE--THEY--ARE!
I SEE BATMAN FOUND YOU FIRST! CAN YOU RE-MERGE?
NOT WITHOUT BREAKING SOMETHING!
HE TIED US INTO A SIAMESE HUMAN KNOT!
HOLY HAMSTRINGS...!
HE'S JETTING THROUGH BINDER ALLEY!
TIGHT FIT!
NOT FOR ME!

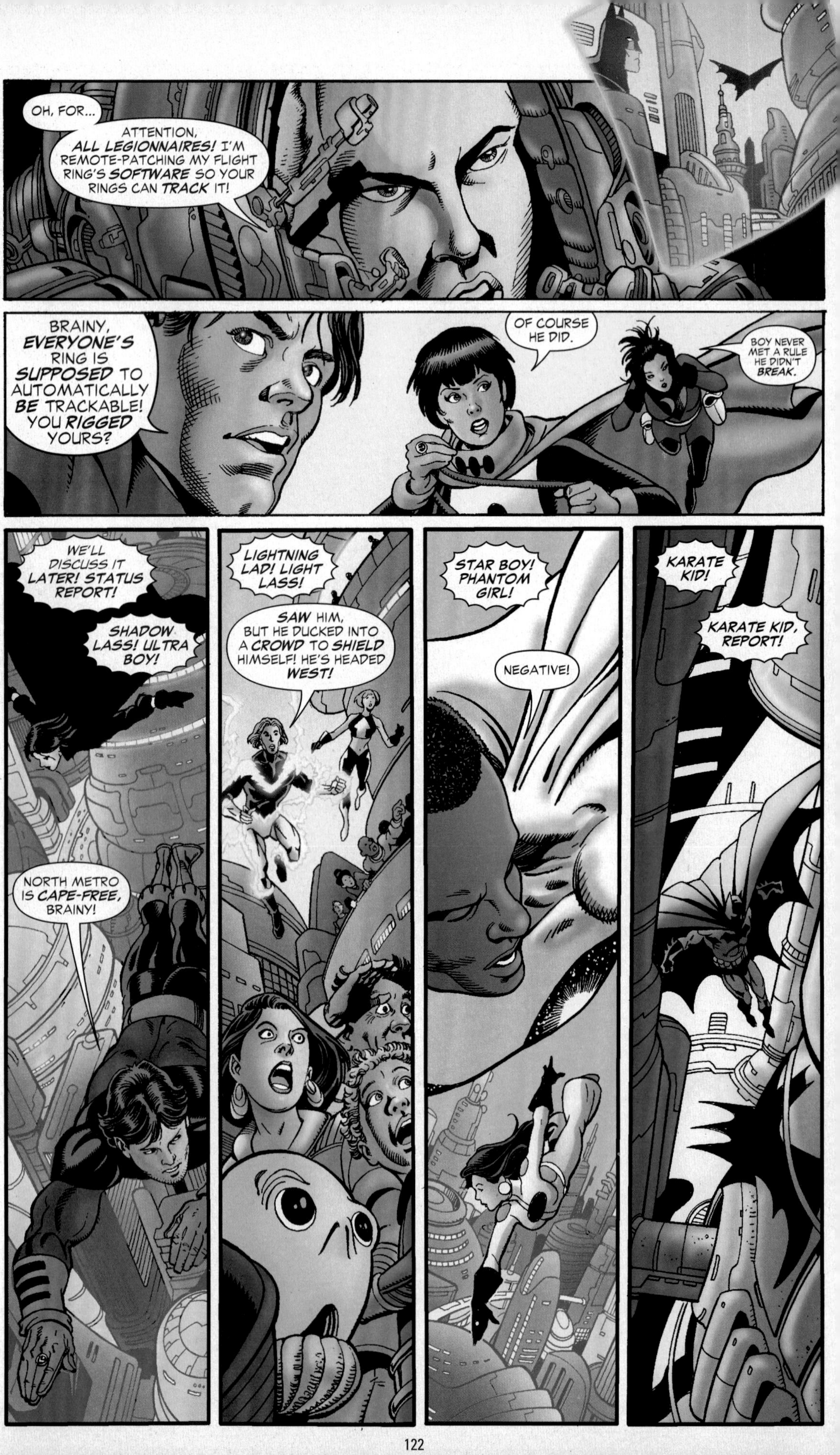
OH, FOR...
ATTENTION, ALL LEGIONNAIRES! I'M REMOTE-PATCHING MY FLIGHT RING'S SOFTWARE SO YOUR RINGS CAN TRACK IT!
BRAINY, EVERYONE'S RING IS SUPPOSED TO AUTOMATICALLY BE TRACKABLE! YOU RIGGED YOURS?
OF COURSE HE DID.
BOY NEVER MET A RULE HE DIDN'T BREAK.
WE'LL DISCUSS IT LATER! STATUS REPORT!
SHADOW LASS! ULTRA BOY!
NORTH METRO IS CAPE-FREE, BRAINY!
LIGHTNING LAD! LIGHT LASS!
SAW HIM, BUT HE DUCKED INTO A CROWD TO SHIELD HIMSELF! HE'S HEADED WEST!
STAR BOY! PHANTOM GIRL!
NEGATIVE!
KARATE KID!
KARATE KID, REPORT!

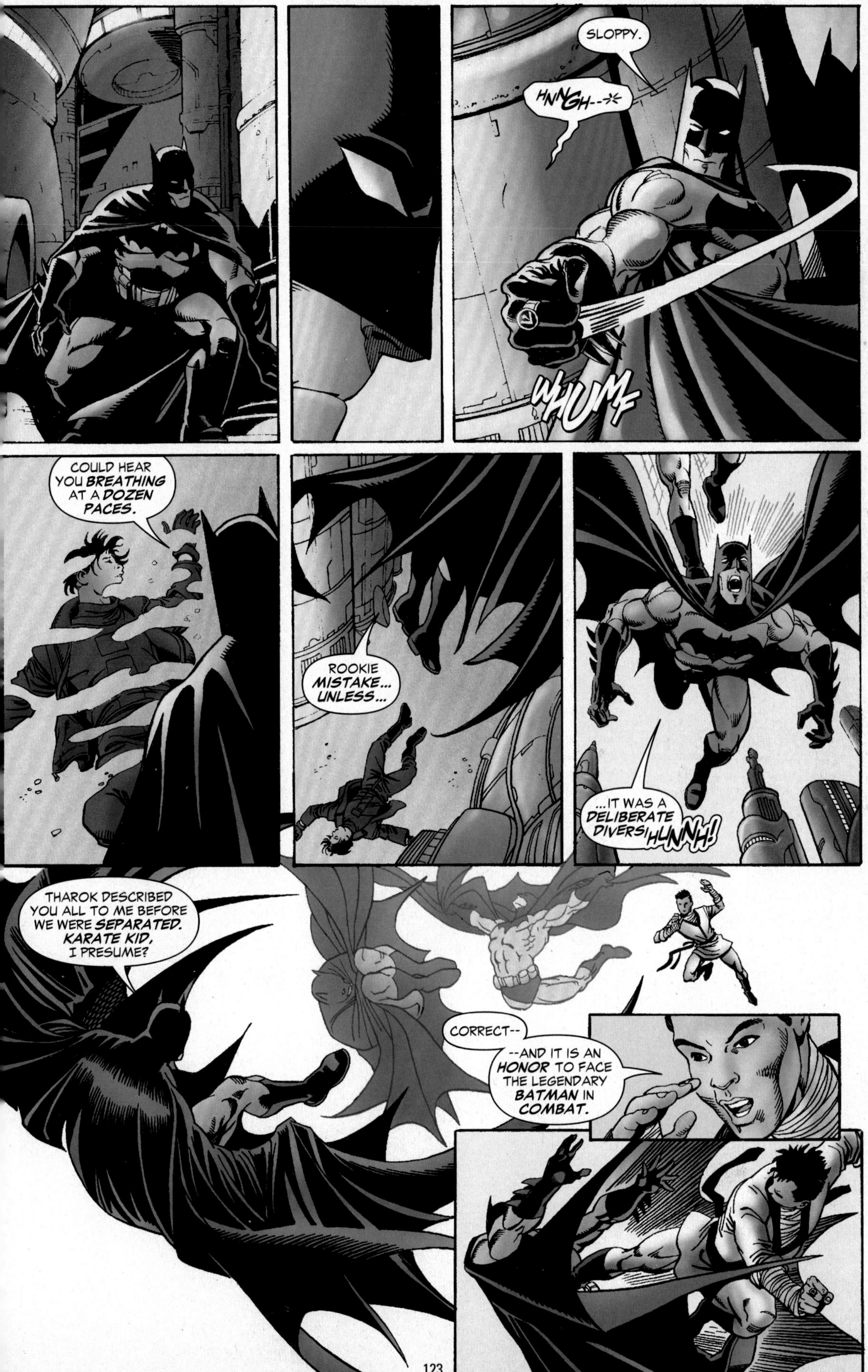
SLOPPY.
HNNGH--
WHUMF
COULD HEAR YOU BREATHING AT A DOZEN PACES.
ROOKIE MISTAKE... UNLESS...
...IT WAS A DELIBERATE DIVERSIHUNNH!
THAROK DESCRIBED YOU ALL TO ME BEFORE WE WERE SEPARATED. KARATE KID, I PRESUME?
CORRECT--
--AND IT IS AN HONOR TO FACE THE LEGENDARY BATMAN IN COMBAT.

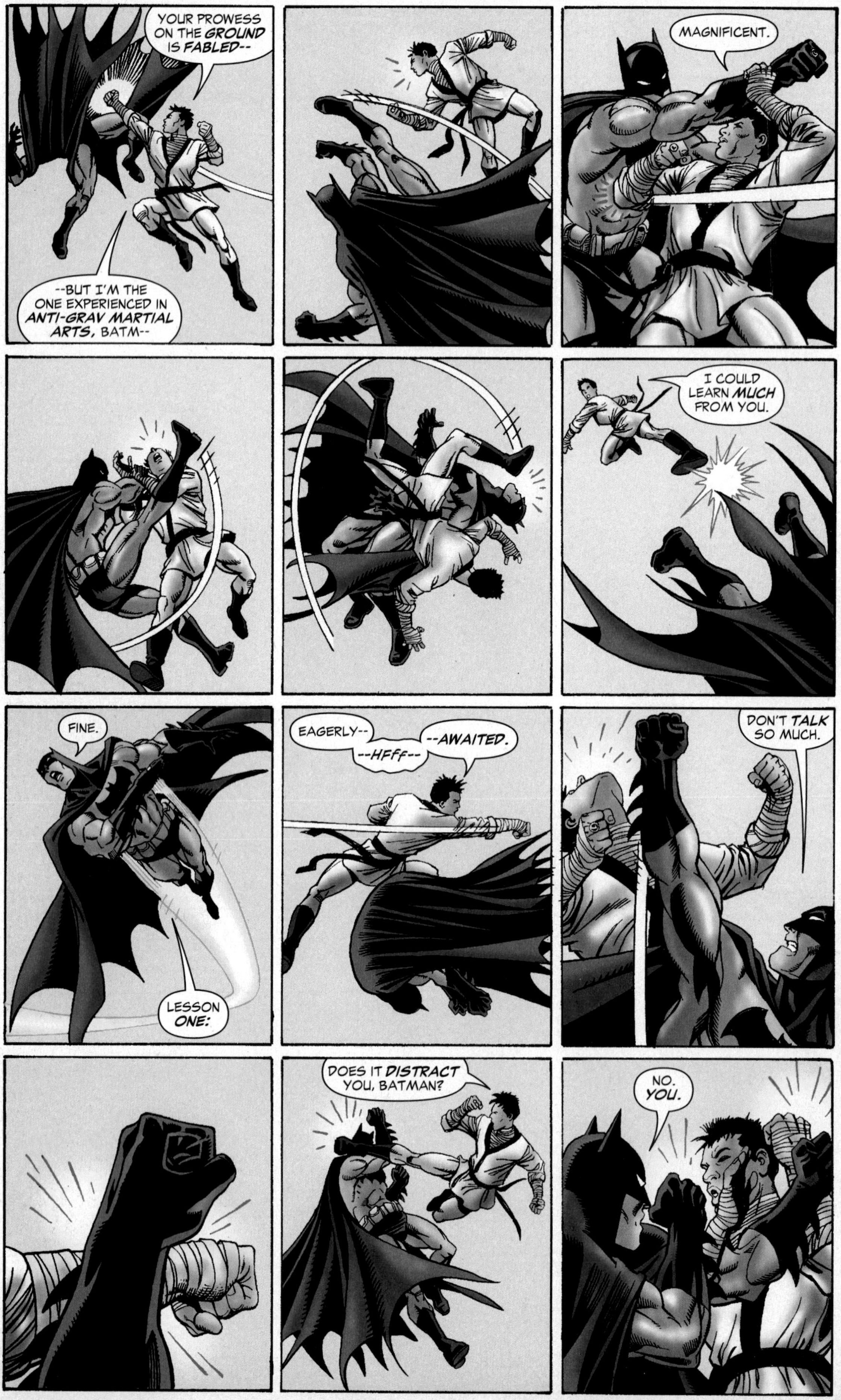
YOUR PROWESS ON THE GROUND IS FABLED--
--BUT I'M THE ONE EXPERIENCED IN ANTI-GRAV MARTIAL ARTS, BATM--
MAGNIFICENT.
I COULD LEARN MUCH FROM YOU.
FINE.
LESSON ONE:
EAGERLY--
--HFff--
--AWAITED.
DON'T TALK SO MUCH.
DOES IT DISTRACT YOU, BATMAN?
NO. YOU.

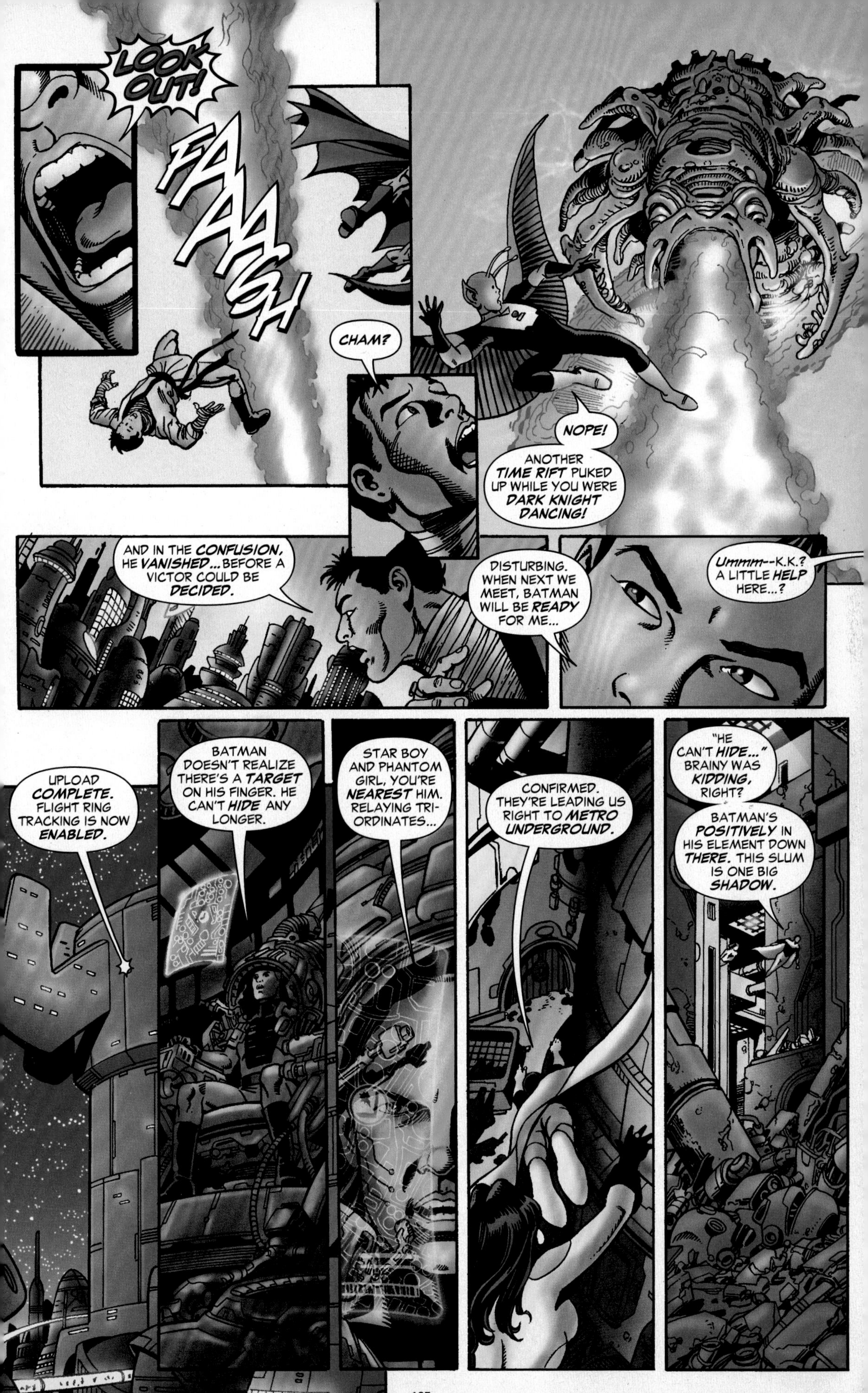
LOOK OUT!
FAAASH
CHAM?
NOPE!
ANOTHER TIME RIFT PUKED UP WHILE YOU WERE DARK KNIGHT DANCING!
AND IN THE CONFUSION, HE VANISHED... BEFORE A VICTOR COULD BE DECIDED.
DISTURBING. WHEN NEXT WE MEET, BATMAN WILL BE READY FOR ME...
Ummm--K.K.? A LITTLE HELP HERE...?
UPLOAD COMPLETE. FLIGHT RING TRACKING IS NOW ENABLED.
BATMAN DOESN'T REALIZE THERE'S A TARGET ON HIS FINGER. HE CAN'T HIDE ANY LONGER.
STAR BOY AND PHANTOM GIRL, YOU'RE NEAREST HIM. RELAYING TRI-ORDINATES...
CONFIRMED. THEY'RE LEADING US RIGHT TO METRO UNDERGROUND.
"HE CAN'T HIDE..." BRAINY WAS KIDDING, RIGHT?
BATMAN'S POSITIVELY IN HIS ELEMENT DOWN THERE. THIS SLUM IS ONE BIG SHADOW.

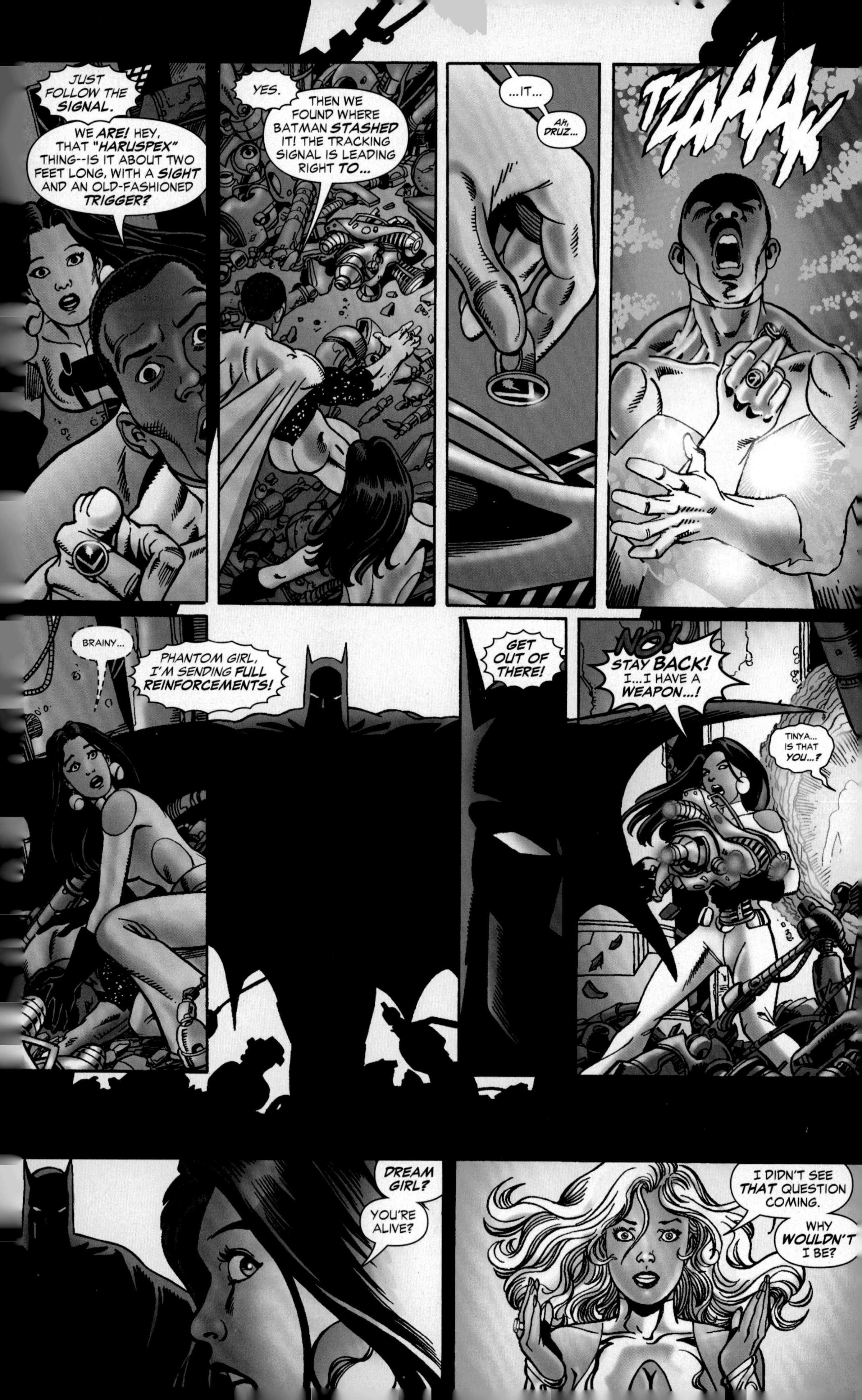
JUST FOLLOW THE SIGNAL.
WE ARE! HEY, THAT "HARUSPEX" THING--IS IT ABOUT TWO FEET LONG, WITH A SIGHT AND AN OLD-FASHIONED TRIGGER?
YES.
THEN WE FOUND WHERE BATMAN STASHED IT! THE TRACKING SIGNAL IS LEADING RIGHT TO...
...IT...
AH, DRUZ...
TZAAAK
BRAINY...
PHANTOM GIRL, I'M SENDING FULL REINFORCEMENTS!
GET OUT OF THERE!
NO! STAY BACK! I...I HAVE A WEAPON...!
TINYA... IS THAT YOU...?
DREAM GIRL?
YOU'RE ALIVE?
I DIDN'T SEE THAT QUESTION COMING.
WHY WOULDN'T I BE?

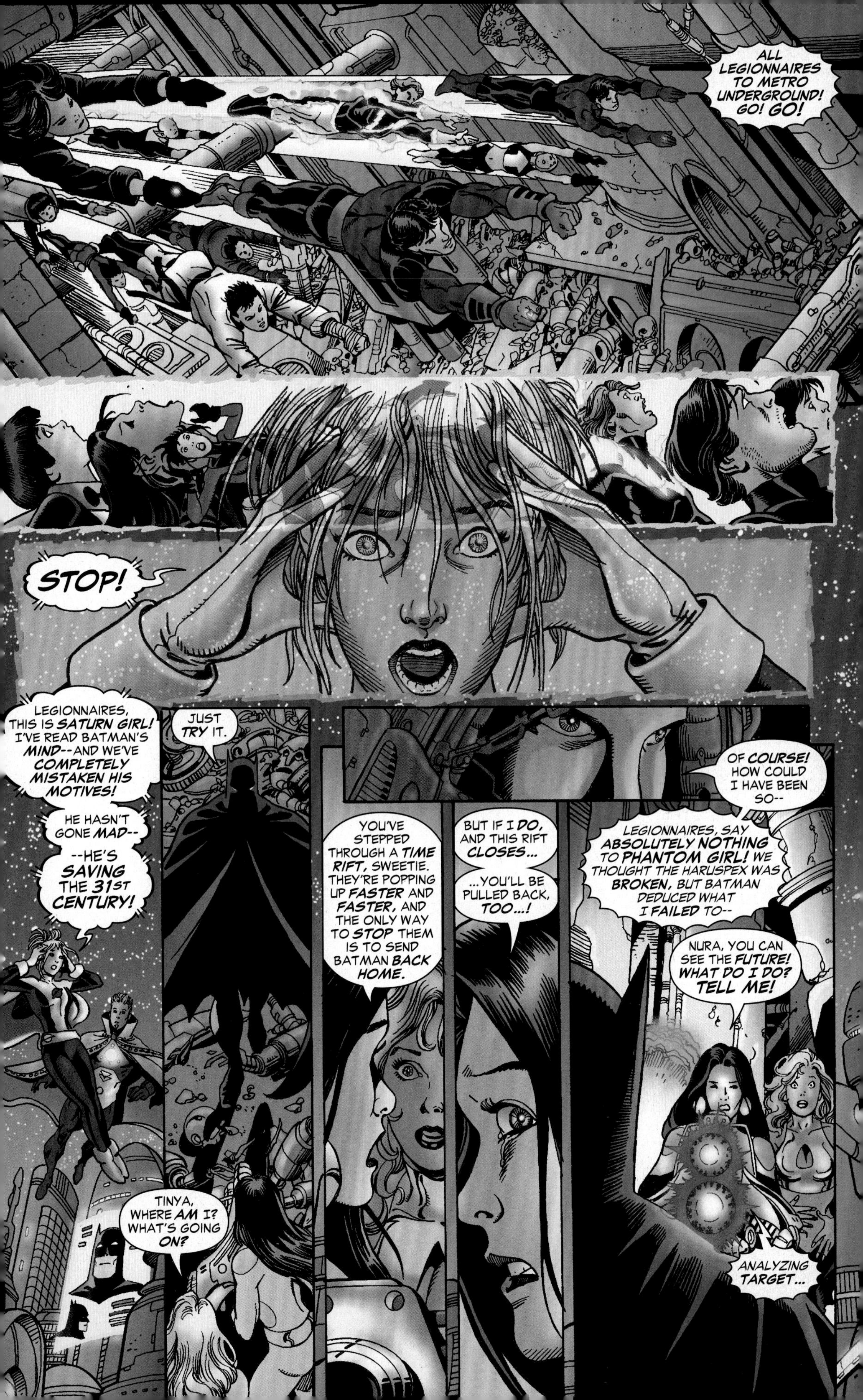
ALL LEGIONNAIRES TO METRO UNDERGROUND! GO! GO!
STOP!
LEGIONNAIRES, THIS IS SATURN GIRL! I'VE READ BATMAN'S MIND--AND WE'VE COMPLETELY MISTAKEN HIS MOTIVES!
HE HASN'T GONE MAD--
--HE'S SAVING THE 31ST CENTURY!
JUST TRY IT.
TINYA, WHERE AM I? WHAT'S GOING ON?
YOU'VE STEPPED THROUGH A TIME RIFT, SWEETIE. THEY'RE POPPING UP FASTER AND FASTER, AND THE ONLY WAY TO STOP THEM IS TO SEND BATMAN BACK HOME.
BUT IF I DO, AND THIS RIFT CLOSES...
...YOU'LL BE PULLED BACK, TOO...!
OF COURSE! HOW COULD I HAVE BEEN SO--
LEGIONNAIRES, SAY ABSOLUTELY NOTHING TO PHANTOM GIRL! WE THOUGHT THE HARUSPEX WAS BROKEN, BUT BATMAN DEDUCED WHAT I FAILED TO--
NURA, YOU CAN SEE THE FUTURE! WHAT DO I DO? TELL ME!
ANALYZING TARGET...

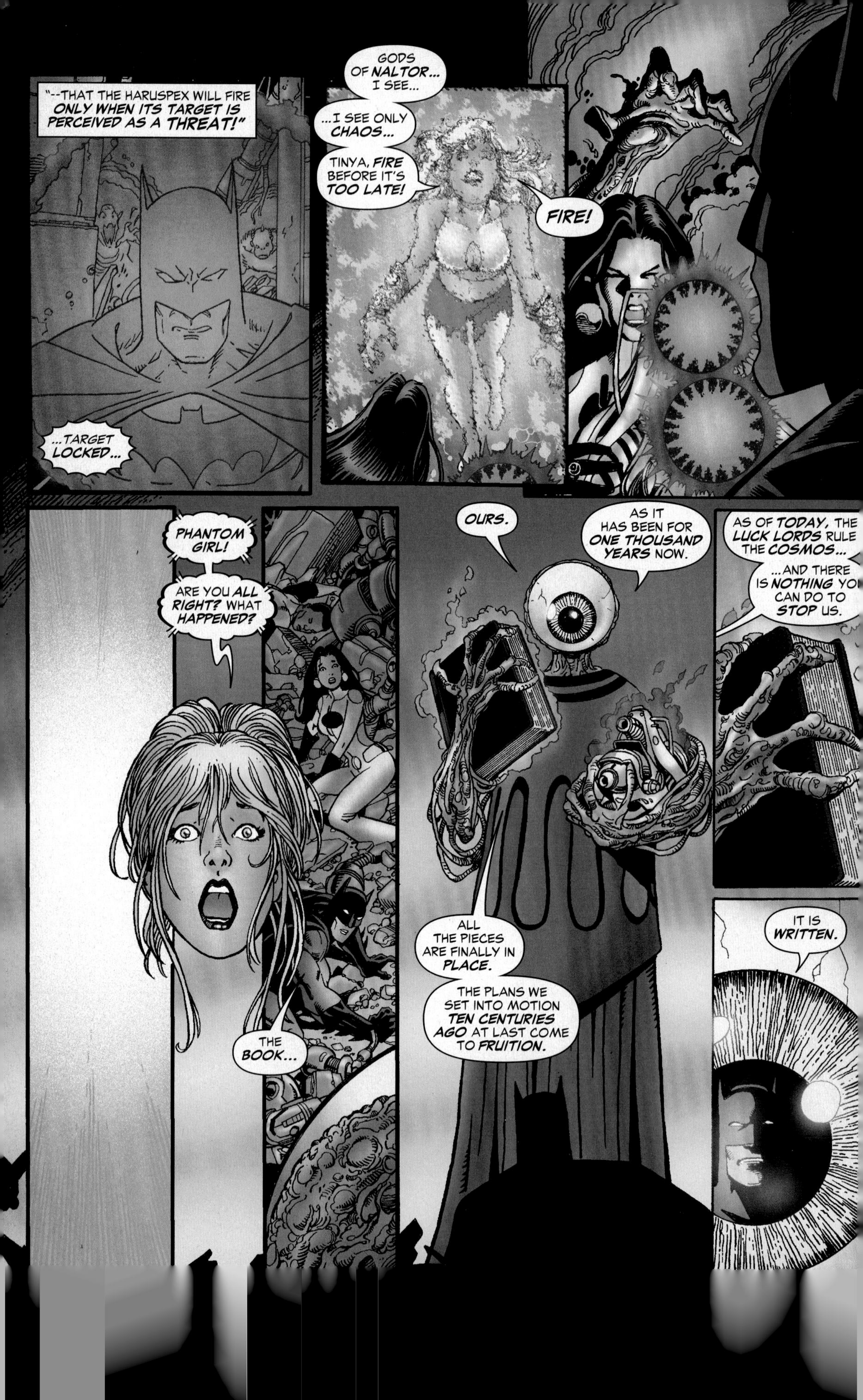
"--THAT THE HARUSPEX WILL FIRE ONLY WHEN ITS TARGET IS PERCEIVED AS A THREAT!"
...TARGET LOCKED...
GODS OF NALTOR... I SEE...
...I SEE ONLY CHAOS...
TINYA, FIRE BEFORE IT'S TOO LATE!
FIRE!
PHANTOM GIRL!
ARE YOU ALL RIGHT? WHAT HAPPENED?
THE BOOK...
OURS.
AS IT HAS BEEN FOR ONE THOUSAND YEARS NOW.
AS OF TODAY, THE LUCK LORDS RULE THE COSMOS...
...AND THERE IS NOTHING YO CAN DO TO STOP US.
ALL THE PIECES ARE FINALLY IN PLACE.
THE PLANS WE SET INTO MOTION TEN CENTURIES AGO AT LAST COME TO FRUITION.
IT IS WRITTEN.

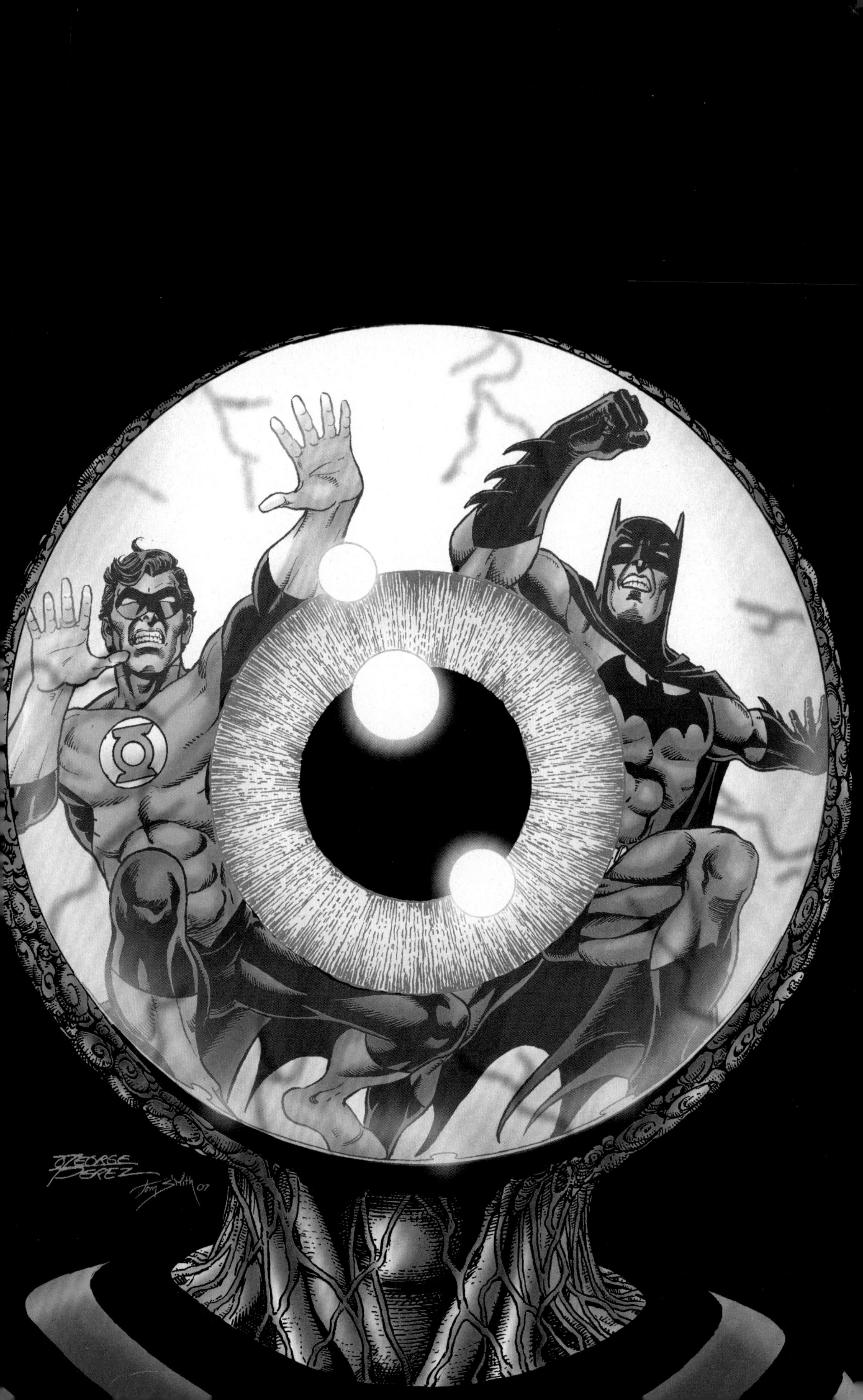
GEORGE PEREZ
Tom Smith '07

GREEN LANTERN and BATMAN

THE LORDS OF LUCK : CHAPTER SIX: THE GIRL WHO KNEW TOO MUCH

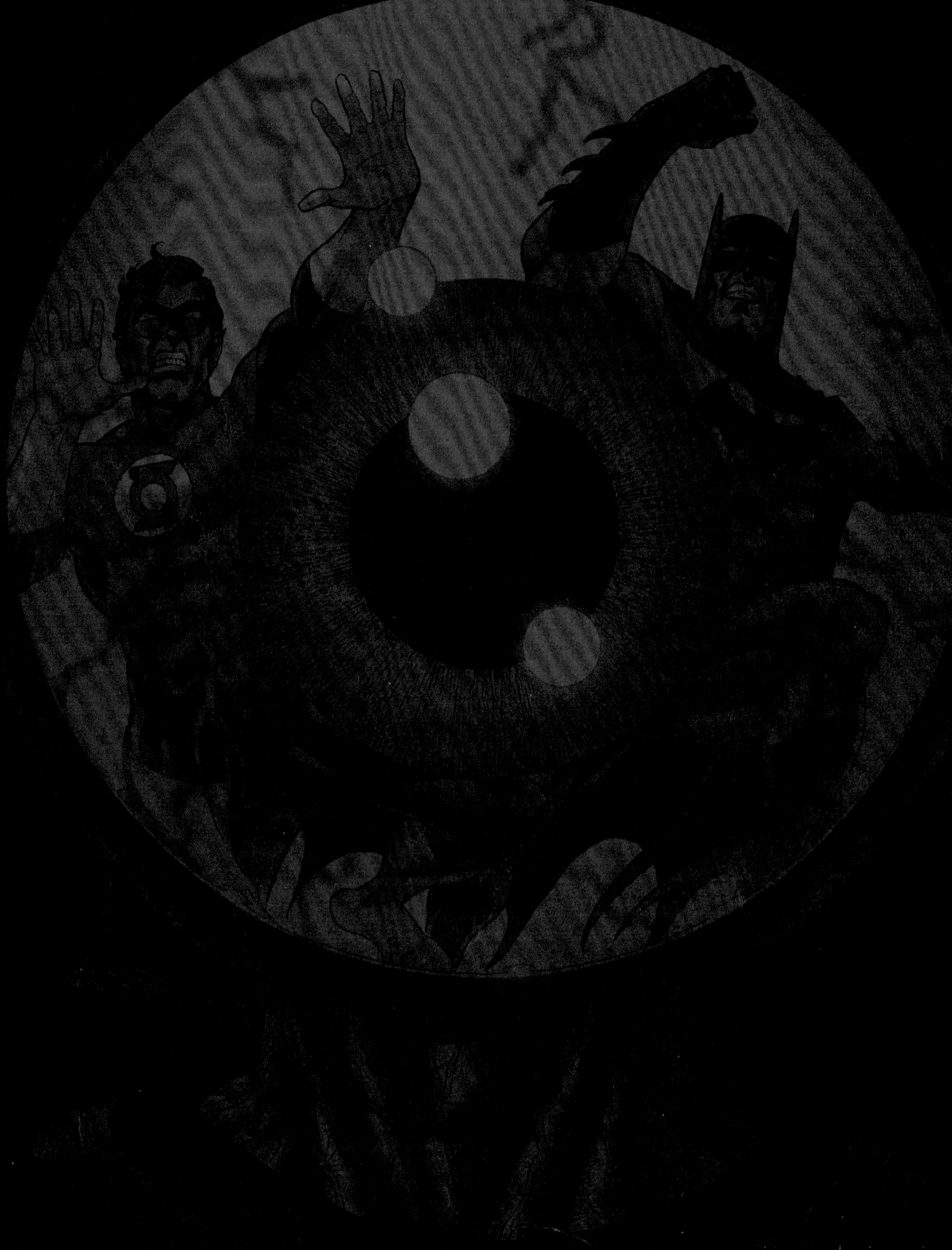

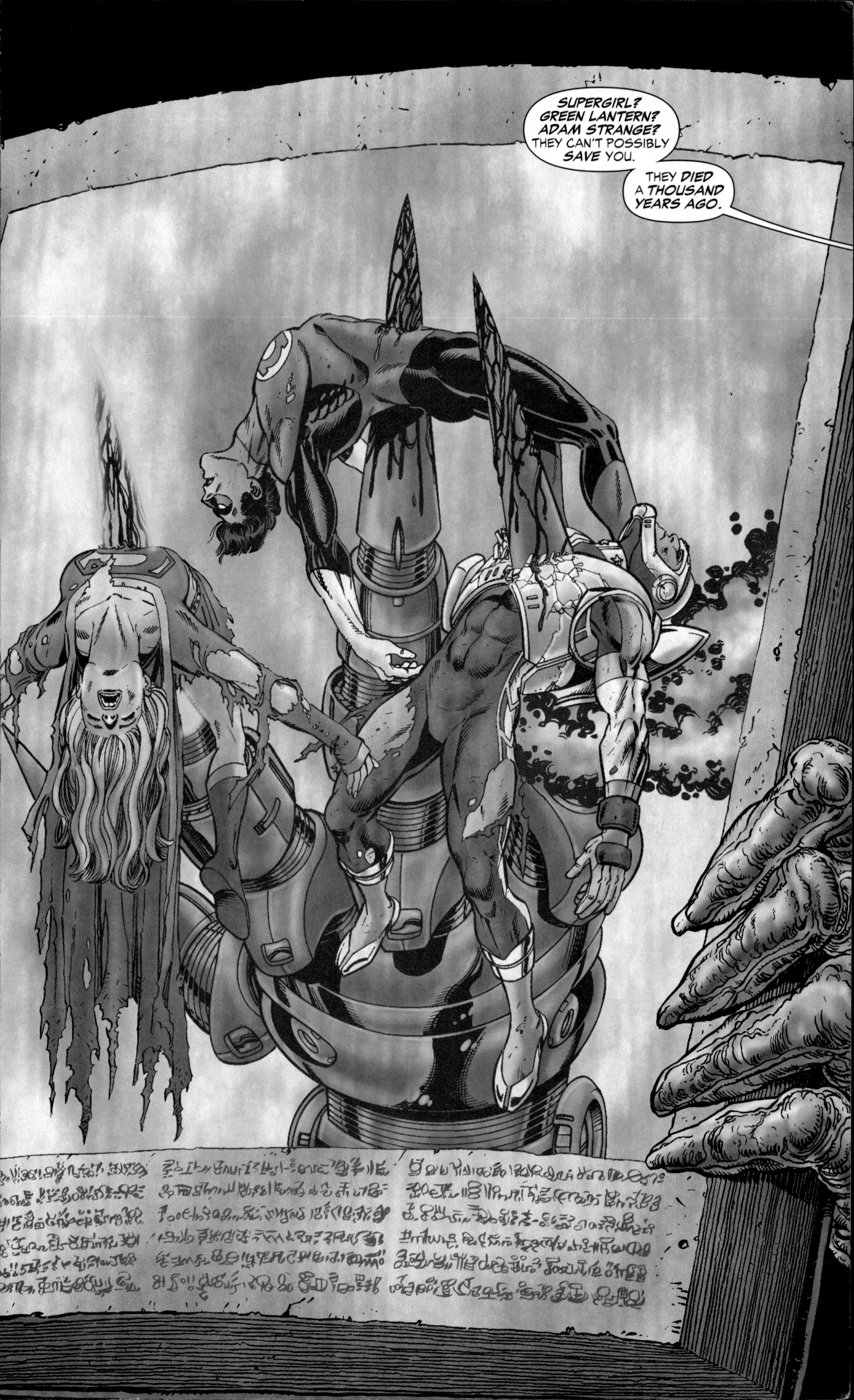
SUPERGIRL? GREEN LANTERN? ADAM STRANGE? THEY CAN'T POSSIBLY SAVE YOU.
THEY DIED A THOUSAND YEARS AGO.

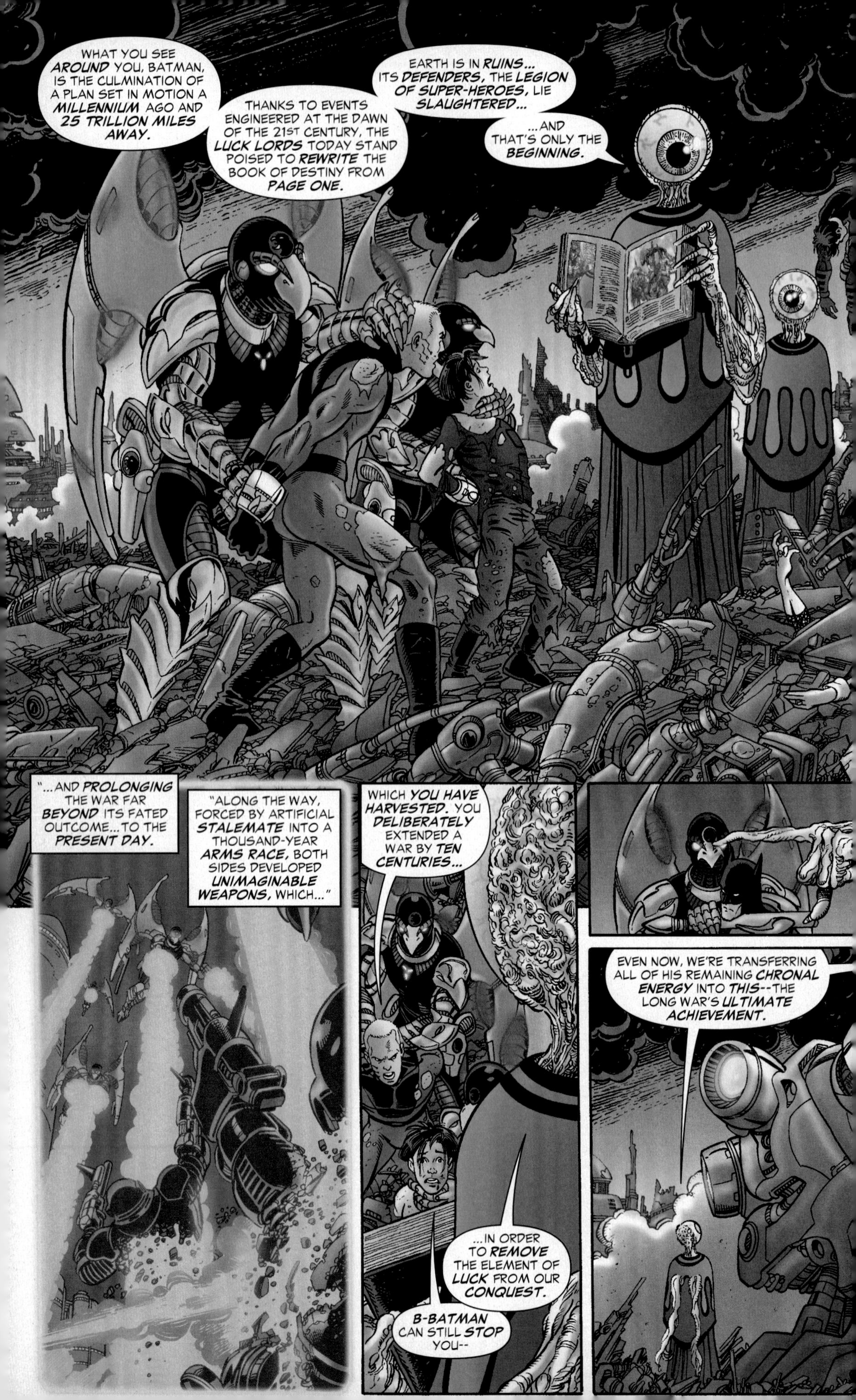
WHAT YOU SEE AROUND YOU, BATMAN, IS THE CULMINATION OF A PLAN SET IN MOTION A MILLENNIUM AGO AND 25 TRILLION MILES AWAY.
THANKS TO EVENTS ENGINEERED AT THE DAWN OF THE 21ST CENTURY, THE LUCK LORDS TODAY STAND POISED TO REWRITE THE BOOK OF DESTINY FROM PAGE ONE.
EARTH IS IN RUINS... ITS DEFENDERS, THE LEGION OF SUPER-HEROES, LIE SLAUGHTERED...
...AND THAT'S ONLY THE BEGINNING.
"...AND PROLONGING THE WAR FAR BEYOND ITS FATED OUTCOME...TO THE PRESENT DAY.
"ALONG THE WAY, FORCED BY ARTIFICIAL STALEMATE INTO A THOUSAND-YEAR ARMS RACE, BOTH SIDES DEVELOPED UNIMAGINABLE WEAPONS, WHICH..."
WHICH YOU HAVE HARVESTED. YOU DELIBERATELY EXTENDED A WAR BY TEN CENTURIES...
...IN ORDER TO REMOVE THE ELEMENT OF LUCK FROM OUR CONQUEST.
B-BATMAN CAN STILL STOP YOU--
EVEN NOW, WE'RE TRANSFERRING ALL OF HIS REMAINING CHRONAL ENERGY INTO THIS--THE LONG WAR'S ULTIMATE ACHIEVEMENT.

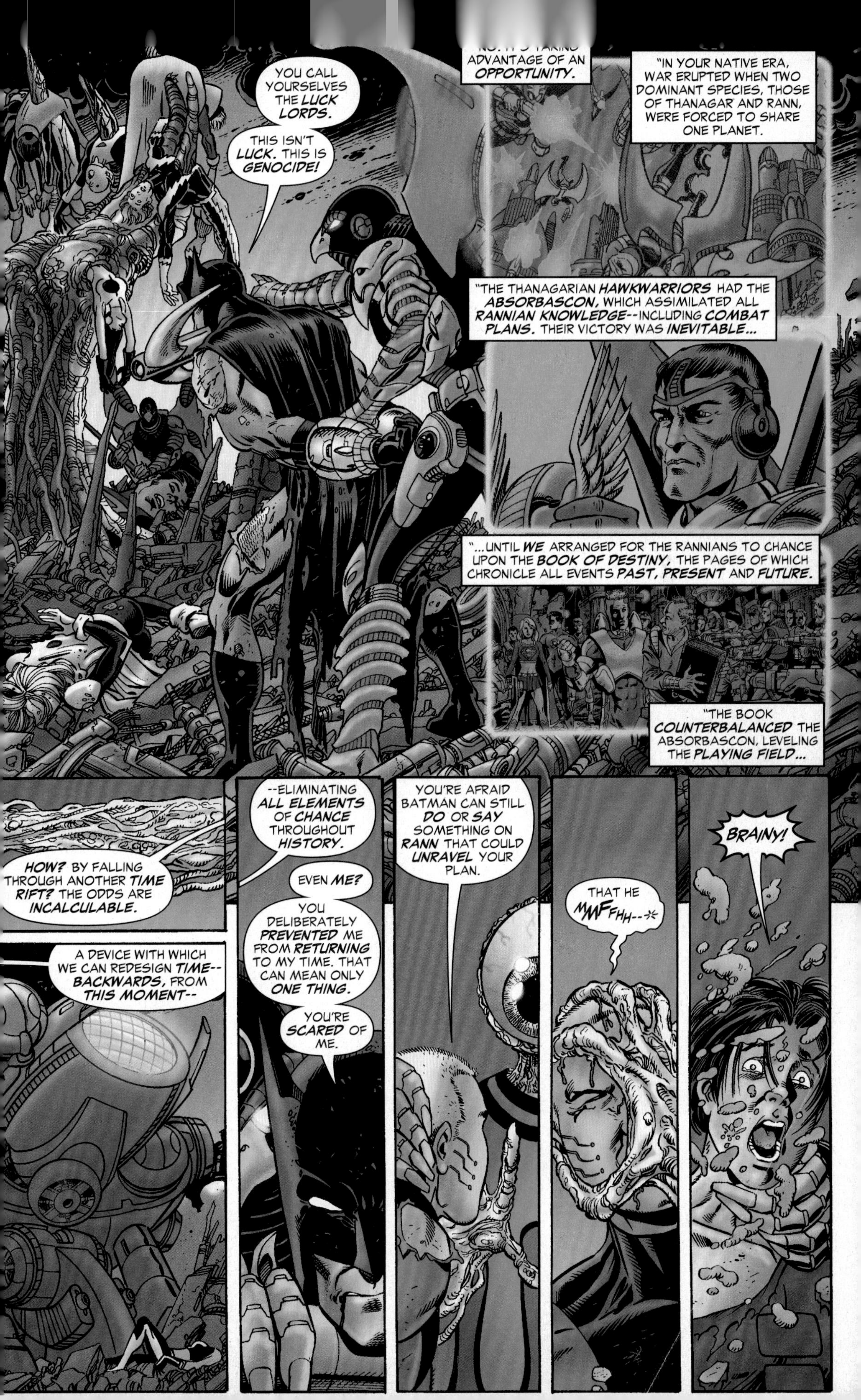

YOU CALL YOURSELVES THE LUCK LORDS.
THIS ISN'T LUCK. THIS IS GENOCIDE!
ADVANTAGE OF AN OPPORTUNITY.
"IN YOUR NATIVE ERA, WAR ERUPTED WHEN TWO DOMINANT SPECIES, THOSE OF THANAGAR AND RANN, WERE FORCED TO SHARE ONE PLANET.
"THE THANAGARIAN HAWKWARRIORS HAD THE ABSORBASCON, WHICH ASSIMILATED ALL RANNIAN KNOWLEDGE--INCLUDING COMBAT PLANS. THEIR VICTORY WAS INEVITABLE...
"...UNTIL WE ARRANGED FOR THE RANNIANS TO CHANCE UPON THE BOOK OF DESTINY, THE PAGES OF WHICH CHRONICLE ALL EVENTS PAST, PRESENT AND FUTURE.
"THE BOOK COUNTERBALANCED THE ABSORBASCON, LEVELING THE PLAYING FIELD...
HOW? BY FALLING THROUGH ANOTHER TIME RIFT? THE ODDS ARE INCALCULABLE.
A DEVICE WITH WHICH WE CAN REDESIGN TIME--BACKWARDS, FROM THIS MOMENT--
--ELIMINATING ALL ELEMENTS OF CHANCE THROUGHOUT HISTORY.
EVEN ME?
YOU DELIBERATELY PREVENTED ME FROM RETURNING TO MY TIME. THAT CAN MEAN ONLY ONE THING.
YOU'RE SCARED OF ME.
YOU'RE AFRAID BATMAN CAN STILL DO OR SAY SOMETHING ON RANN THAT COULD UNRAVEL YOUR PLAN.
THAT HE MMFFHH--*
BRAINY!

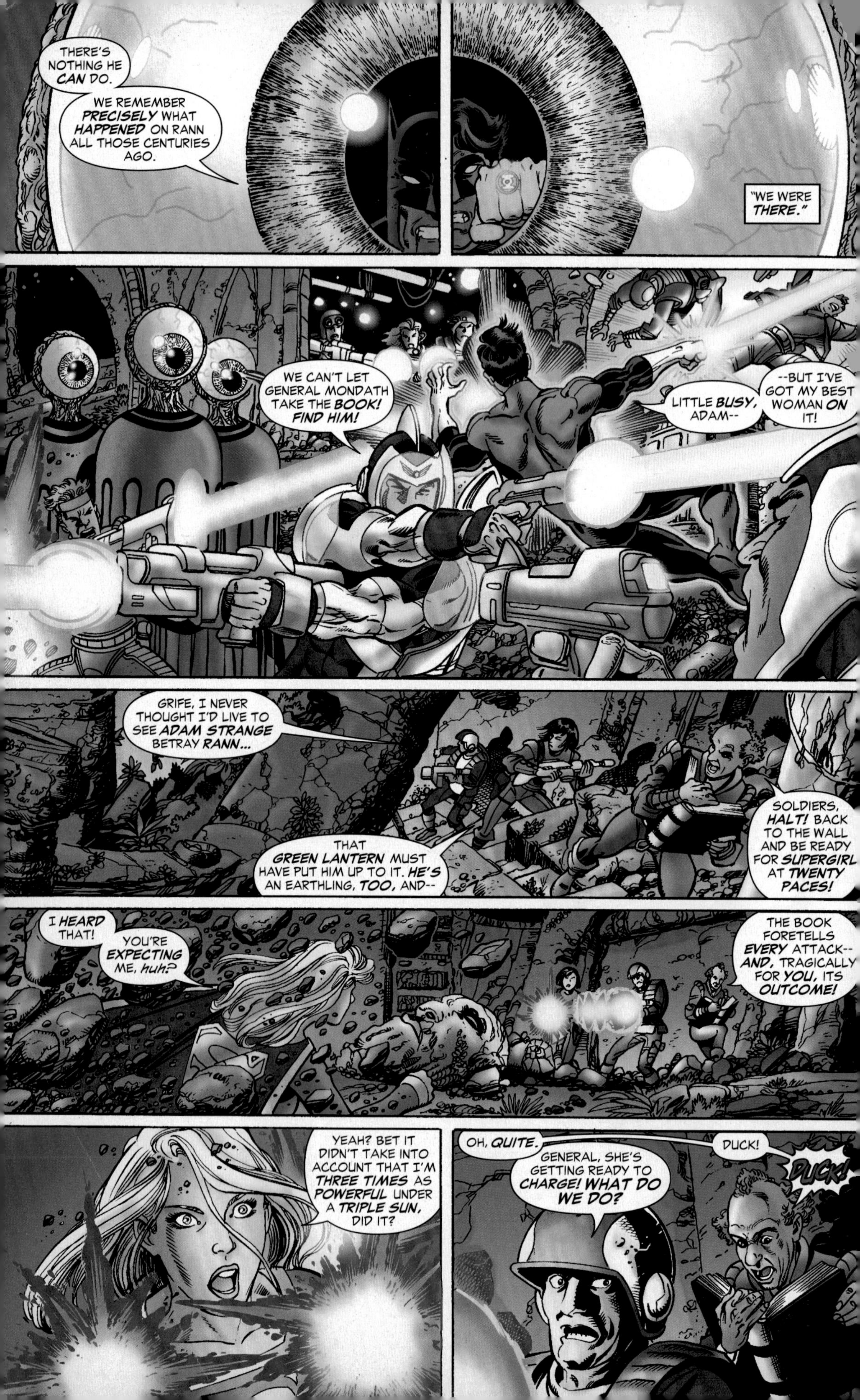
THERE'S NOTHING HE CAN DO.
WE REMEMBER PRECISELY WHAT HAPPENED ON RANN ALL THOSE CENTURIES AGO.
"WE WERE THERE."
WE CAN'T LET GENERAL MONDATH TAKE THE BOOK! FIND HIM!
LITTLE BUSY, ADAM--
--BUT I'VE GOT MY BEST WOMAN ON IT!
GRIFE, I NEVER THOUGHT I'D LIVE TO SEE ADAM STRANGE BETRAY RANN...
THAT GREEN LANTERN MUST HAVE PUT HIM UP TO IT. HE'S AN EARTHLING, TOO, AND--
SOLDIERS, HALT! BACK TO THE WALL AND BE READY FOR SUPERGIRL AT TWENTY PACES!
I HEARD THAT!
YOU'RE EXPECTING ME, huh?
THE BOOK FORETELLS EVERY ATTACK--AND, TRAGICALLY FOR YOU, ITS OUTCOME!
YEAH? BET IT DIDN'T TAKE INTO ACCOUNT THAT I'M THREE TIMES AS POWERFUL UNDER A TRIPLE SUN, DID IT?
OH, QUITE.
GENERAL, SHE'S GETTING READY TO CHARGE! WHAT DO WE DO?
DUCK!
DUCK!

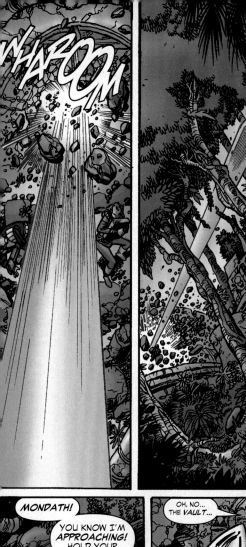

WHAROOM

SHE CAN'T HANDLE
THE OVERLOAD. THAT'S
TO OUR ADVANTAGE.

THROUGH THERE,
YOU'LL FIND "FORBIDDEN"
WEAPONS WE'VE CONFISCATED
FROM VARIOUS INVADERS.
GET THEM. HURRY.

THE SO-CALLED
"THINKING MAN" IS
ON OUR TRAIL.

OH, NO...
THE VAULT...

MONDATH!

YOU KNOW I'M
APPROACHING!
HOLD YOUR
FIRE!

WE BOTH
WANT THE SAME
THING--PEACE ON
RANN! WE CAN
NEGOTIATE!

DIE,
TRAITOR!

...THE
AQUA-RAY...

I'M...
NOT...A...

AND PEOPLE SAY YOU'RE ALL *WASHED UP*...

DOES THAT POWER RING WORK ONLY WHEN YOU'RE *TALKING*? BECAUSE *THAT'S* NEW.

OUR SITUATION ISN'T *IMPROVING*.

WE'RE SURROUNDED BY *MULTIPLE-MENACE* RIFLES.

WHICH DO--?

MANY THINGS, NONE *GOOD*.

OPEN FIRE!

WAIT! MONDATH, WE ARE *NOT* THE ENEMY!

EVEN *I'VE* HEARD OF THE *LUCK LORDS*! WHATEVER THEY *WANT*, THEY'RE PLAYING *YOU* TO *GET* IT!

LIES!

THEY'VE ENTRUSTED ME WITH THE ABILITY TO BE RANN'S *GREATEST* CHAMPION!

NOT *YOU*, YOU EVOLUTIONARY ALIEN *THROWBACK*! *ME*!

WHAT'S *WRONG*, STRANGE?

ASHAMED YOU'RE NO LONGER THE SMARTEST MAN IN THE *ROOM*?

WARNING: AMBUSH ENACTED.

FIRE!

CEASE FIRE!

MISSION *ACCOMPLISHED*. THEY'RE *DEAD*.

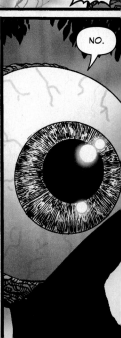

NO.

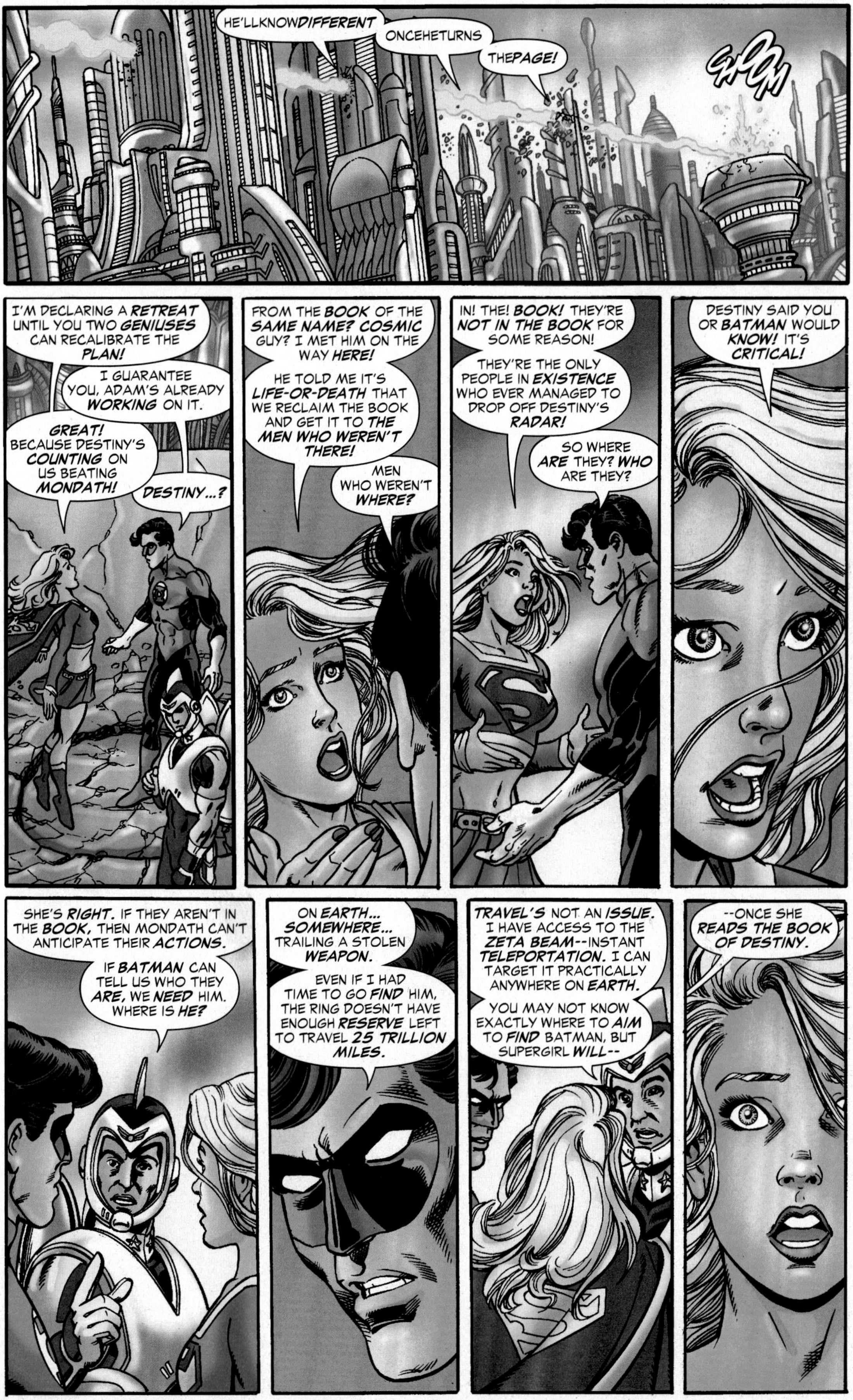

HE'LLKNOWDIFFERENT
ONCEHETURNS
THEPAGE!
SHOOM
I'M DECLARING A RETREAT UNTIL YOU TWO GENIUSES CAN RECALIBRATE THE PLAN!
I GUARANTEE YOU, ADAM'S ALREADY WORKING ON IT.
GREAT! BECAUSE DESTINY'S COUNTING ON US BEATING MONDATH!
DESTINY...?
FROM THE BOOK OF THE SAME NAME? COSMIC GUY? I MET HIM ON THE WAY HERE!
HE TOLD ME IT'S LIFE-OR-DEATH THAT WE RECLAIM THE BOOK AND GET IT TO THE MEN WHO WEREN'T THERE!
MEN WHO WEREN'T WHERE?
IN! THE! BOOK! THEY'RE NOT IN THE BOOK FOR SOME REASON!
THEY'RE THE ONLY PEOPLE IN EXISTENCE WHO EVER MANAGED TO DROP OFF DESTINY'S RADAR!
SO WHERE ARE THEY? WHO ARE THEY?
DESTINY SAID YOU OR BATMAN WOULD KNOW! IT'S CRITICAL!
SHE'S RIGHT. IF THEY AREN'T IN THE BOOK, THEN MONDATH CAN'T ANTICIPATE THEIR ACTIONS.
IF BATMAN CAN TELL US WHO THEY ARE, WE NEED HIM. WHERE IS HE?
ON EARTH... SOMEWHERE... TRAILING A STOLEN WEAPON.
EVEN IF I HAD TIME TO GO FIND HIM, THE RING DOESN'T HAVE ENOUGH RESERVE LEFT TO TRAVEL 25 TRILLION MILES.
TRAVEL'S NOT AN ISSUE. I HAVE ACCESS TO THE ZETA BEAM--INSTANT TELEPORTATION. I CAN TARGET IT PRACTICALLY ANYWHERE ON EARTH.
YOU MAY NOT KNOW EXACTLY WHERE TO AIM TO FIND BATMAN, BUT SUPERGIRL WILL--
--ONCE SHE READS THE BOOK OF DESTINY.

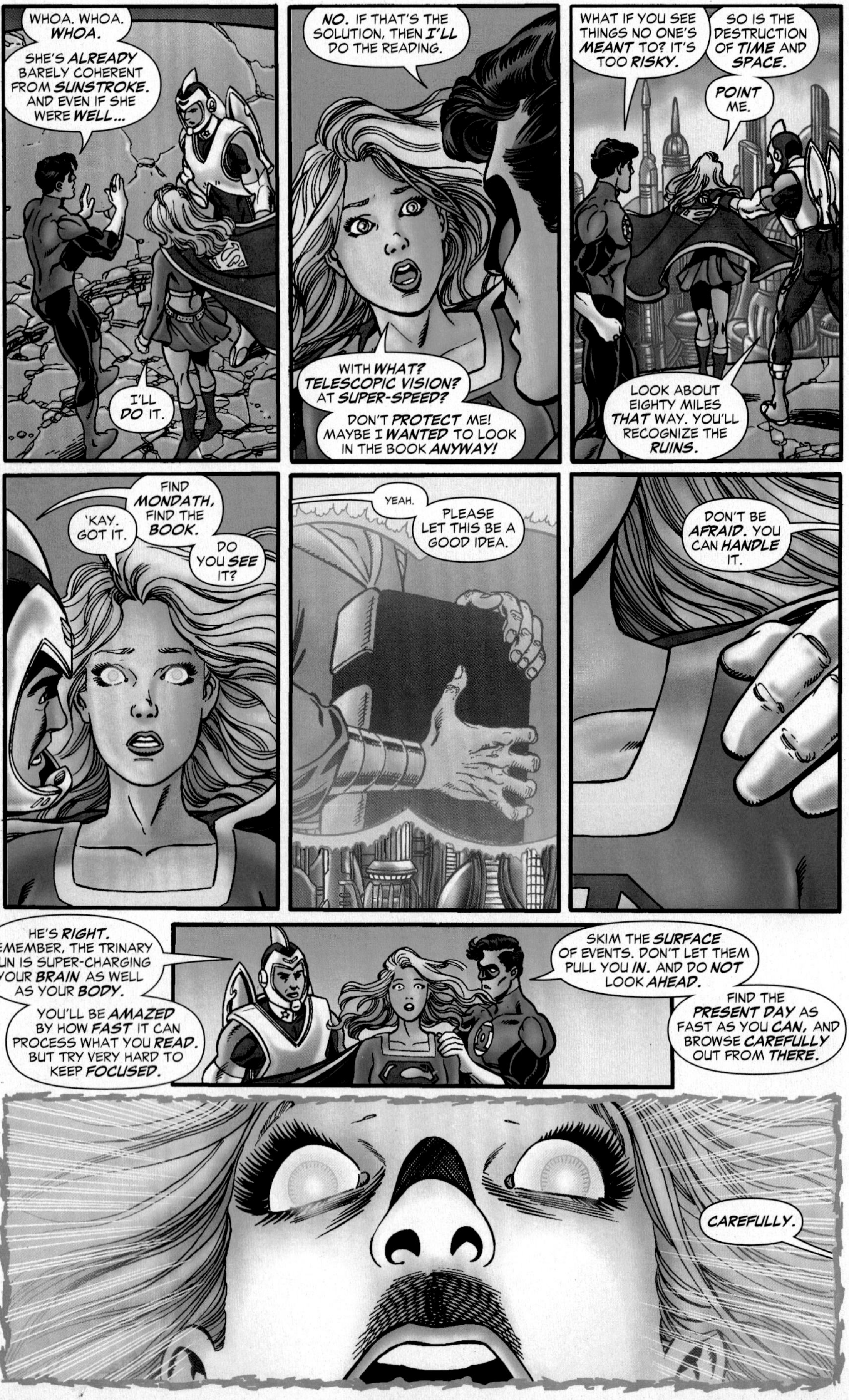
WHOA. WHOA. WHOA.
SHE'S ALREADY BARELY COHERENT FROM SUNSTROKE. AND EVEN IF SHE WERE WELL...
I'LL DO IT.
NO. IF THAT'S THE SOLUTION, THEN I'LL DO THE READING.
WITH WHAT? TELESCOPIC VISION? AT SUPER-SPEED?
DON'T PROTECT ME! MAYBE I WANTED TO LOOK IN THE BOOK ANYWAY!
WHAT IF YOU SEE THINGS NO ONE'S MEANT TO? IT'S TOO RISKY.
SO IS THE DESTRUCTION OF TIME AND SPACE.
POINT ME.
LOOK ABOUT EIGHTY MILES THAT WAY. YOU'LL RECOGNIZE THE RUINS.
FIND MONDATH, FIND THE BOOK.
'KAY. GOT IT.
DO YOU SEE IT?
YEAH.
PLEASE LET THIS BE A GOOD IDEA.
DON'T BE AFRAID. YOU CAN HANDLE IT.
HE'S RIGHT. REMEMBER, THE TRINARY SUN IS SUPER-CHARGING YOUR BRAIN AS WELL AS YOUR BODY.
YOU'LL BE AMAZED BY HOW FAST IT CAN PROCESS WHAT YOU READ. BUT TRY VERY HARD TO KEEP FOCUSED.
SKIM THE SURFACE OF EVENTS. DON'T LET THEM PULL YOU IN. AND DO NOT LOOK AHEAD.
FIND THE PRESENT DAY AS FAST AS YOU CAN, AND BROWSE CAREFULLY OUT FROM THERE.
CAREFULLY.

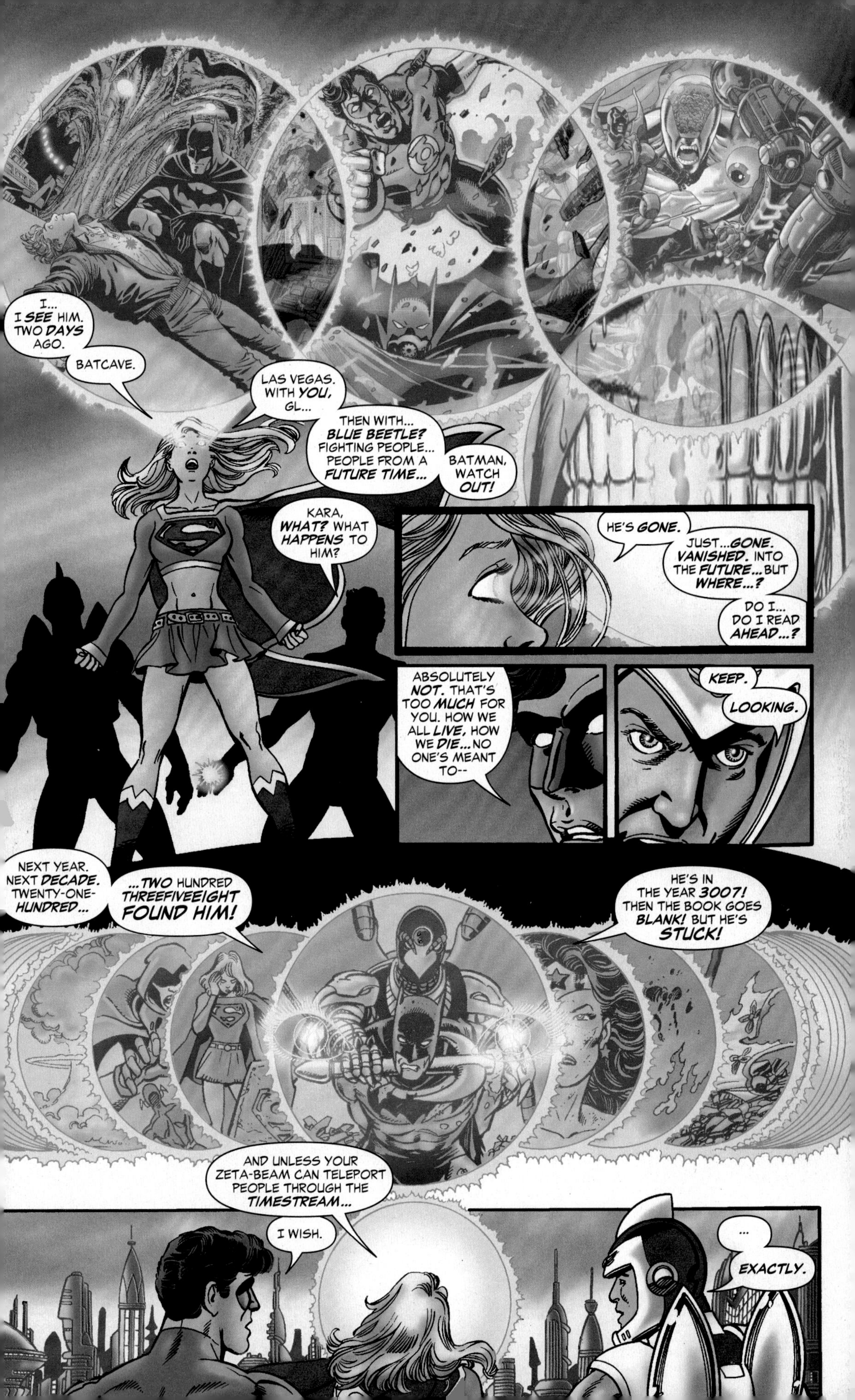
I...
I SEE HIM. TWO DAYS AGO.
BATCAVE.
LAS VEGAS. WITH YOU, GL...
THEN WITH... BLUE BEETLE? FIGHTING PEOPLE... PEOPLE FROM A FUTURE TIME...
BATMAN, WATCH OUT!
KARA, WHAT? WHAT HAPPENS TO HIM?
HE'S GONE.
JUST...GONE. VANISHED. INTO THE FUTURE...BUT WHERE...?
DO I... DO I READ AHEAD...?
ABSOLUTELY NOT. THAT'S TOO MUCH FOR YOU. HOW WE ALL LIVE, HOW WE DIE...NO ONE'S MEANT TO--
KEEP.
LOOKING.
NEXT YEAR. NEXT DECADE. TWENTY-ONE-HUNDRED...
...TWO HUNDRED THREEFIVEEIGHT FOUND HIM!
HE'S IN THE YEAR 3007! THEN THE BOOK GOES BLANK! BUT HE'S STUCK!
AND UNLESS YOUR ZETA-BEAM CAN TELEPORT PEOPLE THROUGH THE TIMESTREAM...
I WISH.
...
EXACTLY.

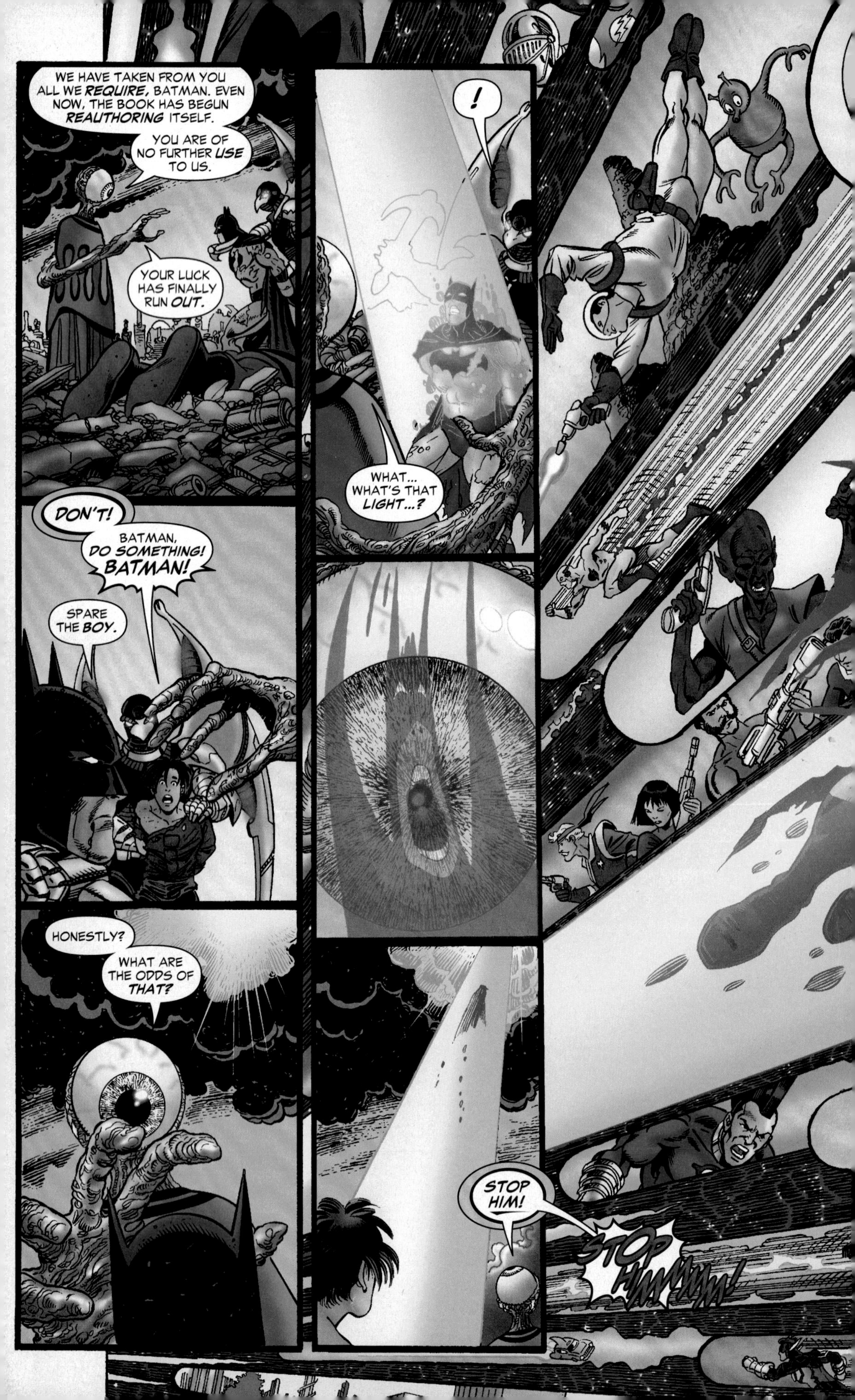
WE HAVE TAKEN FROM YOU ALL WE REQUIRE, BATMAN. EVEN NOW, THE BOOK HAS BEGUN REAUTHORING ITSELF.
YOU ARE OF NO FURTHER USE TO US.
YOUR LUCK HAS FINALLY RUN OUT.
!
WHAT... WHAT'S THAT LIGHT...?
DON'T!
BATMAN, DO SOMETHING! BATMAN!
SPARE THE BOY.
HONESTLY?
WHAT ARE THE ODDS OF THAT?
STOP HIM!
STOP HIMMMM!

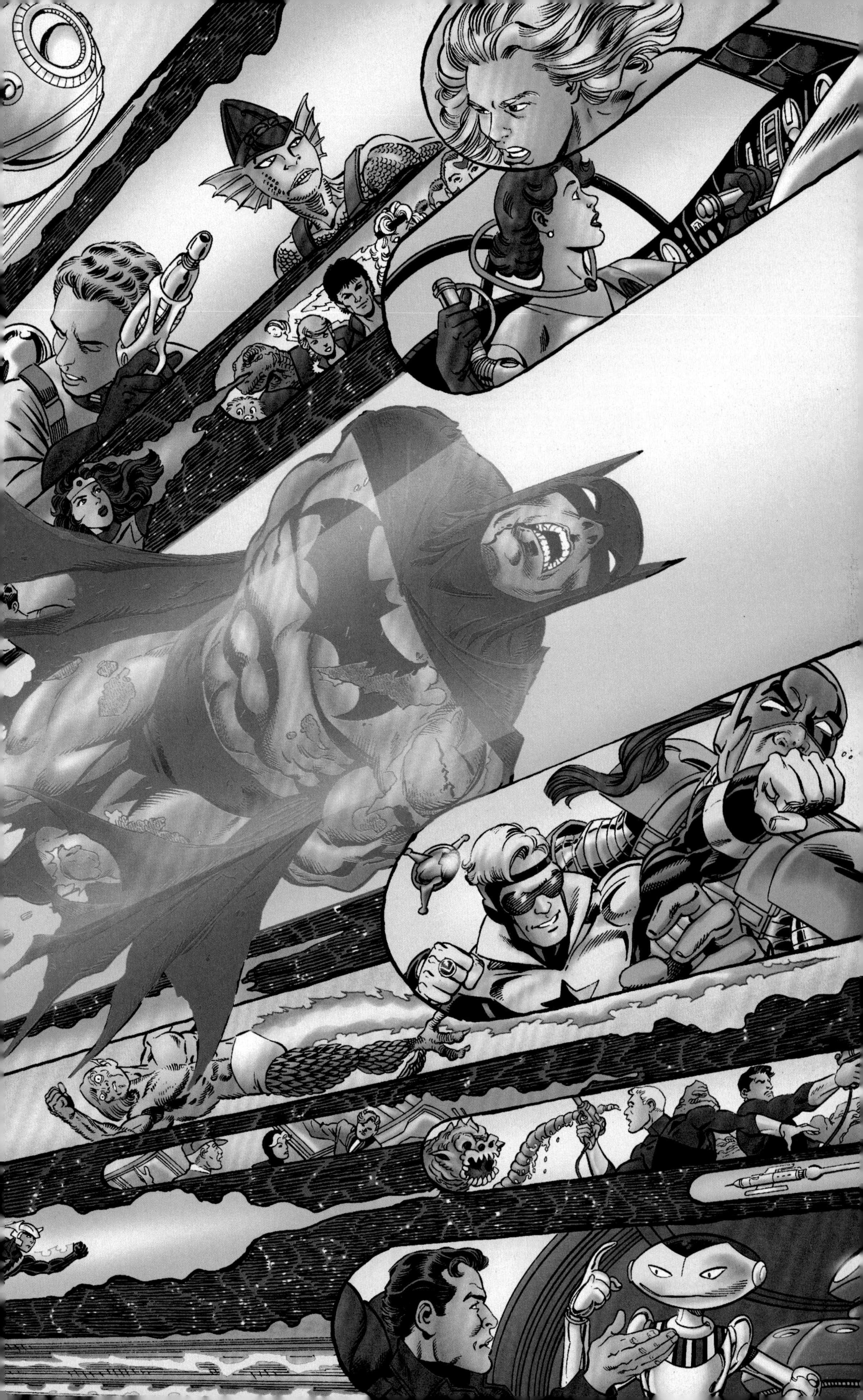

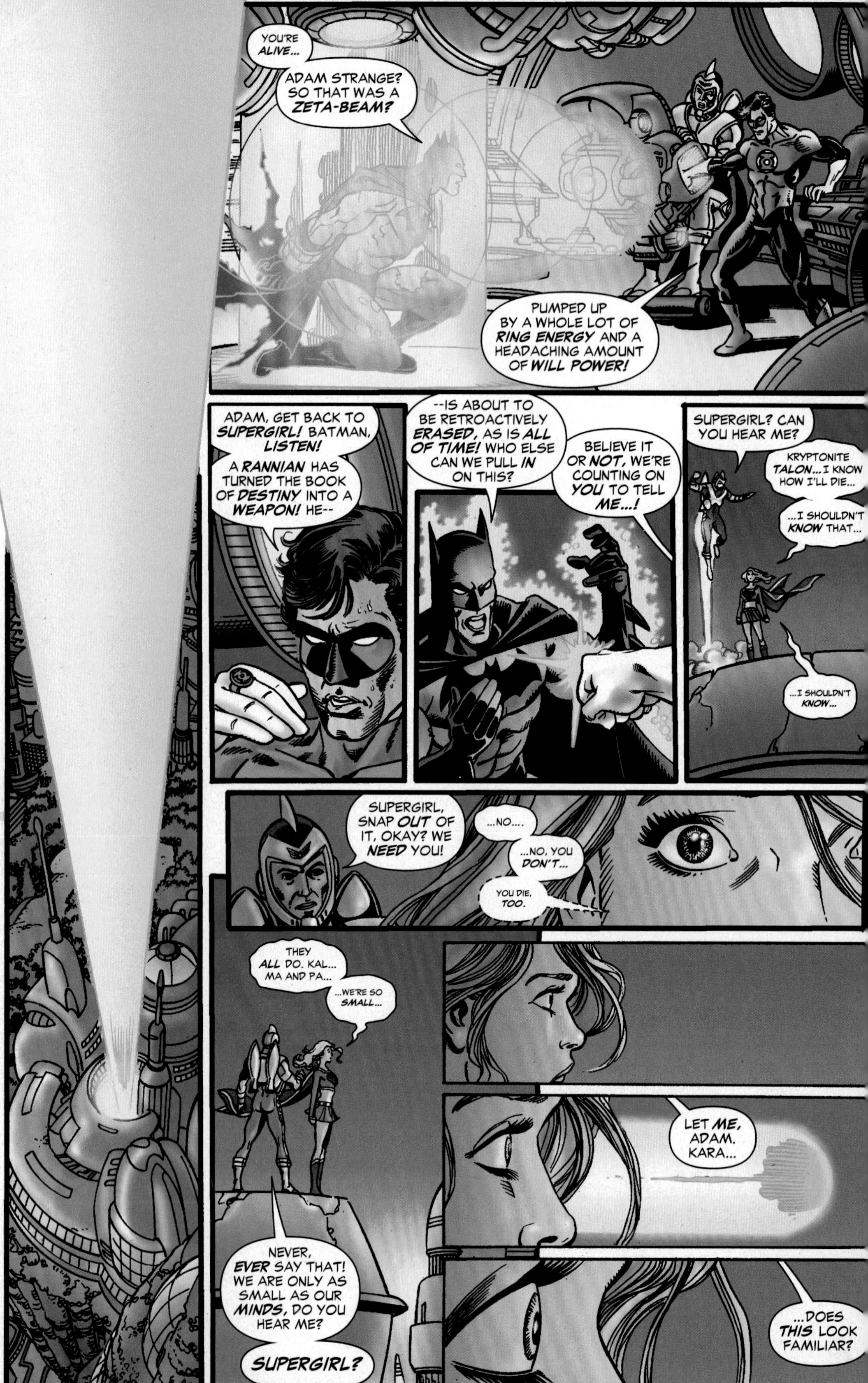

YOU'RE ALIVE...
ADAM STRANGE? SO THAT WAS A ZETA-BEAM?
PUMPED UP BY A WHOLE LOT OF RING ENERGY AND A HEADACHING AMOUNT OF WILL POWER!
ADAM, GET BACK TO SUPERGIRL! BATMAN, LISTEN!
A RANNIAN HAS TURNED THE BOOK OF DESTINY INTO A WEAPON! HE--
--IS ABOUT TO BE RETROACTIVELY ERASED, AS IS ALL OF TIME! WHO ELSE CAN WE PULL IN ON THIS?
BELIEVE IT OR NOT, WE'RE COUNTING ON YOU TO TELL ME...!
SUPERGIRL? CAN YOU HEAR ME?
KRYPTONITE TALON... I KNOW HOW I'LL DIE...
...I SHOULDN'T KNOW THAT...
...I SHOULDN'T KNOW...
SUPERGIRL, SNAP OUT OF IT, OKAY? WE NEED YOU!
...NO....
...NO, YOU DON'T...
YOU DIE, TOO.
THEY ALL DO. KAL... MA AND PA...
...WE'RE SO SMALL...
NEVER, EVER SAY THAT! WE ARE ONLY AS SMALL AS OUR MINDS, DO YOU HEAR ME?
SUPERGIRL?
LET ME, ADAM. KARA...
...DOES THIS LOOK FAMILIAR?

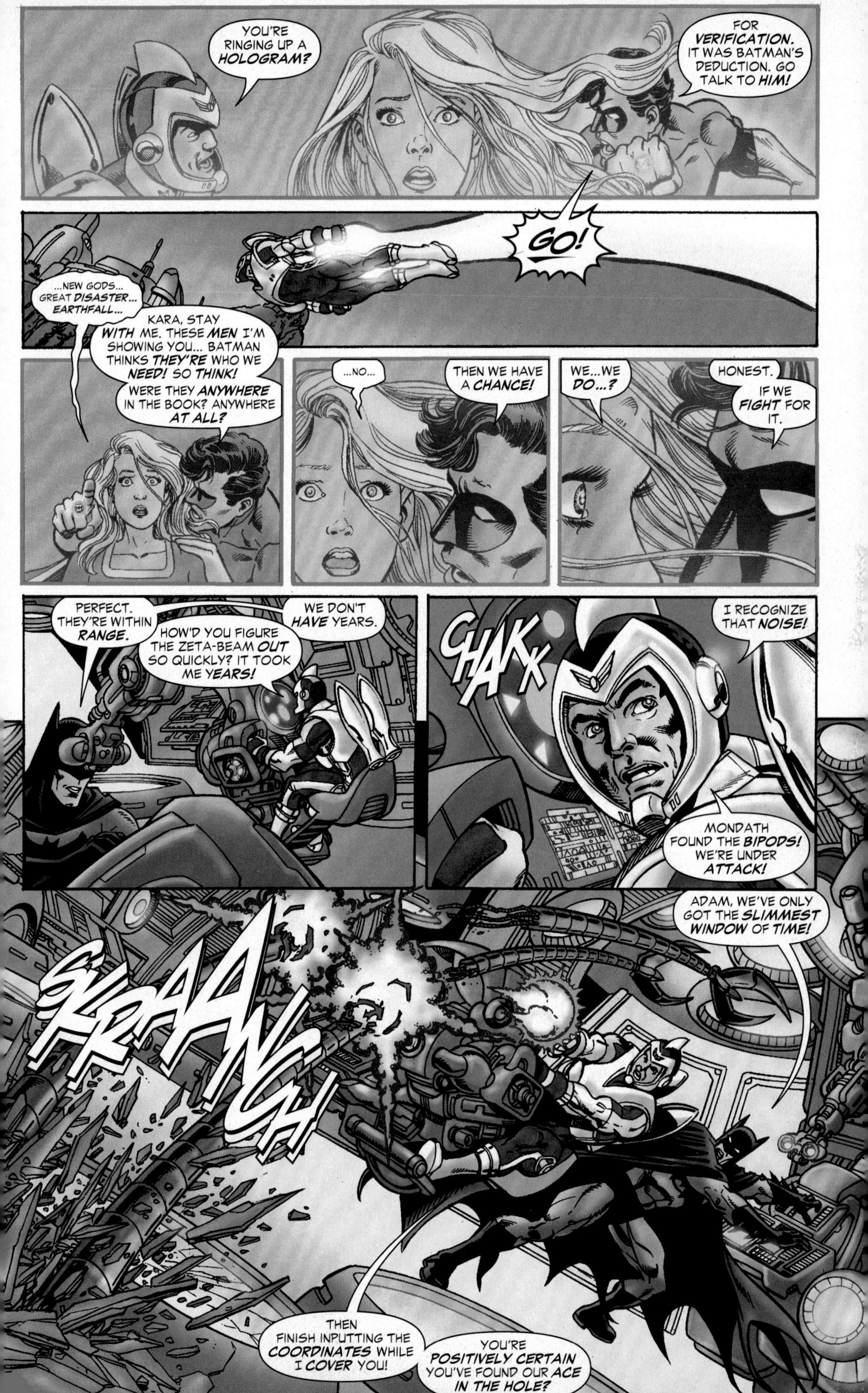
YOU'RE RINGING UP A HOLOGRAM?
FOR VERIFICATION. IT WAS BATMAN'S DEDUCTION. GO TALK TO HIM!
GO!
...NEW GODS... GREAT DISASTER... EARTHFALL...
KARA, STAY WITH ME. THESE MEN I'M SHOWING YOU... BATMAN THINKS THEY'RE WHO WE NEED! SO THINK!
WERE THEY ANYWHERE IN THE BOOK? ANYWHERE AT ALL?
...NO...
THEN WE HAVE A CHANCE!
WE...WE DO...?
HONEST.
IF WE FIGHT FOR IT.
PERFECT. THEY'RE WITHIN RANGE.
HOW'D YOU FIGURE THE ZETA-BEAM OUT SO QUICKLY? IT TOOK ME YEARS!
WE DON'T HAVE YEARS.
CHAKK
I RECOGNIZE THAT NOISE!
MONDATH FOUND THE BIPODS! WE'RE UNDER ATTACK!
SKRAANCH
ADAM, WE'VE ONLY GOT THE SLIMMEST WINDOW OF TIME!
THEN FINISH INPUTTING THE COORDINATES WHILE I COVER YOU!
YOU'RE POSITIVELY CERTAIN YOU'VE FOUND OUR ACE IN THE HOLE?

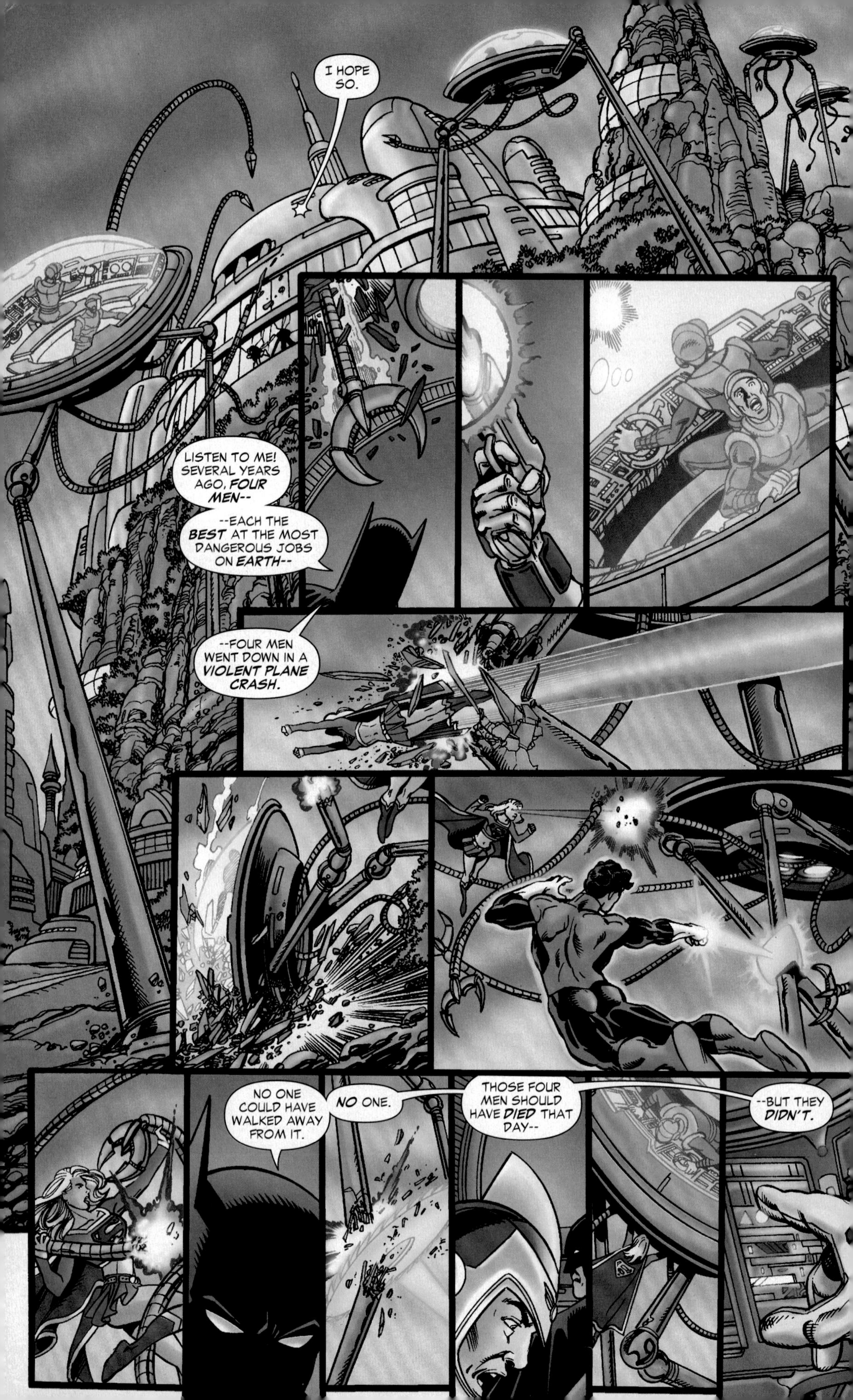
I HOPE SO.
LISTEN TO ME! SEVERAL YEARS AGO, FOUR MEN--
--EACH THE BEST AT THE MOST DANGEROUS JOBS ON EARTH--
--FOUR MEN WENT DOWN IN A VIOLENT PLANE CRASH.
NO ONE COULD HAVE WALKED AWAY FROM IT.
NO ONE.
THOSE FOUR MEN SHOULD HAVE DIED THAT DAY--
--BUT THEY DIDN'T.

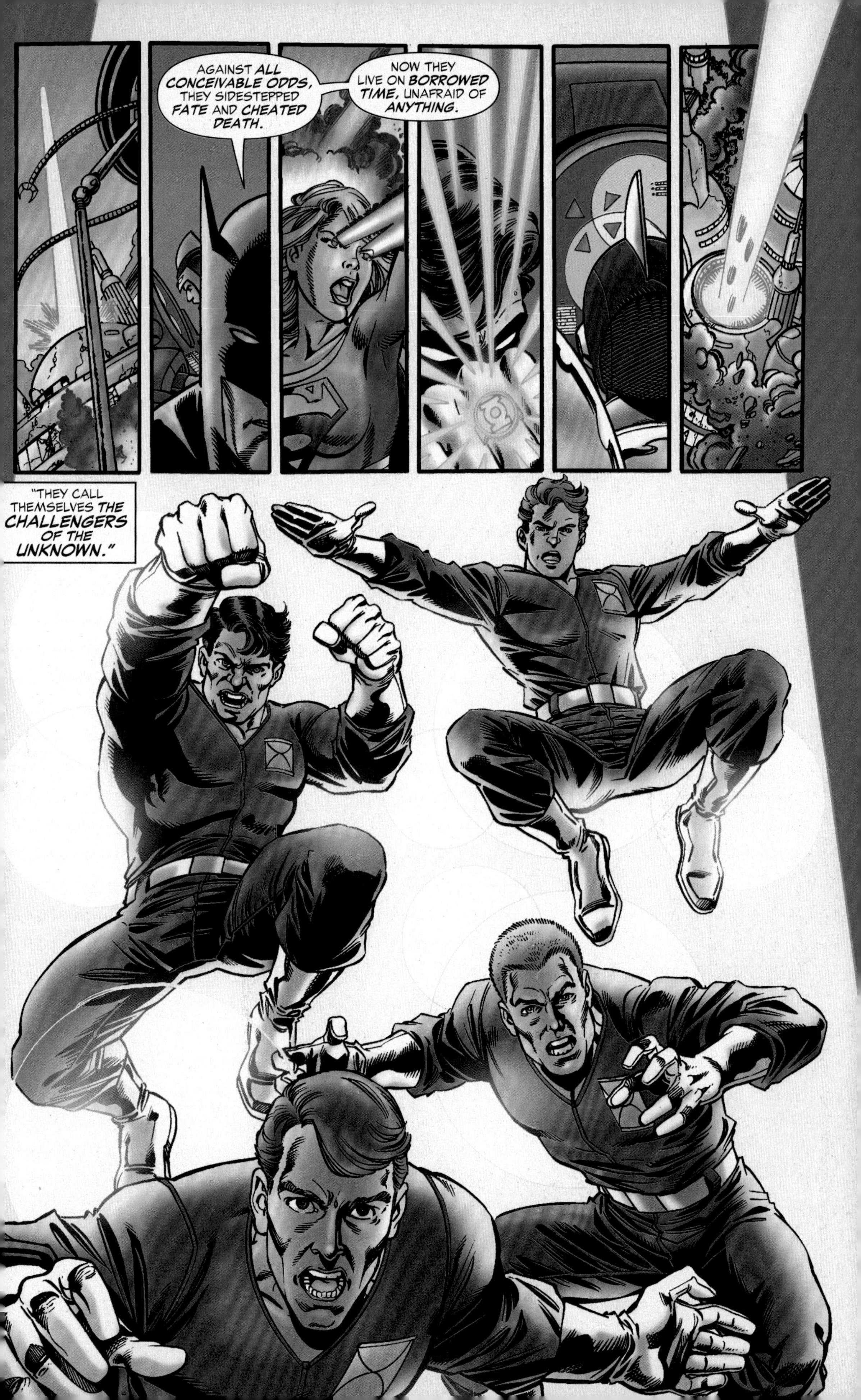
AGAINST ALL CONCEIVABLE ODDS, THEY SIDESTEPPED FATE AND CHEATED DEATH.
NOW THEY LIVE ON BORROWED TIME, UNAFRAID OF ANYTHING.
"THEY CALL THEMSELVES THE CHALLENGERS OF THE UNKNOWN."

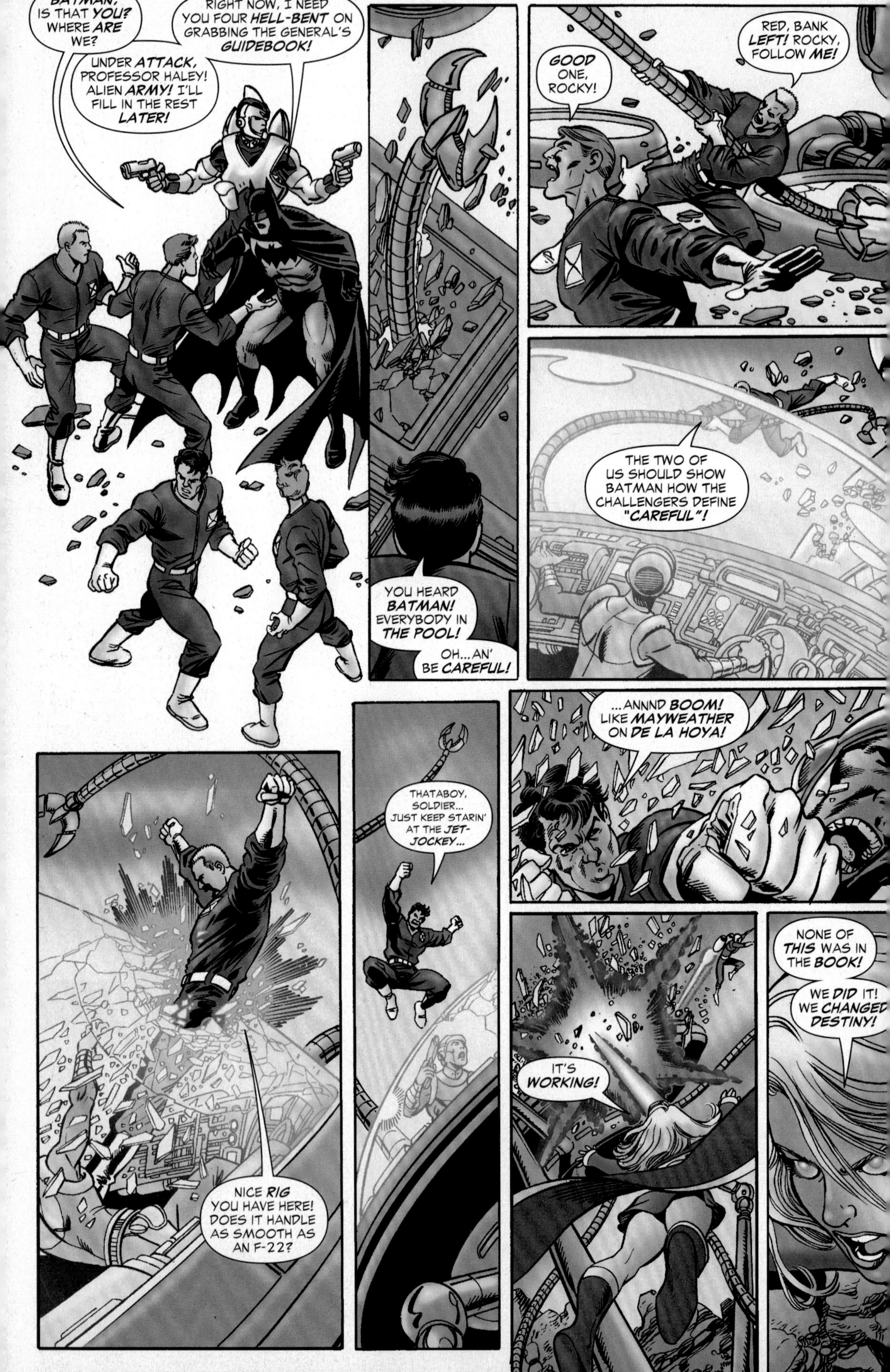

BATMAN, IS THAT YOU? WHERE ARE WE?
UNDER ATTACK, PROFESSOR HALEY! ALIEN ARMY! I'LL FILL IN THE REST LATER!
RIGHT NOW, I NEED YOU FOUR HELL-BENT ON GRABBING THE GENERAL'S GUIDEBOOK!
YOU HEARD BATMAN! EVERYBODY IN THE POOL!
OH...AN' BE CAREFUL!
GOOD ONE, ROCKY!
RED, BANK LEFT! ROCKY, FOLLOW ME!
THE TWO OF US SHOULD SHOW BATMAN HOW THE CHALLENGERS DEFINE "CAREFUL"!
NICE RIG YOU HAVE HERE! DOES IT HANDLE AS SMOOTH AS AN F-22?
THATABOY, SOLDIER... JUST KEEP STARIN' AT THE JET-JOCKEY...
...ANNND BOOM! LIKE MAYWEATHER ON DE LA HOYA!
IT'S WORKING!
NONE OF THIS WAS IN THE BOOK!
WE DID IT! WE CHANGED DESTINY!

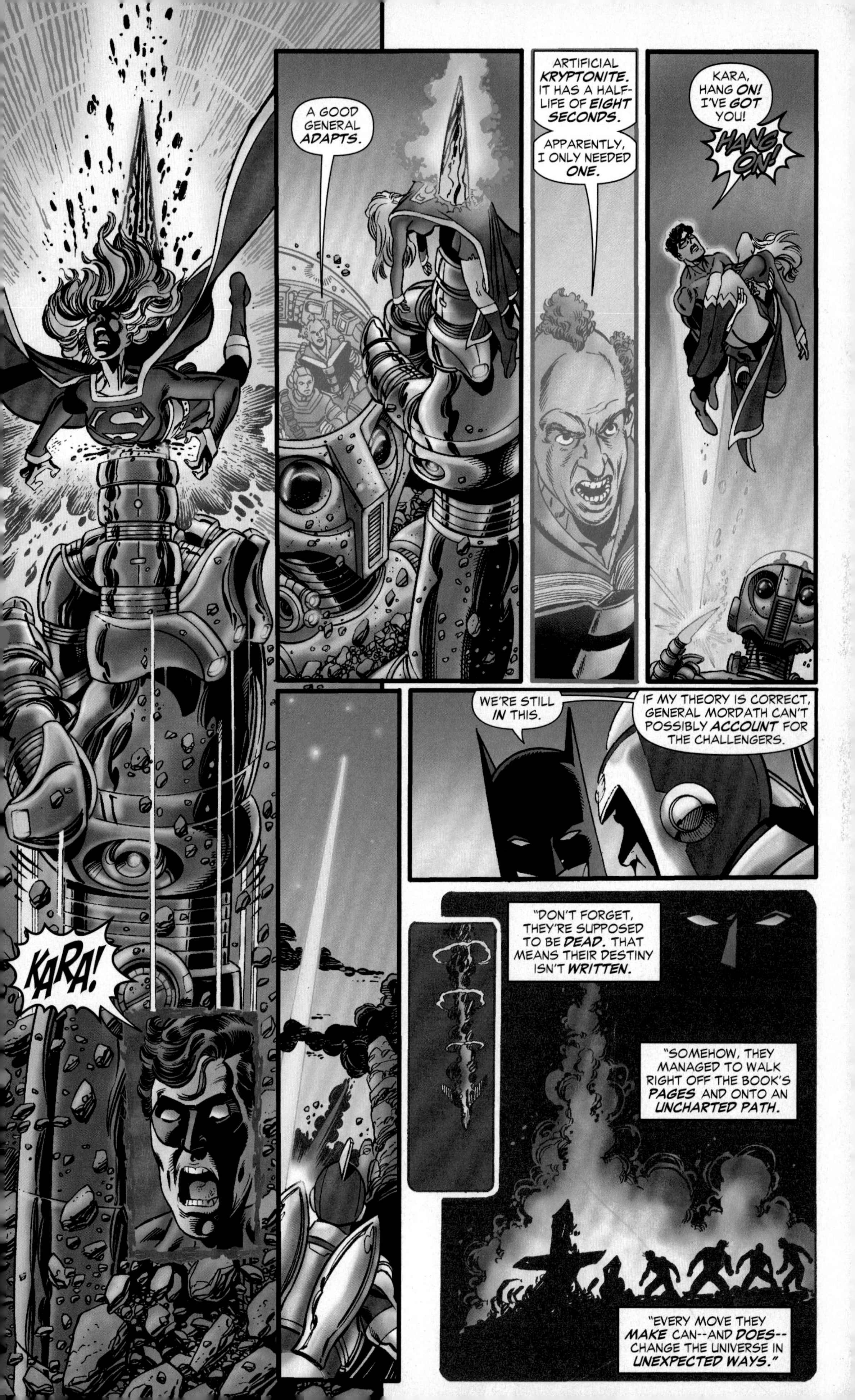

A GOOD GENERAL ADAPTS.
ARTIFICIAL KRYPTONITE. IT HAS A HALF-LIFE OF EIGHT SECONDS.
APPARENTLY, I ONLY NEEDED ONE.
KARA, HANG ON! I'VE GOT YOU!
HANG ON!
KARA!
WE'RE STILL IN THIS.
IF MY THEORY IS CORRECT, GENERAL MORDATH CAN'T POSSIBLY ACCOUNT FOR THE CHALLENGERS.
"DON'T FORGET, THEY'RE SUPPOSED TO BE DEAD. THAT MEANS THEIR DESTINY ISN'T WRITTEN.
"SOMEHOW, THEY MANAGED TO WALK RIGHT OFF THE BOOK'S PAGES AND ONTO AN UNCHARTED PATH.
"EVERY MOVE THEY MAKE CAN--AND DOES--CHANGE THE UNIVERSE IN UNEXPECTED WAYS."

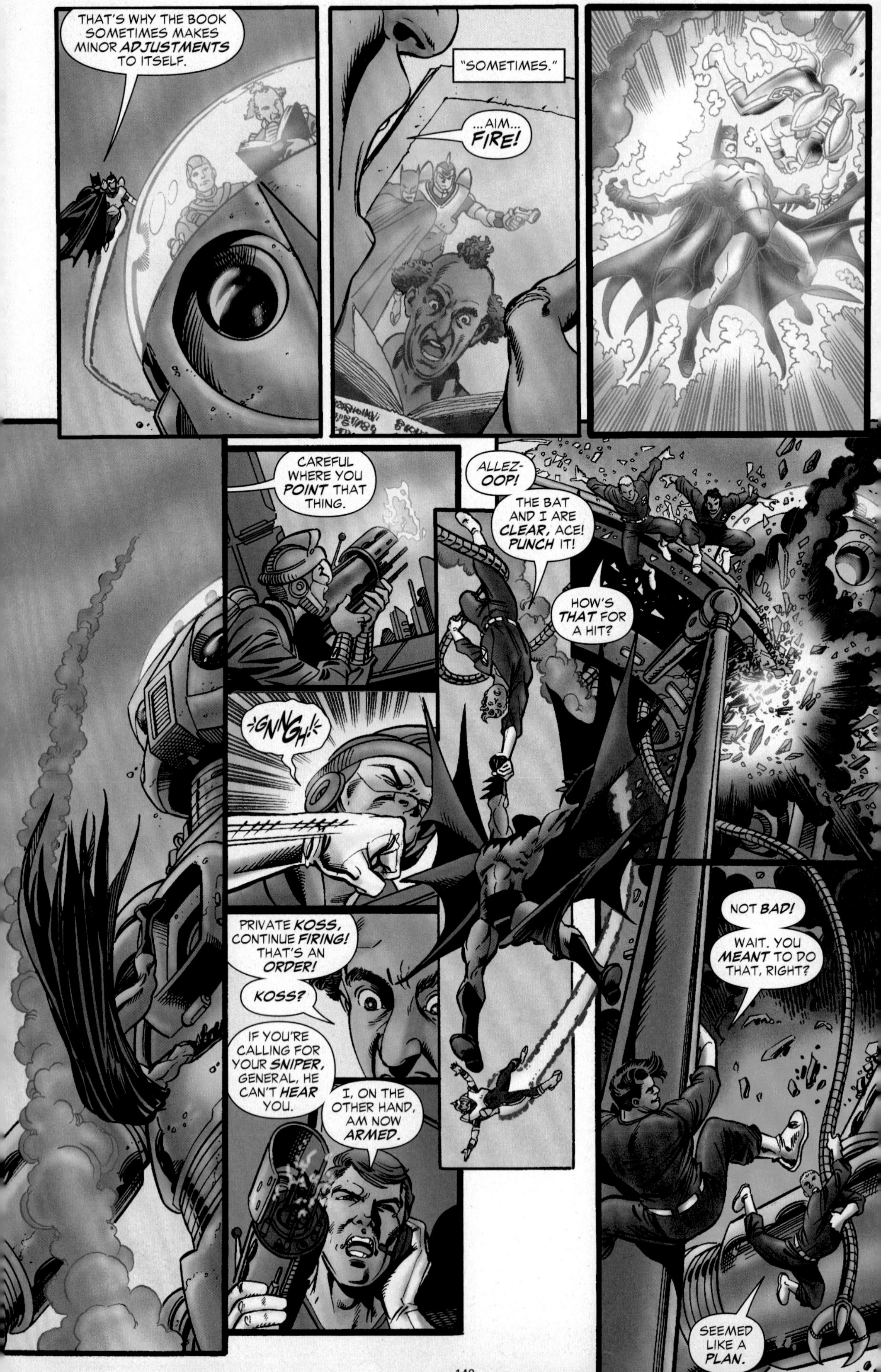
THAT'S WHY THE BOOK SOMETIMES MAKES MINOR ADJUSTMENTS TO ITSELF.
"SOMETIMES."
...AIM... FIRE!
CAREFUL WHERE YOU POINT THAT THING.
ALLEZ-OOP!
THE BAT AND I ARE CLEAR, ACE! PUNCH IT!
HOW'S THAT FOR A HIT?
GNNGH!
PRIVATE KOSS, CONTINUE FIRING! THAT'S AN ORDER!
KOSS?
IF YOU'RE CALLING FOR YOUR SNIPER, GENERAL, HE CAN'T HEAR YOU.
I, ON THE OTHER HAND, AM NOW ARMED.
NOT BAD!
WAIT. YOU MEANT TO DO THAT, RIGHT?
SEEMED LIKE A PLAN.

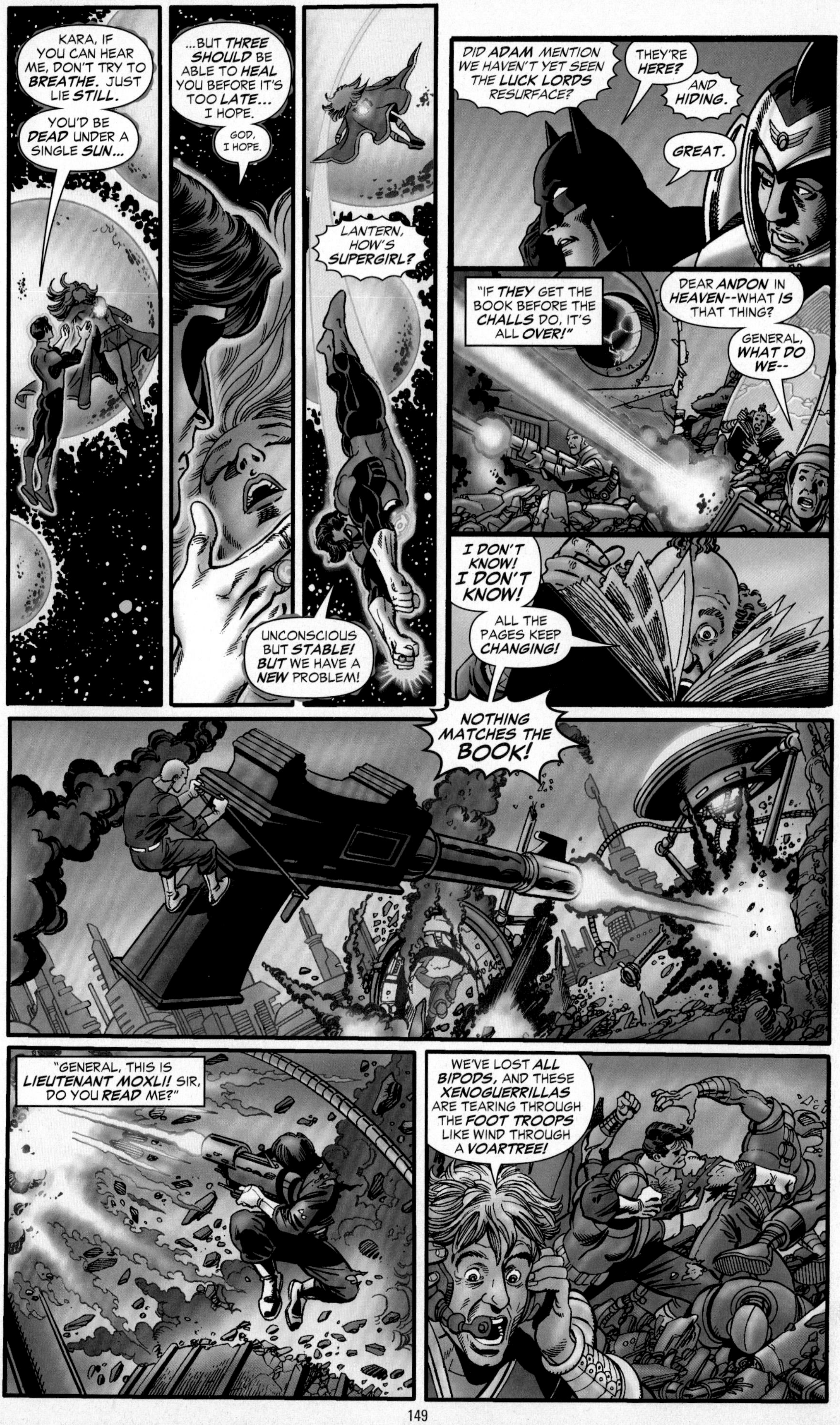

KARA, IF YOU CAN HEAR ME, DON'T TRY TO BREATHE. JUST LIE STILL.
YOU'D BE DEAD UNDER A SINGLE SUN...
...BUT THREE SHOULD BE ABLE TO HEAL YOU BEFORE IT'S TOO LATE... I HOPE.
GOD, I HOPE.
LANTERN, HOW'S SUPERGIRL?
UNCONSCIOUS BUT STABLE! BUT WE HAVE A NEW PROBLEM!
DID ADAM MENTION WE HAVEN'T YET SEEN THE LUCK LORDS RESURFACE?
THEY'RE HERE?
AND HIDING.
GREAT.
"IF THEY GET THE BOOK BEFORE THE CHALLS DO, IT'S ALL OVER!"
DEAR ANDON IN HEAVEN--WHAT IS THAT THING?
GENERAL, WHAT DO WE--
I DON'T KNOW! I DON'T KNOW!
ALL THE PAGES KEEP CHANGING!
NOTHING MATCHES THE BOOK!
"GENERAL, THIS IS LIEUTENANT MOXLI! SIR, DO YOU READ ME?"
WE'VE LOST ALL BIPODS, AND THESE XENOGUERRILLAS ARE TEARING THROUGH THE FOOT TROOPS LIKE WIND THROUGH A VOARTREE!

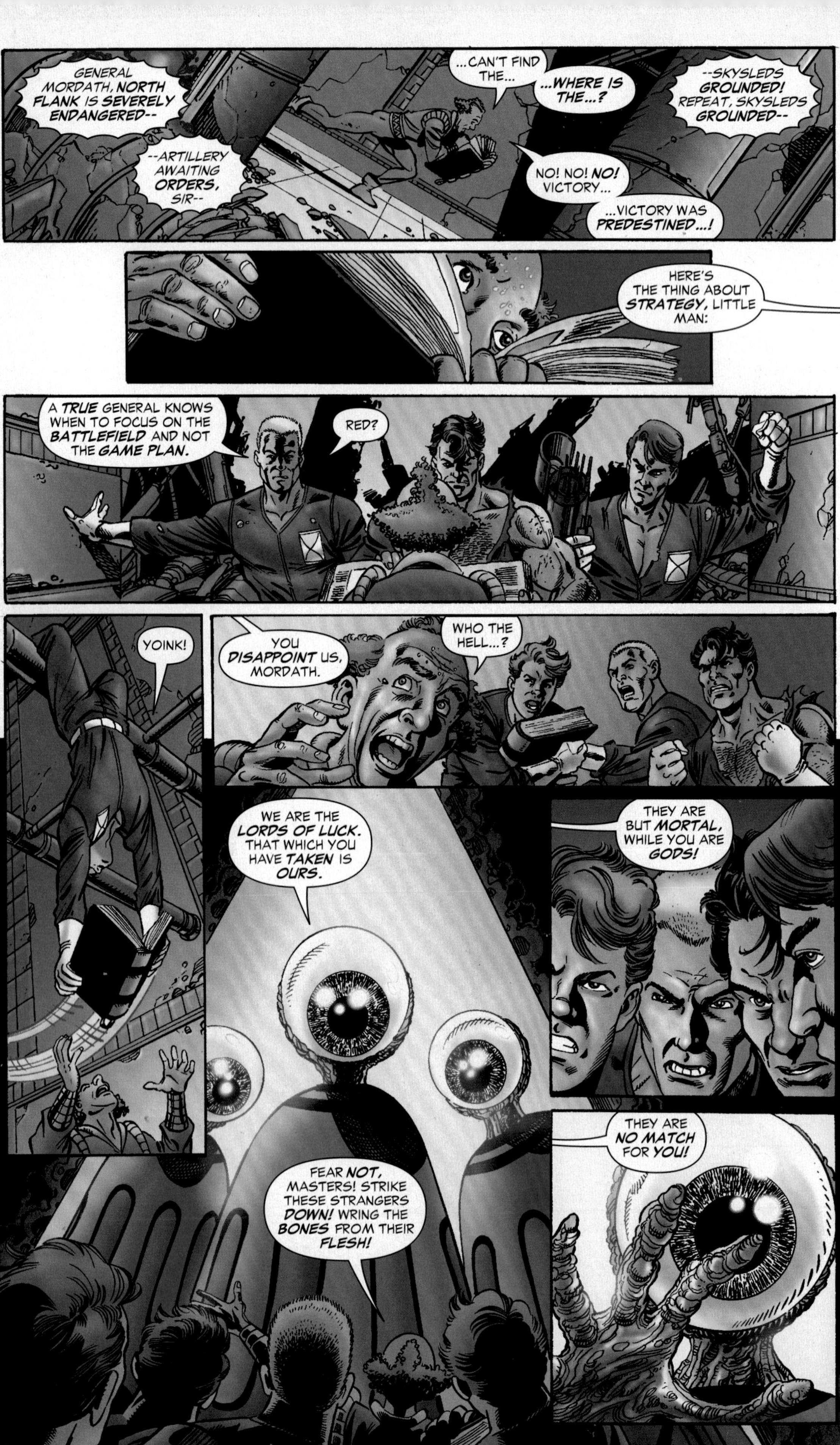
GENERAL MORDATH, NORTH FLANK IS SEVERELY ENDANGERED--
--ARTILLERY AWAITING ORDERS, SIR--
...CAN'T FIND THE...
...WHERE IS THE...?
--SKYSLEDS GROUNDED! REPEAT, SKYSLEDS GROUNDED--
NO! NO! NO! VICTORY...
...VICTORY WAS PREDESTINED...!
HERE'S THE THING ABOUT STRATEGY, LITTLE MAN:
A TRUE GENERAL KNOWS WHEN TO FOCUS ON THE BATTLEFIELD AND NOT THE GAME PLAN.
RED?
YOINK!
YOU DISAPPOINT US, MORDATH.
WHO THE HELL...?
WE ARE THE LORDS OF LUCK. THAT WHICH YOU HAVE TAKEN IS OURS.
THEY ARE BUT MORTAL, WHILE YOU ARE GODS!
THEY ARE NO MATCH FOR YOU!
FEAR NOT, MASTERS! STRIKE THESE STRANGERS DOWN! WRING THE BONES FROM THEIR FLESH!

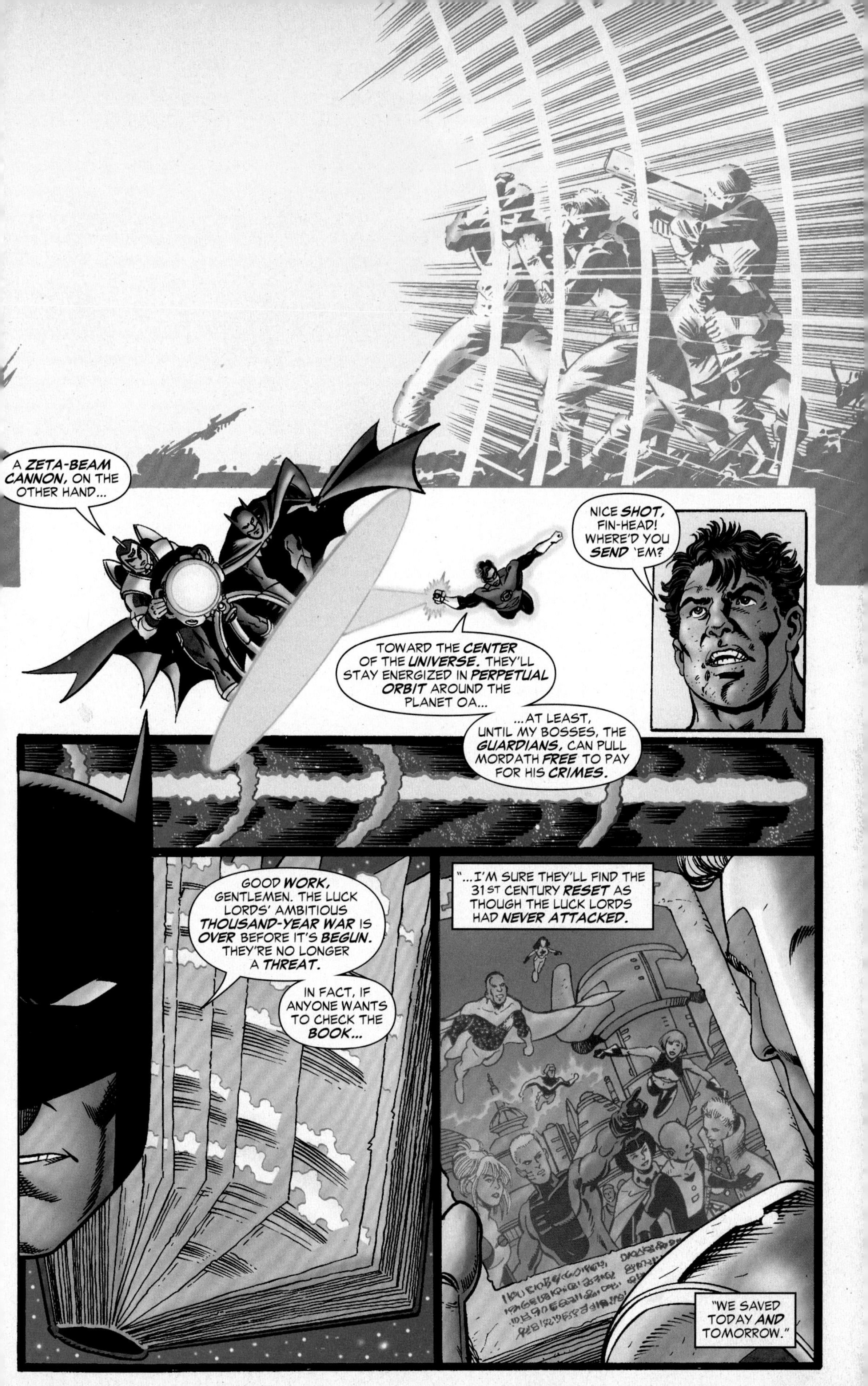
A ZETA-BEAM CANNON, ON THE OTHER HAND...
NICE SHOT, FIN-HEAD! WHERE'D YOU SEND 'EM?
TOWARD THE CENTER OF THE UNIVERSE. THEY'LL STAY ENERGIZED IN PERPETUAL ORBIT AROUND THE PLANET OA...
...AT LEAST, UNTIL MY BOSSES, THE GUARDIANS, CAN PULL MORDATH FREE TO PAY FOR HIS CRIMES.
GOOD WORK, GENTLEMEN. THE LUCK LORDS' AMBITIOUS THOUSAND-YEAR WAR IS OVER BEFORE IT'S BEGUN. THEY'RE NO LONGER A THREAT.
IN FACT, IF ANYONE WANTS TO CHECK THE BOOK...
"...I'M SURE THEY'LL FIND THE 31ST CENTURY RESET AS THOUGH THE LUCK LORDS HAD NEVER ATTACKED.
"WE SAVED TODAY AND TOMORROW."

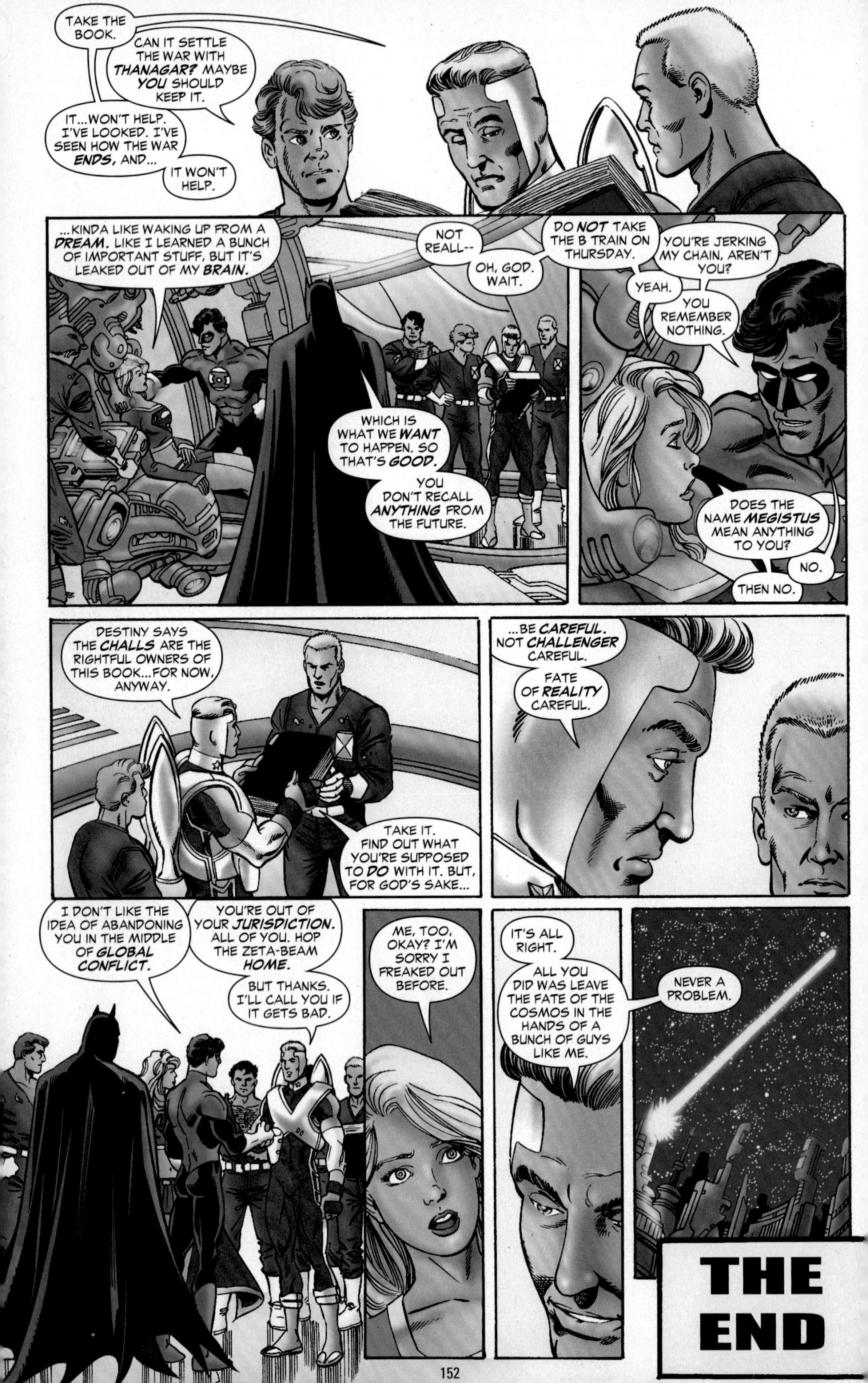

TAKE THE BOOK.
CAN IT SETTLE THE WAR WITH THANAGAR? MAYBE YOU SHOULD KEEP IT.
IT...WON'T HELP. I'VE LOOKED. I'VE SEEN HOW THE WAR ENDS, AND...
IT WON'T HELP.
...KINDA LIKE WAKING UP FROM A DREAM. LIKE I LEARNED A BUNCH OF IMPORTANT STUFF, BUT IT'S LEAKED OUT OF MY BRAIN.
NOT REALL--
OH, GOD. WAIT.
DO NOT TAKE THE B TRAIN ON THURSDAY.
WHICH IS WHAT WE WANT TO HAPPEN. SO THAT'S GOOD.
YOU DON'T RECALL ANYTHING FROM THE FUTURE.
YOU'RE JERKING MY CHAIN, AREN'T YOU?
YEAH.
YOU REMEMBER NOTHING.
DOES THE NAME MEGISTUS MEAN ANYTHING TO YOU?
NO.
THEN NO.
DESTINY SAYS THE CHALLS ARE THE RIGHTFUL OWNERS OF THIS BOOK...FOR NOW, ANYWAY.
TAKE IT. FIND OUT WHAT YOU'RE SUPPOSED TO DO WITH IT. BUT, FOR GOD'S SAKE...
...BE CAREFUL. NOT CHALLENGER CAREFUL.
FATE OF REALITY CAREFUL.
I DON'T LIKE THE IDEA OF ABANDONING YOU IN THE MIDDLE OF GLOBAL CONFLICT.
YOU'RE OUT OF YOUR JURISDICTION. ALL OF YOU. HOP THE ZETA-BEAM HOME.
BUT THANKS. I'LL CALL YOU IF IT GETS BAD.
ME, TOO, OKAY? I'M SORRY I FREAKED OUT BEFORE.
IT'S ALL RIGHT.
ALL YOU DID WAS LEAVE THE FATE OF THE COSMOS IN THE HANDS OF A BUNCH OF GUYS LIKE ME.
NEVER A PROBLEM.
THE END

MARK'S REMARKS

WRITER **MARK WAID** ANNOTATES *THE LORDS OF LUCK*

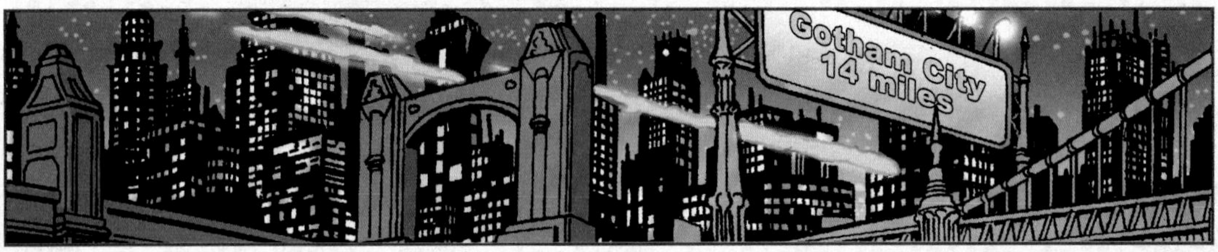
Gotham City
14 miles

Page 10: "Gotham City, 14 miles" was a tip of the hat to the 1960s *Batman* TV series, in which the Batmobile sped past that sign every week as it wheeled out of the Batcave. George misunderstood and put the sign way away from the cave, but it's still a fun in-joke, and not the first one we lifted from the days of Adam West (See also, "...turbines to speed").

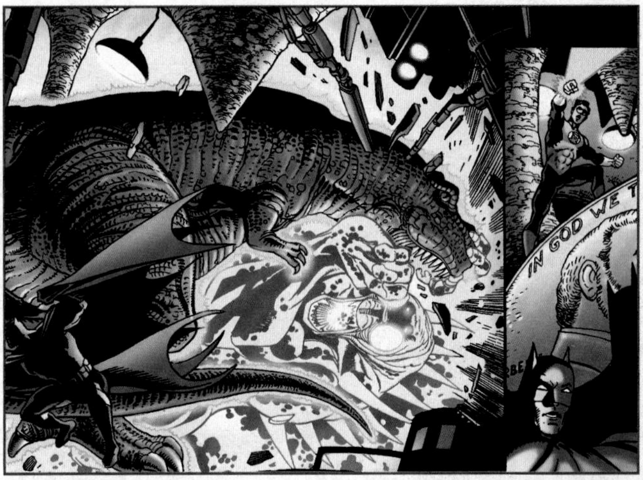

Pages 16-19: The dinosaur and the giant penny are, of course, mainstay trophies of the Batcave and have been since the 1940s. That always seemed like Robin's idea more than Batman's to me.

Pages 21-22: Only after receiving the plot to this issue did George confess to me that he's never played blackjack and had no idea how the game went. I pretended to be appalled at his lack of savoir faire, but in reality I was just grateful he hasn't lost as much at the tables over the years as I have.

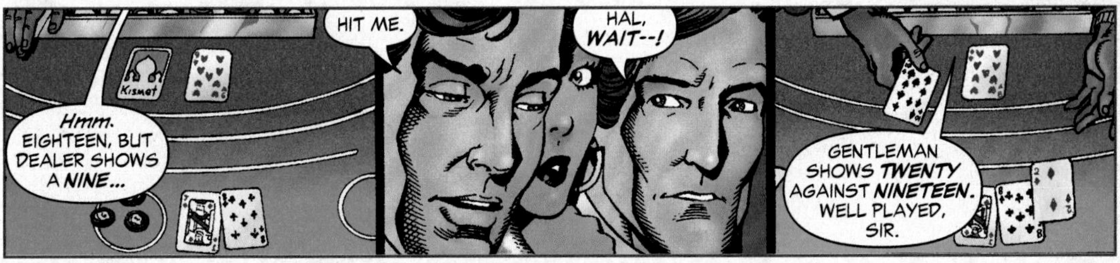
Kismet
Hmm. EIGHTEEN, BUT DEALER SHOWS A *NINE...*
HIT ME.
HAL, *WAIT--!*
GENTLEMAN SHOWS *TWENTY* AGAINST *NINETEEN.* WELL PLAYED, SIR.

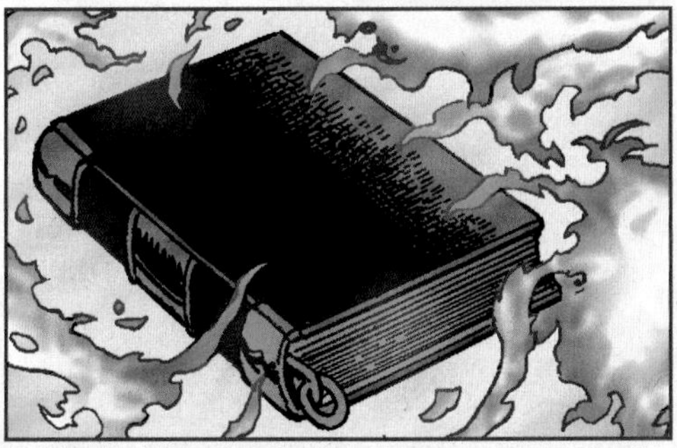

Page 24: The Book of Destiny first appeared, along with its owner Destiny, in WEIRD MYSTERY TALES #1 (August 1972), almost two decades before both were adopted to magnificent effect by Neil Gaiman for his acclaimed SANDMAN series.

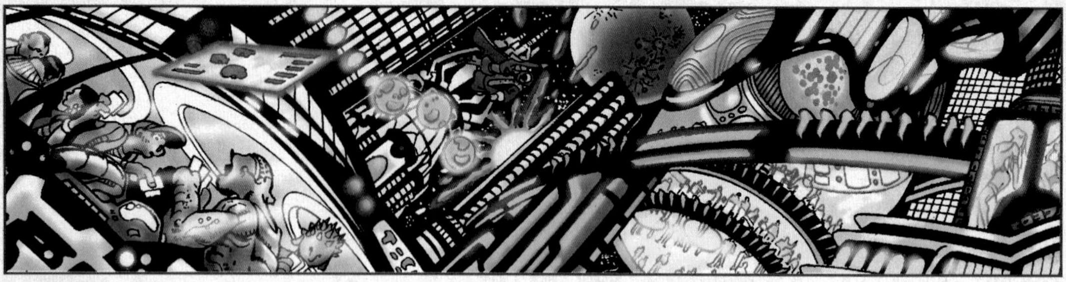

Page 36: Ventura, the casino planet, first appeared in WORLD'S FINEST COMICS #150 (June 1965).

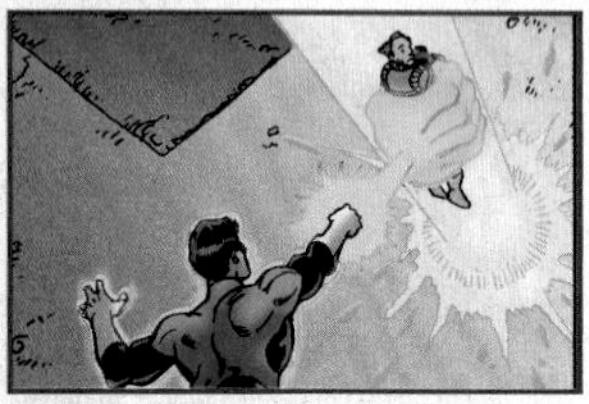

Page 53: The Zeta-Beam first appeared in SHOWCASE #17 (December 1958) in the first Adam Strange story. More about Adam soon.

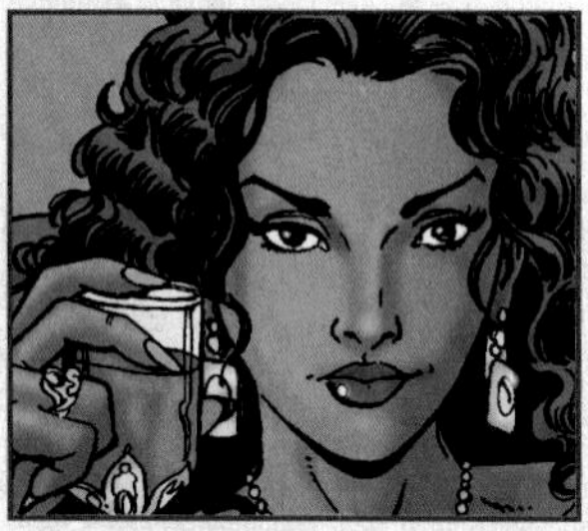

Page 67: La Dama first appeared in BLUE BEETLE (2nd series) #3 (July 2006).

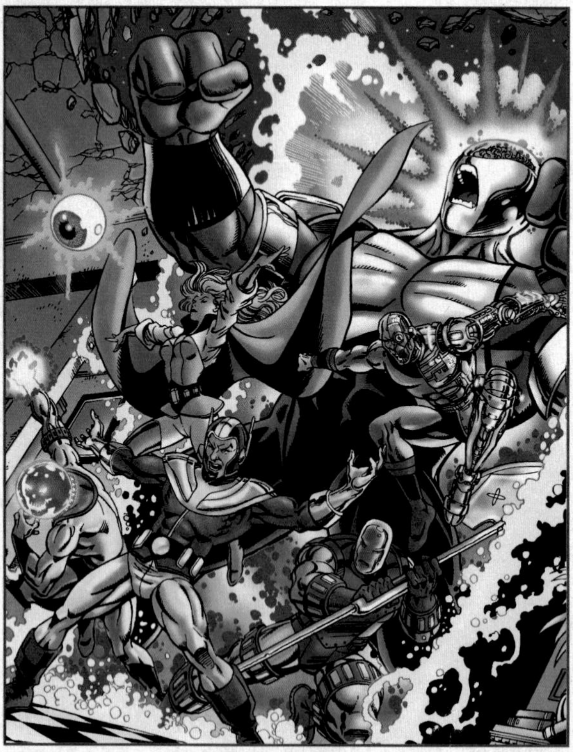

Pages 68-69: The Lord of Time first appeared in JUSTICE LEAGUE OF AMERICA #10 (March 1962). Legion villains The Fatal Five first appeared in ADVENTURE COMICS #352 (January 1967).

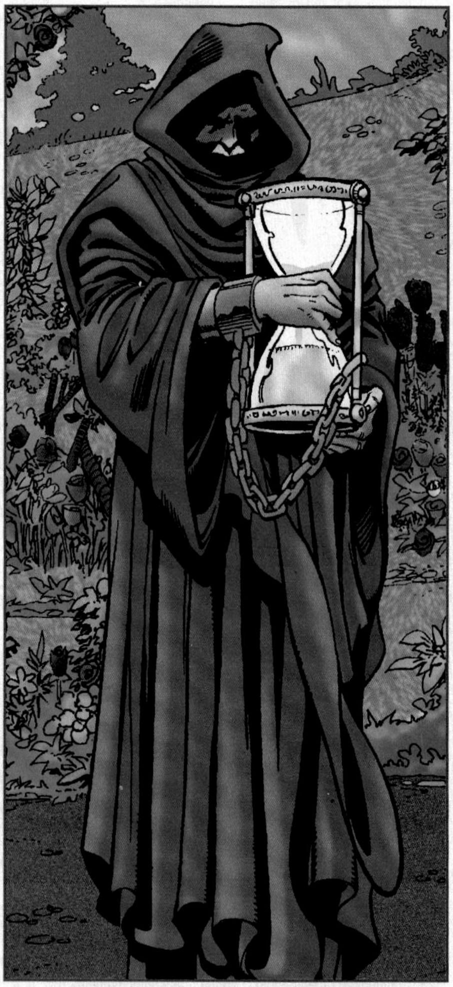

Page 92: If you're foolishly reading these annotations before you finish the actual story, spoiler alert: the hourglass chained to Destiny's wrist is, for astute readers, a big clue to the identity of the Men Who Weren't There.

Page 93: I went through every back issue of (again, spoiler alert!) CHALLENGERS OF THE UNKNOWN looking for the perfect image to have George drop into the Book of Destiny — one that would represent the Challs but wouldn't necessarily be a dead giveaway as to their identities.

I chose the cover to CHALLENGERS OF THE UNKNOWN #24 (March 1962). Needless to say, my attempts at subterfuge slowed down the denizens of the Internet by no more than 45 seconds.

Page 94: The Luck Lords were first referenced in ADVENTURE COMICS #343 (April 1966) but didn't actually appear for over twenty years, when then-writer Paul Levitz defined them in LEGION OF SUPER-HEROES #44-45 (March-April 1988).

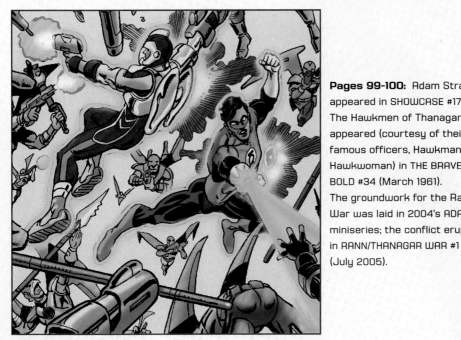

Pages 99-100: Adam Strange first appeared in SHOWCASE #17.

The Hawkmen of Thanagar first appeared (courtesy of their most famous officers, Hawkman and Hawkwoman) in THE BRAVE AND THE BOLD #34 (March 1961).

The groundwork for the Rann/Thanagar War was laid in 2004's ADAM STRANGE miniseries; the conflict erupted in RANN/THANAGAR WAR #1 (July 2005).

Pages 115: A very close continuity call. When I plotted this story, excited that the planet Rann was under a triple-star system, I'd forgotten that RANN/THANA-GAR WAR had established that the entire planet had been moved into the Polaris system. Luckily, parts of that are *also* in a trinary starfield.

The ultra-solar rays wouldn't be as strong here as they were under the Alpha Centauri system, but they'd be strong enough to gradually affect the Maid of Might.

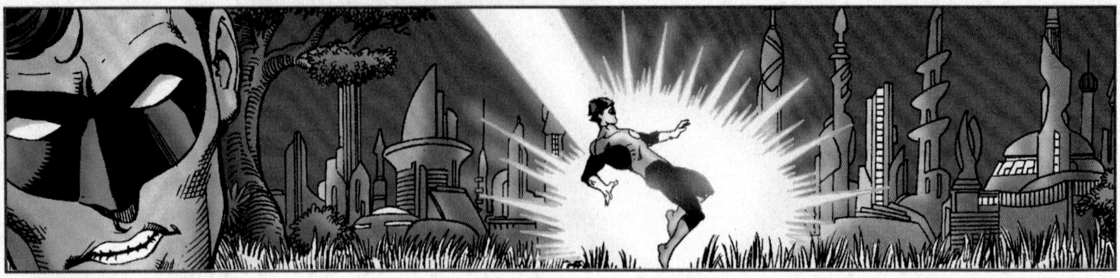

Page 117: Green Lantern's arrival on Rann is George's perfect (and deliberate) homage to Adam Strange artist Carmine Infantino's flair for body language and lush landscapes.

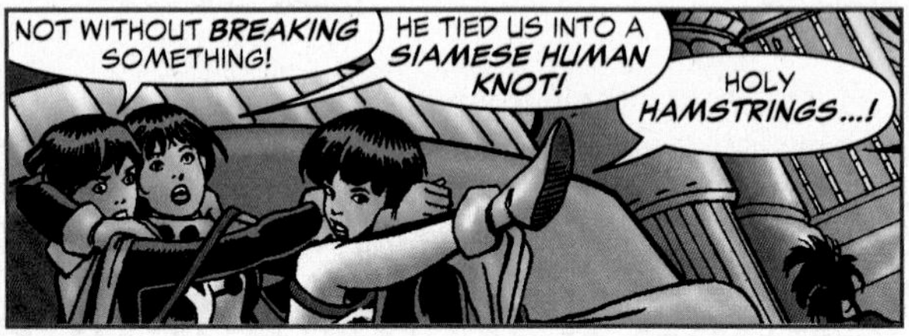

NOT WITHOUT BREAKING SOMETHING!
HE TIED US INTO A SIAMESE HUMAN KNOT!
HOLY HAMSTRINGS...!

Page 121: Entwining characters into a "Siamese Human Knot" is our last direct lift from the 1960s Batman show and so, *so* George's idea and not mine. That said, that didn't keep me from lifting Burt Ward dialogue from 1968.

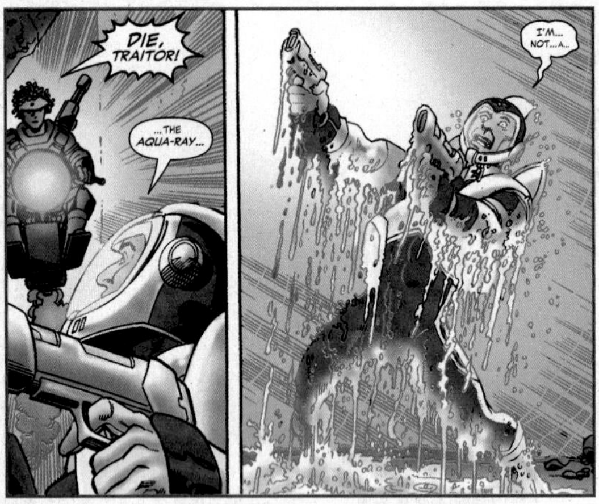

DIE, TRAITOR!
...THE AQUA-RAY...
I'M... NOT... A...

Page 135: The Aqua-Ray Weapon first appeared in MYSTERY IN SPACE #69 (August 1961). In fact, I had fun mining out quite a few artifacts from old Adam Strange stories for George to illustrate in this issue. Also on display: the Multiple Menace Rifles from MYSTERY IN SPACE #72 (December 1961), the Ray-Gun in the Sky from MYSTERY IN SPACE #77 (August 1962), and the tripodial Mechanical Masters of Rann from MYSTERY IN SPACE #65 (February 1961).

Page 140-141: Here's what I wrote in the plot. "SUPERPANEL ACROSS SPREAD: Batman, caught in the Zeta-Beam, is pulled a THOUSAND YEARS BACK THROUGH TIME, across a montage of images of WHATEVER THE HELL YOU FEEL LIKE DRAWING that happened in the DC Universe during that time.
I'll spend Monday pulling together reference, but just off the top of my head, I'm thinking Kamandi, the Atomic Knights, Space Cabby, future Flashes, future Starmen, Chris KL-99, Star Hawkins, the Star Rovers, Space Ranger, Tommy Tomorrow, Astra, Booster Gold, Reverse-Flash, the Tornado Twins... as I say, I'll pull together reference and leave it up to you as to how much or how little you want to do here."
As is always the case, George took the number of characters I offered up and, God bless him, multiplied by three. From top to bottom, here's the full, annotated list:

- In the purple hood, the Time Trapper, who walks all of time and space (ADVENTURE COMICS #318, March 1964).
- In the metal visor, one of the Atomic Knights of the at-the-time-of-publication far-flung future era of...wait for it...1986 (STRANGE ADVENTURES #117, June 1960).
- The chest insignia of Thondor Allen, one of the long line of Flashes who live between the 20th and 30th centuries, as established in the storyline "Chain Lightning" (FLASH #145-150, February-July 1999).
- In red and yellow, Space Ranger and his sidekick Cryll, protectors of the 22nd century (SHOWCASE #15, July 1958).
- The Time Sphere of Rip Hunter, Time Master (SHOWCASE #20, May 1959).
- Professor Zoom, the Reverse-Flash of the 25th century (FLASH #139, September 1963).
- Also in red and yellow – apparently, popular space colors – Chris KL-99 and his friends Halk (magenta) and Jero (green, all appearing first in STRANGE ADVENTURES #1, August 1950).
- Kamandi, the Last Boy on Earth, survivor of the future's Great Disaster (KAMANDI #1, October 1972).

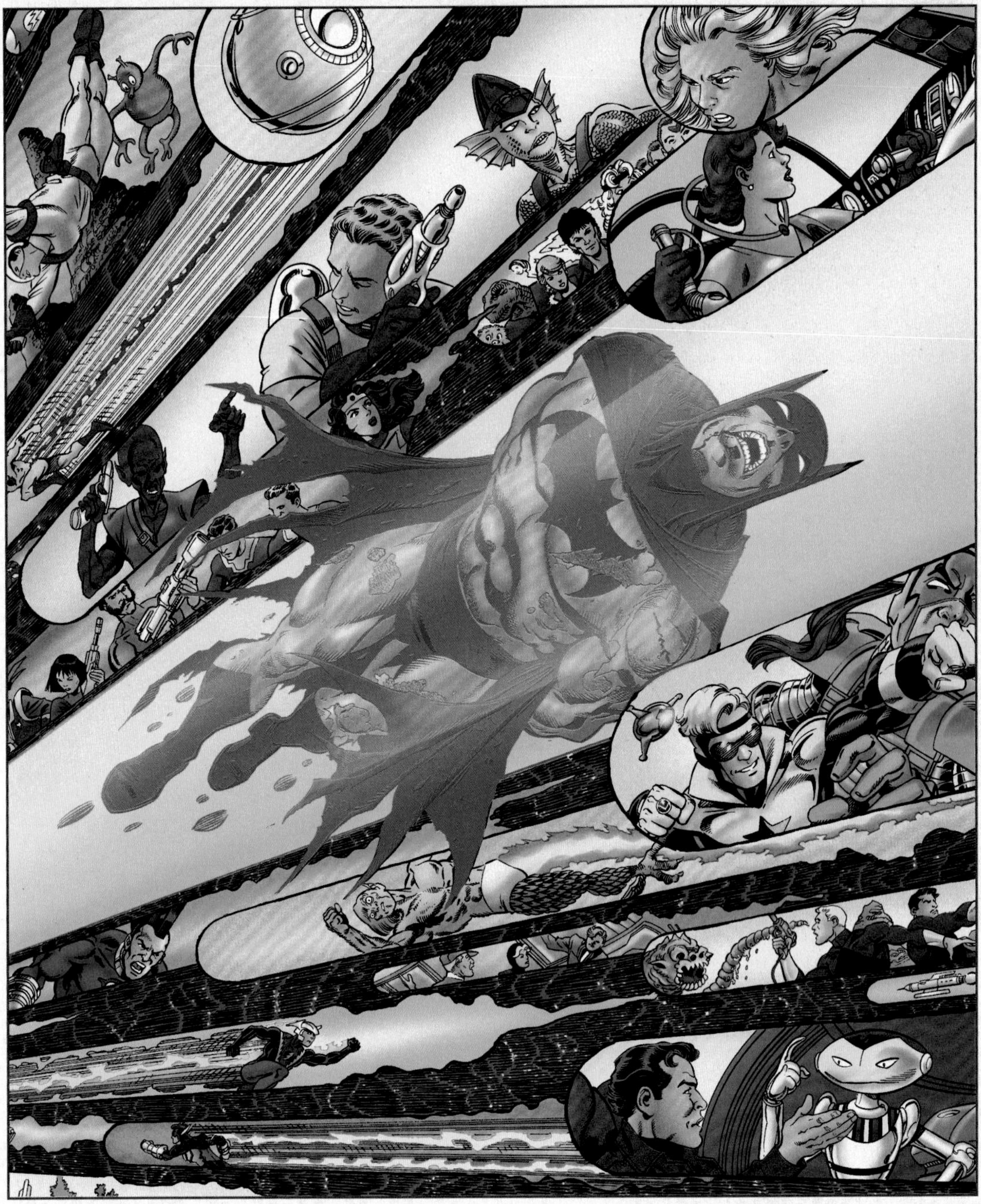

• The freebooters of the 22nd century, Donovan Flint and the Star Hunters (STAR HUNTERS #1, November 1977).

• The Sun Devils, whose individual names even I don't know (but who appeared in SUN DEVILS #1-12, July 1984-June 1985).

• In red and yellow (again!), space-reporter Astra, "the girl of the future!" (SENSATION COMICS #99, October 1950.)

• Beneath Batman, Booster Gold punches out the villain Blackguard as electronic robo-sidekick Skeets cheers him on (a scene from BOOSTER GOLD #1, February 1986).

• In the mohawk, Omac, the One-Man Army Corps (OMAC #1, October 1974).

• One of DC's least fondly remembered heroes, Ultra the Multi-Alien (from MYSTERY IN SPACE #103, November 1965).

• Homer Glint, Karel Sorensen, and Rick Purvis — the Star Rovers, adventurers of the 22nd century (MYSTERY IN SPACE #66, March 1961).

• Captain Tommy Tomorrow and Captain Brent Wood of the 21st century Planeteers (and, yes, Brent should have a mustache; my bad). Tommy first appeared in REAL FACT COMICS #6 (January 1947) but didn't hit it big until he began his own long-running

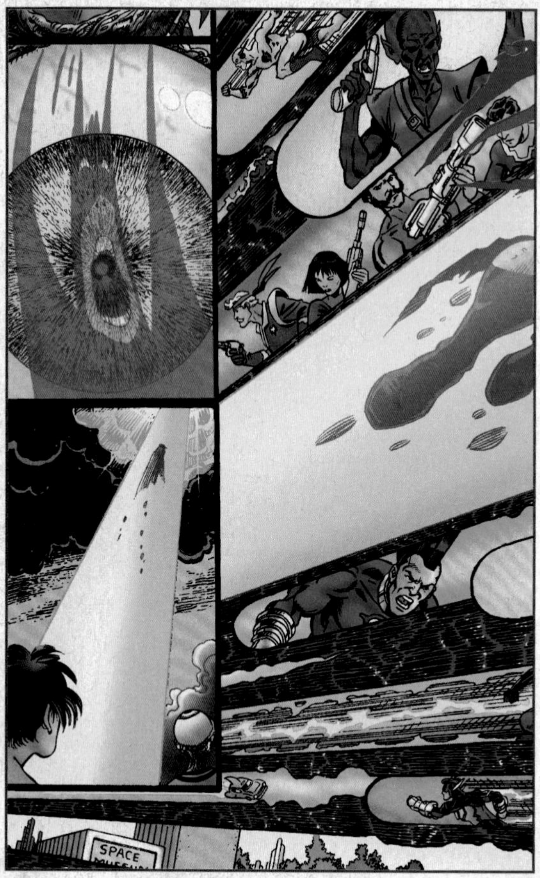
SPACE

series in ACTION COMICS #127-251 (December 1948-April 1959).

• Jace Allen, the Flash of the 28th century (CHAIN LIGHTNING).

• Star Hawkins, crack investigator from the late 21st century, and his assistant Ilda F2324 (STRANGE ADVENTURES #114, March 1960).

• John Fox, Flash of the year 2465 (FLASH 50th ANNIVERSARY SPECIAL, 1990) runs almost headlong towards Taxi #7433, hack of the Space Cabby (MYSTERY IN SPACE #21, August 1954).

• At page bottom, a glimpse of the 25th century's Space Museum (STRANGE ADVENTURES #104, May 1959).

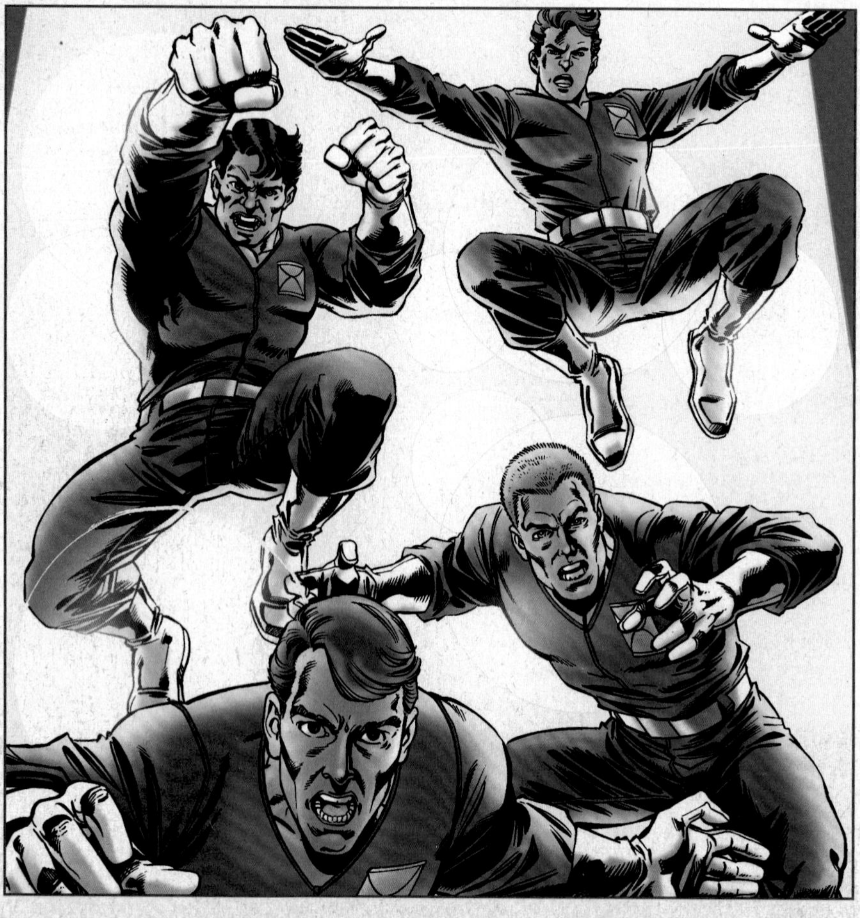

Page 146: The Challengers of the Unknown, DC's famous "Death-Cheaters," began their long careers in SHOWCASE #6, February 1957.